AIR FRYER FOR BEGINNERS COOKBOOK

1001 Easy Recipes with Tips and Tricks for Frying, Roast and Bake Every Day from Appetizers to Desserts. From Traditional to Vegan recipes + 21 Day Meal Plan

Emanuela de Cocina

Thank you very much for choosing this book.
Here you will find many recipes for your Air fryer.

We would like to inform you that this cookbook was **WRITTEN AND TRANSLATED** in its entirety from Spanish to English by children, with the help of teachers, during a twinning initiative between the **USA and Spain** called "Relations Above All", carried out by the "Colegio Privado Internacional" - Spain.
We therefore sincerely hope that you will understand the sometimes imperfect translation or the absence of images.
We have tried to compensate for this with a number of recipes, collected from all the children and their families, creating this fantastic cookbook.
We sincerely hope that you can help us by leaving a positive review, if appropriate, on Amazon.
We trust in your understanding and.... Enjoy!!!

Thank you!

Table of contents

Appetizers and snacks recipes 18
   1. Shrimps with paprika and bacon 18
   2. Broccoli and cheese nuggets 18
   3. Mixed nuts 18
   4. Herb roasted cauliflower 18
   5. Healthy broccoli crisps 18
   6. Baked cheese crisps 18
   7. Cashew nut bowls 19
   8. Baked tortillas 19
   9. Green beans with lemon 19
   10. Pork rinds 19
   11. Cocktail Meatballs for Kids 19
   12. Spinach rolls 19
   13. Crunchy aubergine with cheese 20
   14. Vegetable sandwich 20
   15. Southern cheese straws 20
   16. Sage Radish Chips 21
   17. Courgette rolls 21
   18. Easy carrot dip 21
   19. Cauliflower popcorn with turmeric 21
   20. Sweet potatoes 21
   21. Cajun spiced appetizer 21
   22. Cheese croquettes wrapped in bacon 22
   23. Mexican Zucchini and Bacon Ole Tortas 22
   24. Mozzarella sticks 22
   25. Plain banana chips 22
   26. Brussels sprouts with feta cheese 23
   27. Cumin pork sticks 23
   28. Pepper chips 23
   29. Crispy bacon bites 23
   30. Chips with broccoli and spicy sauce 23
   31. Spicy dip 24
   32. Crispy Broccoli Crisps 24
   33. Courgette sticks with cheese 24
   34. BBQ Lil Smokies 24
   35. Baby corn 24
   36. Summer Meatball Skewers 24
   37. Cauliflower Bombs with Sweet and Sour Sauce 25
   38. French fries with Greek yoghurt sauce 25
   39. Old-fashioned onion rings 25
   40. Cashew nut dip 25
   41. Sweet potato bites 26
   42. Roasted peanuts 26
   43. Crunchy aubergine 26
   44. Chicken party pillows 26
   45. Mixed vegetables 26
   46. Quick and easy popcorn 27
   47. Dill cheese mushrooms 27
   48. Plain horseradish chips 27
   49. Roasted parsnip 27
   50. Apple chips 27
   51. Polenta sticks 27
   52. Fried green tomatoes 28
   53. Coconut biscuits 28
   54. Meat pizza without crust 28
   55. Spinach sauce 28
   56. Tomato and Parmesan fries Italian style 28
   57. Cocktail flanks 29
   58. Bacon croquettes 29
   59. Jalapeño Poppers with Cheese and Bacon 29
   60. Grilled Cheese Sandwiches 29
   61. Cheese pastry 29
   62. Pizza Bites 30
   63. Pineapple Bites with Yoghurt Sauce 30
   64. Chocolate bacon bites 30
   65. Avocado wedges 30
   66. Sauteed Asian Short Ribs 30
   67. Lemon Tofu 31
   68. Mexican rolls 31
   69. Carrots and rhubarb 31
   70. Orange cauliflower 31
   71. Party Time Mixed Nuts 31
   72. Curly's cauliflower 32
   73. Avocado Fries with Chipotle Sauce 32
   74. Bites of veal 32
   75. Egg rolls with tomato and avocado 32
   76. Tomatoes and herbs 32
   77. Olive fritters 33
   78. Vegetarian rolls 33
   79. Deviled eggs, country style 33
   80. Chicken wings in barbecue sauce 34
   81. Spicy avocado fries wrapped in bacon 34
   82. Potato wedges 34
   83. Ranch dipped fillets 34
   84. Mozzarella sandwich 34

85. Asian Teriyaki Chicken 34
86. Ricotta balls 35
87. Cheese pizza with pita bread 35
88. Brussels sprouts 35
89. Puppies of the Poppers' family 35
90. Tasty pork meatballs 36
91. Mushrooms stuffed with vegetable cream ... 36
92. Onion dip 36
93. Mini Cheeseburger Bites 36
94. Lemon Tofu Cubes 36
95. Breadsticks with cheddar cheese 37
96. Easy Habanero Wings 37
97. Roasted Brussels sprouts and bacon 37
98. Okra with sesame 37
99. Vegetable fritters 37
100. Wonton sausage snacks 38
101. Prawn cakes 38
102. Bacon-wrapped shrimps 38
103. Chicken Wings with Sage 38
104. Crispy prawns 38
105. Grandma's green beans 38
106. Pickled bacon bowls 39
107. Tomato Smokies 39
108. Scallop and Bacon Brochettes 39
109. Sausage and vegetable cocktail on a stick 39
110. Aromatic cabbage chips 39

Dessert recipes 40
111. Vanilla-orange custard 40
112. Baileys Butterscotch Brownies with Alcoholic Flavour 40
113. Chocolate cake 40
114. Coconut Cheese Crackers 41
115. Yummy brownies 41
116. Clove biscuits 41
117. Peach cobbler recipe 41
118. Apple wedges 42
119. Chocolate-peanut butter fondants 42
120. Tea biscuits 42
121. Molten lava cake 42
122. Peanut crackers 42
123. Chocolate custard 43
124. Dulce de leche muffins with walnuts 43
Banana cake 43
126. Tasty peach pie 43
127. Hazelnut brownie cups 44
128. Plum Sticks Recipe 44
130. Classic Buttermilk Biscuits 44
131. Pop-tarts Ninja 44
132. Courgette brownies 45
133. Avocado tart 45
134. Vanilla cake 45
135. Coconut and coconut pudding 45
136. Chocolate molten lava cake 46
137. Nut biscuits 46
138. Crème Brulee 46
139. Strawberry shortcakes 46
140. Dark Chocolate Brownies 46
141. Nutella and Banana Cupcakes 47
142. Orange Swiss roll 47
143. Egg custard 47
144. Creamy rice pudding 47
145. Peach plot 48
146. Vanilla Coconut Cheese Crackers 48
147. Mum's orange rolls 48
148. Vanilla mozzarella balls 48
149. Peach slices 49
150. Butter crumble 49
151. Cheesecake with berries and white chocolate 49
152. Strawberry coconut fritters 49
153. Classic white chocolate biscuits 49
154. Lemon Glazed Muffins 50
155. Apple bread pudding 50
156. Blueberry Pancakes 50
157. Lemon curd 51
158. Coconut biscuits 51
159. Almond bars 51
160. Rustic baked apples 51
161. Banana Split 51
162. Greek-style griddle cakes 52
163. Cashew nut cake 52
164. Ricotta and lemon tart recipe 52
165. Classic butter cake 52
166. Rhubarb pie recipe 53
167. Dark chocolate cheesecake 53
168. Lemon Butter Cake 53
170. Strawberry cheesecake 54
171. Zucchini lemon bread 54

172. Sweet coconut cream cake 54
173. Cranberry almond cake 54
174. Mint and mascarpone cake 55
175. Super moist chocolate cake 55
176. Coconut lemon bars 55
177. Stevia cake 55
178. Sweet potato pie 55
179. Pear fritters with cinnamon and ginger 56
180. Avocado Chocolate Brownies 56
181. Blueberry Bread Pudding 56
182. Sugar butter fritters 56
183. Coconut sunflower biscuits 57
184. Stuffed apples 57
185. Cheat Apple Pie 57
187. Delicious Autumn Clafoutis 57
188. Donuts of milk 58
189. Vanilla Rum and Walnut Cookies 58
190. Pumpkin bars 58
191. Chocolate with coconut 59
192. Lemon cake with almond and coconut 59
193. Dulce de leche cake with walnuts 59
194. Easy Spanish Churros 59
195. Angel Cake 60
196. Classic pound cake 60
197. Chocolate muffins with almonds 60
198. Ricotta cheesecake 60
199. Cheese and butter biscuits 60
200. Mandarin tart recipe 61
201. Apple and caramel tart 61
202. Soft buttermilk biscuits 61
Mixed berries with walnut streusel 61
204. Puffed coconut and walnut biscuits 62
205. Berry pudding 62
206. Lemon berry stew 62
207. Blueberry and Whisky Brownies for Father's Day 62
208. Spanish-style doughnut weavings 62
209. Chocolate brownie 63
210. Chocolate lava cake 63

Poultry recipes 63
211. Lemon Pepper Chicken Wings 63
212. Chicken Tarragon Removals 63
213. Crispy stuffed chicken breast 63
214. Cajun Mustard Turkey Fingers 64
215. Hot chicken skin 64
216. Sweet Italian turkey sausage with vegetables . 64
217. Chicken pizzas 64
218. Chicken calves 65
219. Chicken and Onion Kabobs 65
220. Chicken with peanut butter curry 65
221. Buffalo chicken strips 65
222. Impressive sweet turkey pie 65
223. Chicken Wings with Rubber 66
224. Air fried chicken tenderloin 66
225. Easy Thanksgiving Crunchwrap 66
226. Chicken tenderloin rubbed with paprika and cumin 66
227. Chicken fillets 67
228. Chicken and shrimp pasta 67
229. Greek chicken 67
230. Salted egg frittata with meat 67
231. Turkey nuggets with thyme 67
232. chicken kabab 68
233. Ground turkey mixture 68
234. Indian Chicken Calves 68
235. KFC Like Chicken Tenders 68
236. Beastly barbecue sticks 68
237. Chimichurri Turkey 69
238. Moroccan chicken 69
239. Duck in vanilla and pepper sauce 69
240. Traditional Asian sticky chicken 69
241. Turkey bacon with scrambled eggs 69
242. Chicken with honey and spicy orange 70
243. Juicy and spicy chicken wings 70
244. Turkey with almonds and shallots 70
245. Tasty Caribbean chicken 70
246. Duck leg and onion mixture 70
247. Thai red duck with onion confit 71
248. Leftovers 'n Enchilada Bake 71
249. Chicken breasts wrapped in bacon 71
250. Chicken with sweet garlic 71
251. Agave Mustard Glazed Chicken 72
252. Pepper turkey sandwiches 72
253. Chicken Tenders with Parmesan and Lime 72
254. Turkey rolls 72
255. Eggs, cauliflower and broccoli brekky 73
256. Chicken and bacon mix 73
257. Sweet chilli chicken wings 73

258. Glazed chicken wings 73
259. Garlic chicken sausages 74
260. Chicken with cashew nuts 74
261. Turkey breast in buttermilk 74
262. Crispy chicken fingers 74
263. Chicken and Onion Kabobs 74
264. Barbecued chicken with sweet and sour sauce 75
265. Chicken and cream cheese mixture 75
266. Chicken marjoram 75
267. Fried chicken halves 75
268. Chicken Thighs with Thyme and Okra 75
269. Traditional Teriyaki Chicken 76
270. Crispy Chicken Tenders 76
271. Turkey with cheese wrapped in bacon 76
272. Turkey with garlic and lemon asparagus ... 76
273. Duck Oregano Duck Spread 77
274. Chicken in crust 77
275. Strawberry turkey 77
276. Crispy and juicy whole chicken 77
277. Chicken breasts with jalapeños 77
278. Crispy Chicken Noodles with Peanuts 78
279. Vermouth Burgers with Bacon and Turkey . 78
280. Traditional chicken tetrazzini 78
281. Oregano and lemon chicken drumsticks ... 79
282. Chicken with Cauliflower and Pecorino Romano 79
283. Chicken burgers 79
284. Sweet and spicy chicken drumsticks 79
285. Holiday Colby Turkey Meatloaf 79
286. Crispy turkey sandwich with cabbage salad 80
287. Delicious Chicken Fajitas 80
288. Chicken Wings 80
289. Chicken thighs in batter 80
290. Duck and blackberry mixture 81
291. Rice with duck and walnuts 81
292. Parsley duck 81
293. Baked Rice, Black Beans and Cheese 81
294. Chicken Meatballs with Miso-ginger 82
295. Chicken drumsticks with paprika and turnip .. 82
296. Dill chicken quesadilla 82
297. Authentic Mongolian chicken 82
298. Chicken with marinara sauce 82
299. Sweet and spicy chicken drumsticks 83
300. Chicken breasts with spinach 83
301. Sesame chicken wings 83
302. Chicken with Vegetables and Rice 83
303. Ethiopian Style Chicken with Cauliflower 83
304. Sticky Turkey Thighs Chinese Style 84
305. Sweet Lime and Chilli Chicken Barbecue 84
306. Turkey and maple mustard 84
307. Juicy herb thighs 84
308. Spicy Turkey Meatloaf with Cheese 85
309. The best chicken pizza ever 85
310. Dill chicken fritters 85
311. Spinach and Egg Casserole with Coconut Milk 85
312. Chicken and Coconut Meatballs 86
313. Turkey breakfast frittata 86
314. Chicken Dijon with lime 86
315. Chicken with Ginger and Lemon Sauce 86
316. Honey-glazed turkey breast 86
317. Middle-Eastern Chicken Barbecue with Tzatziki Sauce 87
318. Buffalo chicken 87
319. Turkey with Paprika and Shallot Sauce 87
320. Blue cheese chicken mix 87
321. Delicious Whole Chicken 88
322. Legs in batter with lemon butter 88
323. Crispy chicken wings 88
324. Chicken in batter with almond flour and coconut milk 88
325. Easy chicken sliders 88
326. Chicken with carrots 89
327. Cajun Chicken Tenders 89
328. Air Fried Crispy Chicken Tenders 89
329. Spicy chicken and tomato sauce 89
330. Spaghetti Pizza Casserole 90
331. Lemon chicken breast with pepper 90
332. Chicken drumsticks 90
333. Jerk Chicken, Pineapple and Vegetable Kabobs 90
334. Air fried chicken with cheese 91
335. Turkey with butter and mushroom sauce 91
336. Liver spread with paprika 91
337. Eggs Benedict on English muffins 91
338. Chicken and black olives recipe 92
339. Chicken Enchiladas 92

- 340. Mediterranean chicken breasts with roasted tomatoes 92
- 341. Spicy chicken thighs 92
- 342. Old-fashioned chicken drumettes 92
- 343. Garlic chicken 93
- 344. Chicken pesto 93
- 345. Chicken Zaatar 93
- 346. Asian Chicken Fillets with Cheese 93
- 347. Delicious turkey wings 94
- 348. Simple chicken wings 94
- 349. Turkey Meatballs with Manchego Cheese 94
- 350. The Best Chicken Burgers 94
- 351. Malaysian Chicken Satay with Peanut Sauce 94
- 352. Sweet curry chicken cutlets 95
- 353. Chicken pie with coconut milk 95
- 354. Broccoli and Cheese Rice Casserole 95
- 355. Chicken Parmesan and Dill 95
- 356. Mixed Vegetable Breakfast Frittata 96
- 357. Turkey and Coconut Broccoli 96
- 358. Chicken wings with cheese 96
- 359. Maple Glazed Chicken Special 96
- 360. Chinese duck 97

Beef, pork and lamb recipes 97

- 361. Veal cubes with vegetables 97
- 362. Smoked brisket with dill pickles 97
- 363. Kansas City Pork Ribs Recipe 97
- 364. Pepper lamb with rhubarb 98
- 365. Beef with mixed mushrooms and ghee 98
- 366. Pork and garlic sauce 98
- 367. Tasty pork chops with peanut sauce 98
- 368. Meatball and Mushroom Casserole with Cheese 99
- 369. Za'atar lamb loin chops 99
- 370. Grilled sirloin steak 99
- 371. Meat with hot paprika 99
- 372. Garlic and Ginger Sauce 99
- 373. Max's Meatloaf 100
- 374. Wine marinated sirloin steak 100
- 375. Pork roulade 100
- 376. Pork loin with potatoes 100
- 377. Simple beef patties 100
- 378. Salami Rolls with Homemade Mustard Spread 101
- 379. Beef jerky 101
- 380. Sirloin steak with butter 101
- 381. Roast beef with garlic and celery with butter 101
- 382. Top roast with mustard, rosemary and thyme mixture. 101
- 383. Smoked pork 102
- 384. Meat, lettuce and cabbage salad 102
- 385. Lamb kebabs with caraway, sichuan and cumin 102
- 386. Veal schnitzel 102
- 387. Pork Chops and Sage Sauce Recipe 102
- 388. Sausage meatballs 103
- 389. Veal brisket with cumin and paprika 103
- 390. Stuffed peppers 103
- 391. Monterey Jack'n Sausage Brekky Casserole .. 103
- 392. Fig wrapped in grilled prosciutto 104
- 393. Pork with coconut and green beans 104
- 394. Pepper jacket potato with smoked bacon .. 104
- 395. Steak with rattlesnake and garlic sauce 104
- 396. Simple meatballs with garlic and herbs 104
- 397. Moroccan beef kebab 104
- 398. Pork with raspberry jam and balsamic glaze 105
- 399. Filet Mignon with herb crust 105
- 400. Rare lamb chops 105
- 401. Grandma's famous pork chops 105
- 402. Easy corn dog chews 106
- 403. Smoked beef burgers 106
- 404. Spicy and saucy veal fingers 106
- 405. Veal fillets with lemon sauce 106
- 406. Pork tail with herb and garlic sauce 107
- 407. Lamb steak with garlic and lemon 107
- 408. Eggs and Bacon with Brekky's Biscuit 107
- 409. Southwestern meatloaf 107
- 410. Lamb with mustard, chives and basil 108
- 411. Grilled coriander lamb chops 108
- 412. Sausage and cauliflower frittata 108
- 413. Grilled fillet steak with tomato and olive salad 108
- 414. Classic Keto Cheeseburgers 108
- 415. Filet Mignon with butter 109
- 416. Veal and kale omelette 109
- 417. Classic flank steak strips with vegetables .. 109
- 418. Rack of lamb breaded with herbs 109
- 419. Winter veal with garlic mayonnaise sauce 109

420. Beef and courgette stir-fry 110
421. Steak frites with gravy 110
422. Spring meat and onions 110
423. Roast loin of pork with herbs de Provence 110
424. Lemon Osso Bucco 110
425. Sweet pork belly 111
426. Perfect Thai Meatballs 111
427. Orange roast beef 111
428. Meatballs with Cheese and Honey Mustard
.... 111
429. Sweet and sour pork chops 111
430. Nutmeg pork chops 112
431. Plain meat 112
432. Favourite Beef Stroganoff 112
433. Lamb sausages 112
434. Chinese-style creamed veal 112
435. Glazed ham 113
436. Lamb chops with sesame seeds 113
437. Leg of lamb with herbs 113
438. Sirloin steak with yoghurt and curry paprika
.... 113
439. Wet Stuffed Pork Rolls 113
440. Pig and cabbage 114
441. Teriyaki Steak with Fresh Herbs 114
442. Beef with marinade and oregano 114
443. Lamb with mint and rosemary 114
444. Fried pork with sweet and sour glaze 114
445. Pork with chilli and tomato 115
446. Coriander and English mustard veal chops 115
447. Meat and tofu mixture 115
448. Sausage and semolina pie with southern cheese 115
449. Honey-mustard marinated pork chops 116
450. Lamb loin chops in lemon sauce 116
451. Meat and vegetable kebabs 116
452. Tomato riblets 116
453. Rack of lamb in saffron sauce 116
454. Creamy pork schnitzel 117
455. Meatballs with Mexican chilli 117
456. Wrapped pork 117
457. Mint lamb mix 117
458. Peach purée on ribs 117
459. Irish whiskey fillet 118
460. Asian beef patties 118

Fish and seafood recipes 118
461. Grilled tilapia 118
462. Salmon with tarragon and spring onions ... 118
463. Fillet of cod in beer sauce 118
464. Salted fish fillets 119
465. Cod with basil and paprika 119
466. Hot tilapia 119
467. Cajun fish cakes with cheese 119
468. Rice Flour Coated Shrimp 119
469. Salmon and garlic sauce 120
470. Golden cod nuggets 120
471. Fish with Garam Masala sauce 120
472. Tasty crab croquettes 120
473. Trout salad with cream 121
474. Tilapia Ham 121
475. Creamy salmon 121
476. Pistachio-crusted salmon 121
477. Salmon with prawns and pasta 121
478. Cajun Spiced Vegetable and Shrimp Cake .. 122
479. Old bay and dijon seasoned crab cakes 122
480. Salmon with lemon and chilli 122
481. Curried halibut fillets 122
482. Tuna stuffed potato sticks 122
483. Spicy prawn kebab 123
484. Trout and shallots 123
485. Smoked halibut and eggs on brioche 123
486. Salmon fillets, plain 123
487. Grilled fish and celery burgers 123
488. Codfish pie 124
489. Fish packages 124
490. Branzino with lemon 124
491. Shrimps with cheese 124
492. Classic Parmesan Fish Fillets 125
493. Glazed Halibut 125
494. Summer fish packages 125
495. Cod with mustard 125
496. Rosemary and garlic prawns 125
497. Recipe of sea bass with honey 126
498. Hong Kong Cod Fillet Recipe 126
499. Catfish bites 126
500. Cajun lemon salmon 126
501. Fish fillets 126
502. Tuna au gratin with herbs 126

#	Recipe	Page
503.	Herbed squid rings	127
504.	Fried Branzino	127
505.	Spicy shrimps	127
506.	Delicious crab cakes	127
507.	Sunday fish with sticky sauce	128
508.	Easy to make garlic shrimps	128
509.	Squid with paprika and basil	128
510.	Swordfish with butter and paprika	128
511.	Hearty small octopus salad	128
512.	Summer shrimp skewers	129
513.	Grilled and herbed scallops	129
514.	Herbed salmon	129
515.	Tasty tuna empanadas	129
516.	Creamy breaded shrimps	129
517.	Halibut and caper mixture	130
518.	Garlic shrimp mix	130
519.	Big catfish	130
520.	Italian shrimps	130
521.	Pesto shrimp on the grill	130
522.	Salmon fillet with lemon and paprika	131
523.	Haddock coated with sesame seeds	131
525.	Authentic Mediterranean Squid Salad	131
526.	Lobster tails with olives and butter	132
527.	Grilled shrimps	132
528.	Cod and fennel dish	132
529.	Breaded flounder	132
530.	Fisherman's fish fingers	132
531.	Tasty distress fish	133
532.	Frozen sesame fish fillets	133
533.	Charcoal and fennel	133
534.	Greek style grilled fish	133
535.	Shrimps with cumin, thyme and oregano	134
536.	Whitefish cakes	134
537.	Delicious seafood pie	134
538.	Italian mackerel	134
539.	Salmon and blackberry sauce	135
540.	Hake fillets with classic garlic sauce	135
541.	Coconut prawns	135
542.	Lemon breaded shrimps	135
543.	Olives with prawns and parsley	136
544.	Crispy codfish sticks	136
545.	Cod fillets with garlic and herbs	136
546.	Shrimps with cheese	136
547.	Lemon salmon	136
548.	Salmon with green beans	136
549.	Haddock with herbs	137
550.	Big cod fried in the open air	137
551.	Coconut crusted shrimp	137
552.	Salmon with broccoli	137
553.	Salmon with pesto	138
554.	Rosemary Infused Butter Scallops	138
555.	Japanese flounder with chives	138
556.	Filipino steak	138
557.	Pesto sauce on fish fillets	138
558.	Flounder fillets with crust	139
559.	Shrimp and pine nut mixture	139
560.	Shrimps with garlic and goat cheese	139
561.	Breaded fish fillets with tarragon	139
562.	Cod and sauce	139
563.	Flounder stuffed with crab	140
564.	Haddock with chilli	140
565.	Mahi Mahi with green beans	140
566.	Tilapia with Dijon mustard crust and parmesan cheese	140
567.	Prawns in butter with garlic-sriracha sauce	140
568.	Grilled shrimps with butter	141
569.	Tuna coated with sesame seeds	141
570.	Snapper fillets with tomato and walnut sauce	141
571.	Grilled citrus Branzini	141
572.	Rice with turmeric and cauliflower	142
573.	Famous Indian fish curry	142
574.	Fresh tilapia fried in the open air	142
575.	Crab Cake Burgers	142
576.	Trout and Almond Butter Sauce	142
577.	Fish and chips	143
578.	Recipe for salted cod tapas from Portugal	143
579.	Chinese garlic shrimp	143
580.	Prawn skewers	143
581.	Haddock with Kalamata olives and capers	143
582.	Mixed sea bass and olives	144
583.	Super easy scallops	144
584.	Cajun Shrimp	144
585.	Grilled Halibut with lemon and tomatoes	144
586.	Thyme catfish	144
587.	Salmon with turmeric and soy sauce	145

#	Title	Page
588.	Fried shrimps with sweet chilli sauce	145
589.	Mixed trout with herbs	145
590.	Prawn skewers	145
591.	Pesto-crusted salmon	145
592.	Tilapia with capers and cheese sauce	146
593.	Grilled Squid Rings with Kale and Tomatoes	146
594.	Parsley Linguini with Grilled Tuna	146
595.	Grilled salmon with butter and wine	146
596.	Louisiana shrimp	146
597.	Sole and cauliflower fritters	146
598.	Rosemary shrimps	147
599.	Trout and tomato mix with courgettes	147
600.	Crab cakes	147
601.	Tilapia with walnut crust	147
602.	Spiced coconut shrimp kebab	147
603.	Halibut fillets	148
604.	Tilapia with paprika	148
605.	Jumbo shrimps	148
606.	Cajun Cod Fillets with Avocado Sauce	148
607.	Shrimp and celery salad	149
608.	Scallops with butter	149
609.	Trout with butter and chives	149
610.	Ginger Cod	149

Vegetables and garnishes 149

#	Title	Page
611.	Delicious ratatouille	149
612.	Roasted aubergine	150
613.	Green beans and tomatoes recipe	150
614.	Courgette latkes	150
615.	Summer vegetable fritters	150
616.	Rainbow Cheese and Vegetable Cake	150
617.	Broccoli Casserole	150
618.	Coconut Risotto	151
619.	Vegetable and egg salad	151
620.	Chickpeas, fried with herbs	151
621.	Super Cabbage Canapés	151
622.	Crisp and tender Brussels sprouts	151
623.	Amazing cheese sticks	152
624.	Mediterranean vegetable skewers	152
625.	Courgette mix recipe	152
626.	Lemon cabbage	152
627.	Mozzarella Risotto	152
628.	Mushroom pan with thyme	152
629.	Fried asparagus with romesco sauce	153
630.	Aubergine meatballs with almonds	153
631.	Pumpkin rice dish	153
632.	Courgette and Parmesan crisps	153
633.	Spicy jacket potatoes	154
634.	Butter cabbage	154
635.	Japanese tempura bowl	154
636.	Broccoli and cranberry mix	154
637.	Healthy green beans	154
638.	Mediterranean tomatoes with feta cheese	154
639.	Asparagus with paprika	155
640.	Lemon cabbage	155
641.	Roasted cauliflower	155
642.	Coriander pepper mix	155
643.	Italian tomatoes with goat cheese	155
644.	Cauliflower with Buffalo Sauce	156
645.	Potatoes and special tomato sauce recipe	156
646.	Butter fennel	156
647.	Broccoli with cheese and garlic in the open air	156
648.	Sweet and sour vegetable mixture	156
649.	Vegetarian rolls	156
650.	Broccoli and chives with almonds	157
651.	Leeks and spring onions	157
652.	Asparagus with bacon	157
653.	Balsamic Mustard Greens	157
654.	Crispy cauliflower bites	157
655.	Nutmeg and Dill Ravioli	158
656.	Crispy rosemary potatoes	158
657.	Broccoli puree	158
658.	Courgette and rocket mixture	158
659.	Crunchy pickles	158
660.	Cauliflower parmesan risotto	159
661.	Open-air jacket potatoes	159
662.	Pumpkin noodles	159
663.	Cheese and bacon fries	159
664.	Endive and rice mix	159
665.	Fennel with lemon	160
666.	Green celery puree	160
667.	Tamarind Glazed Sweet Potatoes	160
668.	Cauliflower puree	160
669.	Brussels sprouts chips	160
670.	Courgette nests	160
671.	Potato casserole dish	161
672.	Scrambled eggs	161

#	Title	Page
673.	Mushroom melt with cheese simple	161
674.	Cauliflower fritters Mexican style	161
675.	Lime and mozzarella aubergines	161
676.	Veal meatballs	162
677.	Sauteed artichokes	162
678.	Barbecue chicken pizza	162
679.	Balsamic cabbage mix	162
680.	Fried agnolotti	162
681.	Mung bean mix	163
682.	Rice pilaf with cremini mushrooms	163
683.	Portobello mushroom recipe	163
684.	Turmeric and kale mixture	163
685.	Tomato bites with creamy parmesan sauce	163
686.	Grilled cheese	164
687.	Cold chicken croquettes	164
688.	Sweet potato and chickpea tacos	164
689.	Macadamia Rice and Cauliflower	164
690.	Smoked BBQ Toast S	164
691.	Coconut crusted shrimp	164
692.	Mixed courgettes and pumpkins	165
693.	Green beans fried with Pecorino Romano	165
694.	Harissa Broccoli Spread	165
695.	Cabbages and sprouts	165
696.	Pumpkin wedges	165
697.	Mushrooms stuffed with butter and mint	166
698.	Broccoli Empanadas	166
699.	Perfect crispy tofu	166
700.	Roasted almond delight	166
701.	Green beans with spices	166
702.	Kabocha crisps	167
703.	Coconut cabbage and parmesan	167
704.	Roasted beetroot salad	167
705.	Fried green olives stuffed with peppers	167
706.	Low Carbohydrate Pita Crisps	167
707.	Cabbage wedges	167
708.	Rainbow vegetables and parmesan croquettes	168
709.	Cabbage puree	168
710.	Sweet corn fritters with avocado	168
711.	Rosemary olive mix	168
712.	Crunchy wax beans with almonds and blue cheese	169
713.	Almond Brussels sprouts	169
714.	Shredded beans	169
715.	Asparagus Parmesan	169
716.	Cream of broccoli and cauliflower soup	169
717.	Fennel with Shirataki noodles	170
718.	Cranberry salad	170
719.	Greek Roasted Tomatoes with Feta	170
720.	American-style Brussels sprouts salad	170
721.	Crispy asparagus with parmesan cheese	170
722.	Roasted vegetables	171
723.	Sweetcorn fritters	171
724.	Fried asparagus with goat cheese	171
725.	Mushroom pies	171
726.	Simple green beans with butter	171
727.	Dill corn	172
728.	Smoked asparagus	172
729.	Greek-style vegetable pie	172
730.	Coconut mushroom mix	172
731.	Avocados wrapped in bacon	172
732.	Veggie Tots for children	173
733.	Indian Malai Kofta	173
734.	Smoked fish balls	173
735.	Cheese stuffed mushrooms	173
736.	Pumpkin Parm	174
737.	Roasted broccoli	174
738.	Spinach and cheese	174
739.	Celery and coconut sprouts	174
740.	Pepper stuffed with cheese and broccoli	174
741.	Cheese Sticks with Sweet Thai Sauce	175
742.	Easy vegetable fried dumplings	175
743.	Parmesan artichoke hearts	175
744.	Winter vegetable stew	175
745.	Rutabaga Chili	175
746.	Mushrooms stuffed with garlic	176
747.	Leeks with paprika	176
748.	Plum and bacon pumps	176
749.	Balsamic radishes	176
750.	Jalapeño clouds	176
751.	Asparagus and mozzarella mixture	176
752.	Simple tomato and pepper sauce recipe	177
753.	Easy sweet potato pie	177
754.	Roast red potatoes with duck fat	177
755.	Air fried onions and peppers	177
756.	Breaded mushrooms	177

- 757. Spicy ricotta stuffed mushrooms 177
- 758. Vegetable gratin with the family 178
- 759. Garnished with lemon artichokes 178
- 760. Lemongrass rice mixture 178

Vegan and vegetarian recipes 178
- 761. Vegetarian rice 178
- 762. Mushrooms stuffed with vegetables 179
- 763. Carrot and courgette with butter and mayonnaise 179
- 764. Baked Portobello, Pasta 'n Cheese 179
- 765. Simply stunning vegetables 179
- 766. Crispy asparagus dipped in paprika and garlic 180
- 767. Vegetable pie with cheese and olives 180
- 768. Fresh green beans from the garden 180
- 769. Aubergines stuffed with spices 180
- 770. Easy glazed carrots 180
- 771. Vegetable frittata with two cheeses 181
- 772. Potato, aubergine and courgette chips 181
- 773. Drizzle Onion Blossoming 181
- 774. Parsnip and potato pie 181
- 775. Ultimate Vegan Calzone 182
- 776. Cornish Vegetarian Herbed Cornish Pies ... 182
- 777. Tofu Italian style 182
- 778. Tofu in sweet and spicy sauce 182
- 779. Crispy Pumpkin Crisps 183
- 780. Honey-glazed carrots 183
- 781. Cheese rolls 183
- 782. Vegetarian Tandoori Spiced Grill Recipe 183
- 783. Ultra crispy tofu 184
- 784. Baked Aubergines with cheese and marinara 184
- 785. Mexican Baked Courgettes recipe 184
- 786. Ribs with pineapple appetizer 185
- 787. Roasted mushrooms in herb and garlic oil 185
- 788. Hoisin-glazed Bok Choy 185
- 789. Air-fried plain ravioli 185
- 790. Brussels sprouts with cheese 185
- 791. Fried halloumi with vegetables 185
- 792. Delicious asparagus and mushroom fritters 186
- 793. Mint green beans with shallots 186
- 794. Tortilla layer cake 186
- 795. Refreshing and spicy broccoli 186
- 796. Cauliflower in the open air 187
- 797. Vegetable Fingers with Monterey Jack Cheese 187
- 798. Marinated Tofu Bowl with Pearled Onions 187
- 799. Tofu in sweet and sour sauce 187
- 800. Peppers stuffed with oatmeal 187
- 801. Roasted and glazed strawberries 188
- 802. Aubergine caviar 188
- 803. Sweet and sour Brussels sprouts 188
- 804. Asian-style cauliflower 188
- 805. Shallots and almonds in green beans 188
- 806. Rosemary potatoes au gratin 189
- 807. Seasoned Creole vegetables 189
- 808. Tomato sandwiches with feta and pesto 189
- 809. Pepper stuffed with oatmeal 190
- 810. Carrots in abundance 190
- 811. Barbecued Tofu with Green Beans 190
- 812. Thai spicy vegetables recipe 190
- 813. The best falafel ever 190
- 814. Courgette crisps for children 190
- 815. Roasted vegetables restaurant style 191
- 816. Crunchy battered onion rings with almond flour 191
- 817. Crunchy aubergine rounds 191
- 818. Crispy ham rolls 191
- 819. Tofu in rice flour crust 192
- 820. Swiss cheese and aubergine crispies 192
- 821. Open vegan flatbread 192
- 822. Cheese Pizza with Broccoli Crust 192
- 823. Chewy glazed parsnips 192
- 824. Egg and cauliflower rice casserole 193
- 825. Easy roasted winter vegetable delight 193
- 826. Sautéed spinach 193
- 827. Sweet and sour Brussels sprouts 193
- 828. Mushrooms stuffed with cream cheese-pesto sauce 193
- 829. Stuffed aubergine 193
- 830. Roasted broccoli with salted garlic 194
- 831. Brussels sprouts chips with paprika 194
- 832. Spicy cooked vegetables 194
- 833. Corn skewers in the air fryer 194
- 834. Tomatoes stuffed with cheese 194
- 835. Courgette with Mediterranean Dill Sauce .. 195

836. Salad of roasted peppers with goat's cheese ... 195
837. Vegetables au gratin with rosemary ... 195
838. Crunchy and healthy avocado fingers ... 195
839. Air-fried vegetable sushi ... 196
840. Tofu with cauliflower ... 196
841. Courgette pie with garlic and sour cream .. 196
842. The best crispy tofu ... 196
843. Roasted peppers with Greek mayonnaise sauce ... 197
844. Stuffed peppers Greek style ... 197
845. Bread rolls with butter ... 197
846. Perfectly roasted mushrooms ... 197
847. Cheese stuffed mushrooms ... 197
848. Radish salad ... 198
849. Onion rings with spicy ketchup ... 198
850. Spinach quiche without eggs ... 198
851. Classic baked banana ... 199
852. Vegetables flavoured with garlic and wine 199
853. Indian Aloo Tikka ... 199
854. Baked oatmeal with berries ... 199
855. Mushroom and cheese pizza ... 199
856. Crunchy tofu with paprika ... 200
857. Broccoli Shawarma Crispy ... 200
858. Aubergines stuffed with sauce ... 200
859. Delicious potato pancakes ... 200
860. Vegetable kebabs with simple peanut sauce ... 200
861. Vegetable fritters for children ... 201
862. Almond-apple deal ... 201
863. Mushrooms with cheese ... 201
864. Deliciously healthy crisps ... 201
865. Mixed fresh vegetables from the garden 201
866. Curry and Coriander Spiced Bread Rolls 202
867. Coloured vegetable croquettes ... 202
868. Croissant rolls ... 202
869. Barbecued roasted almonds ... 202
870. Bacon sautéed with spinach ... 203
871. Thai sweet potato dumplings ... 203
872. Italian easy to season pasta sheets ... 203
873. Spicy tofu ... 203
874. Cheese balls with mushrooms and cauliflower ... 203
875. Almond Flour Battered Wings ... 204
876. Open-air Falafel ... 204
877. Aubergines stuffed with vegetables ... 204
878. Mushroom and pepper pizza ... 204
879. Twice-fried cauliflower tater tots ... 205
880. Spinach and feta triangles ... 205
881. Crispy and tasty spring rolls ... 205
882. Rice salad with cauli and tomatoes ... 205
883. Corn cakes ... 205
884. Paneer cutlet ... 206
885. Famous buffalo cauliflower ... 206
886. Crispy green beans with Pecorino Romano ... 206
887. Spicy roasted cashew nuts ... 206
888. Quick Crunchy Cheese Larks ... 207
889. Chives 'n Thyme Spiced Veggie Burger ... 207
890. Celery croquettes with chive mayonnaise . 207
891. Bacon and Cheese Stuffed Mushrooms ... 207
892. Fried okra with chilli ... 207
893. Herb roasted potatoes and peppers ... 208
894. Hasselback potatoes ... 208
895. Rosemary roasted pumpkin ... 208
896. Easy granola with sultanas and walnuts ... 208
897. Corn on the Cob with Spicy Avocado Spread ... 208
898. Cauliflower and ricotta fritters ... 209
899. Mediterranean Falafel with Tzatziki ... 209
900. Wasabi Gourmet Popcorn ... 209
901. Radish and mozzarella salad with balsamic vinaigrette ... 209
902. Mediterranean-style fries with vegetable sauce ... 210
903. French fries with polenta ... 210
904. Elegant Garlic Mushroom ... 210
905. Traditional Indian Bhaji ... 210
906. Delicious mushrooms ... 210
907. Okra with green beans ... 211
908. Grilled drunken mushrooms ... 211
909. Vegetable sauce wraps ... 211
910. Versatile stuffed tomato ... 211

Other recipes for the air fryer ... 211

911. Turkey cutlets in Dijon and Curry Sauce 211
912. Egg Salad with Asparagus and Spinach ... 212
913. Peppery egg salad ... 212
914. Famous Western Eggs ... 212

915. Potato and kale croquettes ... 212
916. Fluffy omelette with beef leftovers ... 213
917. Fruit skewers with a Greek twist ... 213
918. Cajun Turkey Meatloaf ... 213
919. Spring chocolate doughnuts ... 213
920. Double Cheese Balls with Mushrooms ... 213
921. Crispy Wontons with Asian Sauce ... 214
922. Bagel 'n' Egg Melts ... 214
923. Homemade pork scratchings ... 214
924. Breakfast eggs with chard and ham ... 214
925. Filipino minced meat omelette (tortang Giniling) ... 215
926. Baked Denver omelette with sausages ... 215
927. Cauliflower and Manchego Croquettes ... 215
928. Keto Rolls with Halibut and Eggs ... 215
929. Apple crisps country style ... 215
930. Creamy Italian Frittata with Kale ... 216
931. Mini sweet monkey rolls ... 216
932. Chicken avocado sliders dinner ... 216
933. Easy broccoli with cheese ... 217
934. Famous Bacon Cheese Rolls ... 217
935. Celery and bacon cakes ... 217
936. The best sweet potato crisps ... 217
937. Stuffed Chicken with Double Cheese ... 217
938. Chicken with super-easy tomato sauce ... 218
939. Quinoa with baked eggs and bacon ... 218
940. Salted pretzel croissants ... 218
941. Toast with blueberries and honey ... 218
942. Winter Baked Eggs with Italian Sausage ... 219
943. Spicy Cheese Risotto Balls ... 219
944. Za'atar Eggs with Chicken and Provolone Cheese ... 219
945. Cajun creamed chicken ... 219
946. Scrambled Eggs with Sausage ... 220
947. Pea fritters with yoghurt and parsley sauce ... 220
948. Spicy paprika chicken ... 220
949. Sweetcorn and grain fritters ... 220
950. Spicy Eggs with Sausage and Swiss Cheese 221
951. Decadent Frittata with roasted garlic and sausage ... 221
952. Deviled eggs for farmer's breakfast ... 221
953. Vegetable casserole with ham and baked eggs ... 222
954. Baked eggs with cheese and cowrie rice ... 222
955. Baked Eggs Florentine style ... 222
956. Baked Eggs with Linguica Sausage ... 222
957. Masala Baked Eggs ... 222
958. Country style pork pie ... 223
959. Jamaican Cornmeal Pudding ... 223
960. Egg muffins for breakfast ... 223
961. Grilled lemon grilled pork chops ... 224
962. Cheese and garlic stuffed chicken breasts . 224
963. Chive, feta cheese and chicken frittata ... 224
964. Rum roasted cherries ... 224
965. Omelette with smoked tofu and vegetables ... 224
966. Eggs Florentine style with spinach ... 225
967. Award-winning breaded chicken ... 225
968. Sausage, Pepper and Fontina Frittata ... 225
969. Nachos with mozzarella sticks ... 225
970. Broccoli bites with spicy sauce ... 226
971. Cheese Sticks with Ketchup ... 226
972. Salted Italian Crespelle ... 226
973. Onion rings with mayonnaise sauce ... 226
974. Two cheese and shrimp dip ... 227
975. Philadelphia mushroom omelette ... 227
976. Delicious hot fruit tart ... 227
977. Omelette with mushrooms and peppers ... 227
978. Broccoli Parmesan Fritters ... 228
979. Cheese and chive stuffed chicken rolls ... 228
980. Asparagus and Creamed Egg Salad ... 228
981. Easy Frittata with chicken sausage ... 228
982. Carrot crisps with romano cheese ... 229
983. Breakfast eggs and seafood casserole ... 229
984. Greek Revithokeftedes easy ... 229
985. Spicy potato wedges ... 229
986. Keto Brioche with Caciocavallo ... 229
987. Baked eggs with meat and tomatoes ... 230
988. Veal and Kale Omelette ... 230
989. Cauliflower balls with cheese ... 230
990. Super easy sage and lime wings ... 231
991. Spring Frittata with Chicken and Goat Cheese ... 231
992. Potatoes with cashew sauce ... 231
993. Potato appetizer with garlic and mayonnaise sauce ... 231
994. The easiest vegan burrito ever ... 231
995. Eggs with turkey bacon and green onions . 232

996. The easiest pork chops to make 232
997. English muffins with a twist 232
998. Easy fried mushrooms 232
999. Onion rings wrapped in bacon 233
1000. Roasted green bean salad with goat's cheese 233
1001. Japanese fried rice with eggs 233
21-DAY MEAL PLAN 234

Introduction

The air fryer is a popular kitchen appliance used to prepare foods such as meat, cakes and chips, but free of oils. It works by circulating hot air around the food to produce a crispy exterior.

Hot air circulation also leads to a chemical reaction known as the Maillard effect, which occurs between an amino acid and a reducing sugar in the presence of heat. This causes alterations in the colour and flavour of the food (Reliable source).

Air-fried foods are promoted as a healthy alternative to fried foods due to their lower fat and calorie content. Instead of completely submerging the food in oil, air frying requires only a tablespoon of oil to achieve a taste and texture similar to fried foods.

The taste and texture of air-fried food is comparable to the results of a deep fryer: crispy on the outside and juicy on the inside. However, only a small amount of oil needs to be used if at all (depending on what is being cooked).

So yes, compared to frying, air frying is definitely a healthier alternative if you commit to using only 1-2 tablespoons of a vegetable-based oil with seasonings, and stick to air frying vegetables more than anything else. Any gadget that helps you and your family improve your vegetable intake is key to controlling weight, reducing the risk of chronic disease and improving long-term health as we age.

What can be cooked in an air fryer?

Air fryers are fast and, once you understand how they work, can be used to heat frozen foods or cook all kinds of fresh foods such as chicken, steak, pork chops, salmon and vegetables. Most meats don't need added oil because they are already so juicy - just season them with salt and your favourite herbs and spices. Make sure the seasonings are dry, as less moisture will result in a crispier result. If you want to drizzle the meats with barbecue sauce or honey, wait until the last two minutes of cooking. Lean cuts of meat, or foods with little or no fat, need oil to brown and crisp. Brush boneless chicken breasts and pork chops with a little oil before seasoning. Vegetable oil or canola oil is often recommended because they have a higher smoke point, which means they can withstand the high heat of the air fryer.

Vegetables should also be sautéed in oil before air-frying. We recommend sprinkling them with salt before air-frying, but use a little less than you are used to: crispy pieces fried in the open air have a lot of flavour. We love air-frying broccoli florets, Brussels sprouts and small potato halves. They get very crispy. Squash, sweet potatoes and beets seem sweeter, and green beans and peppers take no time at all to cook.

The use of an air fryer can help reduce fat content.

Fried foods tend to have more fat than foods prepared by other cooking methods. For example, a fried chicken breast contains about 30% more fat than an equal amount of grilled chicken.

Some manufacturers claim that the use of an air fryer can reduce the fat content of fried foods by up to 75%. This is because air fryers require much less fat than traditional fryers. While many recipes for fried dishes require up to 3 cups (750 ml) of oil, air fried foods require only one tablespoon (15 ml). This means that air fryers use up to 50 times more oil than air fryers and, although not all of that oil is absorbed by the food, using an air fryer can significantly reduce the total fat content of your food.

Air frying resulted in a final product with much less fat, but with a similar colour and moisture content. This may have a major impact on health, as higher consumption of fats from vegetable oils has been associated with an increased risk of conditions such as heart disease and inflammation.

Switching to an air fryer can help with weight loss

Fried foods not only have more fat, but also more calories and may contribute to weight gain. Higher consumption of fried foods was associated with an increased risk of obesity. If you want to reduce your waistline, switching from fried foods to air-fried foods can be a good place to start. At 9 calories per gram of fat, dietary fat contains more than twice as many calories per gram as other macronutrients such as protein and carbohydrates. Since air-fried foods are lower in fat than deep-fried products, switching to an air fryer can be an easy way to reduce calories and promote weight loss.

Air fryers can reduce the formation of harmful compounds.

In addition to more fat and calories, frying foods can create potentially dangerous compounds such as acrylamide. Acrylamide is a compound that forms in carbohydrate-rich foods during high-temperature cooking methods such as frying. According to the International Agency for Research on Cancer, acrylamide is classified as a "probable carcinogen", which means that some research shows that acrylamide may be linked to the development of cancer.

Although results are conflicting, some studies have found an association between dietary acrylamide and an increased risk of kidney, endometrial and ovarian cancer. Air frying foods instead of using a deep fryer may help reduce the acrylamide content of fried foods. In fact, one study found that air frying reduced acrylamide by 90% compared to traditional frying. However, it is important to note that other harmful compounds can be formed during the air frying process.

Aldehydes, heterocyclic amines and polycyclic aromatic hydrocarbons are other potentially hazardous chemicals formed by high-temperature cooking that may be associated with an increased risk of cancer. Further research is needed to determine how outdoor cooking may affect the formation of these compounds.

Appetizers and snacks recipes

1. Shrimps with paprika and bacon

Portions: 10
Cooking time: 45 minutes
Ingredients:
- ½ kilogram of shrimps, peeled and deveined
- 1 teaspoon paprika
- ½ teaspoon ground black pepper
- ½ tsp crushed red pepper flakes
- 1 tablespoon salt
- 1 teaspoon chilli powder
- 1 tablespoon shallot powder
- 1/4 teaspoon cumin powder
- ½ kilogram of thinly sliced bacon

Addresses:
1. Toss the shrimp with all the seasoning until well coated.
2. Then wrap the prawns with a slice of bacon and secure with a toothpick, repeat with the rest of the ingredients, chill for 30 minutes.
3. Place the preparation in the air fryer for 7 to 8 minutes, working in batches. Serve with cocktail sticks if desired. Enjoy.

2. Broccoli and cheese nuggets

Servings: 4
Cooking time: 15 minutes
Ingredients:
- 1/4 cup almond flour
- 2 cups broccoli florets, cooked until tender
- 1 cup shredded cheddar cheese
- 2 egg whites
- 1/8 teaspoon salt

Addresses:
1. Preheat the air fryer to 163°C.
2. Spray the air fryer basket with cooking spray.
3. Add the cooked broccoli to the bowl and using a masher, mash the broccoli into small pieces.
4. Add the rest of the ingredients to the bowl and mix well to combine.
5. Make small nuggets with the broccoli mixture and place them in the basket of the air fryer.
6. Cook the broccoli nuggets for 15 minutes. Turn them over halfway through.
7. Serve and enjoy.

3. Mixed nuts

Servings: 8
Cooking time: 15 minutes
Ingredients:
- 2 cups of mixed nuts
- 1 teaspoon chipotle chili powder
- 1 teaspoon ground cumin
- 1 tablespoon melted butter
- 1 teaspoon pepper
- 1 teaspoon salt

Addresses:
1. In a bowl, combine all the ingredients, coating the walnuts well.
2. Set your Air Fryer to about 175°C and let it heat up for 5 minutes.
3. Place the mixed nuts in the fryer basket and roast for 4 minutes, shaking the basket halfway through cooking.

4. Herb roasted cauliflower

Servings: 2
Cooking time: 20 minutes
Ingredients:
- 3 cups cauliflower florets
- 2 tablespoons sesame oil
- 1 teaspoon onion powder
- 1 teaspoon garlic powder
- 1 teaspoon thyme
- 1 teaspoon sage
- 1 teaspoon rosemary
- Sea salt and ground black pepper, to taste
- 1 teaspoon paprika

Addresses:
1. Start by preheating your fryer to 205°C.
2. Toss cauliflower with remaining ingredients, stir to coat well.
3. Cook for 12 minutes, shaking the cooking basket halfway through cooking. The cauliflower will crisp as it cools, enjoy!

5. Healthy broccoli crisps

Servings: 4
Cooking time: 25 minutes
Ingredients:
- 450 grams of broccoli, chopped
- 1/2 cup almond flour
- 1/4 cup ground flaxseed
- 1/2 teaspoon garlic powder
- 1 teaspoon salt

Addresses:
1. Add the broccoli to the microwave-safe bowl and microwave for 3 minutes.
2. Transfer the steamed broccoli to the food processor and process until it resembles rice.
3. Transfer the broccoli to a large mixing bowl.
4. Add the rest of the ingredients to the bowl and mix until well combined.
5. Spray the air fryer basket with cooking spray.
6. Make small tots with the broccoli mixture and place them in the fryer basket.
7. Cook the broccoli tots for 12 minutes at 3F.
8. Serve and enjoy.

6. Baked cheese crisps

Servings: 4
Cooking time: 15 minutes
Ingredients:

- 1/2 cup grated Parmesan cheese
- 1 cup grated Cheddar cheese
- 1 teaspoon Italian seasoning
- 1/2 cup marinara sauce

Addresses:
1. Start by preheating your Air Fryer to 180°C. Place a piece of parchment paper in the cooking basket.
2. Mix the cheese with the Italian seasoning.
3. Add about 1 tablespoon of the cheese mixture to the basket, making sure they do not touch. Bake for 6 minutes or until golden brown to your liking.
4. Work in batches and place on a large platter to cool slightly. Serve with the marinara sauce and enjoy!

7. Cashew nut bowls

Servings: 4
Cooking time: 5 minutes
Ingredients:
- 115 grams of cashew nuts
- 1 teaspoon ranch seasoning
- 1 teaspoon sesame oil

Addresses:
1. Preheat the air fryer to 190°C. Mix the cashews with the ranch seasoning and sesame oil and place in the preheated air fryer. Cook the cashew nuts for 4 minutes. Then shake well and cook for another minute.

8. Baked tortillas

Servings: 4
Cooking time: 30 minutes
Ingredients:
- 1 large head of cauliflower divided into florets.
- 4 large eggs
- 2 cloves garlic (minced)
- 1 ½ teaspoon herbs (whatever your favourite: basil, oregano, thyme)
- ½ teaspoon salt

Addresses:
1. Preheat your fryer to 190°C/0°C.
2. Place parchment paper on two baking trays.
3. In a food processor, shred the cauliflower into rice.
4. Add ¼ cup of water and the mashed cauliflower to a saucepan.
5. Cook over medium-high heat until tender for 10 minutes. Drain.
6. Dry with a clean kitchen towel.
7. Mix the cauliflower, eggs, garlic, herbs and salt.
8. Make 4 thin circles on the parchment paper.
9. Bake for 20 minutes, until dry.

9. Green beans with lemon

Servings: 4
Cooking time: 20 minutes
Ingredients:
- 1 lemon, squeezed
- 450 grams of green beans, washed and de-stemmed
- ¼ teaspoon extra virgin olive oil
- Sea salt to taste
- Black pepper to taste

Addresses:
1. Preheat the Air Fryer to 200°C.
2. Place the green beans in the basket of the Air Fryer and drizzle the lemon juice over them.
3. Sprinkle with pepper and salt. Pour in the oil and toss to coat the green beans well.
4. Cook for 10 - 12 minutes and serve hot.

10. Pork rinds

Servings: 3
Cooking time: 10 minutes
Ingredients:
- 170 grams of pork skin
- 1 tablespoon keto tomato sauce
- 1 teaspoon olive oil

Addresses:
1. Chop the pork skin into the rinds and drizzle with the sauce and olive oil. Mix well. Then preheat the air fryer to 200°C. Place the pork rinds in the basket of the air fryer in one layer and cook for minutes. Turn the pork rinds over on the other side after 5 minutes of cooking.

11. Cocktail Meatballs for Kids

Servings: 8
Cooking time: 20 minutes
Ingredients:
- ½ teaspoon fine sea salt
- 1 cup grated Romano cheese
- 3 cloves garlic, minced
- 680 grams of ground pork
- ½ cup spring onions, finely chopped
- 2 eggs, well beaten
- 1/3 teaspoon cumin powder
- 2/3 teaspoon ground black pepper, or more to taste
- 2 teaspoons basil

Addresses:
1. Just combine all the ingredients in a large bowl.
2. Shape into bite-sized balls, cook the meatballs in the air fryer for 18 minutes at 175°C. Serve with some sour sauce, such as marinara sauce, if desired. Serve with some tangy sauce, such as marinara sauce, if desired - bon appetit!

12. Spinach rolls

Servings: 6
Cooking time: 4 minutes
Ingredients:

- 1 package of frozen or thawed spinach
- 1 red onion, chopped
- 1 cup chopped fresh parsley
- 1 cup fresh mint leaves, chopped
- 1 egg
- 1 cup crumbled feta cheese
- ½ cup grated Romano cheese
- ¼ teaspoon ground cardamom
- Salt and freshly ground black pepper, as needed
- 1 packet frozen filo dough, thawed
- 2 tablespoons olive oil

Addresses:
1. Place all the ingredients listed, except the filo dough and oil, in a food processor and pulse until smooth.
2. Place a sheet of filo on the cutting board and cut it into three rectangular strips.
3. Coat each strip with the oil.
4. Add a teaspoon of the spinach mixture along with the short side of a strip.
5. Roll the dough to secure the filling.
6. Repeat with the rest of the filo sheets and the spinach mixture.
7. Set the temperature of the Air Fryer to 180°C. Grease the basket of the Air Fryer.
8. Place the rolls in the prepared basket in a single layer.
9. Chill in the open air for about 4 minutes.
10. Enjoy!

13. Crunchy aubergine with cheese

Servings: 4
Cooking time: 45 minutes
Ingredients:
- 1 aubergine, peeled and thinly sliced
- Salt
- 1/2 cup almond flour
- 1/4 cup canola oil
- 1/2 cup water
- 1 teaspoon garlic powder
- 1/2 teaspoon dried dill weed
- 1/2 teaspoon ground black pepper, to taste

Addresses:
1. Salt the aubergine slices and leave for about 30 minutes. Squeeze the aubergine slices and rinse them under cold running water.
2. Mix the aubergine slices with the other ingredients. Cook at 195 °C for 13 minutes, working in batches.
3. Serve with a dipping sauce and enjoy!

14. Vegetable sandwich

Servings: 2
Cooking time: 25 minutes
Ingredients:
For the barbecue sauce:
- 1 teaspoon olive oil
- 1 clove garlic, minced
- ¼ onion, chopped
- ½ cup water
- ½ tablespoon sugar
- ½ tablespoon Worcestershire sauce
- ¼ teaspoon of mustard powder
- 1½ tablespoons tomato ketchup
- salt and ground black pepper, as needed

For the sandwich:
- 2 tablespoons softened butter
- 1 cup sweet corn kernels
- 1 roasted green pepper, chopped
- 4 slices of bread, sliced horizontally

Addresses:
For the barbecue sauce:
1. For the barbecue sauce, place the oil in a medium frying pan and heat over medium heat to sauté the garlic and onion for about 3-5 minutes.
2. Add the rest of the ingredients and bring to the boil over high heat.
3. Reduce heat to medium and simmer for about 8-10 minutes or until desired thickness.
4. For the sandwich: in a frying pan, melt the butter over medium heat and sauté the corn for about 1-2 minutes.
5. In a bowl, mix together the barbecue sauce, corn and pepper.
6. Spread corn mixture on one side of 2 slices of bread.
7. Top with the remaining slices.
8. Set the temperature of the Air Fryer to 180°C.
9. Place the sandwiches in the basket of the Air Fryer in a single layer.
10. Chill in the open air for about 5-6 minutes.
11. Serve.

15. Southern cheese straws

Servings: 6
Cooking time: 30 minutes
Ingredients:
- 1 cup all-purpose flour
- Sea salt and ground black pepper, to taste
- 1/4 teaspoon smoked paprika
- 1/2 teaspoon celery seeds
- 115 grams of freshly grated, cold, mature Cheddar cheese
- 1 stick of butter

Addresses:
1. Start by preheating your air fryer to 165°C. Line the air fryer basket with parchment paper.
2. In a bowl, thoroughly mix the flour, salt, black pepper, paprika and celery seeds.
3. Next, combine the cheese and butter in the bowl of a mixer. Gradually add the flour mixture and mix well.
4. Then put the dough into a biscuit press fitted with a star disc. Place the long strips

of dough on the parchment paper. Then cut into 15-centimetre lengths.
5. Bake in the preheated air fryer for 1 minute.
6. Repeat with the rest of the dough. Leave the cheese straws to cool on a wire rack. You can store them between sheets of parchment in an airtight container. Bon appetit!

16. Sage Radish Chips

Servings: 6
Cooking time: 35 minutes
Ingredients:
- 2 cups of sliced radish
- ½ teaspoon sage
- 2 teaspoons avocado oil
- ½ teaspoon salt

Addresses:
1. In the bowl of a blender, combine the radish, sage, avocado oil and salt. Preheat the air fryer to 160°C. Place the sliced radish in the basket of the air fryer and cook for 35 minutes. Shake the vegetables every minute.

17. Courgette rolls

Servings: 2 - 4
Cooking time: 15 minutes
Ingredients:
- 3 courgettes, thinly sliced lengthwise with a mandolin or a very sharp knife
- 1 tablespoon of olive oil
- 1 cup of goat cheese
- ¼ teaspoon of black pepper

Addresses:
1. Preheat your Air Fryer to 200°C.
2. Coat each courgette strip with a light brushing of olive oil.
3. Combine the sea salt, black pepper and goat's cheese.
4. Place a small amount of goat's cheese in the centre of each courgette strip. Roll up the strips and secure with a toothpick.
5. Transfer to the Air Fryer and cook for minutes until the cheese is hot and the courgette is slightly crisp. If desired, add a little tomato sauce on top.

18. Easy carrot dip

Servings: 6
Cooking time: 15 minutes
Ingredients:
- 2 cups of grated carrots
- 1/4 teaspoon cayenne pepper
- 4 tablespoons melted butter
- 1 tablespoon chopped chives
- Pepper
- Salt

Addresses:
1. Add all ingredients to the baking tray of the air fryer and stir until well combined.
2. Place the dish in the air fryer and cook at 190°C for 15 minutes.
3. Transfer the cooked carrot mixture to a blender and blend until smooth.
4. Serve and enjoy.

19. Cauliflower popcorn with turmeric

Servings: 4
Cooking time: 11 minutes
Ingredients:
- 1 cup cauliflower florets
- 1 teaspoon ground turmeric
- 2 beaten eggs
- 2 tablespoons almond flour
- 1 teaspoon salt
- Cooking spray

Addresses:
1. Cut the cauliflower florets into small pieces and sprinkle with ground turmeric and salt. Then dip the vegetables in the eggs and dredge them in the almond flour. Preheat the air fryer to 200°C. Place the cauliflower popcorn in the air fryer in a single layer and cook for 7 minutes. Give the vegetables a good shake and cook for a further 4 minutes.

20. Sweet potatoes

Portions: 24
Cooking time: 31 minutes
Ingredients:
- 2 peeled potatoes
- 1/2 teaspoon Cajun seasoning
- Salt

Addresses:
1. Add water to a large pot and bring to the boil. Add the sweet potatoes to the pot and boil for a few minutes. Drain well.
2. Grate the boiled sweet potatoes into a large bowl using a grater.
3. Add the Cajun seasoning and salt to the grated sweet potatoes and mix until well combined.
4. Spray the air fryer basket with cooking spray.
5. Make a small batch of the sweet potato mixture and place it in the basket of the air fryer.
6. Cook at 200°C for 8 minutes. Turn the tots over and cook for a further 8 minutes.
7. Serve and enjoy.

21. Cajun spiced appetizer

Portions: 5
Cooking time: 30 minutes
Ingredients:
- 2 tablespoons Cajun or Creole seasoning
- ½ cup melted butter
- 2 cups of peanuts
- 2 cups thin mini wheat crackers
- 2 cups mini pretzels

- 2 teaspoons salt
- 1 teaspoon cayenne pepper
- 4 cups of plain popcorn
- 1 teaspoon paprika
- 1 teaspoon garlic
- ½ teaspoon thyme
- ½ teaspoon oregano
- 1 teaspoon black pepper
- ½ teaspoon onion powder

Addresses:
1. Preheat the Air Fryer to 185°C.
2. In a bowl, combine the Cajun spice with the melted butter.
3. In a separate bowl, mix together the peanuts, crackers, popcorn and pretzels. Top the sandwiches with the butter mixture.
4. Place in the fryer and fry for 8 - 10 minutes, shaking the basket frequently during the cooking time. You will need to complete this step in two batches.
5. Place the snack mixture on a biscuit sheet and allow to cool.
6. The snacks can be stored in an airtight container for up to one week.

22. Cheese croquettes wrapped in bacon

Servings: 6
Cooking time: 8 minutes
Ingredients:
- 450 grams of thin slices of bacon
- 150 grams of strong block cheddar cheese cut into rectangular pieces of approximately 2.5 centimetres
- 1 cup plain flour
- 3 eggs
- 1 cup breadcrumbs
- 1 tablespoon of olive oil
- Salt, to taste

Addresses:
1. Preheat the fryer to 195°C and grease one fryer basket.
2. Wrap 1 piece of cheddar cheese with the bacon slices, covering them completely.
3. Repeat with the rest of the cheese and the bacon slices.
4. Place the croquettes in a baking dish and freeze for about 10 minutes.
5. Place the flour in a shallow dish.
6. Beat the eggs in a second dish.
7. Mix the oil, breadcrumbs and salt in a third shallow dish.
8. Dredge the croquettes evenly in flour and dip them in the eggs.
9. Dredge in the breadcrumb mixture and place the croquettes in the fryer basket.
10. Cook for about 8 minutes and serve hot.

23. Mexican Zucchini and Bacon Ole Tortas

Servings: 4
Cooking time: 22 minutes
Ingredients:
- 1/3 cup grated Swiss cheese
- 1/3 teaspoon fine sea salt
- 1/3 teaspoon baking powder
- 1/3 cup spring onions, finely chopped
- 1/2 tablespoon finely chopped fresh basil
- 1 courgette, chopped.
- 1/2 tsp freshly ground black pepper
- 1 teaspoon of Mexican oregano
- 1 cup chopped bacon
- 1/4 cup almond flour
- 1/4 cup coconut flour
- 2 small eggs, lightly beaten
- 1 cup grated Cotija cheese

Addresses:
1. Mix all the ingredients, except the cheese, until everything is well combined.
2. Then gently flatten each ball. Spray the cakes with non-stick cooking oil.
3. Bake the cakes for 1 minute at 150°C and work in batches. Serve hot with tomato ketchup and mayonnaise.

24. Mozzarella sticks

Servings: 4
Cooking time: 60 minutes
Ingredients:
- 6 mozzarella cheese sticks of about 50 grams
- 1 teaspoon dried parsley
- 100 grams of finely ground pork rind
- ½ cup grated Parmesan cheese
- 2 eggs

Addresses:
1. Cut the mozzarella sticks in half and freeze them for forty-five minutes. Optionally, you can leave them longer and place them in a Ziploc bag to prevent freezer burn.
2. In a small bowl, combine the dried parsley, pork rind and Parmesan cheese.
3. In a separate bowl, beat the eggs with a fork.
4. Take a frozen mozzarella stick and dip it into the eggs, then into the pork rind mixture, making sure to coat it completely. Proceed with the rest of the cheese sticks, placing each coated stick in the basket of your air fryer.
5. Bake at 200 °C for ten minutes, until golden brown.
6. Serve hot, with a little homemade marinara sauce if desired.

25. Plain banana chips

Servings: 8
Cooking time: 10 minutes
Ingredients:
- 2 raw bananas, peeled and cut into slices
- 2 tablespoons olive oil
- Salt and black pepper, to taste

Addresses:

1. Preheat the fryer to 180°C and grease the fryer basket.
2. Drizzle the banana slices with olive oil and place them in the fryer basket.
3. Cook for about 10 minutes and season with salt and black pepper.
4. Serve hot.

26. Brussels sprouts with feta cheese

Servings: 4
Cooking time: 20 minutes
Ingredients:
- 350 grams of Brussels sprouts, trimmed and without ends
- 1 teaspoon kosher salt
- 1 tablespoon lemon zest
- Non-stick cooking spray
- 1 cup feta cheese, cubed

Addresses:
1. First, peel the Brussels sprouts with a small paring knife. Mix the leaves with salt and lemon zest, spray them with cooking spray, covering all sides.
2. Bake at 195°C for 8 minutes, shake the cooking basket halfway through the cooking time and cook for a further 7 minutes.
3. Be sure to work in batches so that everything cooks evenly. Taste and adjust seasonings. Serve with feta cheese - bon appetit!

27. Cumin pork sticks

Servings: 4
Cooking time: 12 minutes
Ingredients:
- 2 beaten eggs
- 4 tablespoons flaxseed meal
- ½ teaspoon chilli powder
- ¼ teaspoon ground cumin
- 225 grams of pork loin
- 1 teaspoon sunflower oil

Addresses:
1. Cut the pork loin into sticks and sprinkle with chilli powder and cumin powder. Then dip the pork sticks into the eggs and coat them with the linseed meal. Place the meat in the air fryer and drizzle with sunflower oil. Cook the sandwich at 200°C for 6 minutes. Then turn the pork sticks on the other side and cook for a further 6 minutes.

28. Pepper chips

Servings: 4
Cooking time: 20 minutes
Ingredients:
- 1 beaten egg
- 1/2 cup grated Parmesan
- 1 teaspoon sea salt
- 1/2 teaspoon crushed red pepper flakes
- 350 grams of peppers, deveined and cut into strips of approximately 5 millimetres
- 2 tablespoons grapeseed oil

Addresses:
1. In a bowl, combine egg, Parmesan, salt and red pepper flakes, stir to combine well.
2. Dip the peppers in the batter and transfer them to the cooking basket. Brush with the grape seed oil.
3. Cook for 4 minutes in the preheated Air Fryer. Shake the basket and cook for a further 3 minutes. Work in batches.
4. Taste, adjust the seasoning and serve - bon appetit!

29. Crispy bacon bites

Servings: 4
Cooking time: 10 minutes
Ingredients:
- 4 strips of bacon, cut in small pieces
- 1/2 cup pork rinds, shredded
- 1/4 cup hot sauce

Addresses:
1. Add the bacon pieces to a bowl.
2. Add the hot sauce and mix well.
3. Add the crushed pork rinds and mix until the bacon pieces are well coated.
4. Place the bacon pieces in the basket of the air fryer and cook at 180°C for 10 minutes.
5. Serve and enjoy.

30. Chips with broccoli and spicy sauce

Servings: 4
Cooking time: 15 minutes
Ingredients:
- 350 grams of broccoli florets
- 1/2 teaspoon onion powder
- 1 teaspoon granulated garlic
- 1/2 tsp cayenne pepper
- Sea salt and ground black pepper, to taste
- 2 tablespoons sesame oil
- 4 tablespoons Parmesan cheese, preferably freshly grated

For the hot sauce you need:
- 1/4 cup mayonnaise
- 1/4 cup Greek yogurt
- 1/4 teaspoon Dijon mustard
- 1 teaspoon hot sauce

Addresses:
1. Start by preheating the fryer to 200°C.
2. Blanch the broccoli in boiling salted water until al dente, about 3 to 4 minutes. Drain well and transfer to the lightly greased basket of the Air Fryer.
3. Add the onion powder, garlic, cayenne pepper, salt, black pepper, sesame oil and Parmesan cheese.
4. Cook for 6 minutes, stirring halfway through cooking.

5. In the meantime, mix all the ingredients for the hot sauce. Serve the broccoli fries with the cold sauce and enjoy!

31. Spicy dip

Servings: 6
Cooking time: 5 minutes
Ingredients:
- 340 grams chopped chilli peppers
- 1 and 1/2 cups apple cider vinegar
- Pepper
- Salt

Addresses:
1. Add all ingredients into the air fryer pan and stir well.
2. Place the dish in the air fryer and cook at 195 °C for 5 minutes.
3. Transfer the pepper mixture to a blender and blend until smooth.
4. Serve and enjoy.

32. Crispy Broccoli Crisps

Servings: 4
Cooking time: 15 minutes
Ingredients:
- 450 grams broccoli florets
- 1/2 teaspoon onion powder
- 1 teaspoon granulated garlic
- 1/2 teaspoon cayenne pepper
- Sea salt and ground black pepper, to taste
- 2 tablespoons sesame oil
- 4 tablespoons Parmesan cheese, preferably freshly grated

Addresses:
1. Start by preheating the fryer to 200°C.
2. Blanch the broccoli in boiling salted water until al dente, about 3 to 4 minutes. Drain well and transfer to the lightly greased basket of the Air Fryer.
3. Add the onion powder, garlic, cayenne pepper, salt, black pepper and sesame oil.
4. Cook for 6 minutes, stirring halfway through cooking. Enjoy!

33. Courgette sticks with cheese

Servings: 2
Cooking time: 20 minutes
Ingredients:
- 1 courgette cut into strips
- 2 tablespoons mayonnaise
- 1/4 cup tortilla chips, crushed
- 1/4 cup grated romano cheese
- Sea salt and black pepper, to taste
- 1 tablespoon garlic powder
- 1/2 teaspoon red pepper flakes

Addresses:
1. Cover the courgettes with mayonnaise.
2. Mix the crushed tortilla chips, cheese and spices in a shallow dish.
3. Then top the courgette sticks with the cheese and chips mixture.
4. Cook for 12 minutes in the preheated air fryer, shaking the basket halfway through the cooking time.
5. Work in batches until the sticks are crispy and golden brown - bon appetit!

34. BBQ Lil Smokies

Servings: 6
Cooking time: 20 minutes
Ingredients:
- 150 grams of meat cocktail sausage
- 280 grams of barbecue sauce with no added sugar

Addresses:
1. Start by preheating your fryer to 195°C.
2. Poke holes in the sausages with a fork and transfer them to the baking tray.
3. Cook for 1 minute. Pour the barbecue sauce into the pan and cook for a further 2 minutes.
4. Serve with chopsticks, enjoy!

35. Baby corn

Servings: 4
Cooking time: 20 minutes
Ingredients:
- 225 grams of boiled tender tripe
- 1 cup flour
- 1 teaspoon garlic powder
- ½ teaspoon carambola seeds
- ¼ teaspoon chilli powder
- A pinch of bicarbonate of soda
- Salt to taste

Addresses:
1. In a bowl, combine flour, chili powder, garlic powder, baking soda, salt and carom seeds. Add a little water to create a dough-like consistency.
2. Dredge each small corn in the batter.
3. Preheat the Air Fryer.
4. Cover the basket of the Air Fryer with aluminium foil before placing the coated tripe on the foil.
5. Cook for 10 minutes.

36. Summer Meatball Skewers

Servings: 6
Cooking time: 20 minutes
Ingredients:
- 225 grams of ground pork
- 225 grams of minced meat
- 1 teaspoon dried onion flakes
- 1 teaspoon chopped fresh garlic
- 1 teaspoon dried parsley flakes
- Salt and black pepper, to taste
- 1 red pepper, chopped into 2.5 cm pieces
- 1 cup pearl onions
- 1/2 cup barbecue sauce

Addresses:

1. Mix the minced meat with the onion, garlic, parsley, salt and black pepper. Form the mixture into balls of a few centimetres.
2. Thread the meatballs, peeled onions and peppers alternately onto the skewers.
3. Heat the barbecue sauce in the microwave for 10 seconds.
4. Cook in the preheated Air Fryer at 195°C for 5 minutes. Turn the skewers halfway through cooking. Brush with the sauce and cook for a further 5 minutes. Work in batches.
5. Serve with the remaining barbecue sauce and enjoy.

37. Cauliflower Bombs with Sweet and Sour Sauce

Servings: 4
Cooking time: 25 minutes
Ingredients:
For the cauliflower bombs:
- 225 grams of cauliflower
- 55 grams of ricotta cheese
- 1/3 cup Swiss cheese
- 1 egg
- 1 tablespoon Italian seasoning

For the sweet and sour sauce:
- 1 canned red pepper
- 1 clove garlic, minced
- 1 teaspoon sherry vinegar
- 1 tablespoon tomato puree
- 2 tablespoons olive oil
- Salt and black pepper, to taste

Addresses:
1. Blanch the cauliflower in boiling salted water for 3-4 minutes until al dente. Drain well and chop in a food processor.
2. Add the rest of the ingredients for the cauliflower bombs and mix to combine well.
3. Bake for 16 minutes in the preheated air fryer, stirring halfway through the cooking time.
4. In the meantime, blend all the ingredients for the sauce in your food processor until well combined. Season to taste and serve the cauliflower bombs with the sweet and sour sauce on the side - bon appetit!

38. French fries with Greek yoghurt sauce

Portions: 5
Cooking time: 20 minutes
Ingredients:
- 1/2 cup maize flour
- 1/2 cup all-purpose flour
- 1 teaspoon cayenne pepper
- 1/2 teaspoon shallot powder
- 1 teaspoon garlic powder
- 1/2 teaspoon boletus powder
- Kosher salt and ground black pepper, to taste
- 2 eggs
- 2 cups of gherkin pieces, dried with kitchen towels

For the Greek yoghurt dip you need:
- 1/2 cup Greek yoghurt
- 1 clove garlic, minced
- 1/4 teaspoon ground black pepper
- 1 tablespoon chopped fresh chives

Addresses:
1. In a shallow bowl, mix together the cornmeal and flour, add the seasonings and mix to combine well. Beat the eggs in another shallow bowl.
2. Dredge the gherkins in the flour mixture and then in the egg mixture. Press the gherkin pieces into the flour mixture again, coating evenly.
3. Cook in the preheated Air Fryer at 200°C for 5 minutes, shake the basket and cook for a further 5 minutes. Work in batches.
4. Meanwhile, mix all the sauce ingredients together until well combined. Serve the fried gherkins with the Greek yoghurt sauce and enjoy.

39. Old-fashioned onion rings

Servings: 4
Cooking time: 10 minutes
Ingredients:
- 1 large onion, cut into rings
- 1¼ cups plain flour
- 1 cup of milk
- 1 egg
- ¾ cup dry bread crumbs
- Salt to taste

Addresses:
1. Preheat the fryer to 185°C and grease the fryer basket.
2. Mix the flour and salt in a dish. Beat the egg with the milk in a second bowl until well blended.
3. Place the breadcrumbs on a third plate.
4. Dredge the onion rings in the flour mixture and dip them in the egg mixture.
5. Finally, dredge them in the breadcrumbs and place the onion rings in the fryer basket.
6. Cook for about 10 minutes and serve hot.

40. Cashew nut dip

Servings: 6
Cooking time: 8 minutes
Ingredients:
- ½ cup of cashew nuts soaked in water for 4 hours and drained
- 3 tablespoons chopped coriander
- 2 cloves garlic, minced
- 1 teaspoon lime juice
- Pinch of salt and black pepper
- 2 tablespoons coconut milk

Addresses:

1. In a blender, mix all the ingredients and transfer them to a pan. Place the ramekin in the basket of your air fryer and cook at 180°C for 8 minutes. Serve as a party dip.

41. Sweet potato bites

Servings: 2
Cooking time: 30 minutes
Ingredients:
- 2 sweet potatoes, cut into 2.5 centimetre cubes
- 1 teaspoon red chilli flakes
- 2 teaspoons cinnamon
- 2 tablespoons olive oil
- 2 tablespoons honey
- ½ cup chopped fresh parsley

Addresses:
1. Preheat the Air Fryer to 180°C.
2. Put all the ingredients in a bowl and stir well to coat the sweet potato cubes completely.
3. Place the sweet potato mixture in the basket of the Air Fryer and cook for 15 minutes.

42. Roasted peanuts

Portions: 10
Cooking time: 14 minutes
Ingredients:
- 2½ cups raw peanuts
- 1 tablespoon of olive oil
- Salt as needed

Addresses:
1. Set the temperature of the Air Fryer to 160°C.
2. Add the peanuts to the basket of the Air Fryer in a single layer.
3. Fry for about 9 minutes, stirring twice.
4. Remove the peanuts from the basket of the Air Fryer and transfer them to a bowl.
5. Add the oil and salt and stir to coat well.
6. Place the nut mixture back into the basket of the Air Fryer.
7. Fry for about 5 minutes.
8. Once done, transfer the hot nuts into a glass or steel bowl and serve.

43. Crunchy aubergine

Servings: 4
Cooking time: 20 minutes
Ingredients:
- 1 aubergine, cut into 2.5 centimetre pieces
- 1/2 teaspoon Italian seasoning
- 1 teaspoon paprika
- 1/2 teaspoon red pepper
- 1 teaspoon garlic powder
- 2 tablespoons olive oil

Addresses:
1. Add all ingredients to the large bowl and mix well.
2. Transfer the aubergine mixture to the fryer basket.
3. Cook for 20 minutes in the air fryer and shake the basket halfway through.
4. Serve and enjoy.

44. Chicken party pillows

Servings: 4
Cooking time: 20 minutes
Ingredients:
- 1 teaspoon olive oil
- 1 cup ground chicken
- 1 can (225 grams) Pillsbury Crescent Roll Dough
- Sea salt and ground black pepper, to taste
- 1 teaspoon onion powder
- 1/2 teaspoon garlic powder
- 4 tablespoons tomato paste
- 115 grams of cream cheese at room temperature
- 2 tablespoons melted butter

Addresses:
1. Heat the olive oil in a skillet over medium-high heat. Then cook the ground chicken until golden brown or about 4 minutes.
2. Roll out the crescent dough. Roll out the dough with a rolling pin and cut it into 8 pieces.
3. Place the browned chicken, salt, black pepper, onion powder, garlic powder, tomato paste and cheese in the centre of each piece.
4. Fold each corner over the filling with wet hands. Press to cover the filling completely and seal the edges.
5. Now, spray the bottom of the Air Fryer basket with cooking oil. Place the chicken pads in a single layer in the cooking basket. Drizzle the melted butter over the chicken pads.
6. Bake at 190°C until golden brown. Work in batches - bon appetit!

45. Mixed vegetables

Servings: 4
Cooking time: 45 minutes
Ingredients:
- 100 grams of radish
- ½ teaspoon parsley
- 100 grams of celery
- 1 yellow carrot
- 1 orange carrot
- 1 red onion
- 100 grams of pumpkin
- 100 grams of parsnips
- Salt to taste
- Pepper to taste
- 1 tablespoon of olive oil
- 4 unpeeled garlic cloves

Addresses:

1. Peel and cut all the vegetables into 2 to 3 cm pieces.
2. Preheat your Air Fryer to 195°C.
3. Pour in the oil and allow it to heat up before placing the vegetables in the fryer, followed by the garlic, salt and pepper.
4. Roast for 18 - 20 minutes.
5. Top with parsley and serve hot with rice if desired.

46. Quick and easy popcorn

Servings: 4
Cooking time: 20 minutes
Ingredients:
- 2 tablespoons dried corn kernels
- 1 teaspoon safflower oil
- Kosher salt to taste
- 1 teaspoon crushed red pepper flakes

Addresses:
1. Add the dried corn kernels to the basket of the Air Fryer and coat it with safflower oil.
2. Cook at 200°C for 15 minutes, shaking the basket every 5 minutes.
3. Sprinkle with salt and red pepper flakes and enjoy!

47. Dill cheese mushrooms

Servings: 6
Cooking time: 5 minutes
Ingredients:
- 255 grams of sliced mushroom stems
- 1 teaspoon dried parsley
- 1 teaspoon dried dill
- 170 grams grated cheddar cheese
- 1 tablespoon butter
- 1/2 teaspoon salt

Addresses:
1. Finely chop the mushroom stems and place in the bowl.
2. Add the parsley, dill, cheese, butter and salt to the bowl and mix until well combined.
3. Preheat the air fryer to 200°C.
4. Fill the mushroom caps with the mixture in the bowl and place them in the fryer basket.
5. Cook the mushrooms for a few minutes.
6. Serve and enjoy.

48. Plain horseradish chips

Portions: 12
Cooking time: 15 minutes
Ingredients:
- 450 grams of radishes, washed and cut into chunks
- 2 tablespoons olive oil
- 1/4 teaspoon pepper
- 1 teaspoon salt

Addresses:
1. Preheat the air fryer to 190°C.
2. Add all ingredients to the large bowl and mix well.
3. Add the radish slices to the fryer basket and cook for 15 minutes. Shake the basket 2 times during cooking.
4. Serve and enjoy.

49. Roasted parsnip

Portions: 5
Cooking time: 55 minutes
Ingredients:
- 900 grams of parsnips [about 6 large parsnips].
- 2 tablespoons maple syrup
- 1 tablespoon coconut oil
- 1 tablespoon dried parsley flakes

Addresses:
1. Melt the coconut oil in your Air Fryer for 2 minutes at 160°C.
2. Rinse the parsnips to clean and dry them. Chop into 2.5 cm cubes. Transfer to the deep fryer.
3. Cook the parsnip cubes in the oil for 35 minutes, stirring regularly.
4. Season the parsnips with parsley and maple syrup and cook for another 5 minutes or more to achieve a smooth texture throughout. Serve immediately.

50. Apple chips

Servings: 2
Cooking time: 16 minutes
Ingredients:
- 1 apple, peeled, cored and thinly sliced
- 1 tablespoon sugar
- ½ teaspoon ground cinnamon
- Pinch of ground cardamom
- Pinch of ground ginger
- A pinch of salt

Addresses:
1. Set the temperature of the Air Fryer to 200°C.
2. In a bowl, add all the ingredients and toss to coat well.
3. Place the apple slices in the basket of the Air Fryer in a single layer in 2 batches.
4. Air fry for about 7-8 minutes, turning once halfway through.
5. Serve.

51. Polenta sticks

Servings: 4
Cooking time: 6 minutes
Ingredients:
- 2½ cups cooked polenta
- Salt as needed
- ¼ cup grated Parmesan cheese

Addresses:
1. Spread the polenta evenly in a greased baking dish and, with the back of a spoon, smooth the top surface.
2. Cover the baking dish and refrigerate for about 1 hour or until set.

3. Remove from the refrigerator and cut the polenta into slices of the desired size.
4. Set the temperature of the Air Fryer to 180°C. Grease a baking tray.
5. Place the polenta sticks in the prepared baking dish in a single layer and sprinkle with salt.
6. Place the baking tray in the basket of the Air Fryer.
7. Chill in the open air for about 5-6 minutes.
8. Top with cheese and serve.

52. Fried green tomatoes

Servings: 2
Cooking time: 10 minutes
Ingredients:
- 2 medium green tomatoes
- 1 egg
- ¼ cup finely ground, bleached flour
- 1/3 cup grated Parmesan cheese

Addresses:
1. Cut the tomatoes into half-centimetre-thick slices.
2. Break the egg into a bowl and beat with a mixer. In another bowl, mix the flour and Parmesan cheese.
3. Dip the tomato slices in the egg and then dredge them in the flour and cheese mixture to coat. Place each slice in the fryer basket. They may need to be cooked in several batches.
4. Cook for seven minutes in the air fryer, turning them over halfway through cooking and serve hot.

53. Coconut biscuits

Servings: 8
Cooking time: 12 minutes
Ingredients:
- 55 grams of icing sugar
- 100 grams of butter
- 1 small egg
- 1 teaspoon vanilla extract
- 140 grams of self-raising flour
- 30 grams of chopped white chocolate
- 3 tablespoons desiccated coconut

Addresses:
1. In a large bowl, add the sugar and butter and beat until fluffy and light.
2. Add the egg and vanilla extract and beat until well combined.
3. Now add the flour and chocolate and mix well.
4. In a shallow bowl, place the coconut.
5. With your hands, roll the mixture into small balls and roll them evenly in the coconut.
6. Place the balls on an ungreased baking sheet 2.5 centimetres apart and gently press down on each ball.
7. Set the fryer temperature to 185°C.
8. Place the baking tray in the fryer basket.
9. Fry in the open air for about 8 minutes and then for another 4 minutes at 160°C.
10. Remove from the fryer and place the baking tray on a wire rack to cool for about 5 minutes.
11. Now invert the biscuits onto a wire rack to cool completely before serving.
12. Serve.

54. Meat pizza without crust

Servings: 1
Cooking time: 15 minutes
Ingredients:
- ½ cup grated mozzarella cheese
- 2 slices of bacon, unsweetened, cooked and crumbled
- ¼ cup ground sausage, cooked
- 7 slices of pepperoni
- 1 tablespoon grated Parmesan cheese

Addresses:
1. Spread the mozzarella in the bottom of a 15 cm baking tin. Place the bacon, sausage and pepperoni, add a sprinkling of parmesan cheese on top.
2. Place the mould inside the air fryer.
3. Cook at 200°C for five minutes. The cheese is ready when it has a brown colour and is bubbling. Take care when removing the pan from the fryer and serve.

55. Spinach sauce

Servings: 8
Cooking time: 40 minutes
Ingredients:
- 225 grams of softened cream cheese
- 1/4 teaspoon garlic powder
- 1/2 cup chopped onion
- 1/3 cup water chestnuts, drained and chopped
- 1 cup mayonnaise
- 1 cup grated Parmesan cheese
- 1 cup frozen spinach, thawed and squeezed to remove all liquid
- 1/2 teaspoon pepper

Addresses:
1. Spray the fryer's baking dish with cooking spray.
2. Add all ingredients to the bowl and mix until well combined.
3. Transfer the mixture from the bowl to the prepared baking dish and place the dish in the fryer basket.
4. Cook at 150°C for 35 minutes. After 20 minutes of cooking, stir the sauce.
5. Serve and enjoy.

56. Tomato and Parmesan fries Italian style

Servings: 4
Cooking time: 20 minutes
Ingredients:
- 4 roma tomatoes cut into slices

- 2 tablespoons olive oil
- Sea salt and white pepper to taste
- 1 teaspoon Italian seasoning mix
- 4 tablespoons grated Parmesan cheese

Addresses:
1. Start by preheating your fryer to 180°C. Generously grease the fryer basket with non-stick cooking oil.
2. Mix the sliced tomatoes with the rest of the ingredients. Transfer to the cooking basket without overlapping.
3. Cook in the preheated Air Fryer for 5 minutes. Shake the cooking basket and cook for a further 5 minutes. Work in batches.
4. Serve with Mediterranean aioli for dipping, if desired - bon appetit!

57. Cocktail flanks

Servings: 4
Cooking time: 45 minutes
Ingredients:
- 1 package of 340 grams of cocktail sausages
- 1 tin of 225 grams of crescent rolls

Addresses:
1. Drain the cocktail sausages and dry them with kitchen paper.
2. Unroll the crescent rolls and cut the dough into rectangular strips of approximately 2.5 by 3.8 centimetres.
3. Wrap the sausages in the strips with the ends sticking out. Leave in the freezer for 5 minutes.
4. Preheat the Air Fryer to 165°C.
5. Remove the sausages from the freezer and place them in the cooking basket. Cook for 6 - 8 minutes.
6. Reduce the air fryer temperature and cook for a further 3 minutes or until a golden colour is achieved.

58. Bacon croquettes

Servings: 6
Cooking time: 8 minutes
Ingredients:
- 450 grams of thinly sliced bacon
- 450 grams of strong cheddar block cheese cut into 2.5 centimetre rectangular pieces.
- 1 cup all-purpose flour
- 3 eggs
- 1 cup breadcrumbs
- Salt as needed
- ¼ cup olive oil

Addresses:
1. Wrap 2 slices of bacon around a piece of cheddar cheese, covering it completely.
2. Repeat with the remaining pieces of bacon and cheese.
3. Place the croquettes in a baking dish and freeze for about 5 minutes.
4. Add the flour in a shallow dish.
5. In a second dish, break the eggs and beat them well.
6. In a third dish, mix the breadcrumbs, salt and oil.
7. Dredge the croquettes in flour, then dip them in the beaten eggs and finally in the breadcrumb mixture.
8. Set the temperature of the Air Fryer to 200°C.
9. Place the croquettes in the basket of the Air Fryer in a single layer.
10. Chill in the open air for about 7-8 minutes.
11. Serve hot.

59. Jalapeño Poppers with Cheese and Bacon

Portions: 5
Cooking time: 5 minutes
Ingredients:
- 10 fresh jalapeño peppers, halved and seeded
- 2 slices of bacon, cooked and crumbled
- 1/4 cup shredded cheddar cheese
- 170 grams of softened cream cheese

Addresses:
1. In a bowl, combine bacon, cream cheese and cheddar cheese.
2. Stuff each jalapeño half with the cheese and bacon mixture.
3. Spray the air fryer basket with cooking spray.
4. Place the halved stuffed jalapeños in the basket of the air fryer and cook at 185°C for 5 minutes.
5. Serve and enjoy.

60. Grilled Cheese Sandwiches

Servings: 2
Cooking time: 5 minutes
Ingredients:
- 4 slices of white bread
- ½ cup melted butter, softened
- ½ cup sharp cheddar cheese, shredded
- 1 tablespoon of mayonnaise

Addresses:
1. Preheat the fryer to 180°C and grease the fryer basket.
2. Spread the mayonnaise and melted butter on one side of each slice of bread.
3. Sprinkle the cheddar cheese on the buttered side of the 2 slices.
4. Cover with the remaining slices of bread and transfer to the fryer basket.
5. Cook for a few minutes and serve hot.

61. Cheese pastry

Servings: 6
Cooking time: 5 minutes
Ingredients:
- 1 egg yolk
- 115 grams of crumbled feta cheese
- 1 finely chopped chive

- 2 tablespoons fresh parsley, finely chopped
- Salt and ground black pepper as necessary
- 2 sheets of frozen filo pastry, thawed
- 2 tablespoons olive oil

Addresses:
1. In a large bowl, place the egg yolk and beat well.
2. Add the feta cheese, spring onions, parsley, salt and black pepper. Mix well.
3. Cut each sheet of filo pastry into three strips.
4. Add about 1 teaspoon of the feta mixture to the bottom of a strip.
5. Fold the tip of the sheet over the filling in a zigzag pattern to form a triangle.
6. Repeat with the remaining strips and fillings.
7. Set the temperature of the Air Fryer to 200°C.
8. Coat each cake evenly with oil.
9. Place the cakes in the basket of the Air Fryer in a single layer.
10. Air fry for about 3 minutes, then air fry for about 2 minutes at 180°C.
11. Serve.

62. Pizza Bites

Portions: 10
Cooking time: 3 minutes
Ingredients:
- 10 slices of mozzarella cheese
- 10 slices of pepperoni

Addresses:
1. Preheat the air fryer to 200°C.
2. Line the air fryer pan with baking paper and place the mozzarella in it in a single layer. After this, place the pan in the air fryer basket and cook the cheese for 3 minutes or until melted.
3. After this, remove the cheese from the air fryer and cool to room temperature. Then remove the melted cheese from the baking paper and place the salami slices on it. Fold the cheese into patties.

63. Pineapple Bites with Yoghurt Sauce

Servings: 4
Cooking time: 10 minutes
Ingredients:
- ½ pineapple cut into 2.5 centimetre-thick long sticks
- ¼ cup desiccated coconut
- 1 tablespoon fresh mint leaves, chopped
- 1 chopped green chilli
- 1 cup vanilla yoghurt
- 1 tablespoon of honey

Addresses:
1. Preheat the fryer to 200°C and grease one fryer basket.
2. Place the coconut in a shallow dish.
3. Dip the pineapple sticks in the honey and then dip them in the coconut.
4. Place the pineapple sticks in the fryer basket and cook for about 10 minutes.
5. For the yoghurt sauce, mix the mint, chilli and vanilla yoghurt in a bowl.
6. Serve these pineapple sticks with yoghurt sauce.

64. Chocolate bacon bites

Servings: 4
Cooking time: 10 minutes
Ingredients:
- 4 slices of bacon cut in halves
- 1 cup melted dark chocolate
- A pinch of pink salt

Addresses:
1. Dip each slice of bacon in a little chocolate, sprinkle pink salt on them, put them in the basket of your air fryer and cook at 180°C.
2. Serve as a snack.

65. Avocado wedges

Servings: 4
Cooking time: 8 minutes
Ingredients:
- 4 avocados, peeled, pitted and cut into wedges
- 1 beaten egg
- 1 ½ cups of almond flour
- Pinch of salt and black pepper
- Cooking spray

Addresses:
1. Put the egg in one bowl and the almond flour in another.
2. Season the avocado chunks with salt and pepper, dip them in the egg and then in the almond flour.
3. Place the avocado bites in the basket of your air fryer, grease with cooking spray and cook at 200°C for 8 minutes.
4. Serve as an appetizer immediately.

66. Sauteed Asian Short Ribs

Servings: 4
Cooking time: 35 minutes
Ingredients:
- 450 grams of meaty ribs
- ½ tablespoon rice vinegar
- 2 tablespoons soy sauce
- 1 tablespoon Sriracha sauce
- 2 cloves garlic, minced
- 1 tablespoon doenjang (soybean paste)
- 1 teaspoon kochukaru (chilli flakes)
- Sea salt and ground black pepper to taste
- 1 tablespoon sesame oil
- 1/4 cup green onions, coarsely chopped

Addresses:
1. Place ribs, vinegar, soy sauce, Sriracha, garlic and spices in a Ziploc bag and marinate overnight.

2. Rub the sides and bottom of the Air Fryer basket with sesame oil. Discard the marinade and transfer the ribs to the prepared cooking basket.
3. Cook the marinated ribs for 17 minutes in the preheated Air Fryer.
4. Turn the ribs over, baste with the reserved marinade and cook for a further 15 minutes.
5. Garnish with green onions and enjoy!

67. Lemon Tofu

Servings: 4
Cooking time: 15 minutes
Ingredients:
- 450 grams tofu, drained and pressed
- 1 tablespoon arrowroot powder
- 1 tablespoon tamari

For the sauce you need:
- 2 teaspoons arrowroot powder
- 2 tablespoons erythritol
- 1/2 cup water
- 1/3 cup lemon juice
- 1 teaspoon lemon zest

Addresses:
1. Cut the tofu into cubes. Add the tofu and tamari to the resealable bag and shake well.
2. Add 1 tablespoon of arrowroot to the bag and shake well to coat the tofu. Leave to stand for 15 minutes.
3. Meanwhile, in a bowl, mix all the sauce ingredients together and set aside.
4. Spray the air fryer basket with cooking spray.
5. Add the tofu to the basket of the air fryer and cook at 200°C for 10 minutes. Stir halfway through.
6. Add the cooked tofu and sauce mixture to the pan and cook over medium-high heat for 3-5 minutes.
7. Serve and enjoy.

68. Mexican rolls

Servings: 4
Cooking time: 15 minutes
Ingredients:
- 1 cup minced meat
- 1 teaspoon taco seasoning
- 55 grams of grated Mexican blend cheese
- 1 teaspoon keto tomato sauce
- Cooking spray

Addresses:
1. Preheat the fryer to 190°C.
2. While the fryer is heating, mix the ground beef and taco seasoning in the bowl.
3. Spray muffin tins with cooking spray. Then transfer the ground beef mixture into the muffin tins and top with cheese and tomato sauce.
4. Transfer the muffin tins into the preheated air fryer and cook for minutes.

69. Carrots and rhubarb

Servings: 4
Cooking time: 35 minutes
Ingredients:
- 450 grams of heirloom carrots
- 450 grams rhubarb
- 1 medium orange
- ½ cup walnuts, halved
- 2 teaspoons walnut oil
- ½ teaspoon sugar or a few drops of sugar extract

Addresses:
1. Rinse the carrots to wash them, dry them and cut them into 2.5 centimetre pieces.
2. Transfer the carrots to the basket of the Air Fryer and drizzle with walnut oil.
3. Cook at 160°C for about 20 minutes.
4. Meanwhile, wash the rhubarb and cut into 1 cm pieces.
5. Coarsely dice the walnuts.
6. Wash the orange and grate the peel into a small bowl. Peel the rest of the orange and cut into wedges.
7. Place the rhubarb, walnuts and sugar in the fryer and cook for a further 5 minutes.
8. Add 2 tablespoons of orange zest, along with the orange pieces. Serve immediately.

70. Orange cauliflower

Servings: 2
Cooking time: 30 minutes
Ingredients:
- Juice of ½ lemon
- 1 head of cauliflower
- ½ tablespoon olive oil
- 1 teaspoon curry powder
- Sea salt to taste
- Ground black pepper to taste

Addresses:
1. Wash the cauliflower. Cut out the leaves and the core.
2. Cut the cauliflower into florets of the same size.
3. Coat the inside of the Air Fryer with the oil and allow to heat for about 2 minutes.
4. In a bowl, mix together the juice of half a fresh lemon and the curry powder. Then add the cauliflower florets.
5. Sprinkle with the pepper and salt and mix again, coating the florets well.
6. Transfer to the fryer, cook for 20 minutes and serve hot.

71. Party Time Mixed Nuts

Servings: 3
Cooking time: 14 minutes
Ingredients:
- ½ cup raw peanuts
- ½ cup raw almonds

- ½ cup raw cashew nuts
- ½ cup sultanas
- ½ cup walnuts
- 1 tablespoon of olive oil
- Salt to taste

Addresses:
1. Preheat the fryer to 160°C and grease the fryer basket.
2. Place the nuts in the fryer basket and cook for about 9 minutes, stirring twice during cooking.
3. Remove the nuts from the fryer basket and transfer them to a bowl.
4. Drizzle with olive oil and salt and toss to coat well.
5. Return the nut mixture to the fryer basket and cook for a few minutes.
6. Serve hot.

72. Curly's cauliflower

Servings: 4
Cooking time: 30 minutes
Ingredients:
- 4 cups of bite-size cauliflower florets
- 1 cup of bread crumbs mixed with 1 teaspoon of salt
- ¼ cup melted butter, can be vegan or other.
- ¼ cup buffalo sauce [vegan/other].
- Mayo [vegan or other] or creamy dipping dressing

Addresses:
1. In a bowl, combine the butter and buffalo sauce to create a creamy paste.
2. Cover each flower completely with the sauce.
3. Coat the florets with the breadcrumb mixture.
4. Cook the florets in the Air Fryer for approximately 15 minutes at 180°C, shaking the basket from time to time.
5. Serve with raw vegetable salad, mayonnaise or a creamy dressing.

73. Avocado Fries with Chipotle Sauce

Servings: 3
Cooking time: 20 minutes
Ingredients:
- 2 tablespoons fresh lime juice
- 1 pitted avocado, peeled and sliced
- Himalayan pink salt and ground white pepper to taste
- 1/4 cup flour
- 1 egg
- 1/2 cup breadcrumbs
- 1 chipotle chilli in adobo sauce
- 1/4 cup light mayonnaise
- 1/4 cup plain Greek yogurt

Addresses:
1. Drizzle the avocado slices with lime juice and set aside.
2. Next, prepare your breading station. Mix the salt, pepper and plain flour in a shallow dish. In another plate, beat the egg.
3. Finally, place the breadcrumbs on a third plate.
4. Start by dredging the avocado slices in the flour mixture. Then dip them in the egg and press the avocado slices into the breadcrumbs, coating them evenly.
5. Cook in the preheated Air Fryer at 190°C for 11 minutes, shaking the cooking basket halfway through the cooking time.
6. Meanwhile, blend the chipotle chilli, mayonnaise and Greek yoghurt in your food processor until the sauce is creamy and smooth.
7. Serve the avocado slices warm with the salsa on the side. Enjoy.

74. Bites of veal

Servings: 2
Cooking time: 15 minutes
Ingredients:
- 1 teaspoon cayenne pepper
- 225 grams of veal loin, minced
- 1 tablespoon coconut flour
- 1 teaspoon walnut oil
- ¼ teaspoon salt
- 1 teaspoon apple cider vinegar

Addresses:
1. Sprinkle the meat with apple cider vinegar and salt. Then sprinkle with cayenne pepper and coconut flour.
2. Shake the meat well and transfer it to the air fryer. Drizzle with walnut oil and cook at 185°C.
3. Shake the meat every 5 minutes to prevent it from burning.

75. Egg rolls with tomato and avocado

Portions: 5
Cooking time: 20 minutes
Ingredients:
- 10 egg roll wrappers
- 3 avocados, peeled and pitted
- 1 diced tomato
- Salt and pepper to taste

Addresses:
1. Preheat your Air Fryer to 180°C.
2. Put the tomato and avocados in a bowl. Sprinkle with a little salt and pepper and mash with a fork until smooth.
3. Spoon equal amounts of the mixture into the wrappers. Wrap the wrappers around the filling, wrapping them completely.
4. Transfer the rolls to a lined baking dish and bake for 5 minutes.

76. Tomatoes and herbs

Servings: 2
Cooking time: 30 minutes

Ingredients:
- 2 large tomatoes, washed and cut into halves
- Herbs, such as oregano, basil, thyme, rosemary and sage, to taste
- Cooking spray
- Pepper to taste
- Grated Parmesan (optional)
- Chopped parsley (optional)

Addresses:
1. Spray both sides of each tomato half with a small amount of cooking spray.
2. Top the tomatoes with a light sprinkling of pepper and herbs of your choice.
3. Place the tomatoes in the basket with the cut side up. Cook for 20 minutes or longer if necessary.
4. Serve them hot, at room temperature or cold as refreshing summer snacks. Optionally, garnish with grated parmesan and chopped parsley before serving.

77. Olive fritters

Servings: 6
Cooking time: 12 minutes
Ingredients:
- Cooking spray
- ½ cup chopped parsley
- 1 egg
- ½ cup almond flour
- Salt and black pepper to taste
- 3 chopped spring onions
- ½ cup kalamata olives, pitted and chopped
- 3 courgettes, grated

Addresses:
1. In a bowl, combine all ingredients except cooking spray, stir well and form medium-sized fritters from this mixture.
2. Place the fritters in the basket of your air fryer, grease with cooking spray and cook at 195°C for 6 minutes on each side.
3. Serve them as an appetizer.

78. Vegetarian rolls

Servings: 8
Cooking time: 33 minutes
Ingredients:
- 5 large, peeled potatoes
- 2 tablespoons vegetable oil, divided
- 2 small onions, finely chopped
- 2 green chillies, seeded and chopped
- 2 curry leaves
- ½ teaspoon ground turmeric
- Salt
- 8 slices of bread

Addresses:
1. Add the potatoes to the pan of boiling water and cook for about 20 minutes.
2. Drain the potatoes well and mash them with a potato masher.
3. In a frying pan, heat 1 teaspoon of oil over medium heat and sauté the onion for about 4-5 minutes.
4. Add the green chillies, curry leaves and turmeric. Sauté for about 1 minute.
5. Add the mashed potatoes and salt and mix well.
6. Once done, remove from the heat and allow to cool completely.
7. Make 8 equal-sized patties from the mixture.
8. Thoroughly wet the bread slices with water.
9. With your hands, press each slice of bread between your hands to remove excess water.
10. Place a slice of bread in the palm of your hand and place a hamburger in the centre.
11. Roll the slice of bread into a spindle shape and seal the edges to secure the filling.
12. Coat the roll with a little oil. Repeat this process with the remaining slices of bread.
13. Set the temperature of the Air Fryer to 200°C. Grease the basket with cooking spray.
14. Add the rolls to the prepared basket in a single layer.
15. Chill in the open air for about 12-13 minutes.
16. Serves.

79. Deviled eggs, country style

Servings: 3
Cooking time: 25 minutes
Ingredients:
- 6 eggs
- 6 slices of bacon
- 2 tablespoons mayonnaise
- 1 teaspoon hot sauce
- 1/2 teaspoon Worcestershire sauce
- 2 tablespoons chopped green onions
- 1 tablespoon pickle relish
- Salt and ground black pepper
- 1 teaspoon smoked paprika

Addresses:
1. Place the rack in the basket of the Air Fryer and lower the eggs onto the rack.
2. Cook for 15 minutes.
3. Place them in an ice water bath to stop the cooking process. Peel the eggs under cold running water and cut them into halves.
4. Cook the bacon for 3 minutes, turn the bacon over and cook for a further 3 minutes, chop the bacon and set aside.
5. Mash the egg yolks with the mayonnaise, hot sauce, Worcestershire sauce, green onions, pickle relish, salt and black pepper, add the reserved bacon and spoon the egg yolk mixture into the egg whites.
6. Garnish with smoked paprika and enjoy!

80. Chicken wings in barbecue sauce

Servings: 6
Cooking time: 20 minutes
Ingredients:
For the sauce you need:
- 1 tablespoon yellow mustard
- 1 tablespoon apple cider vinegar
- 1 tablespoon of olive oil
- 1/4 cup ketchup, no sugar added
- 1 clove garlic, minced
- Salt and ground black pepper
- 1/8 teaspoon ground allspice
- 1/4 cup water

For the wings you need:
- 900 grams of chicken wings
- 1/4 teaspoon celery salt
- 1/4 cup habanero hot sauce
- Fresh chopped parsley

Addresses:
1. In a preheated pan over medium-high heat, place all the sauce ingredients and bring to the boil.
2. When it reaches boiling point, reduce the heat and simmer until it has thickened.
3. Meanwhile, preheat your Air Fryer to 200°C, cook the chicken wings for 6 minutes, turn them over and cook for a further 6 minutes.
4. Season the chicken wings with celery salt.
5. Serve with the prepared sauce and habanero hot sauce, garnish with fresh parsley leaves. Enjoy!

81. Spicy avocado fries wrapped in bacon

Portions: 5
Cooking time: 10 minutes
Ingredients:
- 2 teaspoons chilli powder
- 2 avocados, pitted and cut into 10 pieces
- 1 teaspoon salt
- ½ teaspoon garlic powder
- 1 teaspoon ground black pepper
- 5 slices of bacon cut in halves

Addresses:
1. Place the bacon slices on a clean surface. Then place a piece of avocado on each slice of bacon. Add the salt, black pepper, chilli powder and garlic powder.
2. Then wrap the bacon slice around the avocado and repeat with the remaining rolls, securing with a cocktail stick or toothpicks.
3. Preheat your air fryer and cook the preparation for 5 minutes.
4. Serve with your favourite dipping sauce.

82. Potato wedges

Servings: 4
Cooking time: 30 minutes
Ingredients:
- 4 medium potatoes, cut into chunks
- 1 tablespoon Cajun spice
- 1 tablespoon of olive oil
- Salt and pepper

Addresses:
1. Place the potato pieces in the basket of the Air Fryer and pour in the olive oil.
2. Cook at 185°C for minutes, shaking the basket twice during the cooking time.
3. Place the cooked wedges in a bowl and coat with the Cajun spice, pepper and salt.
4. Serve hot.

83. Ranch dipped fillets

Servings: 2
Cooking time: 13 minutes
Ingredients:
- ¼ cup panko breadcrumbs
- 1 beaten egg
- 2 tilapia fillets
- Garnish: Herbs and chillies
- ½ packet powdered ranch dressing mix
- 1¼ tablespoons vegetable oil

Addresses:
1. Preheat the fryer to 180°C and grease the fryer basket.
2. Mix the ranch dressing with the panko breadcrumbs in a bowl.
3. Beat the eggs in a shallow bowl and dip the fish fillet into the eggs.
4. Dredge in the breadcrumbs and transfer to the fryer basket.
5. Cook for about 13 minutes and garnish with chillies and herbs to serve.

84. Mozzarella sandwich

Servings: 8
Cooking time: 5 minutes
Ingredients:
- 2 cups shredded mozzarella cheese
- ¾ cup almond flour
- 2 teaspoons psyllium husk powder
- ¼ teaspoon sweet paprika

Addresses:
1. Put the mozzarella in a bowl and melt in the microwave for 2 minutes, quickly add all the other ingredients and stir well until a dough is formed.
2. Divide the dough into 2 balls, roll them on 2 baking trays and cut them into triangles.
3. Place the tortillas in the basket of your air fryer and bake at 185°C for 5 minutes.
4. Transfer to bowls and serve as an appetizer.

85. Asian Teriyaki Chicken

Servings: 6
Cooking time: 40 minutes
Ingredients:
- 680 grams of chicken
- Sea salt and ground black pepper

- 2 tablespoons coarsely chopped fresh chives

For the Teriyaki sauce you need:
- 1 tablespoon sesame oil
- 1/4 cup soy sauce
- 1/2 cup water
- 1/2 teaspoon of five-spice powder
- 2 tablespoons rice wine vinegar
- 1/2 teaspoon grated fresh ginger
- 2 cloves garlic, crushed

Addresses:
1. Start by preheating the fryer to 190°C.
2. Rub the chicken drums with salt and ground black pepper.
3. Cook in the preheated Air Fryer for approximately 15 minutes. Turn over and cook for a further 7 minutes.
4. While the chicken drumsticks are roasting, combine the sesame oil, soy sauce, water, five-spice powder, vinegar, ginger and garlic in a frying pan over medium heat. Cook for 5 minutes, stirring occasionally.
5. Now reduce the heat and simmer until the glaze thickens.
6. Then spread the glaze all over the chicken drumsticks. Fry in the open air for another 6 minutes or until the surface is crispy. Serve with the remaining glaze and garnish with fresh chives. Bon appetit!

86. Ricotta balls

Servings: 2 - 4
Cooking time: 25 minutes
Ingredients:
- 2 cups ricotta, grated
- 2 separate eggs
- 2 tablespoons finely chopped chives
- 2 tbsp. finely chopped fresh basil
- 4 tablespoons flour
- ¼ teaspoon salt to taste
- ¼ teaspoon pepper powder to taste
- 1 teaspoon orange zest

For the cladding you need:
- ¼ cup quality bread crumbs
- 1 tablespoon vegetable oil

Addresses:
1. Preheat your Air Fryer to 200°C.
2. In a bowl, combine the egg yolks, flour, salt, pepper, chives and orange zest. Pour in the ricotta and fold in with your hands.
3. Mould equal quantities of the mixture into balls.
4. Mix the oil with the breadcrumbs to a crumbly consistency.
5. Dredge the balls in the breadcrumbs and transfer each one to the fryer basket.
6. Place the basket in the fryer. Air fry for 8 minutes or until golden brown.
7. Serve with a sauce of your choice, such as ketchup.

87. Cheese pizza with pita bread

Servings: 4
Cooking time: 6 minutes
Ingredients:
- 1 pita bread
- ¼ cup mozzarella cheese
- 7 slices of pepperoni
- ¼ cup sausage
- 1 tablespoon yellow onion, thinly sliced
- 1 tablespoon pizza sauce
- 1 splash of extra virgin olive oil
- ½ teaspoon chopped fresh garlic

Addresses:
1. Preheat the fryer to 180°C and grease the fryer basket.
2. Spread pita bread with pizza sauce and add sausage, pepperoni, onion, garlic and cheese.
3. Drizzle with olive oil and place in the fryer basket.
4. Cook for about 6 minutes and serve hot.

88. Brussels sprouts

Servings: 2
Cooking time: 15 minutes
Ingredients:
- 2 cups halved Brussels sprouts
- 1 tablespoon balsamic vinegar
- 1 tablespoon of olive oil
- ¼ teaspoon salt

Addresses:
1. Mix all the ingredients in a bowl and coat the Brussels sprouts well.
2. Place the sprouts in the basket of the Air Fryer and fry at 200°C for 10 minutes, shaking the basket halfway through.

89. Puppies of the Poppers' family

Servings: 50 candies
Cooking time: 25 minutes
Ingredients:
- ½ cup unsweetened applesauce
- 1 cup peanut butter
- 2 cups of oats
- 1 cup flour
- 1 teaspoon baking powder

Addresses:
1. Combine the applesauce and peanut butter in a bowl to create a smooth consistency.
2. Pour in the oats, flour and baking powder. Continue mixing until a smooth dough forms.
3. Form a ball with half a spoonful of dough and continue with the rest of the dough.
4. Preheat the Air Fryer to 180°C.
5. Grease the bottom of the basket with oil.
6. Place the poppers in the fryer and cook for 8 minutes, turning them over halfway through. You may need to cook the poppers in batches.

7. Allow poppers to cool and serve immediately or store in an airtight container for up to 2 weeks.

90. Tasty pork meatballs

Servings: 4
Cooking time: 10 minutes
Ingredients:
- 2 eggs, lightly beaten
- 2 tablespoons capers
- 225 grams of ground pork
- 3 cloves garlic, minced
- 2 tablespoons chopped fresh mint
- 1/2 tablespoon chopped coriander
- 2 teaspoons crushed red pepper flakes
- 1 1/2 tablespoons melted butter
- 1 teaspoon kosher salt

Addresses:
1. Preheat the air fryer to 200°C.
2. Add all ingredients to the mixer bowl and mix until well combined.
3. Spray the air fryer basket with cooking spray.
4. Make small balls of the meat mixture and place them in the fryer basket.
5. Cook the meatballs for 10 minutes. Shake the basket halfway through.
6. Serve and enjoy.

91. Mushrooms stuffed with vegetable cream

Portions: 12
Cooking time: 8 minutes
Ingredients:
- 680 grams of mushrooms, stems chopped
- 1/2 cup sour cream
- 1 cup shredded cheddar cheese
- 1 small diced carrot
- 1/2 pepper, diced
- 1/2 onion, chopped
- 2 slices of bacon cut into cubes

Addresses:
1. Finely chop the mushroom stems.
2. Spray pan with cooking spray and heat over medium heat.
3. Add the chopped mushrooms, bacon, carrot, onion and pepper to the pan and cook until tender.
4. Remove the pan from the heat. Add the cheese and sour cream to the cooked vegetables and stir well.
5. Spoon the vegetable mixture into the mushroom caps and place in the fryer basket.
6. Cook the mushrooms at 180°C for 8 minutes.
7. Serve and enjoy.

92. Onion dip

Servings: 8
Cooking time: 25 minutes
Ingredients:
- 900 grams of chopped onion
- 1/2 teaspoon bicarbonate of soda
- 6 tablespoons softened butter
- Pepper
- Salt

Addresses:
1. Melt the butter in a frying pan over medium heat.
2. Add the onion and bicarbonate and fry for 5 minutes.
3. Transfer the onion mixture to the fryer's baking tray.
4. Place in the air fryer and cook at 185°C for 25 minutes.
5. Serve and enjoy.

93. Mini Cheeseburger Bites

Servings: 4
Cooking time: 20 minutes
Ingredients:
- 1 tablespoon Dijon mustard
- 2 tablespoons chopped spring onions
- 450 grams of minced meat
- 1 ½ teaspoons of chopped green chilli pepper
- 1/2 teaspoon cumin
- Salt and ground black pepper
- 12 cherry tomatoes
- 12 cubes of cheddar cheese

Addresses:
1. In a large bowl, place the mustard, ground beef, cumin, spring onions, garlic, salt and pepper.
2. Mix with your hands or a spatula so that everything is evenly coated.
3. Shape the meatballs and cook them in the preheated air fryer for 15 minutes at 190°C. Air fry until cooked in the centre.
4. Skewer cherry tomatoes, mini burgers and cheese on cocktail sticks - enjoy!

94. Lemon Tofu Cubes

Servings: 2
Cooking time: 7 minutes
Ingredients:
- ½ teaspoon ground coriander
- 1 tablespoon avocado oil
- 1 teaspoon lemon juice
- ½ teaspoon chilli flakes
- 170 grams of tofu

Addresses:
1. In a shallow bowl, mix the ground coriander, avocado oil, lime juice and chilli flakes.
2. Cut the tofu into cubes and sprinkle with the coriander mixture. Shake the tofu.
3. Then preheat the air fryer to 200°C and place the tofu cubes in it. Cook the tofu for 4 minutes.
4. Then turn the tofu on the other side and cook for 3 more minutes.

95. Breadsticks with cheddar cheese

Servings: 6
Cooking time: 30 minutes
Ingredients:
- 1/2 cup almond flour
- Sea salt and ground black pepper
- 1/4 teaspoon smoked paprika
- 1/2 teaspoon celery seeds
- 170 grams of cold, freshly grated mature Cheddar cheese
- 2 tablespoons cream cheese
- 2 tablespoons cold butter

Addresses:
1. Start by preheating your air fryer to 165°C. Line the air fryer basket with parchment paper.
2. In a bowl, thoroughly mix the almond flour, salt, black pepper, paprika and celery seeds.
3. Next, combine the cheese and butter in the bowl of a stand mixer. Slowly add the almond flour mixture and mix to combine well.
4. Then put the dough into a biscuit press fitted with a star disc. Place the long strips of dough on the parchment paper. Then cut them into 15-centimetre pieces.
5. Bake in the preheated air fryer for 1 minute.
6. Repeat with the rest of the dough. Cool the cheese straws on a wire rack. You can store them between sheets of parchment in an airtight container. Bon appetit

96. Easy Habanero Wings

Servings: 6
Cooking time: 25 minutes
Ingredients:
- 3 cloves garlic, peeled and halved
- 2 tablespoons habanero hot sauce
- 1/2 tablespoon soy sauce
- 680 grams of chicken wings
- 1 teaspoon garlic salt
- 1 teaspoon smoked cayenne pepper
- 1 teaspoon ground black pepper

Addresses:
1. Rub the chicken wings with the garlic. Then season them with the salt, black pepper and smoked cayenne pepper.
2. Transfer chicken wings to air fryer basket, add soy sauce, habanero hot sauce and honey. Toss to coat all sides.
3. Air fry the chicken wings for 16 minutes or until heated through.

97. Roasted Brussels sprouts and bacon

Servings: 2
Cooking time: 45 minutes
Ingredients:
- 680 grams of Brussels sprouts
- ¼ cup fish sauce
- ¼ cup bacon grease
- 6 strips of bacon
- Pepper to taste

Addresses:
1. Trim and quarter the Brussels sprouts.
2. Mix the cabbage with the bacon fat and fish sauce.
3. Cut the bacon into small strips and cook.
4. Add the bacon and pepper to the sprouts.
5. Spread in a greased frying pan and cook at 230°C for 35 minutes.
6. Stir every 5 minutes or so.
7. Roast for a few more minutes and serve.

98. Okra with sesame

Servings: 4
Cooking time: 4 minutes
Ingredients:
- 310 grams okra, washed and chopped
- 1 egg, lightly beaten
- 1 teaspoon sesame seeds
- 1 tablespoon sesame oil
- 1/4 teaspoon pepper
- 1/2 teaspoon salt

Addresses:
1. In a bowl, whisk together the egg, pepper and salt.
2. Add the okra to the beaten egg. Sprinkle with sesame seeds.
3. Preheat the air fryer to 200 °C.
4. Stir the okra well. Spray the fryer basket with cooking spray.
5. Place the okra pieces in the basket of the air fryer and cook for 4 minutes.
6. Serve and enjoy.

99. Vegetable fritters

Servings: 4
Cooking time: 15 minutes
Ingredients:
- 1 cup peppers, deveined and chopped
- 1 tsp sea salt flakes
- 1 teaspoon cumin
- ¼ teaspoon paprika
- ½ cup chopped shallots
- 2 cloves garlic, minced
- 1 ½ tablespoons chopped fresh coriander
- 1 beaten egg
- ¾ cup shredded Cheddar cheese
- ¼ cup cooked quinoa
- ¼ cup flour

Addresses:
1. In a bowl, combine all the ingredients well.
2. Divide the mixture into equal portions and form each into a ball. Slightly flatten each ball with the palm of your hand to form patties.
3. Lightly coat the burgers with cooking spray.

4. Place the patties in the cooking basket of the Air Fryer, taking care not to overlap them.
5. Cook at 170°C for 10 minutes, turning halfway through.

100. Wonton sausage snacks

Portions: 5
Cooking time: 20 minutes
Ingredients:
- 225 grams ground sausage
- 2 tablespoons chopped spring onions
- 1 clove garlic, minced
- 1/2 tablespoon fish sauce
- 1 teaspoon Sriracha sauce
- 20 wonton wrappers
- 1 egg beaten with 1 tablespoon of water

Addresses:
1. In a bowl, mix together the ground sausage, spring onions, garlic, fish sauce and Sriracha.
2. Divide the mixture between the wonton wrappers. Dip the fingers in the egg wash.
3. Fold the wonton in half. Bring the 2 ends of the wonton up and use the egg wash to stick them together. Pinch the edges together and cover each wonton with the egg wash.
4. Place the folded wontons in the lightly greased baking basket. Bake at 180°C for 10 minutes. Work in batches and serve hot - bon appetit!

101. Prawn cakes

Servings: 4
Cooking time: 5 minutes
Ingredients:
- 280 grams of chopped shrimps
- 1 beaten egg
- 1 teaspoon of chopped dill
- 1 teaspoon psyllium husk
- 2 tablespoons almond flour
- 1 teaspoon olive oil
- 1 teaspoon chives

Addresses:
1. In a bowl, mix the prawns, egg, dill, psyllium husk, almond flour and chives.
2. When the mixture is homogeneous, make 4 cakes.
3. Preheat the air fryer to 200°C.
4. Place the cakes in the air fryer and drizzle with olive oil. Cook the food for 5 minutes.

102. Bacon-wrapped shrimps

Servings: 6
Cooking time: 7 minutes
Ingredients:
- 450 grams of thinly sliced bacon
- 450 grams of peeled and deveined shrimp
- Salt

Addresses:
1. Preheat the fryer to 200°C and grease the fryer basket.
2. Wrap 1 shrimp with a slice of bacon covering it completely.
3. Repeat with the rest of the prawns and the bacon slices.
4. Place the bacon-wrapped shrimps in a baking dish and freeze for about 15 minutes.
5. Place the prawns in the fryer basket and cook for about 7 minutes.
6. Serve hot.

103. Chicken Wings with Sage

Servings: 4
Cooking time: 1 hour and 10 minutes
Ingredients:
- 1/3 cup almond meal
- 1/3 cup buttermilk
- 680 grams of chicken wings
- 1 tablespoon tamari sauce
- 1/3 teaspoon fresh sage
- 1 tsp mustard seeds
- 1/2 teaspoon garlic paste
- 1/2 tsp freshly ground mixed peppercorns
- 1/2 teaspoon seasoned salt
- 2 teaspoons of fresh basil

Addresses:
1. Place the seasonings together with the garlic paste, chicken wings, buttermilk and tamari sauce in a large bowl.
2. Leave to soak for about 55 minutes. When the time is up, drain the wings.
3. Dredge the wings in the almond flour and transfer them to the cooking basket of the Air Fryer.
4. Fry in the open air for 16 minutes. Serve on a nice platter with a garnish on the side - bon appetit!

104. Crispy prawns

Servings: 4
Cooking time: 8 minutes
Ingredients:
- 1 egg
- 225 grams nacho chips, crushed
- 18 prawns, peeled and deveined

Addresses:
1. In a shallow dish, break the egg and beat it well.
2. Put the crushed nachos on another plate.
3. Dip the prawns in the beaten egg and cover with the nachos.
4. Set the temperature of the Air Fryer to 180°C.
5. Place the prawns in the basket of the Air Fryer in a single layer.
6. Chill in the open air for about 8 minutes.
7. Serve hot.

105. Grandma's green beans

Servings: 4

Cooking time: 10 minutes
Ingredients:
- 450 grams of chopped green beans
- 1 cup butter
- 2 cloves garlic, minced
- 1 cup toasted pine nuts

Addresses:
1. Boil a pot of water.
2. Add the green beans and cook until tender for 5 minutes.
3. Heat the butter in a large frying pan over high heat. Add the garlic and pine nuts and sauté for 2 minutes or until the pine nuts are lightly browned.
4. Transfer the green beans to the frying pan and turn them over until they are coated.
5. It works!

106. Pickled bacon bowls

Servings: 4
Cooking time: 20 minutes
Ingredients:
- 4 gherkin spears cut in halves and quarters
- 8 slices of bacon, cut in halves
- 1 cup avocado mayonnaise

Addresses:
1. Wrap each gherkin loin in a slice of bacon.
2. Place them in the basket of your air fryer and cook at 200°C for 20 minutes.
3. Divide into bowls and serve as an appetizer with the mayonnaise.

107. Tomato Smokies

Portions: 10
Cooking time: 10 minutes
Ingredients:
- 340 grams of smoked pork and beef
- 85 grams of sliced bacon
- 1 teaspoon keto tomato sauce
- 1 teaspoon Erythritol
- 1 teaspoon of avocado oil
- ½ teaspoon cayenne pepper

Addresses:
1. Sprinkle the smoked fish with cayenne pepper and tomato sauce. Then sprinkle with erythritol and olive oil.
2. Then wrap each smokie in the bacon and secure with the toothpick.
3. Preheat the air fryer to 200°C.
4. Place the bacon smokies in the air fryer and cook. Stir them gently during cooking to prevent them from burning.

108. Scallop and Bacon Brochettes

Servings: 6
Cooking time: 40 minutes
Ingredients:
- 450 grams of scallops
- 1/2 cup coconut milk
- 1 tablespoon of vermouth
- Sea salt and ground black pepper
- 225 grams of bacon, diced
- 1 shallot, diced
- 1 teaspoon garlic powder
- 1 teaspoon paprika

Addresses:
1. In a ceramic bowl, place the scallops, coconut milk, vermouth, salt and black pepper, marinate for 30 minutes.
2. Assemble the skewers by alternating the scallops, bacon and shallots. Sprinkle the garlic powder and paprika all over the skewers.
3. Bake in the preheated air fryer at 200°C for 6 minutes. Serve hot and enjoy!

109. Sausage and vegetable cocktail on a stick

Servings: 4
Cooking time: 25 minutes
Ingredients:
- 16 cocktail sausages cut in halves
- 16 pearl onions
- 1 red pepper cut into approximately 3 cm pieces
- 1 green pepper cut into approximately 3 cm pieces
- Salt and ground black pepper
- 1/2 cup tomato chili sauce

Addresses:
1. Thread the cocktail sausages, pearl onions and peppers alternately onto the skewers. Sprinkle with salt and black pepper.
2. Cook in the preheated Air Fryer at 190°C for 15 minutes, turning the skewers once or twice to ensure even cooking.
3. Serve with chilli and tomato sauce on the side, enjoy!

110. Aromatic cabbage chips

Servings: 4
Cooking time: 5 minutes
Ingredients:
- 2 ½ tablespoons olive oil
- 1 ½ teaspoons garlic powder
- 1 bunch of kale, cut into small pieces
- 2 tablespoons lemon juice
- 1 1/2 teaspoons seasoned salt

Addresses:
1. Mix the kale with the other ingredients.
2. Cook at 90°C for 4 to 5 minutes, stirring the kale halfway through.
3. Serve with your favourite dipping sauce.

Dessert recipes

111. Vanilla-orange custard

Servings: 6
Cooking time: 35 minutes + cooling time
Ingredients:
- 6 eggs
- 200 grams of cream cheese at room temperature
- 2 ½ cans sweetened condensed milk
- 1/2 cup swerve
- 1/2 teaspoon grated orange peel
- 1 ½ cardamom pods, crushed
- 2 teaspoons vanilla paste
- 1/4 cup fresh orange juice

Addresses:
1. In a saucepan, melt the icing sugar over moderate heat, this will take about 12 minutes. Immediately, but carefully, pour the melted sugar into six ramekins, tilting them to cover the bottoms, allow to cool slightly.
2. In a mixing bowl, beat the cheese until smooth. Now add the eggs, one at a time, and continue beating until pale and creamy.
3. Add the orange rind, cardamom, vanilla, orange juice and milk. Mix again.
4. Pour the mixture over the caramelised sugar. Air fry, covered, for 28 minutes or until thickened.
5. Refrigerate overnight, garnish with berries or other fruit and serve.

112. Baileys Butterscotch Brownies with Alcoholic Flavour

Servings: 8
Cooking time: 35 minutes
Ingredients:
- 1 cup granulated swerve
- 2 tablespoons of unsweetened cocoa powder, sieved
- 1/2 cup almond flour
- 1/2 cup coconut flour
- 1/4 teaspoon salt
- 1/4 teaspoon baking powder
- 1/2 cup of melted and cooled butter
- 2 eggs at room temperature
- 1 teaspoon vanilla
- 2 tablespoons Baileys
- 55 grams of unsweetened chocolate chips
- 1/2 cup sour cream
- 1/3 cup powdered erythritol
- 85 grams Ricotta cheese, at room temperature

Addresses:
1. In a bowl, thoroughly combine the granulated swerve, cocoa powder, flour, salt and baking powder.
2. Mix the butter, eggs and vanilla together. Add the batter to a lightly greased baking dish.
3. Fry in the open air for 25 minutes. Leave to cool slightly on a wire rack.
4. Microwave the chocolate chips until everything is melted, allow the mixture to cool to room temperature.
5. Then add the ricotta cheese, Baileys, sour cream and erythritol powder, mix until everything is integrated.
6. Spread this mixture over the top of your brownie. Serve well chilled.

113. Chocolate cake

Servings: 4
Cooking time: 40 minutes
Ingredients:
For the cake you need:
- 1/3 cup plain flour
- ¼ teaspoon baking powder
- 1½ tablespoons cocoa powder, unsweetened
- 2 egg yolks
- 15 grams of icing sugar
- 2 tablespoons vegetable oil
- 3¾ tablespoons milk
- 1 teaspoon vanilla extract

For the meringue you need:
- 2 egg whites
- 30 grams of icing sugar
- 1/8 teaspoon of cream of tartar

Addresses:
For the cake:
1. In a bowl, sift together the flour, baking powder and cocoa powder.
2. In another bowl, add the rest of the ingredients and whisk until well combined.
3. Add the flour mixture and whisk until well combined.

For the meringue:
4. In a clean glass bowl, add all ingredients and, using an electric mixer, beat on high speed until stiff peaks form.
5. Put 1/3 of the meringue into the flour mixture and with a whisk, beat well.
6. Fold in the rest of the meringue.
7. Set the fryer temperature to 180°C.
8. Place the mixture in an ungreased gauze mould.
9. With a piece of aluminium foil, cover the pan tightly and poke a few holes with a fork.
10. Place the mould in the basket of the air fryer.
11. Now, set the temperature of the fryer to 160°C.
12. Fry in the open air for about 30-35 minutes.

13. Remove the piece of aluminium foil and set the temperature to 140°C.
14. Air fry for another 5 minutes or until a toothpick inserted in the centre comes out clean.
15. Remove the pan from the air fryer and place it on a rack to cool for about 10 minutes.
16. Now invert the cake onto a wire rack to cool completely before slicing.
17. Cut the cake into slices of the desired size and serve.

114. Coconut Cheese Crackers

Portions: 30
Cooking time: 12 minutes
Ingredients:
- 225 grams of cream cheese
- 1 teaspoon vanilla
- 1 tablespoon baking powder
- ¾ cup coconut flakes
- 1 cup of swerve
- ¾ cup butter, softened
- 1 ¼ cup coconut flour
- A pinch of salt

Addresses:
1. Preheat the air fryer to 160°C.
2. Beat cream cheese, butter and sweetener in a bowl with a hand mixer until fluffy.
3. Add the vanilla and stir well.
4. Add the coconut flour, baking powder and salt and mix until well combined.
5. Add the coconut flakes and mix to combine.
6. Make biscuits from the mixture and place them on a plate.
7. Place the biscuits in batches in the air fryer and cook for 12 minutes.
8. Serve and enjoy.

115. Yummy brownies

Servings: 4
Cooking time: 10 minutes
Ingredients:
- 2 tablespoons cocoa powder
- 1/4 teaspoon baking powder
- 1/2 teaspoon bicarbonate of soda
- 2 tablespoons of unsweetened applesauce
- 1 teaspoon liquid stevia
- 1 tbsp melted coconut oil
- 3 tablespoons almond flour
- 1/2 teaspoon vanilla
- 1 tbsp unsweetened almond milk
- 1/2 cup almond butter
- 1/4 teaspoon sea salt

Addresses:
1. Preheat the air fryer to 180°C.
2. Grease the baking dish of the fryer with cooking spray and set aside.
3. In a small bowl, mix together the almond flour, baking soda, cocoa powder, baking powder and salt. Set aside.
4. In a small bowl, add the coconut oil and almond butter and heat in the microwave until melted.
5. Add the sweetener, vanilla, almond milk and applesauce to the coconut oil mixture and stir well.
6. Add the dry ingredients to the wet ingredients and stir to combine.
7. Pour the batter into the prepared dish and place it in the air fryer and cook for 10 minutes.
8. Cut and serve.

116. Clove biscuits

Servings: 8
Cooking time: 33 minutes
Ingredients:
- 1 cup almond flour
- 1 teaspoon xanthan gum
- 1 teaspoon flaxseed meal
- ½ teaspoon salt
- 1 teaspoon baking powder
- 1 teaspoon lemon juice
- ½ teaspoon ground cloves
- 2 tablespoons erythritol
- 1 beaten egg
- 3 tablespoons coconut oil, softened

Addresses:
1. In the bowl of a mixer, mix the almond flour, xanthan gum, linseed flour, salt, baking powder and ground cloves.
2. Add the erythritol, lemon juice, egg and coconut oil. Stir the mixture gently with a fork. Then knead the mixture into a smooth dough.
3. Line the cutting board with parchment. Place the dough on the parchment and roll it into a thin layer. Cut the thin dough into squares of biscuit sizes.
4. Preheat the air fryer to 180°C.
5. Line the air fryer basket with baking paper. Place the prepared biscuits in the air fryer basket to form a layer and cook until the biscuits are dry and light brown in colour.
6. Repeat the same steps with the remaining uncooked biscuits.

117. Peach cobbler recipe

Servings: 4
Cooking time: 45 minutes
Ingredients:
- 1 pie crust
- 1,130 kilograms of peaches, pitted and chopped.
- 2 tablespoons cornstarch
- 1 tablespoon dark rum
- 1 tablespoon lemon juice

- 1/2 cup sugar
- 2 tablespoons flour
- Pinch of ground nutmeg
- 2 tablespoons melted butter

Addresses:
1. Roll the tart dough into a tart pan that fits your air fryer and press down well.
2. In a bowl, mix the peaches with the cornflour, sugar, flour, nutmeg, rum, lemon juice and butter and stir well.
3. Pour and spread this into a tart pan, place in your air fryer and cook for 35 minutes.
4. Serve hot or cold

118. Apple wedges

Servings: 4
Cooking time: 25 minutes
Ingredients:
- 4 large apples
- 2 tablespoons olive oil
- ½ cup chopped dried apricots
- 1 - 2 tablespoons sugar
- ½ teaspoon ground cinnamon

Addresses:
1. Peel the apples and cut into eight pieces. Discard the core.
2. Brush the apple pieces with the oil.
3. Place each wedge in the Air Fryer and cook for 12 - 15 minutes.
4. Add the apricots and cook for another 3 minutes.
5. Mix the sugar and cinnamon together. Sprinkle this mixture over the cooked apples before serving.

119. Chocolate-peanut butter fondants

Servings: 4
Cooking time: 25 minutes
Ingredients:
- ½ cup crunchy peanut butter
- 2 tablespoons butter, diced
- ¼ cup + ¼ cup sugar
- 4 eggs at room temperature
- ⅛ cup sifted flour
- 1 teaspoon salt
- ¼ cup water
- Cooking spray

Addresses:
1. Make a salted praline to cover the chocolate fondant. Add ¼ cup sugar, a teaspoon of salt and water to a saucepan. Stir and bring to a boil over low heat. Simmer until desired colour is achieved and reduced. Pour into a baking dish and allow to cool and harden.
2. Preheat the air fryer to 150°C.
3. Place a saucepan of water over medium heat and place a heatproof bowl over it. Add the chocolate, butter and peanut butter. Stir continuously until completely melted, combined and smooth.
4. Remove the bowl and allow to cool slightly. Add the eggs to the chocolate and beat. Add the flour and the remaining sugar, mix well.
5. Grease small loaf pans with cooking spray and spread the chocolate mixture between them. Place two moulds at a time in the basket and bake for 7 minutes.
6. Remove and serve the fondants with a piece of salted praline.

120. Tea biscuits

Portions: 15
Cooking time: 25 minutes
Ingredients:
- ½ cup softened salted butter
- 2 cups almond flour
- 1 organic egg
- 1 teaspoon ground cinnamon
- 2 teaspoons sugar
- 1 teaspoon organic vanilla extract

Addresses:
1. Preheat the fryer to 185°C and grease the fryer basket.
2. Mix all ingredients in a bowl until well combined.
3. Make equal-sized balls of the mixture and place them in the fryer basket.
4. Cook for about 5 minutes and press each ball with a fork.
5. Cook for about 20 minutes and allow the biscuits to cool before serving with the tea.

121. Molten lava cake

Servings: 4
Cooking time: 20 minutes
Ingredients:
- 3 ½ tablespoons sugar
- 1 ½ tablespoons wheat flour
- 100 grams of melted dark chocolate
- 2 eggs

Addresses:
1. Grease 4 ramekins with butter.
2. Preheat the fryer to 190°C and beat the eggs and sugar until frothy. Stir in the butter and chocolate, and gently fold in the flour.
3. Divide the mixture between the moulds and bake in the deep fryer for a few minutes.
4. Allow to cool for 2 minutes before turning the molten lava cakes out onto serving plates.

122. Peanut crackers

Servings: 4
Cooking time: 5 minutes
Ingredients:
- 4 tablespoons peanut butter
- 4 teaspoons erythritol
- 1 beaten egg
- ¼ teaspoon vanilla extract

Addresses:
1. In the bowl of a mixer, combine the peanut butter, erythritol, egg and vanilla extract. Stir the mixture with a fork.
2. Then make 4 biscuits.
3. Preheat the air fryer to 180°C.
4. Place the biscuits in the air fryer and cook for 5 minutes.

123. Chocolate custard

Servings: 4
Cooking time: 32 minutes
Ingredients:
- 2 eggs
- 1 teaspoon vanilla
- 1 cup whipping cream
- 1 cup unsweetened almond milk
- 2 tablespoons cocoa powder, unsweetened
- 1/4 cup Swerve
- A pinch of salt

Addresses:
1. Preheat the air fryer to 150°C.
2. Add all ingredients to the blender and blend until well combined.
3. Pour the mixture into the moulds and place them in the fryer.
4. Cook for 32 minutes.
5. Serve and enjoy.

124. Dulce de leche muffins with walnuts

Portions: 10
Cooking time: 10 minutes
Ingredients:
- 1 packet caramel brownie mix
- 1 egg
- 2 teaspoons water
- ¼ cup chopped walnuts
- 1/3 cup vegetable oil

Addresses:
1. Preheat the fryer to 150°C and lightly grease the muffin tins.
2. Mix the brownie mix, egg, oil and water in a bowl.
3. Stir in the walnuts and pour the mixture into the muffin tins.
4. Place the muffin tins in the fryer basket and cook for about 10 minutes.
5. Serve immediately.

Banana cake

Servings: 6
Cooking time: 40 minutes
Ingredients:
- 1½ cups cake flour
- 1 teaspoon bicarbonate of soda
- ½ teaspoon ground cinnamon
- Salt to taste
- ½ cup vegetable oil
- 2 eggs
- ½ cup sugar
- ½ teaspoon vanilla extract
- 3 medium-sized bananas, peeled and mashed
- ¼ cup chopped walnuts
- ¼ cup chopped sultanas

Addresses:
1. In a large bowl, thoroughly mix the flour, baking soda, cinnamon and salt.
2. In another bowl, beat the eggs and oil well.
3. Add the sugar, vanilla extract and bananas. Whisk until well combined.
4. Add the flour mixture and stir until well combined.
5. Set the temperature of the air fryer to 160°C. Grease a cake tin.
6. Spoon the mixture evenly into the prepared mould and top with nuts and sultanas.
7. Cover the pan with a piece of aluminium foil.
8. Place the mould in the basket of the air fryer.
9. Now, set the temperature of the fryer to 150°C.
10. Fry in the open air for about 30 minutes.
11. Remove the piece of aluminium foil and set the temperature to 140°C.
12. Fry in the open air for another 5-10 minutes or until a toothpick inserted in the centre comes out clean.
13. Remove the pan from the air fryer and place it on a rack to cool for about 10 minutes.
14. Now invert the cake onto a wire rack to cool completely before slicing.
15. Cut the cake into slices of the desired size and serve.

126. Tasty peach pie

Servings: 6
Cooking time: 40 minutes
Ingredients:
- 225 grams of peaches, pitted and crushed
- 3 tablespoons honey
- 1/2 teaspoon baking powder
- 1 ¼ cups cake flour
- 1/2 teaspoon orange extract
- 1 teaspoon pure vanilla extract
- 1/4 teaspoon ground cinnamon
- 1/3 cup ghee
- 1/8 teaspoon salt
- 1/2 cup icing sugar
- 2 eggs
- 1/4 teaspoon freshly grated nutmeg

Addresses:
1. First, preheat the air fryer. Spray the pan with non-stick cooking spray.
2. In a bowl, whisk the ghee with the icing sugar until creamy. Stir in the egg, peach puree and honey.

3. Next, prepare the cake batter by mixing the rest of the ingredients together, now stir in the peach and honey mixture.
4. Transfer the prepared dough to the mould, level the surface with a spoon.
5. Bake for 3 minutes or until a tester inserted in the centre of the cake comes out completely dry. Enjoy!

127. Hazelnut brownie cups

Portions: 12
Cooking time: 30 minutes
Ingredients:
- 170 grams of semisweet chocolate chips
- 1 stick of butter at room temperature
- 1 cup sugar
- 2 large eggs
- ¼ cup red wine
- ¼ teaspoon hazelnut extract
- 1 teaspoon pure vanilla extract
- ¾ cup flour
- 2 tablespoons cocoa powder
- ½ cup ground hazelnuts
- A pinch of kosher salt

Addresses:
1. Melt the butter and chocolate chips in the microwave.
2. In a large bowl, mix the sugar, eggs, red wine, hazelnut and vanilla extract with a whisk. Pour in the chocolate mixture.
3. Add the flour, cocoa powder, ground hazelnuts and a pinch of kosher salt, stirring constantly until a smooth, creamy consistency is achieved.
4. Take a muffin tin and place a muffin tin in each cup. Pour an equal amount of batter into each.
5. Bake at 180°C for 28 - 30 minutes, cooking in batches if necessary.
6. Serve with a ganache topping if desired.

128. Plum Sticks Recipe

Servings: 8
Cooking time: 26 minutes
Ingredients:
- 2 cups dried plums
- 6 tablespoons of water
- 2 tablespoons melted butter
- 1 beaten egg
- 2 cups oat flakes
- 1 cup brown sugar
- 1/2 teaspoon bicarbonate of soda
- 1 teaspoon cinnamon powder
- Cooking spray

Addresses:
1. In your food processor, combine the plums with the water and blend to a sticky paste.
2. In a bowl, mix the oats with the cinnamon, baking soda, sugar, egg and butter and beat very well.
3. Press half of the oat mixture into a baking dish that fits your air fryer sprayed with cooking oil, spread out the plum mixture and top with the other half of the oat mixture.
4. Place in your air fryer and cook at 180°C for 16 minutes. Set the mixture aside to cool, cut into medium loaves and serve.

129. Cobbler

Servings: 4
Cooking time: 30 minutes
Ingredients:
- ¼ cup heavy cream
- 1 beaten egg
- ½ cup almond flour
- 1 teaspoon vanilla extract
- 2 tablespoons softened butter
- ¼ cup chopped hazelnuts

Addresses:
1. Mix the heavy cream, egg, almond flour, vanilla extract and butter.
2. Then whisk the mixture gently.
3. Preheat the air fryer to 160°C.
4. Line the frying pan with baking paper.
5. Pour ½ part of the dough into the mould, flatten gently and cover with hazelnuts.
6. Then pour the rest of the batter over the hazelnuts and place the pan in the fryer.
7. Bake the cake for 30 minutes.

130. Classic Buttermilk Biscuits

Servings: 4
Cooking time: 8 minutes
Ingredients:
- ½ cup cake flour
- 1¼ cups plain flour
- ¾ teaspoon baking powder
- ¼ cup + 2 tablespoons butter, cubed
- ¾ cup buttermilk
- 1 teaspoon granulated sugar
- Salt

Addresses:
1. Preheat the fryer to 200°C and lightly grease a cake tin.
2. Sift the flours, baking soda, baking powder, sugar and salt into a large bowl.
3. Add the cold butter and mix until a coarse crumb is formed.
4. Gradually add the buttermilk and mix until a dough forms.
5. Press the dough until it is about 1.5 centimetres thick on a floured surface and cut into circles with a round biscuit cutter of about 4 centimetres.
6. Place the biscuits in a tart pan in a single layer and spread with butter.
7. Transfer to the air fryer and cook for about 8 minutes until golden brown.

131. Pop-tarts Ninja

Servings: 6

Cooking time: 1 hour
Ingredients:
For pop-tarts you need:
- 1 cup coconut flour
- 1 cup almond flour
- ½ cup of ice water
- ¼ teaspoon salt
- 2 tablespoons swerve
- 2/3 cup very cold coconut oil
- ½ teaspoon vanilla extract

For the lemon glaze you will need:
- 1¼ cups whey powder
- 2 tablespoons lemon juice
- Zest of 1 lemon
- 1 tsp melted coconut oil
- ¼ teaspoon vanilla extract

Addresses:
For making pop-tarts:
1. Preheat the fryer to 190°C and grease the fryer basket.
2. Mix all the flours, swerve and salt in a bowl and add the coconut oil.
3. Mix well with a fork until an almond flour mixture forms.
4. Add the vanilla and 1 tablespoon of cold water and mix until a firm dough forms.
5. Cut the dough into two equal pieces and roll out on a thin sheet.
6. Cut each sheet into 12 rectangles of equal size and place 4 rectangles in the fryer basket.
7. Cook for about 10 minutes and repeat with the remaining rectangles.

For the lemon glaze:
8. Meanwhile, mix together all the ingredients for the lemon glaze and pour over the baked cakes.
9. Top with the sprinkles and serve.

132. Courgette brownies

Portions: 12
Cooking time: 35 minutes
Ingredients:
- 1 cup butter
- 1 cup dark chocolate chips
- 1½ cups grated courgette
- ¼ teaspoon bicarbonate of soda
- 1 egg
- 1 teaspoon vanilla extract
- 1/3 cup unsweetened applesauce
- 1 teaspoon ground cinnamon
- ½ teaspoon ground nutmeg

Addresses:
1. Preheat the fryer to 170°C and grease 3 large baking tins.
2. Mix all ingredients in a large bowl until well combined.
3. Pour evenly into the prepared ramekins and smooth the top surface with the back of the spatula.
4. Place the casserole in the fryer basket and cook for about 35 minutes.
5. Plate and cut into slices to serve.

133. Avocado tart

Servings: 4
Cooking time: 30 minutes
Ingredients:
- 115 grams of raspberries
- 2 avocados, peeled, pitted and mashed
- 1 cup almond flour
- 3 teaspoons baking powder
- 1 cup of swerve
- 4 tablespoons melted butter
- 4 beaten eggs

Addresses:
1. In a bowl, mix all ingredients together, stir and pour into a cake pan that fits the air fryer and has been lined with parchment paper.
2. Place the pan in the fryer and cook at 170°C for 30 minutes.
3. Allow the cake to cool, slice and serve.

134. Vanilla cake

Portions: 12
Cooking time: 30 minutes
Ingredients:
- ¼ teaspoon salt
- ½ cup erythritol powder
- 1 scraped vanilla pod
- 1/3 cup water
- 2/3 cup melted butter
- 4 large eggs

Addresses:
1. Preheat the air fryer for 5 minutes.
2. Combine all ingredients in a mixing bowl.
3. Pour into a greased baking dish.
4. Bake in the air fryer for 30 minutes at 190°C.

135. Coconut and coconut pudding

Servings: 1
Cooking time: 65 minutes
Ingredients:
- 1 cup coconut milk
- 2 tablespoons cocoa powder or organic cocoa
- ½ teaspoon icing sugar extract or 2 tablespoons honey or maple syrup
- ½ tablespoon of quality gelatine
- 1 tablespoon of water

Addresses:
1. Over medium heat, combine the coconut milk, cocoa and sweetener.
2. In a separate bowl, mix the gelatine and water.
3. Add to the pan and stir until completely dissolved.
4. Pour into small dishes and refrigerate for 1 hour.

5. It works!

136. Chocolate molten lava cake

Servings: 4
Cooking time: 25 minutes
Ingredients:
- 100 grams of melted butter
- 3 ½ tablespoons sugar
- 100 grams of melted chocolate
- 1 ½ tablespoons flour
- 2 eggs

Addresses:
1. Preheat the Air Fryer to 190°C.
2. Grease four baking tins with a little butter.
3. Thoroughly mix the eggs and butter before incorporating the melted chocolate.
4. Slowly stir in the flour.
5. Put an equal amount of the mixture in each pan.
6. Put them in the air fryer and cook them for 10 minutes.
7. Place the ramekins upside down on the plates and allow the cakes to fall. Serve hot.

137. Nut biscuits

Servings: 6
Cooking time: 10 minutes
Ingredients:
- ½ cup softened butter
- 1 cup coconut flour
- 85 grams of ground macadamia nuts
- ½ teaspoon baking powder
- 3 tablespoons erythritol
- Cooking spray

Addresses:
1. In the bowl of a mixer, combine the butter, coconut flour, ground coconut nuts, baking powder and erythritol.
2. Knead the non-sticky dough. Cut the dough into small pieces and roll them into balls. Press each biscuit ball gently to get the shape of the biscuits.
3. Preheat the air fryer to 185°C.
4. Spray the fryer basket with cooking spray.
5. Place the uncooked biscuits in the air fryer and cook for 8 minutes. Then cook for a further 2 minutes at 200°C to obtain a light brown crust.

138. Crème Brulee

Servings: 3
Cooking time: 60 minutes
Ingredients:
- 1 cup of milk
- 2 vanilla pods
- 10 egg yolks
- 4 tablespoons sugar + a little extra for the topping

Addresses:
1. In a saucepan, add the milk and cream. Slice the vanilla pods and scrape the seeds into the pan with the vanilla pods as well.
2. Place the pan over medium heat on the cooker until almost boiling while stirring regularly. Turn off the heat.
3. Add the egg yolks to a bowl and beat them. Add the sugar and mix well, but do not let it bubble too much.
4. Remove the vanilla pods from the milk mixture, pour the mixture over the egg mixture, stirring constantly. Leave to stand for a few minutes. Fill 2 or 3 ramekins with the mixture.
5. Place the ramekins in the fryer basket and cook at 90°C for 50 minutes.
6. Once ready, remove the moulds and leave to cool. Sprinkle with the remaining sugar and use a blowtorch to melt the sugar, so that it browns on top.

139. Strawberry shortcakes

Servings: 6
Cooking time: 25 minutes
Ingredients:
- 30 grams reduced-fat Philadelphia cream cheese
- 1 teaspoon corn starch
- 1 teaspoon stevia
- 1 teaspoon icing sugar
- 1/2 cup Greek nonfat vanilla yogurt
- 1/3 cup of low-sugar strawberry jam
- 2 refrigerated pie crusts
- Olive oil or coconut oil spray

Addresses:
1. Cut the pie dough into 6 equal rectangles.
2. In a bowl, mix together the cornflour and the preserves. Add the preserves to the centre of the crust. Fold the crust over and crimp the edges with a fork to seal. Repeat the process with the remaining crusts.
3. Lightly grease the air fryer tray with cooking spray. Add pop tarts in a single layer. Cook in batches for 8 minutes.
4. Meanwhile, prepare the glaze by mixing the stevia, cream cheese and yoghurt in a bowl.
5. Spread the glaze on top of the baked chocolate cake and add icing sugar.
6. Serve and enjoy.

140. Dark Chocolate Brownies

Portions: 10
Cooking time: 35 minutes
Ingredients:
- 170 grams of butter
- ¾ cup white sugar
- 3 eggs
- 2 teaspoons vanilla extract
- ¾ cup flour
- ¼ cup cocoa powder

- 1 cup chopped walnuts
- 1 cup white chocolate chips

Addresses:
1. Line a tray inside your air fryer with baking paper.
2. In a saucepan, melt the chocolate and butter over low heat. Keep stirring until the mixture is smooth. Allow to cool slightly and whisk in the eggs and vanilla.
3. Sieve the flour and cocoa and stir to mix well. Sprinkle the walnuts and add the white chocolate to the batter.
4. Pour the batter into the pan and bake for 20 minutes at 170°C.
5. Serve with raspberry syrup and ice cream.

141. Nutella and Banana Cupcakes

Servings: 4
Cooking time: 12 minutes
Ingredients:
- 1 sheet of puff pastry, cut into 4 equal squares
- ½ cup Nutella
- 2 sliced bananas
- 2 tablespoons icing sugar

Addresses:
1. Preheat the fryer to 190°C and grease the fryer basket.
2. Spread each puff pastry square with Nutella and cover with banana slices and icing sugar.
3. Fold each square into a triangle and press the edges lightly with a fork.
4. Place the cakes in the fryer basket and cook for about 12 minutes.
5. Serve immediately.

142. Orange Swiss roll

Servings: 6
Cooking time: 1 hour and 20 minutes
Ingredients:
- 1/2 cup milk
- 1/4 cup swerve
- 1 tablespoon of yeast
- 1/2 stick of butter, at room temperature
- 1 egg at room temperature
- 1/4 teaspoon salt
- 1 cup almond flour
- 1 cup coconut flour
- 2 tablespoons fresh orange juice

For the filling:
- 2 tablespoons butter
- 4 tablespoons swerve
- 1 teaspoon ground star aniseed
- 1/4 teaspoon ground cinnamon
- 1 teaspoon vanilla paste
- 1/2 cup pastry cream

Addresses:
1. Heat the milk in a microwave-safe bowl and transfer the warm milk to the bowl of an electric stand mixer. Add the 4 cups of swerve and the yeast, and mix to combine well. Cover and let stand until the yeast is foamy.
2. Next, beat in the butter at low speed. Add the egg and mix again. Add the salt and flour. Add the orange juice and mix on medium speed until a smooth batter forms.
3. Knead the dough on a lightly floured surface. Cover loosely and leave to rise in a warm place for about 1 hour or until doubled in size.
4. Next, spray the bottom and sides of a baking dish with cooking oil (butter flavoured).
5. Roll out the dough into a rectangle.
6. Spread 2 tablespoons of butter all over the dough.
7. In a mixing bowl, combine 4 tablespoons swerve, ground star anise, cinnamon and vanilla, sprinkle evenly over the batter.
8. Next, roll the dough into a log. Cut it into equal rolls and place them in the parchment-lined basket of the Air Fryer.
9. Bake at 180°C for 12 minutes, turning halfway through baking. Sprinkle with custard and enjoy.

143. Egg custard

Servings: 6
Cooking time: 32 minutes
Ingredients:
- 2 egg yolks
- 3 eggs
- 1/2 cup erythritol
- 2 cups whipping cream
- 1/2 teaspoon vanilla
- 1 teaspoon nutmeg

Addresses:
1. Preheat the air fryer to 160°C.
2. Add all ingredients to the large bowl and whisk until well combined.
3. Pour the custard mixture into the greased baking dish and place in the air fryer.
4. Cook for 32 minutes.
5. Allow to cool completely and then place in the refrigerator for 1 to 2 hours.
6. Serve and enjoy.

144. Creamy rice pudding

Servings: 6
Cooking time: 20 minutes
Ingredients:
- 1 tablespoon melted butter
- 200 grams of white rice
- 450 grams of milk
- 1/3 cup sugar
- 1 tablespoon of cream
- 1 teaspoon vanilla extract

Addresses:

1. Place all ingredients in a pan that fits your air fryer and stir well.
2. Place the frying pan in the deep fryer and cook at 180°C for a few minutes.
3. Stir the pudding, divide into bowls, refrigerate and serve cold.

145. Peach plot

Servings: 2
Cooking time: 15 minutes
Ingredients:
- 1 peach, peeled, cored and halved
- 1 cup prepared vanilla custard
- 2 sheets of puff pastry
- 1 egg, lightly beaten
- 1 tablespoon sugar
- A pinch of ground cinnamon
- 1 tablespoon of whipped cream

Addresses:
1. Preheat the fryer to 170°C and grease the fryer basket.
2. Place a spoonful of vanilla cream and a peach half in the centre of each sheet of puff pastry.
3. Mix the sugar and cinnamon in a bowl and sprinkle over the peach halves.
4. Pinch the corners of the leaves into a packet shape and place them in the fryer basket.
5. Cook for about 1 minute and cover with whipped cream.
6. Serve with the rest of the custard.

146. Vanilla Coconut Cheese Crackers

Portions: 15
Cooking time: 12 minutes
Ingredients:
- 1 egg
- 1/2 teaspoon baking powder
- 1 teaspoon vanilla
- 1/2 cup swerve
- 1/2 cup butter, softened
- 3 tablespoons softened cream cheese
- 1/2 cup coconut flour
- A pinch of salt

Addresses:
1. In a bowl, beat together the butter, sweetener and cream cheese.
2. Add the egg and vanilla and beat until smooth and creamy.
3. Add the coconut flour, salt and baking powder and whisk until combined. Cover and place in the fridge for 1 hour.
4. Preheat the air fryer to 160°C.
5. Make biscuits from the dough and place them in the air fryer and cook for 12 minutes.
6. Serve and enjoy.

147. Mum's orange rolls

Servings: 6
Cooking time: 1 hour and 20 minutes
Ingredients:
- 1/2 cup milk
- 1/4 cup granulated sugar
- 1 tablespoon of yeast
- 1/2 stick of butter at room temperature
- 1 egg at room temperature
- 1/4 teaspoon salt
- 2 cups plain flour
- 2 tablespoons fresh orange juice

For the filling you need:
- 2 tablespoons butter
- 4 tablespoons white sugar
- 1 teaspoon ground star aniseed
- 1/4 teaspoon ground cinnamon
- 1 teaspoon vanilla paste
- 1/2 cup confectioner's sugar

Addresses:
1. Heat the milk in a microwave-safe bowl and transfer the hot milk to the bowl of an electric stand mixer. Add the granulated sugar and yeast, and mix well. Cover and let stand until the yeast is foamy.
2. Next, beat in the butter at low speed. Add the egg and mix again. Add the salt and flour. Add the orange juice and mix on medium speed until a smooth batter forms.
3. Knead the dough on a lightly floured surface. Cover loosely and let it rest in a warm place for about 1 hour or until doubled in size. Then spray the bottom and sides of a baking pan with cooking oil (butter flavoured).
4. Roll out the dough into a rectangle.
5. Spread the dough with 2 tablespoons of butter. In a bowl, mix the white sugar, ground star anise, cinnamon and vanilla, sprinkle evenly over the dough.
6. Next, roll the dough into a log. Cut it into equal rolls and place them in the parchment-lined basket of the Air Fryer.
7. Bake at 180°C for 12 minutes, turning them over halfway through baking. Sprinkle with icing sugar and enjoy.

148. Vanilla mozzarella balls

Servings: 8
Cooking time: 4 minutes
Ingredients:
- 2 beaten eggs
- 1 teaspoon of almond butter, melted
- 200 grams of coconut flour
- 55 grams of almond flour
- 55 grams of shredded mozzarella cheese
- 1 tablespoon butter
- 2 tablespoons swerve
- 1 teaspoon baking powder
- ½ teaspoon vanilla extract
- Cooking spray

Addresses:

1. In the bowl of a blender, mix the butter and mozzarella. Heat the mixture in the microwave for about 15 minutes or until melted.
2. Then add the almond flour and coconut flour. Then add the swerve and baking powder. Then add the vanilla extract and stir the mixture. Knead the dough smooth.
3. Heat the mixture in the microwave for a further 2-5 seconds if it is not melted enough. Then mix the almond butter and eggs in the bowl. Make 8 balls with the almond flour mixture and roll them in the egg mixture.
4. Preheat the fryer to 200°C.
5. Spray the air fryer basket with cooking spray from the inside and place the rolls in one layer. Cook dessert for 4 minutes or until muffin is golden brown.
6. Cool the cooked dessert completely and sprinkle with Splenda if desired.

149. Peach slices

Servings: 4
Cooking time: 40 minutes
Ingredients:
- 4 cups of sliced peaches
- 2 - 3 tablespoons sugar
- 2 tablespoons flour
- ⅓ cup of oatmeal
- 2 tablespoons unsalted butter
- ¼ teaspoon vanilla extract
- 1 teaspoon cinnamon

Addresses:
1. In a large bowl, combine the peach slices, sugar, vanilla extract and cinnamon. Pour the mixture into a baking dish and place in the Air Fryer.
2. Cook in the air fryer at 145°C.
3. Meanwhile, combine the oats, flour and unsalted butter in a separate bowl.
4. Once the peach slices are cooked, pour the butter mixture over them.
5. Cook for a further 10 minutes at 150°C.
6. Remove from the fryer and leave to crisp for 5 to 10 minutes. Serve with ice cream if desired.

150. Butter crumble

Servings: 4
Cooking time: 25 minutes
Ingredients:
- ½ cup coconut flour
- 2 tablespoons softened butter
- 2 tablespoons erythritol
- 85 grams of crushed peanuts
- 1 tablespoon cream cheese
- 1 teaspoon baking powder
- ½ teaspoon lemon juice

Addresses:

1. In the bowl of a mixer, combine the coconut flour, butter, erythritol, baking powder and lemon juice. Stir the mixture until smooth.
2. Then put it in the freezer for a few minutes. In the meantime, mix the peanuts and cream cheese. Grate the frozen dough.
3. Line the air fryer pan with baking paper. Then put half of the shredded dough into the pan and flatten it. Cover with the cream cheese mixture. Now, place the rest of the shredded dough on top of the cream cheese mixture.
4. Place the pan with the crumble in the air fryer and cook for 25 minutes at 165°C.

151. Cheesecake with berries and white chocolate

Servings: 4
Cooking time: 5-10 minutes
Ingredients:
- 225 grams of softened cream cheese
- 55 grams of milk cream
- ½ teaspoon Splenda
- 1 teaspoon raspberries
- 1 tbsp Da Vinci syrup, white chocolate flavour, sugar-free

Addresses:
1. Whisk the ingredients together to a thick consistency.
2. Divide into cups.
3. Refrigerate.
4. Enjoy!

152. Strawberry coconut fritters

Servings: 8
Cooking time: 15 minutes
Ingredients:
- 3 tablespoons coconut oil
- 350 grams of strawberries
- 1/3 cup demerara sugar
- 1/8 teaspoon salt
- 1 ¼ cups soy milk
- 1/2 teaspoon coconut extract
- 1/2 teaspoon baking powder
- 3/4 cup plain flour

Addresses:
1. Mix all ingredients well in a bowl.
2. The next step is to drop teaspoonful quantities of the mixture into the cooking basket of the air fryer, air fry for 4 minutes at 175°C.
3. Sprinkle with ginger sugar if desired - bon appetit!

153. Classic white chocolate biscuits

Portions: 10
Cooking time: 40 minutes
Ingredients:
- 3/4 cup butter
- 1 ⅔ cups of almond flour
- 1/2 cup coconut flour

- 2 tablespoons coconut oil
- 3/4 cup granulated swerve
- 1/3 teaspoon ground star aniseed
- 1/3 teaspoon ground allspice
- 1/3 teaspoon grated nutmeg
- 1/4 teaspoon fine sea salt
- 225 grams of unsweetened white chocolate
- 2 eggs, well beaten

Addresses:
1. Put all the above ingredients, except the egg, in a mixing bowl. Then knead by hand until a smooth dough forms. Place in the fridge for 20 minutes.
2. Roll the chilled dough into balls, flatten the balls and preheat the Air Fryer to 180°C.
3. Make an egg wash using the remaining egg. Then glaze the biscuits with the egg wash, bake for about 11 minutes, bon appetit!

154. Lemon Glazed Muffins

Servings: 6
Cooking time: 30 minutes
Ingredients:
- ½ cup sugar
- 1 small egg
- 1 teaspoon lemon zest
- ¾ teaspoon baking powder
- ¼ teaspoon bicarbonate of soda
- ½ teaspoon salt
- 2 tablespoons vegetable oil
- ½ cup milk
- ½ teaspoon vanilla extract

For the enamel you need:
- ½ cup icing sugar
- 2 teaspoons lemon juice

Addresses:
1. Preheat the fryer to 180°C.
2. Combine all dry muffin ingredients in a bowl. In another bowl, whisk together the wet ingredients. Gently bring the two mixtures together. Divide the batter between 6 greased muffin tins.
3. Place the muffin tins in the air fryer and cook for 1 to 14 minutes.
4. Whisk the icing sugar with the lemon juice. Spread the icing on the cupcakes.

155. Apple bread pudding

Servings: 8
Cooking time: 44 minutes
Ingredients:
For the bread pudding you need:
- 300 grams of bread cut into cubes
- ½ cup apple, peeled, cored and chopped
- ½ cup sultanas
- ¼ cup chopped walnuts
- 1½ cups milk
- ¾ cup water
- 5 tablespoons honey
- 2 teaspoons ground cinnamon
- 2 teaspoons cornstarch
- 1 teaspoon vanilla extract

For coverage you need:
- 1 1/3 cups plain flour
- 3/5 cup brown sugar
- 7 tablespoons butter

Addresses:
1. In a large bowl, mix the bread, apple, sultanas and walnuts well.
2. In another bowl, add the rest of the pudding ingredients and mix until well combined.
3. Add the milk mixture to the bread mixture and mix until well combined.
4. Refrigerate for about 15 minutes, stirring occasionally.
5. For the topping: in a bowl, mix the flour and sugar.
6. Using a pastry cutter, cut in the butter until a crumbly mixture forms.
7. Set the fryer temperature to 180°C.
8. Spoon the mixture evenly into 2 baking tins and spread the topping mixture over each.
9. Place 1 frying pan in the fryer basket.
10. Fry in the open air for about 22 minutes.
11. Repeat with the rest of the pan.
12. Remove from the fryer and serve hot.

156. Blueberry Pancakes

Servings: 4
Cooking time: 20 minutes
Ingredients:
- ½ teaspoon vanilla extract
- 2 tablespoons honey
- ½ cup blueberries
- ½ cup sugar
- 2 cups + 2 tablespoons flour
- 3 beaten eggs
- 1 cup of milk
- 1 teaspoon baking powder
- A pinch of salt

Addresses:
1. Preheat the Air Fryer to 200°C.
2. In a bowl, mix all the dry ingredients.
3. Pour in the wet ingredients and combine with a whisk, making sure the mixture is smooth.
4. Dredge each blueberry in a little flour to lightly coat it before incorporating it into the batter. This is to ensure that they do not change the colour of the batter.
5. Grease the inside of a baking dish with a little oil or butter.
6. Spoon several equal amounts of batter onto the baking sheet, spreading them out into pancake shapes and making sure to space them well. This may need to be done in two batches.

7. Place the dish in the fryer and bake for about 10 minutes.

157. Lemon curd

Servings: 2
Cooking time: 30 minutes
Ingredients:
- 3 tablespoons sugar
- 1 egg
- 1 egg yolk
- Juice of ¾ lemon

Addresses:
1. Add the sugar and butter to a medium saucepan and beat evenly. Gradually add the egg and egg yolk while whisking to achieve a fresh yellow colour. Add the lemon juice and mix.
2. Place the pan in the fryer basket and cook at 120°C for 6 minutes. Increase the temperature back to 160°C and cook for minutes.
3. Remove the bowl onto a flat surface, use a spoon to check for lumps and remove them. Cover the ramekin with plastic wrap and refrigerate overnight or serve immediately.

158. Coconut biscuits

Portions: 12
Cooking time: 20 minutes
Ingredients:
- 1 cup melted butter
- 1 ¾ cups granulated sugar
- 3 eggs
- 2 tablespoons coconut milk
- 1 teaspoon coconut extract
- 1 teaspoon vanilla extract
- 2 ¼ cups plain flour
- 1/2 teaspoon baking powder
- 1/2 teaspoon bicarbonate of soda
- 1/2 teaspoon fine table salt
- 2 cups coconut chips

Addresses:
1. Start by preheating your fryer to 180°C.
2. In the bowl of an electric mixer, beat the butter and sugar until well combined. Now add the eggs one at a time and mix well, add the coconut milk, coconut extract and vanilla, beat until creamy and smooth.
3. Mix the flour with the baking powder, baking soda and salt. Then add the flour mixture to the butter mixture and stir until everything is well incorporated.
4. Finally, stir in the coconut shavings and mix again. Place tablespoon-sized balls of the dough on a biscuit sheet, leaving 5 centimetres between each biscuit.
5. Bake for 10 minutes or until golden brown, turning the pan once or twice during the baking time.
6. Let the biscuits cool on wire racks - bon appetit!

159. Almond bars

Portions: 12
Cooking time: 35 minutes
Ingredients:
- 2 eggs, lightly beaten
- 1 cup erythritol
- ½ teaspoon vanilla
- ¼ cup water
- ½ cup softened butter
- ¾ cup pitted cherries
- 1 ½ cup almond flour
- 1 tablespoon xanthan gum
- ½ teaspoon salt

Addresses:
1. In a bowl, mix the almond flour, erythritol, eggs, vanilla, butter and salt until a dough forms.
2. Press the batter into the baking tray of the air fryer.
3. Place in the air fryer and cook for 10 minutes.
4. Meanwhile, mix the cherries, xanthan gum and water.
5. Pour the cherry mixture over the cooked dough and cook for 2 more minutes.
6. Cut and serve.

160. Rustic baked apples

Servings: 4
Cooking time: 25 minutes
Ingredients:
- 4 Gala apples
- 1/4 cup rolled oats
- 1/4 cup sugar
- 2 tablespoons honey
- 1/3 cup chopped walnuts
- 1 teaspoon cinnamon powder
- 1/2 teaspoon ground cardamom
- 1/2 teaspoon ground cloves
- 2/3 cup water

Addresses:
1. Use a paring knife to remove the stem and seeds from the apples, making deep holes.
2. In a bowl, mix together the rolled oats, sugar, honey, walnuts, cinnamon, cardamom and cloves.
3. Pour the water into an Air Fryer safe dish. Place the apples in the bowl.
4. Bake for 17 minutes. Serve at room temperature, enjoy!

161. Banana Split

Servings: 8
Cooking time: 10 minutes
Ingredients:
- 1 cup panko bread crumbs
- 4 bananas, peeled and cut in half lengthwise

- ½ cup maize flour
- 2 eggs
- 2 tablespoons chopped walnuts
- 3 tablespoons coconut oil
- 3 tablespoons sugar
- ¼ teaspoon ground cinnamon

Addresses:
1. Preheat the fryer to 140°C and lightly grease one fryer basket.
2. Heat the coconut oil in a frying pan over medium heat and add the breadcrumbs.
3. Cook for 4 minutes until golden brown and transfer to a bowl.
4. Put the flour in a shallow dish and beat the eggs in another shallow dish.
5. Dredge the banana slices in flour, dip them in the eggs and dredge them in the breadcrumbs again.
6. Mix the sugar and cinnamon in a small bowl and sprinkle over the banana slices.
7. Place the banana slices in the fryer basket and cook for about 10 minutes.
8. Top with walnuts and serve.

162. Greek-style griddle cakes

Servings: 4
Cooking time: 15 minutes
Ingredients:
- 3/4 cup wheat flour
- 1/4 teaspoon fine sea salt
- 2 tablespoons sugar
- 1/2 cup milk
- 2 eggs, lightly beaten
- 1 tablespoon butter

For coverage you need:
- 1 cup Greek yoghurt
- 1 mashed banana
- 2 tablespoons honey

Addresses:
1. Mix the flour, salt and sugar in a bowl. Then add the milk, eggs and butter. Mix until smooth and even.
2. Drop spoonfuls of the batter into the pan of the Air Fryer.
3. Cook for 4 to 5 minutes or until bubbles form on the top of the griddle cakes. Repeat with the rest of the batter.
4. In the meantime, mix all the ingredients for the topping. Place in the refrigerator until ready to serve. Serve the griddle cakes with the chilled topping - enjoy!

163. Cashew nut cake

Servings: 8
Cooking time: 18 minutes
Ingredients:
- 1 egg
- 55 grams of crushed cashew nuts
- ½ teaspoon bicarbonate of soda
- 1/3 cup heavy cream
- 30 grams of melted dark chocolate
- 1 tablespoon butter
- 1 teaspoon vinegar
- 1 cup coconut flour

Addresses:
1. Add the egg to a bowl and beat with a hand mixer. Add the coconut flour and stir well.
2. Add the butter, vinegar, baking soda, cream and melted chocolate and stir well.
3. Add the cashew nuts and mix well.
4. Preheat the air fryer to 180°C.
5. Add the prepared batter to the fryer's baking dish and flatten into a pie shape.
6. Cook for 18 minutes.
7. Cut and serve.

164. Ricotta and lemon tart recipe

Servings: 4
Cooking time: 1 hour and 10 minutes
Ingredients:
- 8 beaten eggs
- 3 pounds ricotta cheese
- Grated zest of 1 lemon
- Grated peel of 1 orange
- 1/2 pound sugar
- Butter for the frying pan

Addresses:
1. In a bowl, mix the eggs with the sugar, cheese, lemon and orange zest and stir well.
2. Grease a baking pan that fits your air fryer with a little batter, spread the ricotta mixture, place in the fryer at 200°C and bake for 30 minutes.
3. When the specified time is up, reduce the heat and bake for a further 40 minutes.
4. Remove from the oven, allow the cake to cool and serve.

165. Classic butter cake

Servings: 8
Cooking time: 35 minutes
Ingredients:
- 1 stick of butter at room temperature
- 1 cup sugar
- 2 eggs
- 1 cup all-purpose flour
- 1 teaspoon baking powder
- 1/2 teaspoon bicarbonate of soda
- 1/4 teaspoon salt
- A pinch of freshly grated nutmeg
- A pinch of crushed star aniseed
- 1/4 cup buttermilk
- 1 teaspoon vanilla essence

Addresses:
1. Start by preheating your fryer to 160°C. Spray the bottom and sides of a baking dish with cooking spray.
2. Beat the butter and sugar with a hand mixer until creamy. Then add the eggs, one at a time, and mix well until fluffy.

3. Stir in the flour along with the rest of the ingredients. Mix to combine well. Pour the batter into the prepared pan.
4. Bake for 15 minutes, turn the pan and bake for another 15 minutes, until the top of the cake jiggles when pressed with your fingers. Bon appetit!

166. Rhubarb pie recipe

Servings: 6
Cooking time: 1 hour and 15 minutes
Ingredients:
- 1 ¼ cups almond flour
- 5 tablespoons of cold water
- 8 tablespoons butter
- 1 teaspoon sugar

For the filling you need:
- 3 cups chopped rhubarb
- 1/2 teaspoon of ground nutmeg
- 1 tablespoon butter
- 3 tablespoons flour
- 1 ½ cups sugar
- 2 eggs
- 2 tablespoons low-fat milk

Addresses:
1. In a bowl, mix ¼ cup flour with 1 teaspoon sugar, 8 tablespoons butter and cold water, stir and knead into a dough.
2. Transfer the dough to a floured work surface, form into a disc, flatten, wrap in plastic wrap and store in the refrigerator for about 30 minutes.
3. In a bowl, combine rhubarb with 1 ½ cups sugar, nutmeg, 1 tablespoon flour and whisk.
4. In another bowl, beat the eggs with the milk, add to the rhubarb mixture, pour the whole mixture into the pie crust, put in your air fryer and cook at 200°C, for minutes. Slice and serve cold

167. Dark chocolate cheesecake

Servings: 6
Cooking time: 34 minutes
Ingredients:
- 3 eggs, whites and yolks separated
- 1 cup chopped dark chocolate
- ½ cup softened cream cheese
- 2 tablespoons cocoa powder
- ¼ cup date jam
- 2 tablespoons icing sugar

Addresses:
1. Preheat the fryer to 140°C and lightly grease a cake tin.
2. Refrigerate the egg whites in a bowl to cool before use.
3. Heat the chocolate and cream cheese in the microwave on high power for a few minutes.
4. Remove from the microwave and whisk in the egg yolks.
5. Beat the egg whites until stiff peaks form and combine with the chocolate mixture.
6. Transfer the mixture into a cake tin and place it in the fryer basket.
7. Cook for about 30 minutes and serve.
8. Sprinkle with icing sugar and spread the date jam on top to serve.

168. Lemon Butter Cake

Servings: 8
Cooking time: 2 hours and 20 minutes
Ingredients:
- 1 stick of softened butter
- 1 cup sugar
- 1 medium egg
- 1 ¼ cups flour
- 1 teaspoon butter flavouring
- 1 teaspoon vanilla essence
- A pinch of salt
- ¾ cup milk
- Zest of 1 medium lemon

For the glaze you need:
- 2 tablespoons freshly squeezed lemon juice

Addresses:
1. In a large bowl, mix the butter and sugar with a whisk. Stir in the egg and continue mixing.
2. Add the flour, butter flavouring, vanilla essence and salt, combining well.
3. Pour in the milk, followed by the lemon zest, and continue mixing.
4. Lightly brush the inside of a baking tin with the melted butter.
5. Pour the cake batter into the cake tin.
6. Place the pan in the Air Fryer and bake at 180°C for 15 minutes.
7. After removing from the fryer, run a knife around the edges of the cake to remove it from the pan and transfer it to a serving plate.
8. Allow to cool completely.
9. Meanwhile, prepare the glaze by combining it with the lemon juice.
10. Pour the glaze over the cake and leave to set for a further 2 hours before serving.

169. Cheese cake

Servings: 6
Cooking time: 28 minutes
Ingredients:
For the bark you need:
- 2 tablespoons melted butter
- ¼ teaspoon cinnamon
- 1 tablespoon swerve
- ½ cup almond flour
- A pinch of salt

For the cheesecake you need:
- 1 egg
- ½ teaspoon vanilla
- ½ cup of swerve

- 225 grams of cream cheese

Addresses:
1. Preheat the air fryer to 140°C.
2. Spray the fryer's baking dish with cooking spray.
3. Add all the crust ingredients to the bowl and mix until combined. Transfer the crust mixture to the prepared baking dish and press down into the bottom of the dish.
4. Place the dish in the air fryer and cook for 12 minutes.
5. In a large bowl, beat cream cheese with a hand mixer until smooth.
6. Add the egg, vanilla and salt and stir to combine.
7. Pour the cream cheese mixture over the cooked crust and cook for 16 minutes.
8. Allow to cool completely.
9. Cut and serve.

170. Strawberry cheesecake

Servings: 6
Cooking time: 35 minutes
Ingredients:
- 1 cup almond flour
- 3 tablespoons of melted coconut oil
- ½ teaspoon vanilla
- 1 egg, lightly beaten
- 1 tablespoon fresh lime juice
- ¼ cup erythritol
- 1 cup cream cheese, softened
- 450 grams of chopped strawberries
- 2 teaspoons baking powder

Addresses:
1. Add all ingredients to the large bowl and mix until well combined.
2. Spray the cake pan of the air fryer with cooking spray.
3. Pour the batter into the prepared pan and place in the air fryer and cook for 35 minutes.
4. Allow to cool completely.
5. Cut and serve.

171. Zucchini lemon bread

Portions: 12
Cooking time: 40 minutes
Ingredients:
- 2 cups almond flour
- 2 teaspoons baking powder
- ¾ cup of swerve
- ½ cup coconut oil, melted
- 1 teaspoon lemon juice
- 1 teaspoon vanilla extract
- 3 beaten eggs
- 1 cup grated courgette
- 1 tablespoon lemon zest
- Cooking spray

Addresses:
1. In a bowl, combine all the ingredients except the cooking spray and stir well.
2. Grease a loaf pan that fits the air fryer with cooking spray, line it with parchment paper and pour the bread mixture into it.
3. Place the pan in the air fryer and cook at 165°C for 40 minutes.
4. Cool, cut and serve.

172. Sweet coconut cream cake

Servings: 4
Cooking time: 25 minutes
Ingredients:
- 4 tablespoons coconut cream
- 1 teaspoon baking powder
- 1 teaspoon apple cider vinegar
- 1 beaten egg
- ¼ cup coconut flakes
- 1 teaspoon vanilla extract
- ½ cup coconut flour
- 4 teaspoons Splenda
- 1 teaspoon xanthan gum
- Cooking spray

Addresses:
1. Put all the liquid ingredients in the bowl: coconut cream, apple cider vinegar, egg and vanilla extract. Stir the liquid until homogeneous and add the baking powder, coconut flakes, coconut flour, Splenda and xanthan gum. Stir the ingredients until a smooth dough texture is achieved.
2. Spray the cake tin of the air fryer with cooking spray. Pour the batter into the pan. Preheat the air fryer to 165°.
3. Place the cake tin in the basket of the air fryer and cook for 25 minutes.
4. Then cool the baked cake completely and remove it from the tin. Cut the baked cake into portions.

173. Cranberry almond cake

Servings: 6
Cooking time: 16 minutes
Ingredients:
- 4 eggs
- 1 teaspoon grated orange zest
- 2 teaspoons mixed spices
- 2 teaspoons cinnamon
- 1/4 cup swerve
- 1 cup softened butter
- 2/3 cup dried cranberries
- 1 ½ cups of almond flour
- 1 teaspoon vanilla

Addresses:
1. Preheat the air fryer to 160°C.
2. In a bowl, add the sweetener and melted butter and beat until fluffy.
3. Add the cinnamon, vanilla and spice mixture and stir well.
4. Add the eggs and stir until well combined.
5. Add the almond flour, orange zest and cranberries and stir to combine.

6. Pour the batter into a greased cake pan and place it in the air fryer.
7. Bake the cake for 16 minutes.
8. Cut and serve.

174. Mint and mascarpone cake

Servings: 6
Cooking time: 40 minutes
Ingredients:
- 2 tablespoons stevia
- 1/2 cup coconut flour
- 1/2 cup butter
- 1 cup mascarpone cheese at room temperature
- 115 grams baking chocolate, unsweetened
- 1 teaspoon vanilla extract
- 2 drops of peppermint extract

Addresses:
1. Whisk the sugar, coconut flour and butter in a bowl. Press the mixture into the bottom of a lightly greased baking tin.
2. Bake at 180°C for 18 minutes. Place in your freezer for a few minutes.
3. Next, prepare the cheesecake topping by mixing the rest of the ingredients together. Place this topping on top of the crust and chill in the freezer for another 15 minutes. Serve well chilled.

175. Super moist chocolate cake

Servings: 9
Cooking time: 40 minutes
Ingredients:
- 1/3 cup plain flour
- ¼ teaspoon baking powder
- 1½ tablespoons cocoa powder, unsweetened
- 2 eggs with separated yolks and whites
- 3¾ tablespoons milk
- 40 grams castor sugar
- 2 tablespoons vegetable oil
- 1 teaspoon vanilla extract
- 1/8 teaspoon of cream of tartar

Addresses:
1. Preheat the fryer to 165°C and lightly grease a chiffon pan.
2. Mix the flour, baking powder and cocoa powder in a bowl.
3. Combine the rest of the ingredients in another bowl until well combined.
4. Gradually stir in the flour mixture and pour this mixture into the gauze mould.
5. Cover with aluminium foil and make some holes in the foil.
6. Transfer the baking tray to the basket of the air fryer and cook for about 30 minutes.
7. Remove the foil and set the fryer to 140°C.
8. Cook for a further 10 minutes and cut into slices to serve.

176. Coconut lemon bars

Portions: 12
Cooking time: 25 minutes
Ingredients:
- ¼ cup cashews
- ¼ cup fresh lemon juice, freshly squeezed
- ¾ cup coconut milk
- ¾ cup erythritol
- 1 cup desiccated coconut
- 1 teaspoon baking powder
- 2 beaten eggs
- 2 tablespoons coconut oil
- A pinch of salt

Addresses:
1. Preheat the air fryer for 5 minutes.
2. In a mixing bowl, combine all ingredients.
3. Use a hand blender to mix everything together.
4. Pour into an ovenproof dish that will fit in the air fryer.
5. Bake for 2 minutes at 180°C or until a toothpick inserted in the centre comes out clean.

177. Stevia cake

Servings: 6
Cooking time: 40 minutes
Ingredients:
- 2 tablespoons melted ghee
- 1 cup shredded coconut
- 1 cup mashed avocado
- 3 tablespoons stevia
- 1 teaspoon cinnamon powder
- 2 teaspoons cinnamon powder

Addresses:
1. In a bowl, mix all the ingredients together and stir well. Pour into a cake tin lined with parchment paper.
2. Place the preparation in the mould and then in the fryer and cook at 170°C for 40 minutes.
3. Cool the cake, slice and serve.

178. Sweet potato pie

Servings: 4
Cooking time: 1 hour
Ingredients:
- Sweet potato 170 grams
- 1 (about 20 centimetres) prepared and thawed pie crust
- 2 large eggs
- 1 tablespoon melted butter
- 1 teaspoon olive oil
- ¼ cup heavy cream
- 2 tablespoons maple syrup
- 1 tablespoon light brown sugar
- ½ teaspoon ground cinnamon
- 1/8 teaspoon ground nutmeg
- Salt
- ¾ teaspoon vanilla extract

Addresses:

1. Preheat the fryer to 200°C and grease a cake tin.
2. Rub the sweet potato with oil and place it in the fryer basket.
3. Cook for a few minutes and serve in a serving dish.
4. Allow to cool and mash thoroughly.
5. Add the rest of the ingredients and mix until well combined.
6. Place the shell in a tart pan and spoon the mixture into the tart shell.
7. Place the cake tin in the fryer basket and cook for about 30 minutes.
8. Serve hot.

179. Pear fritters with cinnamon and ginger

Servings: 4
Cooking time: 20 minutes
Ingredients:
- 2 pears, peeled, cored and cut into slices
- 1 tbsp melted coconut oil
- 1 ½ cups plain flour
- 1 teaspoon baking powder
- A pinch of fine sea salt
- A pinch of freshly grated nutmeg
- 1/2 teaspoon ginger
- 1 teaspoon cinnamon
- 2 eggs
- 4 tablespoons milk

Addresses:
1. Mix all the ingredients except the pears in a shallow bowl. Dip each slice of pear into the batter until well coated.
2. Cook in the preheated Air Fryer at 180°C for 4 minutes, turning them over halfway through cooking. Repeat with the rest of the ingredients.
3. Sprinkle with icing sugar if desired - bon appetit!

180. Avocado Chocolate Brownies

Portions: 12
Cooking time: 30 minutes
Ingredients:
- 1 cup avocado, peeled and mashed
- ½ teaspoon vanilla extract
- 4 tablespoons cocoa powder
- 3 tablespoons of melted coconut oil
- 2 beaten eggs
- ½ cup dark chocolate, unsweetened and melted
- ¾ cup almond flour
- 1 teaspoon baking powder
- ¼ teaspoon bicarbonate of soda
- 1 teaspoon stevia

Addresses:
1. In a bowl, mix the flour with the stevia, baking powder and baking soda and stir. Add the rest of the ingredients a little at a time, whisk together and pour into a cake tin that will fit in the air fryer after lining it with parchment paper.
2. Place the pan in your air fryer and cook at 180°C for 30 minutes.
3. Cut into squares and serve cold.

181. Blueberry Bread Pudding

Servings: 4
Cooking time: 45 minutes
Ingredients:
- 1-1/2 cups milk
- 2-1/2 eggs
- 1/2 cup cranberries
- 1 teaspoon butter
- 1/4 cup and 2 tablespoons white sugar
- 1/4 cup sultanas
- 1/8 teaspoon ground cinnamon
- 3/4 cup whipping cream
- 3/4 tsp lemon zest
- 3/4 teaspoon kosher salt
- 3/4 French baguettes, cut into about 5 cm slices
- 3/8 vanilla pod, split and seeded

Addresses:
1. Lightly grease the air fryer tray with cooking spray. Spread the baguette slices, cranberries and sultanas.
2. In a blender, thoroughly mix the vanilla pod, cinnamon, salt, lemon zest, eggs, sugar and cream. Pour the mixture over the baguette slices. Let it stand for one hour.
3. Cover the pan with aluminium foil.
4. Cook at 165°C for 35 minutes.
5. Let it stand for 10 minutes.
6. Serve and enjoy.

182. Sugar butter fritters

Portions: 16
Cooking time: 30 minutes
Ingredients:
For the dough you need:
- 4 cups of flour
- 1 teaspoon kosher salt
- 1 teaspoon sugar
- 3 tablespoons butter at room temperature
- 1 packet instant yeast
- 1 ¼ cups of warm water

For the cakes you need:
- 1 cup sugar
- Pinch of cardamom
- 1 teaspoon cinnamon powder
- 1 stick of melted butter

Addresses:
1. Place all ingredients in a large bowl and combine well.
2. Add the lukewarm water and mix until a smooth, elastic dough forms.
3. Place the dough on a lightly floured surface and place a sheet of greased

aluminium foil on top of the dough. Refrigerate for 5 to 10 minutes.
4. Take it out of the fridge and divide it in two. Mould each half into a log and cut into 20 pieces.
5. In a shallow bowl, combine the sugar, cardamom and cinnamon.
6. Brush the slices with a light coating of melted butter and sugar.
7. Spray the Air Fryer basket with cooking spray.
8. Transfer the slices to the fryer and air fry at 180°C for approximately 10 minutes. Turn each slice once during the cooking time.
9. Sprinkle each slice with the sugar before serving.

183. Coconut sunflower biscuits

Servings: 8
Cooking time: 10 minutes
Ingredients:
- 140 grams of sunflower seed butter
- 6 tablespoons coconut flour
- 1 teaspoon vanilla
- ¼ teaspoon olive oil
- 2 tablespoons swerve
- A pinch of salt

Addresses:
1. Add all the ingredients in the bowl and mix until the dough forms.
2. Preheat the air fryer to 180°C.
3. Make the biscuits with the mixture and place them in the air fryer and cook them for 10 minutes.
4. Serve and enjoy.

184. Stuffed apples

Servings: 4
Cooking time: 13 minutes
Ingredients:
- 4 small, firm, cored apples
- ½ cup sultanas
- ½ cup blanched almonds
- 4 tablespoons sugar, divided
- ½ cup whipped cream
- ½ teaspoon vanilla extract

Addresses:
1. Preheat the fryer to 180°C and lightly grease a baking dish.
2. Place the sultanas, almonds and half the sugar in a food processor and pulse until chopped.
3. Stuff the sultana mixture into each apple and place the apples in the prepared baking dish.
4. Place the pan in the fryer basket and cook for about 10 minutes.
5. Place the cream, remaining sugar and vanilla extract over medium heat in a saucepan and cook for about 3 minutes, stirring continuously.
6. Remove from the heat and serve the apple with vanilla sauce.

185. Cheat Apple Pie

Servings: 8
Cooking time: 30 minutes
Ingredients:
- 55 grams of melted butter
- 55 grams of sugar
- 30 grams of brown sugar
- 2 teaspoons cinnamon
- 1 beaten egg
- 3 large sheets of puff pastry
- ¼ teaspoon salt

Addresses:
1. Whisk together the white sugar, brown sugar, cinnamon, salt and butter. Place the apples in a baking dish and cover them with the mixture.
2. Place the baking dish in the air fryer and cook for a few minutes at 180°C.
3. Meanwhile, roll out the dough on a floured flat surface and cut each sheet into 6 equal pieces. Divide the apple filling between the pieces. Brush the edges of the puff pastry squares with the egg.
4. Fold them over and seal the edges with a fork. Place on a lined baking sheet and cook in the fryer for 8 minutes.
5. Turn over, increase the temperature to 200°C and cook for a further 2 minutes.

186. Churros

Servings: 1
Cooking time: 15 minutes
Ingredients:
- ½ cup water
- ¼ cup butter
- ½ cup flour
- 3 eggs
- 2 ½ teaspoons sugar

Addresses:
1. In a saucepan, bring the water and butter to the boil. Once it is bubbling, add the flour and mix to create a paste-like consistency.
2. Remove from the heat, leave to cool and crack the eggs into the saucepan. Beat with a hand mixer until fluffy.
3. Transfer the dough to a piping bag.
4. Preheat the fryer to 190°C.
5. Put the dough into the fryer in several segments approximately 6 cm long. Cook for 10 minutes before removing from the fryer and dipping in sugar.
6. Serve with the low-carb chocolate sauce of your choice.

187. Delicious Autumn Clafoutis

Servings: 6

Cooking time: 30 minutes
Ingredients:
- 3/4 cup extra fine flour
- 1 ½ cups plums, stoned and pitted
- 4 medium pears, cored and sliced
- 1/2 cup coconut cream
- 3/4 cup coconut milk
- 3 beaten eggs
- 1/2 cup icing sugar for sprinkles
- 3/4 cup white sugar
- 1/2 teaspoon bicarbonate of soda
- 1/2 teaspoon baking powder
- 1/3 teaspoon ground cinnamon
- 1/2 teaspoon crystallised ginger
- 1/4 teaspoon grated nutmeg

Addresses:
1. Lightly grease 2 mini cake tins with non-stick spray. Place the plums and pears in the bottom of the moulds.
2. In a preheated saucepan over moderate heat, heat the cream together with the coconut milk until very hot.
3. Remove the pan from the heat, mix the flour together with the baking soda and baking powder.
4. In a medium bowl, whisk together the eggs, white sugar and spices, beat until the mixture is creamy.
5. Add the creamy milk mixture. Carefully spread this mixture over the fruit.
6. Bake at 160°C for about 25 minutes. To serve, sprinkle with icing sugar.

188. Donuts of milk

Portions: 12
Cooking time: 24 minutes
Ingredients:
For the doughnuts you need:
- 1 cup all-purpose flour
- 1 cup whole wheat flour
- 2 teaspoons baking powder
- Salt
- ¾ cup sugar
- 1 egg
- 1 tablespoon softened butter
- ½ cup milk
- 2 teaspoons vanilla extract

For the enamel you need:
- 2 tablespoons icing sugar
- 2 tablespoons condensed milk
- 1 tablespoon cocoa powder

Addresses:
1. In a large bowl, thoroughly mix the flours, baking powder and salt.
2. In another bowl, add the sugar and egg. Beat until fluffy and light.
3. Add the flour mixture and stir until well combined.
4. Add the butter, milk and vanilla extract and mix until a smooth dough forms.
5. Refrigerate the dough for at least 1 hour.
6. Now place the dough on a lightly floured surface and roll it out to a thickness of 1.25 centimetres.
7. Using a small doughnut cutter, cut 24 small doughnuts from the rolled dough.
8. Set the temperature of the air fryer to 200°C. Grease the air fryer basket.
9. Place the doughnuts in the prepared air fryer basket in 3 batches.
10. Fry in the open air for about 6-8 minutes.
11. Remove from the air fryer and transfer the doughnuts to a tray to cool completely.
12. In a small bowl, mix the condensed milk and cocoa powder.
13. Spread the glaze over the doughnuts and sprinkle with icing sugar.
14. Serves.

189. Vanilla Rum and Walnut Cookies

Servings: 6
Cooking time: 35 minutes
Ingredients:
- 1/2 cup almond flour
- 1/2 cup coconut flour
- 1/2 teaspoon baking powder
- 1/4 teaspoon fine sea salt
- 1 stick unsalted butter, softened
- 1/2 cup swerve
- 1 egg
- 1/2 teaspoon vanilla
- 1 teaspoon buttermilk rum flavouring
- 85 grams of finely chopped walnuts

Addresses:
1. Start by preheating the fryer to 180°C.
2. In a mixing bowl, thoroughly combine the flour with the baking powder and salt.
3. Beat the butter and swerve with a hand mixer until pale and fluffy, add the beaten egg, vanilla and buttermilk rum flavouring, mix again to combine well. Now fold in the dry ingredients.
4. Stir in the chopped walnuts. Divide the mixture into small balls, flatten each ball with a fork and transfer to a baking tin lined with aluminium foil.
5. Bake in the preheated Air Fryer for 14 minutes. Work in several batches and transfer to wire racks to cool completely - bon appetit!

190. Pumpkin bars

Servings: 6
Cooking time: 25 minutes
Ingredients:
- ¼ cup almond butter
- 1 tbsp unsweetened almond milk
- ½ cup coconut flour
- ¾ teaspoon of bicarbonate of soda
- ½ cup divided unsweetened dark chocolate chips

- 1 cup canned, unsweetened pumpkin puree
- ¼ cup swerve
- 1 teaspoon cinnamon
- 1 teaspoon vanilla extract
- ¼ teaspoon nutmeg
- ½ teaspoon ginger
- 1/8 teaspoon salt
- 1/8 tsp ground cloves

Addresses:
1. Preheat the fryer to 180°C and line a baking tray with wax paper.
2. Mix the pumpkin puree, swerve, vanilla extract, milk and butter in a bowl.
3. Combine the coconut flour, spices, salt and baking soda in another bowl.
4. Combine the two mixtures and mix well until homogeneous.
5. Add about 1/3 cup of the unsweetened chocolate chips and transfer this mixture to the pan.
6. Transfer to the fryer basket and cook for about 25 minutes.
7. Microwave the unsweetened chocolate chips on low heat and remove the baked cake from the pan.
8. Cover with melted chocolate and cut into slices to serve.

191. Chocolate with coconut

Servings: 2
Cooking time: 7 minutes
Ingredients:
- ¼ teaspoon vanilla extract
- 1/3 cup coconut milk
- 1 teaspoon butter
- 1 tablespoon cocoa powder
- 15 grams of dark chocolate
- 1 teaspoon monk fruit

Addresses:
1. In a large bowl, whisk together the coconut milk and cocoa powder. When the liquid is smooth, add the vanilla extract and Monk fruit. Stir gently.
2. Then add the dark chocolate and butter.
3. Place the cup with the chocolate mixture in the air fryer and cook at 190°C for 3 minutes.
4. Remove the liquid and cook for a further 4 minutes. Carefully remove the hot chocolate cups from the air fryer. Stir the hot chocolate gently with a spoon.

192. Lemon cake with almond and coconut

Portions: 10
Cooking time: 48 minutes
Ingredients:
- 4 eggs
- 2 tablespoons lemon zest
- 1/2 cup softened butter
- 2 teaspoons baking powder
- 1/4 cup coconut flour
- 2 cups almond flour
- 1/2 cup fresh lemon juice
- 1/4 cup swerve
- 1 tablespoon vanilla

Addresses:
1. Preheat the air fryer to 140°C.
2. Spray the fryer's baking dish with cooking spray and set aside.
3. In a large bowl, beat all ingredients with a hand blender until smooth.
4. Pour the batter into the prepared dish and place it in the air fryer and cook for minutes.
5. Cut and serve.

193. Dulce de leche cake with walnuts

Servings: 6
Cooking time: 30 minutes
Ingredients:
- 1/2 cup melted butter
- 1/2 cup swerve
- 1 teaspoon vanilla essence
- 1 egg
- 1/2 cup almond flour
- 1/2 teaspoon baking powder
- 1/4 cup cocoa powder
- 1/2 teaspoon ground cinnamon
- 1/4 teaspoon fine sea salt
- 30 grams of baking chocolate, unsweetened
- 1/4 cup walnuts, finely chopped

Addresses:
1. Start by preheating your Air Fryer to 180°C. Now, lightly grease six silicone moulds.
2. In a bowl, beat the melted butter with the swerve until fluffy. Then add the vanilla and egg and beat again.
3. Then add the almond flour, baking powder, cocoa powder, cinnamon and salt. Mix until everything is well combined.
4. Stir in the chocolate and walnuts, mix to combine. Bake in preheated fryer for 20 to 22 minutes. Enjoy.

194. Easy Spanish Churros

Servings: 4
Cooking time: 20 minutes
Ingredients:
- 3/4 cup water
- 1 tablespoon swerve
- 1/4 teaspoon sea salt
- 1/4 teaspoon grated nutmeg
- 1/4 teaspoon ground cloves
- 6 tablespoons butter
- 3/4 cup almond flour
- 2 eggs

Addresses:
1. To make the batter, boil the water in a saucepan over medium-high heat, now add

the swerve, salt, nutmeg and cloves, cook until dissolved.
2. Add the butter and lower the heat. Gradually add the almond flour, whisking continuously, until the mixture forms a ball.
3. Remove from the heat and add the eggs one at a time, stirring to combine well.
4. Pour the mixture into a piping bag with a large star tip. Press a few centimetre strips of dough into the greased Air Fryer pan.
5. Cook at 210°C for 6 minutes, working in batches, enjoy!

195. Angel Cake

Portions: 12
Cooking time: 30 minutes
Ingredients:
- ¼ cup melted butter
- 1 cup erythritol powder
- 1 teaspoon strawberry extract
- 12 egg whites
- 2 teaspoons cream of tartar
- A pinch of salt

Addresses:
1. Preheat the air fryer for 5 minutes.
2. Mix the egg whites and cream of tartar.
3. Use a hand mixer and beat until white and fluffy.
4. Add the rest of the ingredients, except the butter, and beat for another minute.
5. Pour into a baking dish.
6. Place in the basket of the air fryer and cook for 30 minutes at 200°C or if a toothpick inserted in the centre comes out clean.
7. Drizzle with melted butter once cooled.

196. Classic pound cake

Servings: 8
Cooking time: 35 minutes
Ingredients:
- 1 stick of butter at room temperature
- 1 cup of swerve
- 4 eggs
- 1 ½ cups coconut flour
- 1/2 teaspoon baking powder
- 1/2 teaspoon bicarbonate of soda
- 1/4 teaspoon salt
- A pinch of freshly grated nutmeg
- A pinch of crushed star aniseed
- 1/2 cup buttermilk
- 1 teaspoon vanilla essence

Addresses:
1. Start by preheating your fryer to 160°C. Spray the bottom and sides of a baking dish with cooking spray.
2. Beat the butter and swerve with a hand mixer until creamy. Then add the eggs, one at a time, and mix well until fluffy.
3. Stir in the flour along with the rest of the ingredients. Mix to combine well. Pour the batter into the prepared pan.
4. Bake for 15 minutes, turn the pan and bake for another 15 minutes, until the top of the cake jiggles when pressed with your fingers. Bon appetit!

197. Chocolate muffins with almonds

Servings: 6
Cooking time: 20 minutes
Ingredients:
- 3/4 cup wheat flour
- 1 cup icing sugar
- 1/4 teaspoon salt
- 1/4 teaspoon nutmeg, preferably freshly grated
- 1 tablespoon cocoa powder
- 55 grams of softened butter
- 1 beaten egg
- 2 tablespoons almond milk
- 1/2 teaspoon vanilla extract
- 40 grams of dark chocolate in pieces
- 1/2 cup chopped almonds

Addresses:
1. In a bowl, combine the flour, sugar, salt, nutmeg and cocoa powder. Mix to combine well.
2. In another bowl, whisk together the butter, egg, almond milk and vanilla.
3. Now add the wet egg mixture to the dry ingredients. Then carefully fold in the chocolate chips and almonds, stirring gently to combine.
4. Spoon the batter mixture into the cupcake tins. Bake your cupcakes at 180°C for 12 minutes until a toothpick comes out clean.
5. Garnish with chocolate chips if desired. Serve and enjoy.

198. Ricotta cheesecake

Servings: 8
Cooking time: 30 minutes
Ingredients:
- 3 eggs, lightly beaten
- 1 teaspoon baking powder
- ½ cup melted ghee
- 1 cup almond flour
- 1/3 cup erythritol
- 1 cup soft ricotta cheese

Addresses:
1. Add all ingredients to the bowl and mix until well combined.
2. Pour the batter into the greased baking dish and place in the air fryer.
3. Cook for 30 minutes.
4. Cut and serve.

199. Cheese and butter biscuits

Servings: 8
Cooking time: 12 minutes

Ingredients:
- 2 eggs
- 5 tablespoons melted butter
- 1/3 cup sour cream
- 1/3 cup shredded mozzarella cheese
- 1 1/4 cups almond flour
- 1/2 teaspoon baking powder
- 1/2 teaspoon salt

Addresses:
1. Preheat the air fryer to 190°C.
2. Add all the ingredients in a large bowl and mix with a hand blender.
3. Pour the batter into the mini silicone muffin moulds and place them in the air fryer and cook for 12 minutes.
4. Serve and enjoy.

200. Mandarin tart recipe

Servings: 8
Cooking time: 30 minutes
Ingredients:
- 3/4 cup sugar
- 2 cups flour
- 1/2 teaspoon vanilla extract
- 1/4 cup olive oil
- 1/2 cup milk
- 1 teaspoon cider vinegar
- Juice and zest of 2 lemons
- Juice and zest of 1 mandarin orange
- Mandarin segments, to serve

Addresses:
1. In a bowl, mix the flour with the sugar and stir.
2. In a separate bowl, mix the oil with the milk, vinegar, vanilla extract, lemon juice and zest and tangerine zest and whisk well.
3. Add the flour, stir well, pour into a cake tin that fits your air fryer, place in the fryer and cook for 20 minutes. Serve immediately with tangerine segments on top.

201. Apple and caramel tart

Servings: 9
Cooking time: 30 minutes
Ingredients:
- ¼ cup almond butter
- ¼ cup sunflower oil
- ½ cup chopped walnuts
- ¾ cup + 3 tbsp. coconut sugar
- ¾ cup water
- 1 ½ teaspoon mixed spices
- 1 cup plain flour
- 1 lemon with peel
- 1 teaspoon bicarbonate of soda
- 1 teaspoon vinegar
- 3 baking apples, cored and sliced

Addresses:
1. Preheat the fryer to 200°C.
2. In a frying pan, melt the almond butter and 3 tablespoons of sugar. Pour the mixture into a baking dish that will fit into the air fryer. Place the apple slices on top. Set aside.
3. In a bowl, combine flour, ¾ cup sugar and baking soda. Add the spice mixture.
4. In another bowl, mix the oil, water, vinegar and lemon zest. Stir in the chopped walnuts.
5. Combine the wet ingredients with the dry ingredients until well combined.
6. Pour into the mould with apple slices.
7. Bake for 30 minutes or until a toothpick inserted comes out clean.

202. Soft buttermilk biscuits

Servings: 4
Cooking time: 25 minutes
Ingredients:
- ½ teaspoon bicarbonate of soda
- ½ cup cake flour
- ¾ teaspoon salt
- ½ teaspoon baking powder
- 4 tablespoons butter, chopped
- 1 teaspoon sugar
- ¾ cup buttermilk

Addresses:
1. Preheat the air fryer to 200°C and combine all the dry ingredients in a bowl. Put the chopped butter in the bowl, and rub it into the flour mixture, until crumbly. Stir in the buttermilk.
2. Flour a flat, dry surface and roll out with a rolling pin to a thickness of 1.25 centimetres. Cut out 10 circles with a small biscuit cutter.
3. Place the biscuits on a lined baking tray. Bake for 8 minutes.

Mixed berries with walnut streusel

Servings: 3
Cooking time: 20 minutes
Ingredients:
- 3 tablespoons chopped walnuts
- 3 tablespoons of slivered almonds
- 2 tablespoons chopped walnuts
- 3 tablespoons of granulated swerve
- 1/2 teaspoon ground cinnamon
- 1 egg
- 2 tablespoons cold salted butter, cut into chunks
- 1/2 cup mixed berries

Addresses:
1. Mix the walnuts, swerve, cinnamon, egg and butter until well combined.
2. Place the mixed berries in the bottom of a lightly greased Air Fryer safe dish. Cover with the prepared topping.
3. Bake for 17 minutes. Serve at room temperature, enjoy!

204. Puffed coconut and walnut biscuits

Portions: 10
Cooking time: 30 minutes
Ingredients:
- 3/4 cup coconut oil, at room temperature
- 1 ½ cups coconut flour
- 1 cup pecans, unsalted, coarsely chopped
- 3 eggs plus one yolk, beaten
- 1 ½ cups extra fine almond flour
- 3/4 cup monk fruit
- 1/4 teaspoon freshly grated nutmeg
- 1/3 teaspoon ground cloves
- 1/2 teaspoon baking powder
- 1/3 teaspoon bicarbonate of soda
- 1/2 tsp pure vanilla extract
- 1/2 teaspoon pure coconut extract
- 1/8 teaspoon fine sea salt

Addresses:
1. In a bowl, combine the two types of flour, the baking soda and the baking powder. In another bowl, beat the eggs with the coconut oil. Combine the egg mixture with the flour mixture.
2. Fold in the remaining ingredients, mixing well. Form the mixture into biscuit shapes.
3. Bake in the oven for about 25 minutes, enjoy!

205. Berry pudding

Servings: 6
Cooking time: 15 minutes
Ingredients:
- 2 cups coconut cream
- 1/3 cup blackberries
- 1/3 cup blueberries
- 3 tablespoons swerve
- Zest of 1 lime, grated

Addresses:
1. In a blender, combine all ingredients and blend well.
2. Divide this into 6 small ramekins, put them in your air fryer and cook at 170°C for minutes.
3. Serve them cold.

206. Lemon berry stew

Servings: 4
Cooking time: 20 minutes
Ingredients:
- 450 grams strawberries, halved
- 4 tablespoons stevia
- 1 tablespoon lemon juice
- 1 and ½ cups of water

Addresses:
1. In a frying pan that fits your air fryer, mix all the ingredients, stir them together and put them in the fryer.
2. Bake at 170°C for 20 minutes.
3. Divide the stew into cups and serve cold.

207. Blueberry and Whisky Brownies for Father's Day

Portions: 10
Cooking time: 50 minutes
Ingredients:
- 1/3 cup blueberries
- 3 tablespoons whisky
- 225 grams of white chocolate
- 3/4 cup wheat flour
- 3 tablespoons coconut flakes
- 1/2 cup coconut oil
- 2 eggs plus one yolk, beaten
- 3/4 cup white sugar
- 1/4 teaspoon ground cardamom
- 1 teaspoon pure rum extract

Addresses:
1. Microwave the white chocolate and coconut oil until melted, allow the mixture to cool to room temperature.
2. Then whisk together the eggs, sugar, rum extract and cardamom.
3. Add the rum and egg mixture to the chocolate mixture. Fold in the flour and coconut flakes, stir to combine.
4. Mix the cranberries with the whisky and leave to soak for 15 minutes. Incorporate them into the batter. Press the dough into a lightly buttered tart tin.
5. Air fry them for 3 minutes at 170°C. Leave to cool slightly on a wire rack before slicing and serving.

208. Spanish-style doughnut weavings

Servings: 4
Cooking time: 20 minutes
Ingredients:
- 3/4 cup water
- 1 tablespoon sugar
- 1/4 teaspoon sea salt
- 1/4 teaspoon grated nutmeg
- 1/4 teaspoon ground cloves
- 6 tablespoons butter
- 3/4 cup plain flour
- 2 eggs

Addresses:
1. To make the batter, boil the water in a saucepan over medium-high heat, now add the sugar, salt, nutmeg and cloves, cook until dissolved.
2. Add the butter and lower the heat. Gradually stir in the flour, whisking continuously, until the mixture forms a ball.
3. Remove from the heat and add the eggs one at a time, stirring to combine well.
4. Pour the mixture into a piping bag with a large star tip. Press a few centimetre strips of dough into the greased Air Fryer pan.
5. Cook at 210°C for 6 minutes, working in batches - bon appetit!

209. Chocolate brownie

Servings: 4
Cooking time: 16 minutes
Ingredients:
- 1 cup bananas, very ripe
- 1 scoop protein powder
- 2 tablespoons cocoa powder, unsweetened
- 1/2 cup almond butter, melted

Addresses:
1. Preheat the air fryer to 160°C.
2. Spray the baking tray of the air fryer with cooking spray.
3. Add all ingredients to the blender and blend until smooth.
4. Pour the batter into the prepared pan and place it in the fryer basket.
5. Bake the brownie for 16 minutes.
6. Serve and enjoy.

210. Chocolate lava cake

Servings: 4
Cooking time: 20 minutes
Ingredients:
- 1 cup dark cocoa candy melts
- 1 stick of butter
- 2 eggs
- 4 tablespoons sugar
- 1 tablespoon of honey
- 4 tablespoons flour
- A pinch of kosher salt
- A pinch of ground cloves
- ¼ teaspoon grated nutmeg
- ¼ teaspoon cinnamon powder

Addresses:
1. Spray the inside of four custard cups with cooking spray.
2. Melt the cocoa candy melts and butter in the microwave for 30 seconds to 1 minute.
3. In a large bowl, mix the eggs, sugar and honey with a whisk until frothy. Pour in the melted chocolate mixture.
4. Add the rest of the ingredients and mix well with an electric or hand mixer.
5. Transfer equal portions of the mixture to the prepared custard cups.
6. Place in the air fryer and bake at 180°C for 12 minutes.
7. Remove from the fryer and leave to cool for 5 to 6 minutes.
8. Place each cup upside down on a dessert plate and let the cake slide. Serve with fruit and chocolate syrup if desired.

Poultry recipes

211. Lemon Pepper Chicken Wings

Servings: 4
Cooking time: 16 minutes
Ingredients:
- 450 grams of chicken wings
- 1 teaspoon lemon pepper
- 1 tablespoon of olive oil
- 1 teaspoon salt

Addresses:
1. Add the chicken wings to the large mixing bowl.
2. Add the rest of the ingredients over the chicken and stir well to coat.
3. Place the chicken wings in the fryer basket.
4. Cook the chicken wings for 8 minutes.
5. Turn the chicken wings to the other side and cook for a further 8 minutes.
6. Serve and enjoy.

212. Chicken Tarragon Removals

Servings: 2
Cooking time: 15 minutes
Ingredients:
- Salt and pepper to taste
- ½ cup dried tarragon
- 1 tablespoon butter

Addresses:
1. Preheat the fryer to 200°C.
2. Place a 30-centimetre cut of aluminium foil on a flat surface.
3. Place the chicken on the foil, sprinkle the tarragon over both and spread the butter over both breasts. Sprinkle with salt and pepper.
4. Wrap the breasts in aluminium foil to allow air to circulate.
5. Place the wrapped chicken in the basket and cook for 1 minute.
6. Remove the chicken and carefully unwrap the foil. Serve with the sauce extract and steamed vegetables.

213. Crispy stuffed chicken breast

Servings: 2
Cooking time: 45 minutes
Ingredients:
- 1 medium-sized aubergine, cut in half lengthwise
- ¼ cup pomegranate seeds
- 2 chicken breasts, skinless and boneless
- 2 egg whites
- ¼ cup breadcrumbs
- Salt
- Freshly ground black pepper
- ½ tablespoon olive oil

Addresses:
1. Preheat the fryer to 200°C and grease one fryer basket.
2. Season the aubergine halves with a little salt and set aside for a few minutes.
3. Place the aubergine halves in the fryer basket, cut side up, and cook for about 20 minutes.

4. Plate and remove the flesh from each aubergine half.
5. Place the aubergine flesh and a pinch of salt and black pepper in the food processor and pulse until a puree forms.
6. Pour the aubergine puree into a bowl and add the pomegranate seeds.
7. Cut the chicken breasts lengthwise to make a pocket and stuff with the aubergine mixture.
8. Whisk the egg whites, a pinch of salt and black pepper in a shallow dish.
9. Mix the breadcrumbs, thyme and olive oil in another dish.
10. Dip the chicken breasts in the egg white mixture and then dredge them in flour.
11. Set the fryer to 180°C and transfer the chicken breasts to the fryer.
12. Cook for about 25 minutes and plate to serve hot.

214. Cajun Mustard Turkey Fingers

Servings: 4
Cooking time: 20 minutes
Ingredients:
- 1/2 cup corn flour mix
- 1/2 cup all-purpose flour
- 1 ½ tablespoons Cajun seasoning
- 1 ½ tablespoons wholegrain mustard
- 1 ½ cups buttermilk
- 1 teaspoon soy sauce
- 350 grams of turkey loins, cut into finger-sized strips
- Salt and ground black pepper

Addresses:
1. In three bowls, combine the cornmeal, flour and Cajun seasoning in the first bowl. Mix the whole grain mustard, buttermilk and soy sauce in the second bowl.
2. Season the turkey fingers with the salt and black pepper. Now dip each strip in the buttermilk mixture, then coat them with the cornflour mixture on all sides.
3. Transfer the prepared turkey fingers to the baking tray of the Air Fryer and cook for 15 minutes, serve with hot tomato ketchup and enjoy!

215. Hot chicken skin

Servings: 4
Cooking time: 30 minutes
Ingredients:
- ½ teaspoon chilli paste
- 225 grams of chicken skin
- 1 teaspoon sesame oil
- ½ teaspoon chilli powder
- ½ teaspoon salt

Addresses:
1. In a shallow bowl, mix together the chilli paste, sesame oil, chilli powder and salt. Then coat the chicken skin well with the chilli mixture and marinate for a few minutes.
2. Meanwhile, preheat the air fryer to 185°C.
3. Place the marinated chicken skin in the air fryer and cook for 20 minutes.
4. When the time has elapsed, turn the chicken skin on the other side and cook for a further 10 minutes or until the chicken skin is crispy.

216. Sweet Italian turkey sausage with vegetables

Servings: 4
Cooking time: 40 minutes
Ingredients:
- 1 onion, diced
- 2 carrots, trimmed and cut into slices
- 1 parsnip, trimmed and cut into slices
- 2 potatoes, peeled and diced
- 1 teaspoon dried thyme
- 1/2 teaspoon dried marjoram
- 1 teaspoon basil, dried
- 1/2 teaspoon celery seeds
- Sea salt and ground black pepper
- 1 tablespoon melted butter
- 350 grams of sweet Italian turkey sausage

Addresses:
1. Mix the vegetables with all the seasonings and the melted butter. Place the vegetables in the bottom of the Air Fryer cooking basket. Lower the sausage over the top of the vegetables.
2. Roast at 180°C for 33 to 37 minutes or until the sausages are no longer pink. Work in batches as needed, shaking halfway through the roasting time. Bon appetit!

217. Chicken pizzas

Servings: 1
Cooking time: 35 minutes
Ingredients:
- ½ cup grated mozzarella cheese
- ¼ cup grated Parmesan cheese
- 450 grams of ground chicken

Addresses:
1. In a large bowl, combine all the ingredients and then spread the mixture, dividing it into four equal-sized parts.
2. Cut a sheet of parchment paper into four circles about 15 centimetres in diameter and place some of the chicken mixture in the centre of each piece, flattening the mixture to fill the circle.
3. Depending on the size of your fryer, cook one or two circles at a time for 25 minutes. Halfway through, turn the crust over to cook on the other side. Keep each batch warm as you move on to the next.
4. Once all the crusts are cooked, top with cheese and toppings of your choice. If

desired, cook crusts covered for an additional five minutes.
5. Serve hot, or freeze and store for later.

218. Chicken calves

Servings: 4
Cooking time: 30 minutes
Ingredients:
- 450 grams of chicken fillets
- 1 teaspoon chopped ginger
- 4 cloves garlic, minced
- 2 tablespoons sesame oil
- 6 tablespoons pineapple juice
- 2 tablespoons soy sauce
- ½ teaspoon pepper

Addresses:
1. Place all the ingredients, except the chicken, in a bowl and combine well.
2. Thread the chicken onto the skewers and coat with the seasoning. Leave to marinate for hours.
3. Preheat the Air Fryer
4. Place the marinated chicken in the fryer basket and cook for 18 minutes. Serve hot.

219. Chicken and Onion Kabobs

Servings: 4
Cooking time: 24 minutes
Ingredients:
- ¼ cup light soy sauce
- 1 tablespoon mirin
- 1 teaspoon garlic salt
- 1 teaspoon sugar
- 4 boneless skinless chicken thighs, cut into 2.5 centimetre cubes
- 5 spring onions, cut into 2.5 centimetre pieces lengthwise

Addresses:
1. In a baking dish, mix together the soy sauce, mirin, garlic salt and sugar.
2. Thread the chicken and spring onions onto the soaked wooden skewers.
3. Place the skewers in the baking dish and generously coat them with the marinade.
4. Cover and refrigerate for about 3 hours.
5. Grease the basket of the Air Fryer.
6. Place the skewers in the prepared Air Fryer basket in 2 batches in a single layer.
7. Air cool for about 10-12 minutes.
8. Once done, remove from the Air Fryer and transfer the chicken skewers to a serving platter.
9. Serve hot.

220. Chicken with peanut butter curry

Servings: 3
Cooking time: 12 minutes
Ingredients:
- 225 grams boneless, skinless chicken thigh, cut into 5-centimetre pieces
- 1 medium pepper, seeded and cut into chunks
- 1 tablespoon lime juice
- 1 tablespoon Thai curry paste
- 1 teaspoon salt
- 2/3 cup coconut milk
- 3 tablespoons peanut butter

Addresses:
1. In a shallow dish, mix well all ingredients except chicken and pepper. Place half of the sauce in a small basting bowl.
2. Add the chicken to the dish and mix well to coat. Marinate in the refrigerator for 3 hours.
3. Thread the pepper and chicken pieces onto the skewers. Place on the skewer rack of the fryer.
4. Cook at 180°C for 12 minutes. Halfway through the cooking time, turn the skewers over and baste them with the sauce. If necessary, cook in batches.
5. Serve and enjoy.

221. Buffalo chicken strips

Servings: 1
Cooking time: 30 minutes
Ingredients:
- ¼ cup hot sauce
- 450 grams of boneless, skinless chicken fillets
- 1 teaspoon garlic powder
- 115 grams pork rind, finely ground
- 1 teaspoon chilli powder

Addresses:
1. Mix the hot sauce and chicken fillets in a bowl, making sure the chicken is completely covered.
2. In another bowl, combine the garlic powder, ground pork rind and chili powder. Use this mixture to coat the fillets, coating them well. Place the chicken in the fryer, being careful not to overlap the pieces.
3. Cook the chicken for 20 minutes until cooked through and golden brown. Serve hot with your favourite sauces and side dishes.

222. Impressive sweet turkey pie

Servings: 3
Cooking time: 50 minutes
Ingredients:
- Salt and pepper for seasoning
- ¼ cup of cream of chicken soup
- ¼ cup mayonnaise
- 2 tablespoons lemon juice
- ¼ cup chopped slivered almonds, chopped
- ¼ cup breadcrumbs
- 2 tablespoons chopped green onion
- 2 tablespoons chopped peppers
- 2 boiled eggs, chopped

- ½ cup chopped celery
- Cooking spray

Addresses:
1. Preheat the fryer to 200°C.
2. Place turkey breasts on a clean flat surface and season with salt and pepper. Grease with cooking spray and place in the fryer basket, cook for minutes. Remove the turkey back to the cutting board, allow to cool and dice. In a bowl, add the celery, eggs, peppers, green onions, almonds, lemon juice, mayonnaise, turkey cubes and cream of chicken soup and mix well.
3. Grease a pan with cooking spray, pour the turkey mixture into the pan, sprinkle with breadcrumbs and spray with cooking spray. Place the dish in the fryer basket, and bake the ingredients at 200°C for minutes. Remove and serve with a garnish of steamed asparagus.

223. Chicken Wings with Rubber

Servings: 4
Cooking time: 25 minutes
Ingredients:
- 1 tablespoon of olive oil
- 1 tablespoon sesame oil
- 4 tablespoons honey
- 3 tablespoons light soy sauce
- 2 cloves garlic, crushed
- 1 pinch of grated fresh ginger
- 2 tablespoons toasted sesame seeds

Addresses:
1. Add all the ingredients in a freezer bag, except the sesame. Seal and massage until the thighs are well coated.
2. Preheat the air fryer to 200°C.
3. Place the thighs in the cooking basket and cook for minutes. Turn and cook for a further 10 minutes.
4. Sprinkle with some sesame seeds and coriander.

224. Air fried chicken tenderloin

Servings: 8
Cooking time: 15 minutes
Ingredients:
- ½ cup almond flour
- 1 beaten egg
- 2 tablespoons coconut oil
- 8 chicken tenderloins
- Salt and pepper

Addresses:
1. Preheat the air fryer for 5 minutes.
2. Season the chicken tenderloin with salt and pepper to taste.
3. Dredge in the beaten eggs and then in the almond flour.
4. Place in air fryer and brush with coconut oil.
5. Cook for 1 minute at 190°C.
6. Halfway through the cooking time, shake the fryer basket to ensure even cooking.

225. Easy Thanksgiving Crunchwrap

Servings: 4
Cooking time: 1 hour and 15 minutes
Ingredients:
- 2 tablespoons sesame oil
- 450 grams of turkey breasts
- 1 tablespoon taco seasoning
- 2 onions, sliced
- 2 bell peppers, cut into slices
- 1 habanero chilli, sliced
- 8 corn tortillas, approximately 15 centimetres in diameter
- 1/2 cup quesadilla cheese
- 1 cup grated manchego cheese
- 1 ½ cups tortilla chips
- 1/2 cup mayonnaise
- 2 tablespoons lemon juice
- 1 teaspoon yellow mustard
- 1 1/2 cups pickled jalapeños, chopped
- 1/4 teaspoon dried dill herb
- 1/2 teaspoon Mexican oregano

Addresses:
1. Start by preheating your Air Fryer to 180°C.
2. Drizzle a tablespoon of sesame oil all over the turkey breasts and cook for 30 minutes, turning them over halfway through.
3. Let stand for 7 minutes, then cut the turkey breast into strips, add the taco seasoning and set aside.
4. Place the onions and peppers in the cooking basket. Cook in the Air Fryer preheated to 200°C for a few minutes, set aside.
5. Spray the base of a baking sheet with cooking spray. Divide the roast turkey, pepper mixture and cheese between the tortillas. Top with the tortilla chips.
6. Fold the tortillas and place them in the pan. Drizzle the remaining tablespoon of sesame oil over each tortilla. Bake for 24 minutes.
7. Meanwhile, make the sauce by mixing the mayonnaise with the lemon juice, mustard, jalapeño, dill and oregano. Serve with warm tortillas. Enjoy.

226. Chicken tenderloin rubbed with paprika and cumin

Servings: 6
Cooking time: 25 minutes
Ingredients:
- ¼ cup coconut flour
- ¼ cup olive oil
- ½ teaspoon garlic powder
- ½ teaspoon ground cumin
- ½ teaspoon onion powder

- ½ teaspoon smoked paprika
- Chicken fillets 450 grams
- Salt and pepper to taste

Addresses:
1. Preheat the air fryer for 5 minutes.
2. Soak the chicken tenderloins in olive oil.
3. Mix in the rest of the ingredients and stir with your hands to combine everything.
4. Place the chicken pieces in the fryer basket.
5. Cook for 2 minutes at 160°C.

227. Chicken fillets

Servings: 3
Cooking time: 30 minutes
Ingredients:
- 8 pieces of chicken fillet (approximate dimensions 7.6 x 2.5 x 2.5 centimetres)
- 1 egg
- 30 grams of salted butter, melted
- 1 cup of breadcrumbs
- 1 teaspoon garlic powder
- ½ cup Parmesan cheese
- 1 teaspoon Italian herbs

Addresses:
1. Coat the chicken pieces with the beaten egg, melted butter, garlic powder and Italian herbs. Leave to marinate for a few minutes.
2. In a bowl, mix together the Panko breadcrumbs and Parmesan. Use this mixture to coat the marinated chicken.
3. Place the aluminium foil in the basket of your Air Fryer.
4. Set the fryer to 200°C and let it heat up briefly. Line the basket with aluminium foil.
5. Place 4 pieces of chicken in the basket. Cook for 6 minutes until golden brown. Do not turn the chicken over.
6. Repeat with the rest of the chicken pieces.
7. Serve the chicken fillets hot.

228. Chicken and shrimp pasta

Servings: 2
Cooking time: 30 minutes
Ingredients:
- 2 tablespoons maize flour
- ½ tablespoon of wine
- 1 tablespoon shrimp paste
- 1 tablespoon ginger
- ½ tablespoon olive oil

Addresses:
1. Preheat the fryer to 180°C.
2. In a bowl, mix the oil, ginger and wine. Coat the chicken wings with the prepared marinade and roll in flour. Add the floured chicken to the shrimp paste and coat.
3. Place the chicken in the cooking basket of your air fryer and cook for 20 minutes, until crispy on the outside.

229. Greek chicken

Servings: 4
Cooking time: 24 minutes
Ingredients:
- 900 grams of chicken fillets
- 1 cup cherry tomatoes
- 2 tablespoons olive oil
- 3 sprigs of dill
- 1 large courgette

For coverage you need:
- 2 tablespoons crumbled feta cheese
- 1 tablespoon chopped fresh dill
- 1 tablespoon of olive oil
- 1 tablespoon fresh lemon juice

Addresses:
1. Preheat the air fryer to 190°C.
2. Spray the air fryer basket with cooking spray.
3. Add the chicken, courgette, dill and tomatoes to the fryer basket. Drizzle with olive oil and season with salt.
4. Cook the chicken for 2 minutes.
5. Meanwhile, in a small bowl, mix all the topping ingredients together.
6. Place the chicken in the serving dish, then top with the vegetables and discard the dill sprigs.
7. Sprinkle the coating mixture over the chicken and vegetables.
8. Serve and enjoy.

230. Salted egg frittata with meat

Servings: 3
Cooking time: 20 minutes
Ingredients:
- 225 grams of minced meat
- 1 onion, chopped
- 3 cloves garlic, minced
- 3 beaten eggs
- 3 tablespoons olive oil
- Salt and pepper to taste

Addresses:
1. Heat the oil in a frying pan over medium heat.
2. Sauté the garlic and onion until fragrant.
3. Add the minced meat and sauté for 5 minutes or until lightly browned. Set aside.
4. Preheat the air fryer for 5 minutes.
5. In a mixing bowl, combine the rest of the ingredients
6. Place the sautéed meat in an ovenproof dish that fits into the air fryer chamber.
7. Pour over the egg mixture.
8. Cook for 20 minutes at 160°C.

231. Turkey nuggets with thyme

Servings: 2
Cooking time: 20 minutes
Ingredients:
- 1 beaten egg
- 1 cup breadcrumbs

- 1 tablespoon dried thyme
- ½ tablespoon dried parsley
- Salt and pepper, to taste

Addresses:
1. Preheat the fryer to 180°C.
2. In a bowl, mix the ground chicken, thyme, parsley, salt and pepper. Form the mixture into balls.
3. Dredge the chicken in the breadcrumbs, then in the egg and then in the breadcrumbs again.
4. Place the nuggets in the basket of the air fryer, spray with cooking spray and cook for minutes, shaking once.

232. chicken kabab

Servings: 3
Cooking time: 6 minutes
Ingredients:
- 450 grams of ground chicken
- 1 tablespoon fresh lemon juice
- ¼ cup almond flour
- 2 green onions, chopped
- 1 egg, lightly beaten
- 1/3 cup fresh parsley, chopped
- 3 cloves garlic
- 115 grams of chopped onion
- ¼ teaspoon turmeric powder
- ½ teaspoon pepper

Addresses:
1. Add all ingredients to the food processor and process until well combined.
2. Transfer the chicken mixture to the container and place in the refrigerator for 1 hour.
3. Divide the mixture into the 6 equal portions and roll them around the soaked wooden skewers.
4. Spray the air fryer basket with cooking spray.
5. Place the skewers in the basket of the air fryer and cook at 200°C for 6 minutes.
6. Serve and enjoy.

233. Ground turkey mixture

Servings: 4
Cooking time: 25 minutes
Ingredients:
- 450 grams ground turkey meat
- Pinch of salt and black pepper
- 2 tablespoons olive oil
- 2 teaspoons parsley flakes
- 450 grams of green beans, trimmed and cut in halves
- 2 teaspoons garlic powder

Addresses:
1. Heat a frying pan that fits the air fryer with the oil over medium-high heat, add the meat and brown for 5 minutes.
2. Add the rest of the ingredients, mix, place the pan in the air fryer and cook at 185°C for 20 minutes.
3. Divide between the plates and serve.

234. Indian Chicken Calves

Servings: 4
Cooking time: 15 minutes
Ingredients:
- 450 grams of chicken fillets, cut in halves
- ¼ cup chopped parsley
- 1/2 tablespoon minced garlic
- 1/2 tablespoon chopped ginger
- ¼ cup yogurt
- 3/4 teaspoon paprika
- 1 teaspoon garam masala
- 1 teaspoon turmeric
- 1/2 tsp cayenne pepper
- 1 teaspoon salt

Addresses:
1. Preheat the air fryer to 180°C.
2. Add all the ingredients in the large bowl and mix well. Place in the fridge for 30 minutes.
3. Spray the air fryer basket with cooking spray.
4. Add the marinated chicken to the fryer basket and cook for 10 minutes.
5. Turn the chicken to the other side and cook for a few more minutes.
6. Serve and enjoy.

235. KFC Like Chicken Tenders

Servings: 4
Cooking time: 25 minutes
Ingredients:
For breading you need:
- 2 whole eggs, beaten
- ½ cup seasoned breadcrumbs
- ½ cup plain flour
- 1 tablespoon black pepper
- 2 tablespoons olive oil

Addresses:
1. Preheat your air fryer to 165°C.
2. Add the breadcrumbs, eggs and flour in three separate bowls. Mix the breadcrumbs with the oil and season with salt and pepper. Dredge the fillets in the flour, eggs and breadcrumbs.
3. Add the chicken to the air fryer and cook for 10 minutes. Increase to 200°C, and cook for a further 5 minutes.

236. Beastly barbecue sticks

Servings: 4
Cooking time: 45 minutes
Ingredients:
- 4 chicken thighs
- ½ tablespoon mustard
- 1 crushed garlic clove
- 1 teaspoon chilli powder

- 2 teaspoons sugar
- 1 tablespoon of olive oil
- Freshly ground black pepper

Addresses:
1. Preheat the Air Fryer to 200°C.
2. Mix the garlic, sugar, mustard, a pinch of salt, freshly ground pepper, chilli powder and oil.
3. Apply this mixture to the thighs and leave to marinate for at least 20 minutes.
4. Place the thighs in the fryer basket and cook for 10 minutes.
5. Lower the temperature to 150°C and continue cooking the thighs for a further 10 minutes.
6. When cooked, serve with bread and corn salad.

237. Chimichurri Turkey

Servings: 1
Cooking time: 70 minutes
Ingredients:
- 450 grams of turkey breast
- ½ cup chimichurri sauce
- ½ cup butter
- ¼ cup grated Parmesan cheese
- ¼ teaspoon garlic powder

Addresses:
1. Massage the turkey breast with the chimichurri sauce, then refrigerate in an airtight container for at least half an hour.
2. Meanwhile, prepare the herb butter. Mix the butter, parmesan and garlic powder together, using a hand mixer if desired (this will make it creamier).
3. Preheat your fryer and place a rack inside.
4. Remove the turkey from the fridge and leave it at room temperature for about twenty minutes while the fryer heats up.
5. Place the turkey in the fryer and cook for twenty minutes. Turn it over and cook on the other side for another twenty minutes.
6. Be careful when removing the turkey from the fryer. Place on a platter and enjoy with the herb butter.

238. Moroccan chicken

Servings: 2
Cooking time: 25 minutes
Ingredients:
- 225 grams of shredded chicken
- 1 cup of broth
- 1 carrot
- 1 broccoli, chopped
- A pinch of cinnamon
- A pinch of cumin
- Pinch of red pepper
- A pinch of sea salt

Addresses:
1. In a bowl, coat the shredded chicken with cumin, red pepper, sea salt and cinnamon.
2. Cut the carrots into small pieces. Put the carrot and broccoli in the bowl with the chicken.
3. Add the stock and stir well. Leave to stand for a few minutes.
4. Transfer to the air fryer. Cook for about 15 minutes at 200°C. Serve hot.

239. Duck in vanilla and pepper sauce

Servings: 4
Cooking time: 30 minutes
Ingredients:
- 4 duck legs with skin
- Juice of ½ lemon
- 1 teaspoon cinnamon powder
- 1 teaspoon vanilla extract
- 10 peppercorns, crushed
- 1 tablespoon balsamic vinegar
- 1 tablespoon of olive oil
- Pinch of salt and black pepper

Addresses:
1. Heat a frying pan with the oil over medium-high heat, add the duck legs and brown them for 3 minutes on each side.
2. Transfer to a frying pan that fits the air fryer, add the rest of the ingredients, stir, place the pan in the air fryer and cook at 190°C for 22 minutes.
3. Divide the duck legs and the cooking juices between the plates and serve.

240. Traditional Asian sticky chicken

Servings: 3
Cooking time: 25 minutes
Ingredients:
- 1 tbsp. chopped coriander leaves
- Salt and black pepper, to taste
- 1 tablespoon roasted peanuts, chopped
- ½ tablespoon apple cider vinegar
- 1 clove garlic, minced
- ½ tablespoon chilli sauce
- 1 chopped ginger
- 1 ½ tablespoons soy sauce
- 2 ½ tablespoons honey

Addresses:
1. Preheat the fryer to 180°C.
2. Wash the chicken wings thoroughly and season with salt and pepper.
3. In a bowl, combine the ginger, garlic, chilli sauce, honey, soy sauce, coriander and vinegar. Coat the chicken with the honey sauce.
4. Place the prepared chicken in the cooking basket of your air fryer and cook for 20 minutes. Serve sprinkled with peanuts.

241. Turkey bacon with scrambled eggs

Servings: 4
Cooking time: 25 minutes
Ingredients:
- 225 grams of turkey bacon

- 4 eggs
- 1/3 cup milk
- 2 tablespoons yoghurt
- 1/2 teaspoon sea salt
- 1 pepper, finely chopped
- 2 green onions, finely chopped
- 1/2 cup Colby cheese, grated

Addresses:
1. Place the turkey bacon in the cooking basket.
2. Bake at 180°C for 9 to 11 minutes. Work in batches. Reserve the fried bacon.
3. In a bowl, beat the eggs well with the milk and yoghurt. Add the salt, pepper and green onions.
4. Spread the sides and bottom of the pan with the reserved teaspoon of bacon fat.
5. Pour the egg mixture into the baking dish. Cook for about 5 minutes. Top with grated Colby cheese and bake for 5 to 6 minutes more.
6. Serve the scrambled eggs with the reserved bacon and enjoy.

242. Chicken with honey and spicy orange

Servings: 4
Cooking time: 20 minutes
Ingredients:
- 1 cup shredded coconut
- ¾ cup breadcrumbs
- 2 whole eggs, beaten
- ½ cup flour
- ½ teaspoon pepper
- Salt to taste
- ½ cup orange marmalade
- 1 tablespoon red pepper flakes
- ¼ cup honey
- 3 tablespoons Dijon mustard

Addresses:
1. Preheat the fryer to 200°C.
2. In a bowl, mix the coconut, flour, salt and pepper. In another bowl, add the beaten eggs. Place the breadcrumbs in a third bowl.
3. Dredge the chicken in the egg mixture, the flour and finally in the breadcrumbs. Place the chicken in the cooking basket of the air fryer and bake for a few minutes.
4. In a separate bowl, mix the honey, orange marmalade, mustard and pepper flakes. Coat the chicken with the marmalade mixture and fry for a further 5 minutes.

243. Juicy and spicy chicken wings

Servings: 4
Cooking time: 25 minutes
Ingredients:
- 900 grams of chicken wings
- 155 grams of hot sauce
- 1 teaspoon Worcestershire sauce
- 1 teaspoon Tabasco
- 6 tablespoons melted butter

Addresses:
1. Spray the air fryer basket with cooking spray.
2. Add the chicken wings to the basket of the air fryer and cook at 190°C for minutes. Shake the basket after every 5 minutes.
3. Meanwhile, in a bowl, mix together the hot sauce, Worcestershire sauce and butter. Set aside.
4. Add the chicken wings to the sauce and mix well.
5. Serve and enjoy.

244. Turkey with almonds and shallots

Servings: 2
Cooking time: 25 minutes
Ingredients:
- 1 large turkey breast, skinless, boned and halved
- 1/3 cup chopped almonds
- Salt and black pepper to taste
- 2 tablespoons olive oil
- 1 tablespoon sweet paprika
- 2 chopped shallots

Addresses:
1. In a frying pan that fits the air fryer, combine the turkey with all the other ingredients and stir.
2. Place the pan in the air fryer and cook at 185°C for 25 minutes.
3. Divide between the plates and serve.

245. Tasty Caribbean chicken

Servings: 8
Cooking time: 10 minutes
Ingredients:
- 1,360 kilograms of boneless, skinless, boneless chicken leg
- 1 tablespoon coriander powder
- 3 tablespoons of melted coconut oil
- ½ teaspoon ground nutmeg
- ½ teaspoon ground ginger
- 1 tablespoon cayenne
- 1 tablespoon cinnamon
- Pepper
- Salt

Addresses:
1. In a small bowl, mix all the spices together and rub them all over the chicken.
2. Spray the air fryer basket with cooking spray.
3. Place the chicken in the basket of the air fryer and cook for 10 minutes.
4. Serve and enjoy.

246. Duck leg and onion mixture

Servings: 2
Cooking time: 16 minutes
Ingredients:
- 2 duck legs

- 1 teaspoon olive oil
- ½ teaspoon ground cumin
- 1 teaspoon salt
- 1 tablespoon chopped spring onions

Addresses:
1. In a shallow bowl, mix the ground cumin and salt. Next, rub the duck legs with the spice mixture. Then mix in the spring onions and olive oil.
2. Sprinkle the duck legs with the spring onion mixture.
3. Preheat the air fryer to 195°C.
4. Place the duck legs in the fryer and cook for 8 minutes. Turn the duck legs over on the other side and cook for 8 minutes.

247. Thai red duck with onion confit

Servings: 4
Cooking time: 25 minutes
Ingredients:
- 680 grams duck breasts, skinless
- 1 teaspoon kosher salt
- 1/2 tsp cayenne pepper
- 1/3 teaspoon of black pepper
- 1/2 teaspoon smoked paprika
- 1 tablespoon Thai red curry paste
- 1 cup caramel onions, halved
- 1/4 small packet chopped coriander

Addresses:
1. Place the duck breasts between 2 sheets of aluminium foil, then use a rolling pin to pound the duck to a thickness of one centimetre.
2. Preheat your air fryer to 200°C.
3. Rub the duck breasts with salt, cayenne pepper, black pepper, paprika and red curry paste. Place the duck breast in the cooking basket.
4. Cook for 11 to 12 minutes. Top with caramelised onions and cook for another 10 to 11 minutes.
5. Serve garnished with coriander and enjoy.

248. Leftovers 'n Enchilada Bake

Servings: 3
Cooking time: 45 minutes
Ingredients:
- 1 egg
- 1/2 can (425 grams) black beans, drained
- 1/2 can (425 grams) tomato sauce
- 1/2 packet (210 grams) cornbread mix
- 1/2 cup shredded Mexican-style cheese, or more to taste
- 1/2 sachet of taco seasoning
- 225 grams chicken breast fillets
- 1-1/2 teaspoons vegetable oil
- 2 tablespoons creman cheese
- 2 tablespoons of water
- 2-1/4 teaspoons chili powder
- 3 tablespoons milk

Addresses:
1. Lightly grease the air fryer tray with vegetable oil. Add chicken and cook for 5 minutes per side at 180°C.
2. Stir in the chili powder, taco seasoning mix, water and tomato sauce. Cook for 10 minutes, while stirring and turning the chicken halfway through the cooking time.
3. Remove chicken from skillet and shred with two forks. Return it to the pan and add the cream cheese and black beans. Mix well.
4. Top with Mexican cheese.
5. In a bowl, whisk together the egg and milk. Add the cornbread mixture and mix well. Pour over the chicken.
6. Cover the pan with aluminium foil.
7. Cook for another 15 minutes. Remove the foil and cook for a further 10 minutes or until the topping is lightly browned.
8. Let it stand for 5 minutes.
9. Serve and enjoy.

249. Chicken breasts wrapped in bacon

Servings: 4
Cooking time: 23 minutes
Ingredients:
- 6-7 fresh basil leaves
- 2 tablespoons of water
- 2 chicken breasts (225 grams), cut in half horizontally
- 12 strips of bacon
- 2 tablespoons fish sauce
- 1 tablespoon of palm sugar
- salt and ground black pepper, as needed
- 1½ teaspoons honey

Addresses:
1. Preheat the fryer to 185°C and grease the fryer basket.
2. Cook the palm sugar in a small, heavy-bottomed frying pan over medium-low heat for about 3 minutes until caramelised.
3. Stir in the basil, fish sauce and water and place in a bowl.
4. Season each chicken breast with salt and black pepper and coat with the palm sugar mixture.
5. Refrigerate to marinate for about 6 hours and wrap each piece of chicken with 3 strips of bacon.
6. Dip it in the honey and place it in the basket of the Air Fryer.
7. Cook for about 20 minutes, turning once in between.
8. Place on a platter and serve hot.
9. Refrigerate to marinate for about 4-6 hours.

250. Chicken with sweet garlic

Servings: 4
Cooking time: 14 minutes
Ingredients:

- 4 onions, chopped
- 2 teaspoons sesame seeds, toasted
- 450 grams of chicken fillets
- Wooden skewers, as needed
- 1 tablespoon fresh ginger, finely grated
- 4 cloves garlic, minced
- ½ cup pineapple juice
- ½ cup soy sauce
- ¼ cup sesame oil
- Pinch of black pepper

Addresses:
1. Preheat the fryer to 200°C and grease one fryer basket.
2. Mix all the ingredients together in a large baking dish, except the chicken.
3. Thread the chicken onto the skewer and place the skewers in the baking dish.
4. Cover evenly with the marinade and cover to refrigerate for about 3 hours.
5. Place half of the chicken skewers in the fryer basket and cook for about 7 minutes.
6. Repeat with the rest of the skewers and plate to serve hot.

251. Agave Mustard Glazed Chicken

Servings: 4
Cooking time: 30 minutes
Ingredients:
- 1 tablespoon avocado oil
- 900 grams of chicken breasts, boneless and skin on
- 1 tablespoon Jamaican seasoning
- 1/2 teaspoon salt
- 3 tablespoons agave syrup
- 1 tablespoon mustard
- 2 tablespoons chopped spring onions

Addresses:
1. Start by preheating your fryer to 185°C.
2. Drizzle the avocado oil all over the chicken breast. Then rub the chicken breast with the Jamaican Jerk rub.
3. Cook in the preheated Air Fryer for approximately 15 minutes. Turn over and cook for a further 8 minutes.
4. While the chicken breasts are roasting, combine the salt, agave syrup and mustard in a skillet over medium heat. Allow to simmer until the glaze thickens.
5. Then spread the glaze all over the chicken breast. Fry in the open air for another 6 minutes or until the surface is crispy. Serve garnished with fresh spring onions - bon appetit!

252. Pepper turkey sandwiches

Servings: 4
Cooking time: 25 minutes
Ingredients:
- 1 cup leftover turkey, cut into bite-sized pieces
- 2 bell peppers, deveined and chopped
- 1 serrano pepper, deveined and chopped
- 1 leek, sliced
- 1/2 cup sour cream
- 1 teaspoon hot paprika
- 3/4 teaspoon kosher salt
- 1/2 teaspoon ground black pepper
- 1 heaped tablespoon of chopped fresh coriander
- Pinch of Tabasco sauce
- 4 hamburger buns

Addresses:
1. Combine all ingredients, minus the hamburger buns, in an Air Fryer baking dish, mixing until everything is well coated.
2. Now, roast it for a few minutes at 195°C.
3. Serve on hamburger buns, add a little more sour cream and Dijon mustard if you like, enjoy!

253. Chicken Tenders with Parmesan and Lime

Servings: 6
Cooking time: 20 minutes
Ingredients:
- 900 grams of chicken tenderloins, cut into pieces
- 1/2 cup pork rinds, shredded
- 1/2 cup grated Parmesan cheese
- 1 tablespoon of olive oil
- Sea salt and ground black pepper, to taste
- 1 teaspoon cayenne pepper
- 1/3 teaspoon ground cumin
- 1 teaspoon chilli powder
- 1 egg

Addresses:
1. Squeeze the lime juice all over the chicken.
2. Spray the cooking basket with non-stick spray.
3. In a bowl, thoroughly mix together the pork rinds, Parmesan, olive oil, salt, black pepper, cayenne pepper, cumin and chilli powder.
4. In another shallow bowl, beat the egg until well beaten. Dip the chicken fillets into the egg and then into the pork rind mixture.
5. Transfer the breaded chicken to the prepared cooking basket. Cook in the preheated Air Fryer at 190°C for 12 minutes.
6. Turn them over halfway through cooking. Work in batches. Serve immediately.

254. Turkey rolls

Servings: 3
Cooking time: 40 minutes
Ingredients:
- 450 grams of turkey breast fillet
- 1 crushed garlic clove
- 1½ teaspoons ground cumin
- 1 teaspoon ground cinnamon
- ½ teaspoon red chilli powder

- Salt, to taste
- 2 tablespoons olive oil
- 3 tablespoons fresh parsley, finely chopped
- 1 small red onion, finely chopped

Addresses:
1. Place the turkey fillet on a cutting board.
2. Carefully cut horizontally starting 1 centimetre from the top and stopping 5 millimetres from the edge.
3. Open this part to have a long piece of fillet.
4. In a bowl, mix the garlic, spices and oil.
5. In a small cup, reserve about 1 tablespoon of the oil mixture.
6. In the remaining oil mixture, add the parsley and onion and mix well.
7. Set the temperature of the Air Fryer to 180°C. Grease the basket of the Air Fryer.
8. Coat the open side of the fillet with the onion mixture.
9. Roll the fillet tightly from the short side.
10. With kitchen string, tie the roll at intervals of 1 to 1.25 centimetres.
11. Coat the outside of the roll with the reserved oil mixture.
12. Place the roll in the prepared fryer basket.
13. Chill in the open air for about 40 minutes.
14. Remove from the Air Fryer and place the turkey roll on a cutting board for about 5-10 minutes before slicing.
15. With a sharp knife, cut the turkey roll into slices of the desired size and serve.

255. Eggs, cauliflower and broccoli brekky

Servings: 3
Cooking time: 20 minutes
Ingredients:
- ½ cup milk
- ½ cup grated Cheddar cheese
- 1 cup broccoli, finely chopped or pureed
- 1 cup cauliflower, mashed
- 1 teaspoon salt
- 1/2 teaspoon ground black pepper
- 1/2 lb. hot pork sausage, diced
- 3 large eggs

Addresses:
1. Lightly grease the air fryer tray with cooking spray. And cook the pork sausage for 5 minutes at 180°C.
2. Remove the basket and stir the mixture a little. Add the cauliflower and broccoli. Cook for a further 5 minutes.
3. In the meantime, beat the eggs, salt, pepper and milk well. Stir in the cheese.
4. Remove the basket and pour in the egg mixture.
5. Cook for another 10 minutes.
6. Serve and enjoy.

256. Chicken and bacon mix

Servings: 2
Cooking time: 25 minutes
Ingredients:
- 2 chicken thighs
- 115 grams of bacon, sliced
- ½ teaspoon salt
- ½ teaspoon ground black pepper
- 1 teaspoon sesame oil

Addresses:
1. Sprinkle the chicken thighs with salt and ground black pepper and wrap with the sliced bacon.
2. Then preheat the air fryer to 195°C. Place the chicken thighs in the air fryer and drizzle with sesame oil.
3. Cook the chicken thighs with bacon for 25 minutes.

257. Sweet chilli chicken wings

Servings: 4
Cooking time: 20 minutes
Ingredients:
- 1 teaspoon garlic powder
- 1 tablespoon tamarind powder
- ¼ cup sweet chili sauce

Addresses:
1. Preheat your air fryer to 200°C.
2. Spray the air fryer basket with cooking spray.
3. Rub the chicken wings with the tamarind and garlic powders. Spray with cooking spray and place in the cooking basket.
4. Cook for 6 minutes, slide the basket out of the fryer and cover with the sweet chilli sauce, cook for a further 8 minutes. Serve cooled.

258. Glazed chicken wings

Servings: 4
Cooking time: 19 minutes
Ingredients:
- 8 chicken wings
- 2 tablespoons plain flour
- 1 teaspoon garlic, finely chopped
- 1 tablespoon fresh lemon juice
- 1 tablespoon soy sauce
- ½ teaspoon crushed dried oregano
- Salt and freshly ground black pepper, to taste

Addresses:
1. Preheat the fryer to 180°C and grease the fryer basket.
2. Mix all ingredients except wings in a large bowl.
3. Cover the wings generously with the marinade and refrigerate for about 2 hours.
4. Remove the chicken wings from the marinade and dust them evenly with flour.
5. Place the wings in the fryer pan and cook for about 6 minutes, turning once in between.

6. Arrange the chicken wings on a platter and serve hot.

259. Garlic chicken sausages

Servings: 4
Cooking time: 10 minutes
Ingredients:
- 1 clove garlic, minced
- 1 chopped spring onion
- 1 cup ground chicken
- ½ teaspoon salt
- ½ teaspoon ground black pepper
- 4 sausage links
- 1 teaspoon olive oil

Addresses:
1. In the bowl of a blender, combine the chopped garlic clove, onion, ground chicken, salt and ground black pepper.
2. Then fill the sausage links with the ground chicken mixture.
3. Cut each sausage into halves and secure the ends.
4. Preheat the air fryer to 185°C.
5. Brush the sausages with olive oil and place them in the air fryer. Cook for a few minutes.
6. Turn the sausages on the other side and cook for a further 5 minutes.
7. Increase the cooking time to 200°C and cook for 8 minutes for faster results.

260. Chicken with cashew nuts

Servings: 4
Cooking time: 30 minutes
Ingredients:
- 2 tablespoons soy sauce
- 1 tablespoon maize flour
- 2 ½ cups onion cubes
- 1 carrot, chopped
- ⅓ cup fried cashew nuts
- 1 pepper, chopped
- 2 tablespoons crushed garlic
- Salt and white pepper to taste

Addresses:
1. Marinate the chicken cubes in a mixture of white pepper, salt, soy sauce and cornflour. Leave to stand for 25 minutes.
2. Preheat the fryer to 190°C and place the marinated chicken. Add the garlic, onion, pepper and carrot and fry for 5-6 minutes.
3. Dredge in the cashew nuts before serving.

261. Turkey breast in buttermilk

Servings: 8
Cooking time: 20 minutes
Ingredients:
- ¾ cup brine from a can of olives
- 1,580 kilograms of boneless, skinless turkey breast
- 2 sprigs of fresh thyme
- 1 sprig of fresh rosemary
- ½ cup buttermilk

Addresses:
1. Mix the olive brine and buttermilk in a bowl until well combined.
2. Place the turkey breast, buttermilk mixture and herb sprigs in a resealable plastic bag.
3. Seal the bag and refrigerate for about 12 hours.
4. Preheat the fryer to 180°C and grease the fryer basket.
5. Remove the turkey breast from the bag and place it in the fryer basket.
6. Cook for about 20 minutes, turning once in between.
7. Place the turkey breast on a cutting board and cut into desired size slices to serve.

262. Crispy chicken fingers

Servings: 2
Cooking time: 8 minutes
Ingredients:
- 3 tablespoons Parmesan cheese
- ¼ tablespoon chopped fresh chives
- ⅓ cup breadcrumbs
- 1 egg white
- 2 tablespoons plum sauce, optional
- ½ tablespoon chopped fresh thyme
- 1 tablespoon of water

Addresses:
1. Preheat the fryer to 180°C.
2. Mix together the chives, Parmesan cheese, thyme and breadcrumbs. In another bowl, whisk the egg white with the water.
3. Dip the chicken strips in the egg mixture and breadcrumb mixture.
4. Place the strips in the fryer basket and cook for a few minutes.
5. Serve with plum sauce.

263. Chicken and Onion Kabobs

Servings: 4
Cooking time: 24 minutes
Ingredients:
- 4 boneless skinless chicken thighs, cut into 2.5 centimetre cubes
- 2 bell peppers, cut into 2.5 centimetre lengths
- Wooden skewers, previously soaked
- ¼ cup light soy sauce
- 1 tablespoon mirin
- 1 teaspoon garlic salt
- 1 teaspoon sugar

Addresses:
1. Preheat the fryer to 180°C and grease a frying pan.
2. Mix the soy sauce, mirin, garlic salt and sugar in a large baking dish.
3. Thread the chicken and peppers onto the soaked wooden skewers.

4. Generously coat the skewers with the marinade and refrigerate for about 3 hours.
5. Place the skewers in the frying pan of the deep fryer in a single layer and cook for about 12 minutes.
6. Place on a platter and serve hot.

264. Barbecued chicken with sweet and sour sauce

Servings: 6
Cooking time: 40 minutes
Ingredients:
- ¼ cup minced garlic
- ¼ cup tomato paste
- ¾ cup chopped onion
- ¾ cup sugar
- 1 cup soy sauce
- 1 cup of water
- 1 cup white vinegar
- 6 chicken thighs
- Salt and pepper to taste

Addresses:
1. Place all ingredients in a Ziploc bag.
2. Leave to marinate for at least hours in the refrigerator.
3. Preheat the air fryer.
4. Place the grill pan attachment on the air fryer.
5. Roast the chicken for 40 minutes.
6. Turn the chicken every 10 minutes so that it cooks evenly.
7. Meanwhile, pour the marinade into a saucepan and heat over medium heat until the sauce thickens.
8. Before serving, brush the chicken with the glaze.

265. Chicken and cream cheese mixture

Servings: 4
Cooking time: 16 minutes
Ingredients:
- Chicken wings of about 450 grams each
- ¼ cup cream cheese
- 1 tablespoon apple cider vinegar
- 1 teaspoon Truvia
- ½ teaspoon smoked paprika
- ½ teaspoon ground nutmeg
- 1 teaspoon of avocado oil

Addresses:
1. In the bowl of a mixer, mix the cream cheese, Truvia, apple cider vinegar, smoked paprika and ground nutmeg.
2. Next, add the chicken wings and dredge them well in the cream cheese mixture. Leave the chicken wings in the cream cheese mixture for 15 minutes to marinate.
3. Meanwhile, preheat the air fryer to 190°C. Place the chicken wings in the air fryer and cook for 8 minutes. Then turn the chicken wings over and baste them with the cream cheese marinade.
4. Cook the chicken wings for a further 8 minutes.

266. Chicken marjoram

Servings: 2
Cooking time: 1 hour
Ingredients:
- 2 small boneless, skinless, skinless chicken breasts
- 2 tablespoons butter
- 1 teaspoon sea salt
- ½ teaspoon crushed red pepper flakes
- 2 teaspoons marjoram
- ¼ teaspoon lemon pepper

Addresses:
1. In a bowl, cover the chicken breasts with all the other ingredients. Marinate for 30-60 minutes.
2. Preheat your Air Fryer to 200°C.
3. Cook for 20 minutes, turning halfway through cooking.
4. Check for doneness with an instant-read thermometer. When the recipe is ready, serve over jasmine rice.

267. Fried chicken halves

Servings: 4
Cooking time: 75 minutes
Ingredients:
- 450 grams of whole chicken
- 1 tablespoon dried thyme
- 1 teaspoon ground cumin
- 1 teaspoon salt
- 1 tablespoon avocado oil

Addresses:
1. Cut the chicken into halves and sprinkle with dried thyme, cumin and salt. Then brush the chicken halves with avocado oil.
2. Preheat the air fryer to 185°C.
3. Place the chicken halves in the air fryer and cook for 60 minutes.
4. Then turn the chicken halves on the other side and cook for another few minutes.

268. Chicken Thighs with Thyme and Okra

Servings: 4
Cooking time: 30 minutes
Ingredients:
- 4 chicken drumsticks, bone in and skin removed
- Pinch of salt and black pepper
- 1 cup okra
- ½ cup melted butter
- Zest of 1 lemon
- 4 cloves garlic, minced
- 1 tablespoon chopped thyme
- 1 tablespoon chopped parsley

Addresses:

1. Heat a frying pan that fits your air fryer with half the butter over medium heat, add the chicken thighs and brown them for 2-3 minutes on each side.
2. Add the rest of the butter, the okra and all the remaining ingredients, stir.
3. Place the pan in the air fryer and cook at 185°C for 20 minutes. Divide among the plates and serve.

269. Traditional Teriyaki Chicken

Servings: 4
Cooking time: 50 minutes
Ingredients:
- 680 grams of chicken breast, cut in halves
- 1 tablespoon lemon juice
- 2 tablespoons Mirin
- 1/4 cup milk
- 2 tablespoons soy sauce
- 1 tablespoon of olive oil
- 1 teaspoon ginger, peeled and grated
- 2 cloves garlic, minced
- 1/2 teaspoon salt
- 1/2 teaspoon ground black pepper
- 1 teaspoon cornstarch

Addresses:
1. In a large ceramic dish, place the chicken, lemon juice, Mirin, milk, soy sauce, olive oil, ginger and garlic. Marinate for 30 minutes in your refrigerator.
2. Spray the sides and bottom of the cooking basket with non-stick cooking spray.
3. Place the chicken in the cooking basket of the air fryer and cook at 185°C for 10 minutes.
4. Turn the chicken over, drizzle with the reserved marinade and cook for a further 4 minutes. Check for doneness, season with salt and pepper and set aside.
5. Mix cornstarch with 1 tablespoon water. Add the marinade to the preheated skillet over medium heat, cook for 3 minutes. Now add the cornstarch slurry and cook until the sauce thickens.
6. Pour the sauce over the reserved chicken and serve immediately.

270. Crispy Chicken Tenders

Servings: 3
Cooking time: 30 minutes
Ingredients:
- 2 boneless, skinless chicken breasts, pounded to a thickness of 1.25 centimetres and cut into strips
- ¾ cup buttermilk
- 1½ teaspoons Worcestershire sauce, divided
- ½ teaspoon smoked paprika, divided
- salt and ground black pepper, as needed
- ½ cup plain flour
- 1½ cups panko breadcrumbs
- ¼ cup parmesan cheese, finely grated
- 2 tablespoons melted butter
- 2 large eggs

Addresses:
1. In a large bowl, combine buttermilk, ¾ teaspoon Worcestershire sauce, ¼ teaspoon paprika, salt and black pepper.
2. Add the chicken fillets and refrigerate overnight.
3. In another bowl, mix together the flour, remaining paprika, salt and black pepper.
4. Place the remaining Worcestershire sauce and eggs in a third bowl and whisk until well combined.
5. Mix the panko, Parmesan and butter well in a fourth bowl.
6. Remove the chicken fillets from the bowl and discard the buttermilk.
7. Dredge the chicken fillets in the flour mixture, then dredge them in the egg mixture and finally coat them in the panko mixture.
8. Set the temperature of the air fryer to 200°C. Grease the air fryer basket.
9. Place the chicken fillets in the prepared air fryer basket in 2 batches in a single layer.
10. Fry in the open air for about 13-15 minutes, turning once halfway through.
11. Remove from the fryer and transfer the chicken fillets to a serving platter.
12. Serve hot.

271. Turkey with cheese wrapped in bacon

Portions: 12
Cooking time: 20 minutes
Ingredients:
- 1 ½ small-sized turkey breast, cut into 12 pieces
- 12 thin slices of Asiago cheese
- Paprika, to taste
- Fine sea salt and ground black pepper, to taste
- 12 bacon banners

Addresses:
1. Place the bacon slices and a slice of Asiago cheese on top of each piece of bacon.
2. Top with turkey, season with paprika, salt and pepper, and roll up, securing with a cocktail stick.
3. Air fry for 13 minutes - bon appetit!

272. Turkey with garlic and lemon asparagus

Servings: 4
Cooking time: 25 minutes
Ingredients:
- 450 grams of turkey breast loins, cut into strips
- 450 grams of asparagus, trimmed and cut in medium pieces
- Pinch of salt and black pepper
- 1 tablespoon lemon juice

- 1 teaspoon coconut aminos
- 2 tablespoons olive oil
- 2 cloves garlic, minced
- ¼ cup chicken broth

Addresses:
1. Heat a frying pan that fits the air fryer with the oil over medium-high heat, add the meat and brown for 2 minutes on each side.
2. Add the rest of the ingredients to the pan, stir, put the pan in the machine and cook at 190°C for 20 minutes.
3. Divide between the plates and serve

273. Duck Oregano Duck Spread

Servings: 6
Cooking time: 10 minutes
Ingredients:
- ½ cup butter, softened
- 340 grams of duck liver
- 1 tablespoon sesame oil
- 1 teaspoon salt
- 1 tablespoon dried oregano
- ½ peeled onion

Addresses:
1. Preheat the air fryer to 200°C.
2. Chop the onion.
3. Place the duck liver in the air fryer, add the onion and cook the ingredients for minutes. Then put the duck pâté in the food processor and process for 2 to 3 minutes or until the liver is smooth (depends on the power of the food processor).
4. Then add the onion and stir the mixture for a further 2 minutes. Transfer the liver mixture to the bowl. Then add the oregano, salt, sesame oil and butter. Stir the duck liver with the help of the spoon and transfer it to the bowl.
5. Refrigerate the pâté for 10-20 minutes before serving.

274. Chicken in crust

Servings: 2
Cooking time: 30 minutes
Ingredients:
- ¼ cup almonds
- 2 boneless and skinless chicken breasts
- 2 tablespoons whole mayonnaise
- 1 tablespoon Dijon mustard

Addresses:
1. Grind the almonds in a food processor until finely chopped.
2. Spread the chopped almonds on a plate and set aside.
3. Cut each chicken breast in half lengthwise.
4. Mix the mayonnaise and mustard together and spread evenly over the chicken slices.
5. Place the chicken on the chopped s plate to cover it completely, placing each coated slice in the basket of your fryer.
6. Cook for 2 minutes at 180°C until golden brown. Test the temperature, making sure the chicken has reached 75°C. Serve hot.

275. Strawberry turkey

Servings: 2
Cooking time: 50 minutes
Ingredients:
- 900 grams of turkey breast
- 1 tablespoon of olive oil
- Salt and pepper
- 1 cup fresh strawberries

Addresses:
1. Preheat your fryer to 190°C.
2. Massage the turkey breast with olive oil, before seasoning with a generous amount of salt and pepper.
3. Cook the turkey in the fryer for fifteen minutes. Turn the turkey over and cook for another fifteen minutes.
4. During the last fifteen minutes, blend the strawberries in a food processor to a smooth consistency.
5. Place the strawberries on top of the turkey, then cook for a further seven minutes and enjoy.

276. Crispy and juicy whole chicken

Servings: 8
Cooking time: 60 minutes
Ingredients:
- 2.25 kilograms chicken (wash and remove giblets before preparation)
- 1/2 teaspoon onion powder
- 1/2 teaspoon pepper
- 1 teaspoon paprika
- 1 teaspoon dried oregano
- 1 teaspoon basil, dried
- 1 ½ teaspoon salt

Addresses:
1. Preheat the air fryer to 180°C.
2. Mix all the spices together and rub over the chicken.
3. Place the chicken in the fryer basket. Make sure the chicken breast is facing down.
4. Cook the chicken for 30 minutes and then turn it over to the other side and cook for a further 30 minutes.
5. Cut and serve.

277. Chicken breasts with jalapeños

Servings: 2
Cooking time: 25 minutes
Ingredients:
- 55 grams of full cream cheese, softened
- 4 slices of unsweetened bacon, cooked and crumbled
- ¼ cup pickled jalapeño peppers, sliced

- ½ cup sharp cheddar cheese, shredded and divided
- 2 boneless, skinless chicken breasts (weighing approximately 170 grams each breast)

Addresses:
1. In a bowl, mix cream cheese, bacon, jalapeño slices and half of the cheddar cheese until well combined.
2. Cut parallel cuts into the chicken breasts about ¾ of the length - make sure you don't cut all the way through (you should be able to make six to eight cuts, depending on the size of the chicken breast).
3. Spoon evenly sized tablespoons of the cheese mixture into the crevices of the chicken breasts. Top the chicken with the remaining cheddar cheese. Place the chicken in the fryer basket.
4. Set the fryer to 180°C and cook the chicken breasts for twenty minutes.
5. Test with a meat thermometer. The chicken should be 70°C when fully cooked.
6. Serve hot and enjoy.

278. Crispy Chicken Noodles with Peanuts

Servings: 4
Cooking time: 25 minutes
Ingredients:
- 680 grams of chicken loins
- 2 tablespoons peanut oil
- 1/2 cup tortilla chips, crushed
- Sea salt and ground black pepper, to taste
- 1/2 teaspoon garlic powder
- 1 teaspoon red pepper flakes
- 2 tablespoons of roasted and chopped peanuts

Addresses:
1. Start by preheating your fryer to 180°C.
2. Brush the chicken tenderloins with peanut oil on all sides.
3. In a bowl, thoroughly mix together the crushed crisps, salt, black pepper, garlic powder and red pepper flakes. Dredge the chicken in the breading, shaking off any remaining coating.
4. Place the chicken tenderloins in the cooking basket. Cook for 12 to 13 minutes or until no longer pink in the centre. Working in batches, an instant-read thermometer should read at least 70°C.
5. Serve garnished with roasted peanuts - bon appetit!

279. Vermouth Burgers with Bacon and Turkey

Servings: 4
Cooking time: 30 minutes
Ingredients:
- 2 tablespoons vermouth
- 1 tablespoon of honey
- 2 strips of Canadian bacon in slices
- 450 grams of ground turkey
- 1/2 chopped shallot
- 2 cloves garlic, minced
- 2 tablespoons fish sauce
- Sea salt and ground black pepper, to taste
- 1 teaspoon red pepper flakes
- 4 soft hamburger rolls
- 4 tablespoons tomato ketchup
- 4 tablespoons mayonnaise
- 4 slices of Cheddar cheese (each slice should weigh about 30 grams)
- 4 lettuce leaves

Addresses:
1. Start by preheating your fryer to 200°C.
2. Whisk the vermouth and honey in a bowl, brush the Canadian bacon with the vermouth mixture.
3. Cook for a few minutes. Turn the bacon over and cook for a further 3 minutes.
4. Next, thoroughly combine the ground turkey, shallots, garlic, fish sauce, salt, black pepper and red pepper. Form the meat mixture into patties.
5. Bake in the preheated Air Fryer at 185°C for 10 minutes. Turn them over and bake for another 10 minutes.
6. Spread the ketchup and mayonnaise on the inside of the hamburger buns and place the burgers on the buns, top with bacon, cheese and lettuce, serve immediately.

280. Traditional chicken tetrazzini

Servings: 4
Cooking time: 55 minutes
Ingredients:
- 280 grams of cooked noodles
- 2 tablespoons olive oil
- 450 grams of chicken breast
- Sea salt and pepper, to taste
- 1 onion, sliced
- 2 cloves garlic, minced
- 1 can of cream of chicken
- 1 can of cream of mushroom soup
- 1 cup sour cream
- 1/2 cup grated mozzarella cheese

Addresses:
1. Bring a large pot of lightly salted water to a boil.
2. Cook the noodles for a few minutes or until al dente, drain and set aside, keeping them warm.
3. Preheat your Air Fryer to 185°C.
4. Coat the cooking basket of the air fryer with 1 teaspoon of olive oil.
5. Sprinkle the chicken breasts with salt and pepper. Cook for 25 minutes or until the chicken breasts are lightly browned.
6. Preheat your Air Fryer to 185°C. Lightly grease the bottom and sides of the baking

tray with the remaining tablespoon of olive oil.
7. Add the onion, garlic, chicken stock, mushroom soup and sour cream. Add the reserved noodles and chicken.
8. Cook for 12 minutes in the preheated Air Fryer. Top with mozzarella and cook for a few more minutes until bubbly. Serve hot.

281. Oregano and lemon chicken drumsticks

Servings: 4
Cooking time: 21 minutes
Ingredients:
- 4 chicken drumsticks, skin on, boneless
- 1 teaspoon dried coriander
- ½ teaspoon dried oregano
- ½ teaspoon salt
- 1 teaspoon lemon juice
- 1 teaspoon softened butter
- 2 cloves garlic, minced

Addresses:
1. In the bowl of a blender, mix the dried coriander, oregano and salt. Then fill the skin of the chicken thigh with the coriander mixture. Add the butter and minced garlic.
2. Drizzle the chicken with lemon juice.
3. Preheat the air fryer to 190°C.
4. Place the chicken thighs in the air fryer and cook for 2 minutes.

282. Chicken with Cauliflower and Pecorino Romano

Servings: 4
Cooking time: 30 minutes
Ingredients:
- 900 grams of chicken thighs
- 2 tablespoons olive oil
- 1 teaspoon sea salt
- 1/2 teaspoon ground black pepper
- 1 teaspoon smoked paprika
- 1 teaspoon dried marjoram
- 1 head of cauliflower (450 g), cut into small florets
- 2 cloves garlic, minced
- 1/3 cup Pecorino Romano cheese, freshly grated
- 1/2 teaspoon dried thyme
- Salt, to taste

Addresses:
1. Mix the chicken thighs with the olive oil, salt, black pepper, paprika and marjoram.
2. Cook in the preheated Air Fryer at 190°C for 11 minutes. Turn the chicken thighs over and cook for a further 5 minutes.
3. Mix the cauliflower florets with the garlic, cheese, thyme and salt.
4. Increase the temperature, add the cauliflower florets and cook for a further 12 minutes. Serve hot.

283. Chicken burgers

Servings: 4
Cooking time: 25 minutes
Ingredients:
- ½ onion, chopped
- 2 cloves garlic, minced
- 1 beaten egg
- ½ cup breadcrumbs
- ½ tablespoon ground cumin
- ½ tablespoon paprika
- ½ tablespoon coriander seeds, crushed
- Salt and pepper to taste

Addresses:
1. In a bowl, mix the chicken, onion, garlic, egg, breadcrumbs, cumin, paprika, coriander, salt and black pepper, and form 4 patties with your hands.
2. Grease the fryer with oil and place the patties inside. Do not layer them. Cook in batches if necessary.
3. Cook for minutes at 190°C, turning once halfway through.

284. Sweet and spicy chicken drumsticks

Servings: 4
Cooking time: 20 minutes
Ingredients:
- 1 crushed garlic clove
- 1 tablespoon mustard
- 2 teaspoons brown sugar
- 1 teaspoon cayenne pepper
- 1 teaspoon red chili powder
- salt and ground black pepper, as needed
- 1 tablespoon vegetable oil
- 4 chicken thighs

Addresses:
1. In a bowl, combine garlic, mustard, brown sugar, oil and spices.
2. Spread the marinade on the chicken thighs and refrigerate to marinate for about 30 minutes.
3. Preheat the air fryer and grease the air fryer basket.
4. Place the thighs in the prepared Air Fryer basket in a single layer.
5. Air fry for about 10 minutes and then 10 more minutes at 150°C.
6. Remove from the Air Fryer and transfer the chicken thighs to a serving platter.
7. Serve hot.

285. Holiday Colby Turkey Meatloaf

Servings: 6
Cooking time: 50 minutes
Ingredients:
- 450 grams of minced turkey meat
- 1/2 cup spring onions, finely chopped
- 2 cloves garlic, finely chopped
- 1 teaspoon dried thyme
- 1/2 teaspoon dried basil
- 3/4 cup Colby cheese, grated

- 3/4 cup crushed saltine crackers
- 1 tablespoon tamari sauce
- Salt and black pepper, to taste
- 1/4 cup tomato sauce with roasted red peppers
- 1 teaspoon brown sugar
- 3/4 tablespoons olive oil
- 1 medium egg, well beaten

Addresses:
1. In a non-stick frying pan, preheated over medium heat, sauté the turkey mince, spring onions, garlic, thyme and basil until tender and fragrant.
2. Next, set your Air Fryer to cook at 180°C. Combine the sautéed mixture with the cheese, crackers and tamari sauce, then form the mixture into a loaf.
3. Mix the remaining elements together and pour over the meatloaf. Bake in the Air Fryer pan for 45 to 47 minutes. Eat warm.

286. Crispy turkey sandwich with cabbage salad

Servings: 4
Cooking time: 20 minutes
Ingredients:
- 450 grams of turkey fillets
- ½ cup milk
- 1 cup flour
- 1 teaspoon paprika
- Salt and black pepper to taste
- ½ teaspoon garlic powder
- 4 hamburger buns
- 1 cup coleslaw

Addresses:
1. Preheat the Air Fryer to 180°C.
2. In a bowl, whisk together the eggs and milk. In another bowl, mix the flour, paprika, garlic, turkey, salt and pepper.
3. Dredge the turkey in the egg mixture and then in the flour mixture.
4. Spray the fryer basket with cooking spray and place the turkey in the fryer.
5. Cook for 7 minutes. Remove the basket and turn over, cook for a further 5 minutes until golden brown.
6. Serve on buns with coleslaw.

287. Delicious Chicken Fajitas

Servings: 4
Cooking time: 15 minutes
Ingredients:
- 4 chicken breasts
- 1 onion, sliced
- 1 pepper, sliced
- 1 ½ tablespoons fajita seasoning
- 2 tablespoons olive oil
- 3/4 cup shredded cheddar cheese

Addresses:
1. Preheat the air fryer to 190°C.
2. Coat the chicken with oil and rub with the seasoning.
3. Place the chicken in the baking dish of the air fryer and top with the peppers and onion.
4. Cook for 15 minutes.
5. Top with grated cheese and cook for 1-2 minutes until the cheese melts.
6. Serve and enjoy.

288. Chicken Wings

Servings: 4
Cooking time: 55 minutes
Ingredients:
- 1,360 kilograms of chicken wings on the bone
- ¾ cup flour
- 1 tbsp. old bay seasoning
- 4 tablespoons butter
- A couple of fresh lemons

Addresses:
1. In a bowl, combine all-purpose flour and Old Bay seasoning.
2. Toss the chicken wings with the mixture to coat each wing well.
3. Preheat the Air Fryer.
4. Shake the wings to remove excess flour and place them in the fryer. You may need to do this in several batches, so that there is no overlapping.
5. Cook for 30 - 40 minutes, shaking the basket frequently, until the wings are cooked through and crisp.
6. Meanwhile, melt the butter in a frying pan over a low heat. Squeeze one or two lemons and add the juice to the pan. Mix well.
7. Serve the wings topped with the sauce.

289. Chicken thighs in batter

Servings: 4
Cooking time: 4 hours and 45 minutes
Ingredients:
- 2 cups buttermilk
- 3 teaspoons salt
- 1 teaspoon cayenne pepper
- 1 tablespoon paprika
- 680 grams of chicken thighs
- 2 teaspoons black pepper
- 2 cups flour
- 1 tablespoon garlic powder
- 1 tablespoon baking powder

Addresses:
1. Place the chicken thighs in a large bowl.
2. In a separate bowl, combine buttermilk, salt, cayenne and black pepper.
3. Coat the thighs with the buttermilk mixture. Place a sheet of aluminium foil over the bowl and place in the refrigerator for 4 hours.
4. Preheat your Air Fryer.

5. Mix the flour, baking powder and paprika in a shallow bowl. Cover a baking tray with a layer of parchment paper.
6. Dredge the chicken thighs in the flour mixture and bake them in the deep fryer for 10 minutes. Turn the thighs over and air fry for a further 8 minutes. You will need to do this in two batches.

290. Duck and blackberry mixture

Servings: 4
Cooking time: 25 minutes
Ingredients:
- 4 duck breasts, boneless and skin-striped
- Pinch of salt and black pepper
- 2 tablespoons olive oil
- 1 and ½ cups of chicken stock
- 2 spring onions, chopped
- 4 cloves garlic, minced
- 1 and ½ cups blackberries, pureed
- 2 tablespoons melted butter

Addresses:
1. Heat a frying pan suitable for a deep fryer with the oil and butter over medium-high heat, add the duck breasts, skin side down, and brown for 5 minutes.
2. Add the rest of the ingredients, mix, place the pan in the air fryer and cook at 185°C for 20 minutes.
3. Divide the duck and sauce among the plates and serve.

291. Rice with duck and walnuts

Servings: 4
Cooking time: 20 minutes
Ingredients:
- 55 grams of mushrooms, cut into slices
- 2 tablespoons olive oil
- 2 cups of cauliflower florets, shredded
- ½ cup walnuts, toasted and chopped
- 2 cups chicken stock
- Pinch of salt and black pepper
- ½ cup chopped parsley
- 900 grams of duck breasts, boned and with skin marked

Addresses:
1. Heat a frying pan suitable for a deep fryer with the oil over medium-high heat, add the duck breasts, skin side down, and brown for 4 minutes.
2. Add the mushrooms, cauliflower, salt and pepper, and cook for another minute.
3. Stir in the stock, place the pan in the fryer and cook at 190°C for 15 minutes.
4. Divide the mixture among the plates, sprinkle the parsley and walnuts on top and serve.

292. Parsley duck

Servings: 4
Cooking time: 25 minutes
Ingredients:
- 4 duck breast fillets, boneless, skin on, trimmed and shredded
- 2 tablespoons olive oil
- 2 tablespoons chopped parsley
- Salt and black pepper to taste
- 1 cup chicken stock
- 1 teaspoon balsamic vinegar

Addresses:
1. Heat a frying pan that fits your deep fryer with the oil over medium heat, add the duck breasts, skin side down, and brown for 5 minutes.
2. Add the rest of the ingredients, stir, put the pan in the fryer and cook at 190°C for 20 minutes.
3. Divide between the plates and serve.

293. Baked Rice, Black Beans and Cheese

Servings: 4
Cooking time: 62 minutes
Ingredients:
- 1 cooked boneless, skinless, boneless chicken breast, minced
- 1 cup grated Swiss cheese
- 1/2 can (425 grams) black beans, drained
- 1/2 can (115 g) chopped green chillies, drained
- 1/2 cup vegetable stock
- 1/2 medium-sized courgette, thinly sliced
- 1/4 cup sliced mushrooms
- 1/4 teaspoon cumin
- 1 or ½ teaspoons olive oil
- 2 tablespoons 2 teaspoons chopped onion
- 3 tablespoons brown rice
- 3 tablespoons of grated carrots
- Ground cayenne pepper to taste
- Salt to taste

Addresses:
1. Lightly grease the air fryer tray with cooking spray. Add rice and broth.
2. Cover the pan with aluminium foil and cook for minutes at 200°C. Lower the heat to 150°C and fluff the rice. Cook for another 10 minutes. Leave to stand for 10 minutes and transfer to a bowl and set aside.
3. Add oil to the same baking sheet. Add the onion and cook for 5 minutes at 165°C.
4. Stir in the mushrooms, chicken and courgette. Mix well and cook for 5 minutes.
5. Add the cayenne pepper, salt and cumin. Mix well and cook for another 2 minutes.
6. Add ½ of the Swiss cheese, carrots, chillies, beans and rice. Stir well to mix. Spread evenly in skillet. Top with remaining cheese.
7. Cover the pan with aluminium foil.
8. Cook for 15 minutes at 200°C and then remove the foil and cook for another 5 to

10 minutes or until the top is lightly browned.
9. Serve and enjoy.

294. Chicken Meatballs with Miso-ginger

Servings: 4
Cooking time: 10 minutes
Ingredients:
- 1 ½ teaspoons white miso paste
- 1 large egg
- 1 teaspoon finely grated ginger
- 1/4 cup panko (Japanese bread crumbs), or fresh breadcrumbs
- 1/4 teaspoon kosher salt
- 2 tablespoons sliced onions
- 2 teaspoons low sodium soy sauce
- 350 grams of ground chicken

Addresses:
1. In a medium bowl, whisk together the soy sauce, miso paste and ginger. Set aside.
2. In a large bowl, mix the ground chicken, large egg, spring onions and salt well with your hands. Add the panko and half of the sauce. Mix well.
3. Divide evenly into 12 balls. Thread onto 4 skewers equally.
4. Place on the skewer rack.
5. Cook for 2 minutes at 200°C. Baste with the rest of the sauce, turn and cook for another 2 minutes. Brush with the sauce once more and cook for a further minute.
6. Serve and enjoy.

295. Chicken drumsticks with paprika and turnip

Servings: 3
Cooking time: 30 minutes
Ingredients:
- 450 grams of chicken thighs
- 1 teaspoon Himalayan salt
- 1 teaspoon paprika
- 1/2 teaspoon ground black pepper
- 1 teaspoon melted butter
- 1 turnip, trimmed and cut into slices

Addresses:
1. Spray the sides and bottom of the cooking basket with non-stick cooking spray.
2. Season the chicken thighs with salt, paprika and ground black pepper.
3. Cook for 10 minutes. Set the temperature to 190°C.
4. Drizzle the turnip slices with melted butter and transfer them to the cooking basket with the chicken. Cook the turnips and chicken for a further 15 minutes, turning them halfway through cooking.
5. As for chicken, an instant-read thermometer should read at least 70°C.
6. Serve and enjoy.

296. Dill chicken quesadilla

Servings: 2
Cooking time: 10 minutes
Ingredients:
- 2 low-carb tortillas
- 200 grams chicken breast, skinless and boneless, boiled
- 1 tablespoon cream cheese
- 1 teaspoon melted butter
- 1 teaspoon chopped garlic
- 1 teaspoon chopped fresh dill
- ½ teaspoon salt
- 55 grams Monterey Jack cheese, grated
- Cooking spray

Addresses:
1. Shred the chicken breast with a fork and place it in the bowl. Add the cream cheese, butter, minced garlic, dill and salt.
2. Then add the grated Monterey Jack cheese and stir in the shredded chicken.
3. Next, place the tortilla in the air fryer pan. Top with the shredded chicken mixture and cover with the second corn tortilla.
4. Cook the food for 5 minutes at 200°C.

297. Authentic Mongolian chicken

Portions: 5
Cooking time: 15 minutes
Ingredients:
- 225 grams of flour
- 225 grams of breadcrumbs
- 3 beaten eggs
- 4 tablespoons canola oil
- Salt and pepper to taste
- 2 tablespoons sesame seeds
- 2 tablespoons red pepper paste
- 1 tablespoon apple cider vinegar
- 2 tablespoons honey
- 1 tablespoon soy sauce
- Sesame seeds, to serve

Addresses:
1. Separate the chicken wings into wings and thighs.
2. In a bowl, mix the salt, oil and pepper.
3. Preheat the air fryer to a temperature of 180°C.
4. Dredge the chicken in the beaten eggs and then in the breadcrumbs and flour. Place the chicken in the cooking basket of the air fryer. Drizzle with a little oil and cook for a few minutes.
5. Combine the red pepper paste, apple cider vinegar, soy sauce, honey and ¼ cup water in a saucepan and bring to a boil.
6. Transfer chicken to sauce mixture and toss to coat. Garnish with sesame seeds to serve.

298. Chicken with marinara sauce

Servings: 2
Cooking time: 25 minutes
Ingredients:
- 1 beaten egg
- ½ cup breadcrumbs

- Pinch of salt and black pepper
- 2 tablespoons marinara sauce
- 2 tablespoons grated Grana Padano cheese
- 2 slices mozzarella cheese

Addresses:
1. Dip the breasts in the egg, then in the crumbs and place them in the fryer.
2. Cook for 5 minutes at 200°C.
3. Then turn them over and sprinkle with marinara sauce, Grana Padano and mozzarella.
4. Cook for 5 minutes.

299. Sweet and spicy chicken drumsticks

Servings: 4
Cooking time: 20 minutes
Ingredients:
- 4 chicken thighs
- 1 crushed garlic clove
- 1 tablespoon mustard
- 2 teaspoons brown sugar
- 1 teaspoon cayenne pepper
- 1 teaspoon red chilli powder
- salt and ground black pepper, as needed
- 1 tablespoon vegetable oil

Addresses:
1. Preheat the fryer to 190°C and grease the fryer basket.
2. Mix the garlic, mustard, brown sugar, oil and spices in a bowl.
3. Rub the chicken thighs with the marinade and refrigerate for a few minutes.
4. Place the thighs in the basket of the Air Fryer in a single layer and cook for about 10 minutes.
5. Set the fryer to 150°C and cook for a further 10 minutes.
6. Place the chicken thighs on a platter and serve hot.

300. Chicken breasts with spinach

Servings: 4
Cooking time: 15 minutes
Ingredients:
- 4 tablespoons of cottage cheese
- 2 boneless, skinless chicken breasts
- Juice of ½ lime
- 2 tablespoons Italian seasoning
- 2 tablespoons olive oil

Addresses:
1. Preheat your air fryer to 200°C.
2. Spray the air fryer basket with cooking spray.
3. Mix the spinach with the ricotta in a bowl.
4. Cut the chicken breasts in half with a knife and pound them with a meat mallet. Season with Italian seasoning.
5. Divide the spinach and cheese mixture between the four pieces of chicken. Roll into cylinders and use toothpicks to secure.
6. Brush with olive oil and transfer to the fryer basket. Cook for 6 minutes, turn over and cook for a further 6 minutes.
7. Serve with salad.

301. Sesame chicken wings

Servings: 4
Cooking time: 25 minutes
Ingredients:
- 2 tablespoons sesame oil
- 2 tablespoons maple syrup
- Salt and black pepper
- 3 tablespoons sesame seeds

Addresses:
1. In a bowl, add the wings, oil, maple syrup, salt and pepper and toss to coat well.
2. In another bowl, add the sesame seeds and roll the wings in the seeds to coat them well.
3. Place the wings in an even layer inside your air fryer and cook for minutes at 180°C, turning once halfway through.

302. Chicken with Vegetables and Rice

Servings: 3
Cooking time: 20 minutes
Ingredients:
- 3 cups of cold boiled white rice
- 1 cup cooked chicken, diced
- ½ cup frozen carrots
- ½ cup frozen peas
- ½ cup chopped onion
- 6 tablespoons soy sauce
- 1 tablespoon vegetable oil

Addresses:
1. Preheat the fryer to 180°C and grease an 18-centimetre non-stick frying pan.
2. Mix the rice, soy sauce and vegetable oil in a bowl.
3. Add the rest of the ingredients and mix until well combined.
4. Transfer the rice mixture to the frying pan and place in the fryer.
5. Cook for about 20 minutes and serve immediately.

303. Ethiopian Style Chicken with Cauliflower

Servings: 6
Cooking time: 30 minutes
Ingredients:
- 2 handfuls fresh Italian parsley, coarsely chopped
- ½ cup chopped fresh chives
- 2 sprigs of thyme
- 6 chicken thighs
- 1 ½ heads of cauliflower, small, cut into large florets

For the Berbere spice mix you need:
- 2 teaspoons mustard powder
- 1/3 teaspoon boletus powder
- 1 ½ teaspoons berbere spice

- 1/3 teaspoon sweet paprika
- 1/2 teaspoon shallot powder
- 1 tablespoon granulated garlic
- 1 teaspoon freshly ground pink peppercorns
- 1/2 teaspoon sea salt

Addresses:
1. Simply combine all the elements for the berbere spice mixture. Then coat the chicken thighs with this rub mixture on all sides. Place them in the baking dish.
2. Now, lower the cauliflower over the chicken thighs. Add the thyme, chives and Italian parsley and spray everything with pan spray. Transfer the baking sheet to the preheated Air Fryer.
3. The next step is to set the timer for 28 minutes and roast, turning occasionally. Bon appetit!

304. Sticky Turkey Thighs Chinese Style

Servings: 6
Cooking time: 35 minutes
Ingredients:
- 1 tablespoon sesame oil
- 900 grams of turkey legs
- 1 teaspoon Chinese five-spice powder
- 1 teaspoon Himalayan pink salt
- 1/4 teaspoon Sichuan pepper
- 6 tablespoons honey
- 1 tablespoon Chinese rice vinegar
- 2 tablespoons soy sauce
- 1 tablespoon sweet chilli sauce
- 1 tablespoon mustard

Addresses:
1. Preheat your air fryer to 180°C.
2. Rub the turkey legs with the sesame oil. Season with the spices.
3. Cook for 2 minutes, turning once or twice. Be sure to work in batches to ensure even cooking.
4. Meanwhile, combine the remaining ingredients in a wok (or similar pan preheated over medium-high heat). Cook and stir until the sauce is reduced by about a third.
5. Add the fried turkey legs to the wok, stir gently to coat them with the sauce.
6. Let the turkey rest for 10 minutes before carving and serving - enjoy!

305. Sweet Lime and Chilli Chicken Barbecue

Servings: 2
Cooking time: 40 minutes
Ingredients:
- ¼ cup soy sauce
- 1 cup sweet chili sauce
- Chicken breasts 450 grams
- Juice from 2 limes, freshly squeezed

Addresses:
1. In a Ziploc bag, combine all ingredients and shake well. Marinate for at least 2 hours in the refrigerator.
2. Preheat the fryer to 200°C.
3. Place the grill pan attachment on the air fryer.
4. Place the chicken on the grill and cook for 30 minutes. Be sure to turn the chicken every 10 minutes so that it cooks evenly.
5. Meanwhile, use the remaining marinade and place in a saucepan. Simmer until the sauce thickens.
6. Once the chicken is cooked, baste it with the thickened marinade.

306. Turkey and maple mustard

Servings: 6
Cooking time: 70 minutes
Ingredients:
- 2 ½ kilograms of whole turkey breast
- 1 tablespoon of olive oil
- 1 teaspoon dried thyme
- ½ teaspoon smoked paprika
- ½ teaspoon dried sage
- 1 teaspoon sea salt
- ½ teaspoon black pepper
- 1 tablespoon unsalted butter, melted
- 2 tablespoons Dijon mustard
- ¼ cup maple syrup

Addresses:
1. Preheat the fryer to 180°C.
2. Rub the turkey breast with the olive oil.
3. Mix the thyme, paprika, sage, salt and pepper. Coat the turkey breast all over with this mixture.
4. Place the turkey breast in the basket of the Air Fryer and cook for 25 minutes.
5. Turn over and cook on the other side for another 12 minutes. Turn once more and cook for another 12 minutes.
6. Check the temperature with a meat thermometer and make sure it has reached 75°C before removing it from the fryer.
7. Meanwhile, combine the maple syrup, mustard and melted butter in a saucepan over medium heat. Stir continuously until a smooth consistency is achieved.
8. Pour the sauce over the cooked turkey in the fryer.
9. Cook for the last 5 minutes, making sure the turkey is browned and crispy.
10. Allow the turkey to rest, under a layer of foil, before carving and serving.

307. Juicy herb thighs

Servings: 4
Cooking time: 22 minutes
Ingredients:
- ½ tablespoon fresh rosemary, chopped
- 1 tablespoon chopped fresh thyme
- 4 boneless chicken thighs

84

- ¼ cup Dijon mustard
- 1 tablespoon of honey
- 2 tablespoons olive oil
- Salt and freshly ground black pepper, to taste

Addresses:
1. Preheat the fryer to 160°C and grease the fryer basket.
2. Mix all the ingredients in a bowl, except the drumsticks, until well combined.
3. Stir in the thighs and coat them generously with the mixture.
4. Cover and refrigerate to marinate overnight.
5. Transfer to the fryer basket and cook for about 12 minutes.
6. Set the fryer to 180°C and cook for about 10 minutes.
7. Serve hot.

308. Spicy Turkey Meatloaf with Cheese

Servings: 6
Cooking time: 55 minutes
Ingredients:
- 900 grams of ground turkey breasts
- 1/2 lb. Cheddar cheese, cubed
- 1/2 cup turkey stock
- 1/3 teaspoon hot paprika
- 3 eggs, lightly beaten
- 1 ½ tablespoons olive oil
- 2 cloves garlic, crushed
- 1 ½ teaspoons dried rosemary
- 1/2 cup chopped yellow onion
- 1/3 cup ground almonds
- 1/2 teaspoon black pepper
- Pinch of Tabasco sauce
- 1 teaspoon seasoned salt
- 1/2 cup tomato sauce

Addresses:
1. Heat the olive oil in a medium saucepan over medium heat, and sauté the onions, garlic and dried rosemary until just tender, 3 to 4 minutes.
2. Meanwhile, set the Air Fryer to cook at 195°C.
3. Place all the ingredients, except the tomato sauce, in a bowl along with the sautéed mixture, mixing well to combine.
4. Shape into a meatloaf and cover with the tomato sauce. Fry in the open air for a few minutes and enjoy!

309. The best chicken pizza ever

Servings: 4
Cooking time: 20 minutes
Ingredients:
- 4 small-sized chicken breasts, boneless and skinless
- 1/4 cup pizza sauce
- 1/2 cup Colby cheese, grated
- 16 slices of pepperoni
- Salt and pepper
- 1 ½ tablespoons olive oil
- 1 ½ tablespoons dried oregano

Addresses:
1. Carefully flatten the chicken breast with a rolling pin.
2. Divide the ingredients between four chicken fillets. Roll the chicken fillets in the stuffing and seal them with a skewer or two toothpicks.
3. Grill on the preheated Air Fryer grill for 1 to 15 minutes at 185°C. Enjoy!

310. Dill chicken fritters

Servings: 8
Cooking time: 16 minutes
Ingredients:
- 450 grams of chicken breast, skinned and boneless
- 85 grams of coconut flakes
- 1 tablespoon ricotta cheese
- 1 teaspoon mascarpone
- 1 teaspoon dried dill
- ½ teaspoon salt
- 1 egg yolk
- 1 teaspoon of avocado oil

Addresses:
1. Cut the chicken breast into small pieces and place in the bowl. Add the coconut flakes, ricotta cheese, mascarpone, dried dill, salt and egg yolk.
2. Next, make the chicken fritters with the help of your fingertips.
3. Preheat the air fryer to 180°C.
4. Line the basket of the air fryer with baking paper and place the chicken fritters in the air fryer.
5. Drizzle the chicken fritters with avocado oil and cook for 8 minutes.
6. Turn the chicken fritters on the other side and cook for a further 8 minutes.

311. Spinach and Egg Casserole with Coconut Milk

Servings: 6
Cooking time: 20 minutes
Ingredients:
- ¼ cup coconut milk
- 1 onion, chopped
- 1 teaspoon garlic powder
- 12 large eggs, beaten
- 2 tablespoons coconut oil
- 3 cups chopped spinach
- Salt and pepper to taste

Addresses:
1. Preheat the air fryer for 5 minutes.
2. In a bowl, combine all ingredients except spinach. Whisk until well incorporated.
3. Place the spinach in a baking dish and pour over the egg mixture.
4. Place in the chamber of the air fryer and cook for 20 minutes at 150°C.

312. Chicken and Coconut Meatballs

Servings: 4
Cooking time: 10 minutes
Ingredients:
- 450 grams of ground chicken
- 1 ½ teaspoons sriracha
- 1/2 tablespoon soy sauce
- 1/2 tablespoon hoisin sauce
- ¼ cup shredded coconut
- 1 teaspoon sesame oil
- ½ cup fresh cilantro, chopped
- 2 green onions, chopped
- Pepper
- Salt

Addresses:
1. Spray the air fryer basket with cooking spray.
2. Add all ingredients to the large bowl and mix until well combined.
3. Make small balls of the meat mixture and place them in the fryer basket.
4. Bake at 180°C for 10 minutes. Turn over halfway through.
5. Serve and enjoy.

313. Turkey breakfast frittata

Servings: 4
Cooking time: 50 minutes
Ingredients:
- 1 tablespoon of olive oil
- 450 grams of turkey breast, sliced
- 6 large eggs
- 3 tablespoons Greek yoghurt
- 3 tablespoons crumbled cottage cheese
- 1/4 teaspoon ground black pepper
- 1/4 teaspoon crushed red pepper flakes
- Himalayan salt
- 1 red pepper, seeded and sliced
- 1 green pepper, seeded and sliced

Addresses:
1. Grease the cooking basket with olive oil. Add the turkey and cook in the preheated Air Fryer at 180°C for 30 minutes, turning them halfway through. Cut into bite-sized strips and set aside.
2. Now beat the eggs with the Greek yoghurt, cheese, black pepper, red pepper and salt. Add the peppers to a baking dish previously greased with cooking spray.
3. Add turkey strips, pour egg mixture over all ingredients.
4. Bake in the preheated Air Fryer at 180°C for 15 minutes. Serve immediately.

314. Chicken Dijon with lime

Servings: 6
Cooking time: 20 minutes
Ingredients:
- 8 chicken thighs
- 1 lime juice
- 1 lime zest
- Kosher salt to taste
- 1 tablespoon light mayonnaise
- ¾ teaspoon of black pepper
- 1 crushed garlic clove
- 3 tablespoons Dijon mustard
- 1 teaspoon dried parsley

Addresses:
1. Preheat the Air Fryer to 190°C.
2. Remove the skin from the chicken and sprinkle the chicken with the salt.
3. In a bowl, mix the Dijon mustard with the lime juice, before adding the lime zest, pepper, parsley and garlic.
4. Coat the chicken with the lime mixture. Leave to marinate for about 10-15 minutes.
5. Drizzle a little oil in the bottom of your Air Fryer. Place the chicken thighs inside and cook for a few minutes.
6. Shake the basket and fry for a further 5 minutes.
7. Serve immediately, garnished with mayonnaise.

315. Chicken with Ginger and Lemon Sauce

Servings: 4
Cooking time: 25 minutes
Ingredients:
- 2 tablespoons chopped spring onions
- 1 tablespoon grated ginger
- 4 cloves garlic, minced
- 2 tablespoons coconut aminos
- 8 chicken thighs
- ½ cup chicken stock
- Salt and black pepper to taste
- 1 teaspoon olive oil
- ¼ cup chopped coriander
- 1 tablespoon lemon juice

Addresses:
1. Heat a frying pan with the oil over medium-high heat, add the chicken thighs, brown for 2 minutes on each side and transfer to a frying pan that fits the fryer.
2. Stir in all the other ingredients, mix everything together, put the pan in the fryer and cook at 185°C for 20 minutes.
3. Divide the chicken and lemon sauce between the plates and serve.

316. Honey-glazed turkey breast

Servings: 6
Cooking time: 55 minutes
Ingredients:
- 2 teaspoons softened butter
- 1 teaspoon dried sage
- 2 sprigs of rosemary, chopped
- 1 teaspoon salt
- ¼ teaspoon freshly ground black pepper, or more if desired
- 1 whole turkey breast
- 2 tablespoons turkey stock

- ¼ cup honey
- 2 tablespoons wholegrain mustard
- 1 tablespoon butter

Addresses:
1. Preheat your Air Fryer to 180°C.
2. Mix together the tablespoon of butter, sage, rosemary, salt and pepper.
3. Rub the turkey breast with this mixture.
4. Place the turkey in the cooking basket of your deep fryer and roast for 20 minutes. Turn the turkey breast over and let it cook for another 15 to 16 minutes.
5. Finally, turn once more and roast for another 12 minutes.
6. Meanwhile, mix the rest of the ingredients in a saucepan with a whisk.
7. Coat the turkey breast with the glaze.
8. Return the turkey to the air fryer and cook for a further 5 minutes. Remove from the fryer, allow to rest and carve before serving.

317. Middle-Eastern Chicken Barbecue with Tzatziki Sauce

Servings: 6
Cooking time: 24 minutes
Ingredients:
- 680 grams boneless, skinless chicken breasts, cut into bite-sized pieces
- 1 teaspoon dried oregano
- ½ teaspoon salt
- ¼ cup olive oil
- 2 cloves garlic, minced
- 2 tablespoons lemon juice
- Ingredients of Tzatziki Dip
- 1 container (170 grams) plain Greek-style yoghurt
- 1 tablespoon of olive oil
- 2 teaspoons white vinegar
- 1 clove garlic, minced
- 1 pinch of salt
- ½ peeled, seeded and grated cucumber

Addresses:
1. In a medium bowl, mix all the Tzatziki dip ingredients together well. Refrigerate for at least 2 hours to allow flavours to blend.
2. In a resealable bag, thoroughly mix the salt, oregano, garlic, lemon juice and olive oil. Add the chicken, squeeze out excess air, seal and marinate for at least hours.
3. Thread the chicken onto the skewers and place on the skewer rack. Cook in batches.
4. Cook at 180°C for 12 minutes. Halfway through the cooking time, turn the skewers over and baste them with the marinade from the resealable bag.
5. Serve and enjoy with the Tzatziki sauce.

318. Buffalo chicken

Servings: 4
Cooking time: 25 minutes
Ingredients:
- ½ cup yoghurt
- 450 grams of chicken breasts cut into strips
- 1 tablespoon ground cayenne
- 1 tablespoon hot sauce
- 2 beaten eggs
- 1 tablespoon sweet paprika
- 1 tablespoon garlic powder

Addresses:
1. Preheat the fryer to 200°C.
2. Beat the eggs together with the hot sauce and yoghurt. In a shallow bowl, combine the breadcrumbs, paprika, pepper and garlic powder. Line a baking dish with parchment paper.
3. Dip the chicken in the egg-yoghurt mixture first, then dredge in the breadcrumbs.
4. Place on the tray and bake in the fryer for 8 minutes. Turn the chicken over and bake for a further 8 minutes.
5. Serve.

319. Turkey with Paprika and Shallot Sauce

Servings: 4
Cooking time: 30 minutes
Ingredients:
- 1 large turkey breast, skinless, boneless and cut into cubes
- 1 tablespoon of olive oil
- ¼ teaspoon sweet paprika
- Salt and black pepper to taste
- 1 cup chicken stock
- 3 tablespoons melted butter
- 4 chopped shallots

Addresses:
1. Heat a frying pan that fits the fryer and place the olive oil and butter in it. Set the heat to medium-high.
2. Add the turkey cubes and brown for 3 minutes on each side.
3. Add the shallots, stir and sauté for a further 5 minutes. Add the paprika, stock, salt and pepper, mix, put the pan in the fryer and cook at 185°C for 20 minutes.
4. Divide into bowls and serve.

320. Blue cheese chicken mix

Servings: 4
Cooking time: 20 minutes
Ingredients:
- 450 grams of chicken breasts, skinless, boneless and cut into thin strips
- 1 small yellow onion, cut into slices
- ½ cup buffalo sauce
- ½ cup chicken stock
- ¼ cup blue cheese, crumbled

Addresses:
1. In a skillet that fits your air fryer, combine the chicken with the onions, buffalo sauce and broth.

2. Mix everything together and then place the pan in the fryer, cook at 185°C for a few minutes.
3. Sprinkle the cheese on top, divide between the plates and serve.

321. Delicious Whole Chicken

Servings: 4
Cooking time: 50 minutes
Ingredients:
- 1.36 kilograms of whole chicken, remove giblets and pat dry.
- 1 teaspoon Italian seasoning
- 1/2 teaspoon garlic powder
- 1/2 teaspoon onion powder
- 1/4 teaspoon paprika
- 1/4 teaspoon pepper
- 1 ½ teaspoon salt

Addresses:
1. In a small bowl, mix together the Italian seasoning, garlic powder, onion powder, paprika, pepper and salt.
2. Rub the spice mixture inside and outside the chicken.
3. Place the chicken breast side down in the fryer basket.
4. Roast the chicken for 30 minutes at 180°C.
5. Turn the chicken over and roast for a further 20 minutes or the internal temperature of the chicken reaches 70°C.
6. Serve and enjoy.

322. Legs in batter with lemon butter

Servings: 8
Cooking time: 35 minutes
Ingredients:
- ½ cup chicken stock
- 1 cup almond flour
- 1 beaten egg
- 1 onion, diced
- 900 grams of chicken thighs
- 2 tablespoons capers
- 3 tablespoons olive oil
- 4 tablespoons butter
- juice of 2 lemons, freshly squeezed
- Salt and pepper to taste

Addresses:
1. Preheat the air fryer for 5 minutes.
2. Combine all ingredients in a baking dish. Be sure to remove all lumps.
3. Place the baking dish in the fryer chamber.
4. Bake for 35 minutes at 160°C.

323. Crispy chicken wings

Servings: 2
Cooking time: 25 minutes
Ingredients:
- 2 stalks of lemongrass (white part), chopped
- 1 onion, finely chopped
- 1 tablespoon soy sauce
- 1½ tablespoons honey
- salt and ground white pepper, as needed
- 450 grams of chicken wings, rinsed and trimmed
- ½ cup corn starch

Addresses:
1. In a bowl, mix together the lemongrass, onion, soy sauce, honey, salt and white pepper.
2. Add the wings and cover generously with the marinade.
3. Cover and refrigerate to marinate overnight.
4. Set the temperature of the Air Fryer to 180°C. Grease the basket of the Air Fryer.
5. Remove the chicken wings from the marinade and coat them with the cornflour.
6. Place the chicken wings in the prepared Air Fryer basket in a single layer.
7. Fry in the open air for about 25 minutes, turning once halfway through.
8. Remove from the air fryer and transfer the chicken wings to a serving platter.
9. Serve hot.

324. Chicken in batter with almond flour and coconut milk

Servings: 4
Cooking time: 30 minutes
Ingredients:
- ¼ cup coconut milk
- ½ cup almond flour
- 1 ½ tablespoons old bay cajun seasoning
- 1 beaten egg
- 4 small chicken thighs
- Salt and pepper to taste

Addresses:
1. Preheat the air fryer for 5 minutes.
2. Mix the egg and coconut milk in a bowl.
3. Dip the chicken thighs into the beaten egg mixture.
4. In a bowl, combine the almond flour, Cajun seasoning, salt and pepper.
5. Dredge the chicken thighs in the almond flour mixture.
6. Place in the fryer basket.
7. Bake for 30 minutes at 180°C.

325. Easy chicken sliders

Servings: 3
Cooking time: 30 minutes
Ingredients:
- 1/2 cup all-purpose flour
- 1 teaspoon garlic salt
- 1/2 teaspoon black pepper, preferably freshly ground
- 1 teaspoon celery seeds
- 1/2 teaspoon of mustard seeds
- 1/2 teaspoon dried basil
- 1 egg

- 2 chicken breasts, cut into thirds
- 6 small rolls

Addresses:
1. In a mixing bowl, thoroughly combine the flour and seasonings.
2. In another shallow bowl, beat the egg until frothy.
3. Dredge the chicken in the flour mixture, then in the egg, then dredge them in the flour mixture again.
4. Spray the chicken pieces with cooking spray on all sides. Transfer them to the cooking basket.
5. Cook in the preheated air fryer at 190°C for 1 minute, turn over and cook for a further 10 to 12 minutes.
6. Check the level of doneness and adjust the seasoning. Serve immediately on buns.

326. Chicken with carrots

Servings: 2
Cooking time: 25 minutes
Ingredients:
- 1 carrot, peeled and cut into thin slices
- 2 tablespoons butter
- 2 chicken breast halves (weighing approximately 115 grams)
- 1 tablespoon chopped fresh rosemary
- Salt and black pepper, as needed
- 2 tablespoons fresh lemon juice

Addresses:
1. Preheat the fryer to 190°C and grease the fryer basket.
2. Place square parchment papers on a smooth surface and arrange the carrot slices evenly in the centre of each parchment paper.
3. Drizzle ½ tablespoon of butter over the carrot slices and season with salt and black pepper.
4. Layer the chicken breasts and top with rosemary, lemon juice and the remaining butter.
5. Fold the parchment paper on all sides and transfer it to the fryer.
6. Cook for about 25 minutes and arrange in a serving dish.

327. Cajun Chicken Tenders

Servings: 4
Cooking time: 25 minutes
Ingredients:
- 3 eggs
- 2 ¼ cups flour, divided
- 1 tablespoon of olive oil
- ½ tablespoon more
- ½ tablespoon garlic powder, divided
- 1 tablespoon salt
- 3 tablespoons cajun seasoning, divided
- ¼ cup milk

Addresses:
1. Season chicken with salt, pepper, ½ tablespoon garlic powder and 2 tablespoons Cajun seasoning. Combine 2 cups flour, remaining cajun seasoning and remaining garlic powder in a bowl.
2. In a separate bowl, whisk together the eggs, milk, olive oil and 1/4 cup flour. Preheat the fryer to 190°C.
3. Line a baking tray with parchment paper.
4. Dip the chicken into the egg mixture and then into the flour mixture. Place on the tray with the parchment paper.
5. If there is not enough space, work in two batches. Cook for 1 minute.

328. Air Fried Crispy Chicken Tenders

Servings: 3
Cooking time: 30 minutes
Ingredients:
- 2 (170 grams) boneless, skinless chicken breasts, pounded to 1.25 centimetres thick and cut into strips
- ½ cup plain flour
- 1½ cups panko breadcrumbs
- ¼ cup parmesan cheese, finely grated
- 2 large eggs
- 1½ teaspoons Worcestershire sauce, divided
- ¾ cup buttermilk
- ½ teaspoon smoked paprika, divided
- salt and ground black pepper, as needed

Addresses:
1. Preheat the fryer to 200°C and grease the fryer basket.
2. Mix the buttermilk, ¾ teaspoon Worcestershire sauce, ¼ teaspoon paprika, salt and black pepper in a bowl.
3. Combine the flour, remaining paprika, salt and black pepper in another bowl.
4. Beat the egg and the remaining Worcestershire sauce in a third bowl.
5. Mix the panko breadcrumbs and Parmesan cheese in a fourth bowl.
6. Place the chicken fillets in the buttermilk mixture and refrigerate overnight.
7. Remove the chicken fillets from the buttermilk mixture and dredge them in the flour mixture.
8. Dip in the egg and coat with the breadcrumb mixture.
9. Place half of the chicken fillets in the basket of the Air Fryer and cook for about 15 minutes, turning once in between.
10. Repeat with the rest of the mixture and serve hot.

329. Spicy chicken and tomato sauce

Servings: 8
Cooking time: 18 minutes
Ingredients:
- 8 chicken thighs

- ½ teaspoon cayenne pepper
- ½ teaspoon chilli powder
- ¼ teaspoon chopped jalapeño pepper
- ½ teaspoon ground cumin
- 1 teaspoon dried thyme
- 1 teaspoon keto tomato sauce
- 1 tablespoon walnut oil
- ½ teaspoon salt

Addresses:
1. In the bowl of a blender, combine the tomato sauce and walnut oil.
2. Then add the chopped jalapeño pepper and stir the mixture until smooth.
3. Rub chicken thighs with chili powder, cayenne pepper, dried cumin, thyme and sprinkle with salt. Then rub the chicken with the tomato sauce mixture and marinate overnight or for at least 8 hours.
4. Preheat the air fryer to 190°C.
5. Place the marinated chicken thighs in the air fryer and cook for minutes.

330. Spaghetti Pizza Casserole

Servings: 4
Cooking time: 30 minutes
Ingredients:
- 225 grams of spaghetti
- 450 grams smoked chicken sausage, sliced
- 2 tomato puree
- 1/2 cup grated Asiago cheese
- 1 tablespoon Italian seasoning
- 3 tablespoons grated romano cheese
- 1 tablespoon fresh basil leaves, chiffonade shaped

Addresses:
1. Bring a large pan of lightly salted water to the boil. Cook the spaghetti for a few minutes or until al dente, drain and set aside, keeping warm.
2. Stir in the chicken sausage, tomato puree, Asiago cheese and Italian seasoning mix.
3. Next, spray a baking pan with cooking spray, add the spaghetti mixture to the pan. Bake in the preheated Air Fryer for 11 minutes.
4. Top with the grated Romano cheese. Turn the air fryer up to 200°C and cook for a further 5 minutes or until heated through and the cheese is melted.
5. Garnish with fresh basil leaves and enjoy!

331. Lemon chicken breast with pepper

Servings: 1
Cooking time:
Ingredients:
- 1 chicken breast
- 1 teaspoon chopped garlic
- 2 lemons, peel and juice reserved
- Salt and pepper to taste

Addresses:
1. Preheat the air fryer.
2. Place all ingredients in a baking dish that will fit in the air fryer.
3. Place in the basket of the air fryer.
4. Close and cook for 20 minutes at 200°C.

332. Chicken drumsticks

Servings: 4
Cooking time: 35 minutes
Ingredients:
- 8 chicken thighs
- 1 teaspoon cayenne pepper
- 2 tablespoons mustard powder
- 2 tablespoons oregano
- 2 tablespoons thyme
- 3 tablespoons coconut milk
- 1 large egg, lightly beaten
- ⅓ cup cauliflower
- ⅓ cup of oatmeal
- Pepper and salt to taste

Addresses:
1. Preheat the Air Fryer to 180°C.
2. Season the chicken thighs with salt and pepper and massage in the coconut milk.
3. Place all the ingredients, except the egg, in the food processor and pulse to create a breadcrumb-like mixture.
4. Transfer to a bowl.
5. In a separate bowl, beat the egg. Dredge each chicken thigh in the breadcrumb mixture before dipping in the egg. Dredge once more in the breadcrumbs.
6. Place the coated chicken thighs in the basket of the Air Fryer and cook for 20 minutes. Serve hot.

333. Jerk Chicken, Pineapple and Vegetable Kabobs

Servings: 8
Cooking time: 18 minutes
Ingredients:
- 8 chicken thigh fillets (115 grams each) boneless and skinless, cut into cubes
- 1 tablespoon jerk seasoning
- 2 large courgettes, cut into slices
- 225 grams of white mushrooms, stems removed
- salt and ground black pepper, as needed
- 1 can (570 grams) pineapple chunks, drained
- 1 tablespoon jerk sauce

Addresses:
1. In a bowl, mix the chicken cubes and jerk seasoning.
2. Cover the bowl and refrigerate overnight.
3. Sprinkle the courgette slices and mushrooms evenly with salt and black pepper.
4. Thread the chicken, vegetables and pineapple onto the greased metal skewers.
5. Set the temperature of the Air Fryer to 185°C and grease the basket of the Air Fryer.

6. Place the skewers in the prepared Air Fryer basket in 2 batches.
7. Air fry for about 8-9 minutes, turning and coating with jerk sauce once halfway through.
8. Remove from the fryer and transfer the chicken skewers to a serving platter.
9. Serve hot.

334. Air fried chicken with cheese

Servings: 6
Cooking time: 15 minutes
Ingredients:
- 6 tablespoons seasoned breadcrumbs
- 2 tablespoons grated Parmesan cheese
- 1 tablespoon melted butter
- ½ cup grated mozzarella cheese
- 1 tablespoon marinara sauce
- Cooking spray as needed

Addresses:
1. Preheat your fryer to 200°C.
2. Grease the cooking basket with cooking spray.
3. In a small bowl, mix the breadcrumbs and Parmesan cheese. Rub chicken pieces with butter and dredge in breadcrumbs.
4. Add the chicken to the cooking basket and cook for 6 minutes.
5. Turn and top with marinara sauce and shredded mozzarella, cook for a further 3 minutes.

335. Turkey with butter and mushroom sauce

Servings: 4
Cooking time: 25 minutes
Ingredients:
- 6 cups leftover turkey meat, skinless, boneless and shredded
- Pinch of salt and black pepper
- 1 tablespoon chopped parsley
- 1 cup chicken stock
- 3 tablespoons melted butter
- 450 grams of mushrooms, cut into slices
- 2 spring onions, chopped

Addresses:
1. Heat a frying pan that fits the air fryer and set the heat to medium-high.
2. Add the butter to the mushrooms and sauté for 5 minutes.
3. Add the rest of the ingredients, mix, place the pan in the air fryer and cook at 185°C for 20 minutes.
4. When ready, divide between the plates and serve.

336. Liver spread with paprika

Servings: 6
Cooking time: 8 minutes
Ingredients:
- 450 grams of chicken liver
- 2 tablespoons ghee
- 1 teaspoon salt
- 1 teaspoon smoked paprika
- ¼ cup hot water

Addresses:
1. Preheat the air fryer to 200°C.
2. Wash and trim the chicken liver and place in the fryer basket. Cook the ingredients for 5 minutes. Then turn them over on the other side and cook for a further 3 minutes.
3. When the chicken liver is cooked, transfer it to a blender. Add the ghee, salt and smoked paprika. Add hot water and blend until smooth.
4. Then transfer the cooked chicken pâté to the bowl and store in the refrigerator for up to 3 days.

337. Eggs Benedict on English muffins

Portions: 5
Cooking time: 40 minutes
Ingredients:
- ½ teaspoon onion powder
- 1 cup of milk
- 1 stalk green onions, chopped
- 1/2 packet hollandaise sauce (25 grams)
- 1/2 cup milk
- 1/2 teaspoon salt
- 1/4 teaspoon paprika
- 2 tablespoons margarine
- 3 English muffins, diced into approximately 1.25 centimetre cubes
- 4 large eggs
- 170 grams of Canadian bacon, diced into cubes of approximately 1.25 centimetres.

Addresses:
1. Lightly grease the air fryer tray with cooking spray.
2. Place half of the bacon in the bottom of the pan, spread the English muffins evenly over the top. Evenly distribute the rest of the bacon on top.
3. In a large bowl, whisk together eggs, 1 cup milk, green onions, onion powder and salt. Pour over English muffin mixture.
4. Sprinkle the top with paprika. Cover with aluminium foil and refrigerate overnight.
5. Preheat the fryer to 200°C.
6. Cook in the fryer covered with aluminium foil for 2 minutes. Remove the foil and continue cooking for another 15 minutes or until set.
7. Meanwhile, prepare the hollandaise sauce by melting the margarine in a frying pan. Combine the remaining milk and hollandaise sauce in a small bowl and whisk in the melted margarine.
8. Simmer until thickened, stirring constantly.
9. Serve and enjoy with the sauce.

338. Chicken and black olives recipe

Servings: 2
Cooking time: 18 minutes
Ingredients:
- 1 chicken breast cut into 4 pieces
- 2 tablespoons olive oil
- 3 cloves garlic, minced

For the sauce you need:
- 1 cup pitted black olives
- 2 tablespoons olive oil
- 1/4 cup chopped parsley
- 1 tablespoon lemon juice
- Salt and black pepper to taste

Addresses:
1. In your food processor, combine the olives with the salt, pepper, 2 tablespoons olive oil, lemon juice and parsley, blend very well and transfer to a bowl.
2. Season the chicken with salt and pepper, rub it with the oil and garlic, place it in your preheated air fryer and cook at 190°C for 8 minutes.
3. Divide the chicken among the plates, cover with the olive sauce and serve.

339. Chicken Enchiladas

Servings: 6
Cooking time: 65 minutes
Ingredients:
- 2 cups grated cheese
- ½ cup sauce
- 1 can chopped green chillies
- 12 flour tortillas
- 2 cans enchilada sauce

Addresses:
1. Preheat your fryer to 200°C.
2. In a bowl, mix together salsa and enchilada sauce. Stir in the chopped chicken to coat.
3. Place chicken in tortillas and roll up, top with cheese.
4. Place the prepared tortillas in the cooking basket of the fryer and cook for 60 minutes.
5. Serve with guacamole

340. Mediterranean chicken breasts with roasted tomatoes

Servings: 8
Cooking time: 1 hour
Ingredients:
- 2 teaspoons olive oil, melted
- 3 pounds bone-in chicken breasts
- 1/2 teaspoon freshly ground black pepper
- 1/2 teaspoon salt
- 1 teaspoon cayenne pepper
- 2 tablespoons fresh parsley, chopped
- 1 teaspoon chopped fresh basil
- 1 teaspoon fresh rosemary, chopped
- 4 medium Roma tomatoes, halved

Addresses:
1. Start by preheating your Air Fryer to 185°C.
2. Brush the cooking basket with a teaspoon of olive oil.
3. Sprinkle the chicken breasts with all the seasonings mentioned above.
4. Cook for 25 minutes or until chicken breasts are lightly browned. Work in batches.
5. Place the tomatoes in the cooking basket and brush with the remaining teaspoon of olive oil. Season with sea salt.
6. Cook the tomatoes for 10 minutes, stirring halfway through cooking.
7. Serve with the chicken breasts and enjoy!

341. Spicy chicken thighs

Servings: 3
Cooking time: 25 minutes
Ingredients:
- 3 chicken thighs
- 1 cup buttermilk
- 2 cups white flour
- 1 teaspoon garlic powder
- 1 teaspoon onion powder
- 1 teaspoon ground cumin
- 1 teaspoon paprika
- salt and ground black pepper, as needed
- 1 tablespoon of olive oil

Addresses:
1. Preheat the fryer to 180°C and grease the basket.
2. Mix the chicken thighs and buttermilk in a bowl and refrigerate for a few hours.
3. Combine the flour and spices in another bowl and dredge the chicken thighs in this mixture.
4. Now dip the chicken in the buttermilk and dredge it again in the flour mixture.
5. Place the chicken thighs in the fryer basket and drizzle them with the oil.
6. Cook for about 25 minutes and place in a hot serving dish.

342. Old-fashioned chicken drumettes

Servings: 3
Cooking time: 30 minutes
Ingredients:
- 1/3 cup plain flour
- 1/2 teaspoon ground white pepper
- 1 teaspoon seasoning salt
- 1 teaspoon garlic paste
- 1 teaspoon rosemary
- 1 whole egg + 1 egg white
- 6 drums of chicken
- 1 heaped tablespoon chopped fresh chives

Addresses:
1. Start by preheating your Air Fryer to 200°C.
2. Mix the flour with the white pepper, salt, garlic paste and rosemary in a small bowl.

3. In another bowl, beat the eggs until frothy.
4. Dip the chicken into the flour mixture, then into the beaten eggs, dredge in the flour mixture once more.
5. Cook the chicken drumettes for 22 minutes. Serve hot, garnished with chives.

343. Garlic chicken

Servings: 4
Cooking time: 32 minutes
Ingredients:
- 900 grams of chicken thighs
- 1 fresh lemon juice
- 9 cloves garlic, cut into slices
- 4 tablespoons melted butter
- 2 tablespoons chopped parsley
- 2 tablespoons olive oil
- Pepper
- Salt

Addresses:
1. Preheat the air fryer to 200°C.
2. Add all ingredients to the large bowl and mix well.
3. Place the chicken wings in the fryer basket and cook for a few minutes. Stir halfway through.
4. Serve and enjoy.

344. Chicken pesto

Servings: 2
Cooking time: 20 minutes
Ingredients:
- 4 chicken thighs
- 6 cloves of garlic
- 1/2 jalapeño pepper
- 2 tablespoons lemon juice
- 2 tablespoons olive oil
- 1 tablespoon sliced ginger
- 1/2 cup coriander
- 1 teaspoon salt

Addresses:
1. Add all the ingredients, except the chicken, to the blender and blend until smooth.
2. Pour the whipped mixture into the large bowl.
3. Add the chicken and stir well to coat. Place in the refrigerator for 2 hours.
4. Spray the fryer basket with cooking spray.
5. Place the marinated chicken in the basket of the air fryer and cook at 200°C for 20 minutes. Turn it over halfway through.
6. Serve and enjoy.

345. Chicken Zaatar

Servings: 4
Cooking time: 35 minutes
Ingredients:
- 4 chicken thighs
- 2 sprigs of thyme
- 1 onion, cut into pieces
- 2 ½ tablespoons zaatar
- ½ teaspoon cinnamon
- 2 cloves garlic, crushed
- 1 lemon juice
- 1 lemon peel
- ¼ cup olive oil
- ¼ teaspoon pepper
- 1 teaspoon salt

Addresses:
1. Add the oil, lemon juice, lemon zest, cinnamon, garlic, pepper, 2 tablespoons of zaatar and salt to a large zip-top bag and shake well.
2. Add chicken, thyme and onion to bag and shake well to coat. Place in the refrigerator overnight.
3. Preheat the fryer.
4. Add the marinated chicken to the basket of the air fryer and cook at 190°C for 15 minutes.
5. Turn the chicken to the other side and sprinkle with the remaining zaatar spice and cook at 190°C for a further 118 minutes.
6. Serve and enjoy.

346. Asian Chicken Fillets with Cheese

Servings: 2
Cooking time: 50 minutes
Ingredients:
- 4 smoked bacon pancakes
- 2 chicken fillets
- 1/2 teaspoon coarse sea salt
- 1/4 teaspoon black pepper, preferably freshly ground
- 1 teaspoon chopped garlic
- 1 piece of ginger (5 centimetres), peeled and minced
- 1 teaspoon black mustard seeds
- 1 teaspoon mild curry powder
- 1/2 cup coconut milk
- 1/3 cup tortilla chips, crushed
- 1/2 cup freshly grated Pecorino Romano cheese

Addresses:
1. Start by preheating your Air Fryer to 200°C.
2. Add the smoked bacon and cook in the preheated Air Fryer for 5 to 7 minutes. Set aside.
3. In a bowl, place the chicken fillets, salt, black pepper, garlic, ginger, mustard seeds, curry powder and milk. Leave to marinate in your fridge for about 30 minutes.
4. In another bowl, mix the crushed potato crisps and grated Pecorino Romano cheese.
5. Dredge the chicken fillets in the fried potato mixture and transfer to the cooking basket. Reduce the temperature to 190°C and cook the chicken for 6 minutes.

6. Turn them over and cook for another 6 minutes. Repeat the process until you run out of ingredients.
7. Serve with the reserved bacon. Enjoy.

347. Delicious turkey wings

Servings: 4
Cooking time: 26 minutes
Ingredients:
- 900 grams of turkey wings
- 4 tablespoons chicken seasoning
- 3 tablespoons olive oil

Addresses:
1. Preheat the fryer to 190°C and grease the fryer basket.
2. Mix the turkey wings, chicken rub and olive oil in a bowl until well combined.
3. Place the turkey wings in the fryer basket and cook for about 26 minutes, turning once in between.
4. Arrange the turkey wings on a platter and serve hot.

348. Simple chicken wings

Servings: 2
Cooking time: 25 minutes
Ingredients:
- 450 grams of chicken wings
- Salt and black pepper, to taste

Addresses:
1. Preheat the fryer to 190°C and grease the fryer basket.
2. Season the chicken wings evenly with salt and black pepper.
3. Place the thighs in the basket of the Air Fryer and cook for about 25 minutes.
4. Place the chicken thighs on a platter and serve hot.

349. Turkey Meatballs with Manchego Cheese

Servings: 4
Cooking time: 15 minutes
Ingredients:
- 450 grams of ground turkey
- 225 grams of ground pork
- 1 egg, well beaten
- 1 teaspoon basil, dried
- 1 teaspoon dried rosemary
- 1/4 cup grated manchego cheese
- 2 tablespoons yellow onions, finely chopped
- 1 teaspoon fresh garlic, finely chopped
- Sea salt and ground black pepper, to taste

Addresses:
1. In a mixing bowl, combine all ingredients until well incorporated.
2. Form the mixture into 2.5 cm balls.
3. Cook the meatballs in the preheated Air Fryer at 200°C for 7 minutes. Stir halfway through the cooking time. Work in batches.
4. Serve with your favourite pasta and enjoy!

350. The Best Chicken Burgers

Servings: 4
Cooking time: 20 minutes
Ingredients:
- 1 tablespoon of olive oil
- 1 onion, peeled and finely chopped
- 2 cloves garlic, minced
- Sea salt and ground black pepper, to taste
- 1/2 teaspoon paprika
- 1/2 teaspoon ground cumin
- 450 grams of ground chicken breast
- 4 soft rolls
- 4 tablespoons ketchup
- 4 tablespoons mayonnaise
- 2 teaspoons Dijon mustard
- 4 tablespoons chopped green onions
- 4 gherkins, cut into slices

Addresses:
1. Heat the olive oil in a frying pan over high heat. Then sauté the onion until golden brown and translucent, about 4 minutes.
2. Add the garlic and cook for a further 30 seconds or until aromatic. Season with salt, pepper, paprika and cumin, set aside.
3. Add the chicken and cook for 2 to 2 minutes, stirring and shredding with a fork. Add the onion mixture and mix to combine well.
4. Form the mixture into patties and transfer to the cooking basket. Cook in the preheated Air Fryer at 180°C for 6 minutes. Turn them over and cook for a further 5 minutes. Work in batches.
5. Spread the base of the roll with ketchup, mayonnaise and mustard. Top with chicken, green onions and pickles. Enjoy.

351. Malaysian Chicken Satay with Peanut Sauce

Servings: 4
Cooking time: 25 minutes
Ingredients:
- 1 tablespoon fish sauce
- 1 tablespoon lime juice
- 1 tablespoon white sugar
- 1 tablespoon yellow curry powder
- 1 teaspoon fish sauce
- 1 teaspoon white sugar
- 1/2 cup chicken stock
- 1/2 cup unsweetened coconut milk
- 1/2 teaspoon granulated garlic
- 1/4 cup creamy peanut butter
- 450 grams boneless, skinless, boneless chicken breasts, cut into strips
- 2 tablespoons olive oil
- 2 teaspoons yellow curry powder
- 3/4 cup unsweetened coconut milk

Addresses:
1. In a zip-top bag, thoroughly mix garlic, 1 teaspoon fish sauce, 1 teaspoon sugar, 2 teaspoons curry powder and ½ cup

coconut milk. Add chicken and mix well to coat. Remove excess air and seal bag. Marinate for 2 hours.
2. Thread the chicken onto the skewer and place on the skewer rack.
3. Cook for 10 minutes. Halfway through the cooking time, turn the skewers over.
4. Meanwhile, prepare the peanut sauce by bringing the remaining coconut milk to a simmer in a medium saucepan. Add the curry powder and cook for a few minutes. Add a tablespoon of fish sauce, the lime juice, a tablespoon of sugar, the peanut butter and the chicken stock. Mix well and cook until heated through. Transfer to a small bowl.
5. Serve and enjoy with the peanut sauce.

352. Sweet curry chicken cutlets

Servings: 3
Cooking time: 35 minutes
Ingredients:
- 1 tablespoon of mayonnaise
- 2 eggs
- 1 tbsp chilli
- 1 tablespoon curry powder
- 1 tablespoon sugar
- 1 tablespoon soy sauce

Addresses:
1. Lay the chicken cutlets on a clean, flat surface and use a knife to cut them into diagonal pieces. Gently flatten them with a rolling pin to make them thinner. Place them in a bowl and add the soy sauce, sugar, curry powder and chilli.
2. Mix well and refrigerate for 1 hour, preheat the fryer to 180°C.
3. Remove the chicken and break the eggs. Add the mayonnaise and mix. Remove each piece of chicken and shake well to remove as much liquid as possible.
4. Place in the fryer basket and cook for 8 minutes. Turn over and continue cooking for 6 minutes. Remove to a platter and continue cooking with the rest of the chicken. Serve.

353. Chicken pie with coconut milk

Servings: 8
Cooking time: 30 minutes
Ingredients:
- ¼ small onion, chopped
- ½ cup chopped broccoli
- ¾ cup coconut milk
- 1 cup chicken stock
- 1/3 cup coconut flour
- 450 grams of ground chicken
- 2 cloves garlic, minced
- 2 tablespoons butter
- 4 ½ tablespoons melted butter
- 4 eggs
- Salt and pepper to taste

Addresses:
1. Preheat the air fryer for 5 minutes.
2. Place the tablespoons of butter, broccoli, onion, garlic, coconut milk, chicken stock and ground chicken in a baking dish that will fit in the air fryer. Season with salt and pepper to taste.
3. In a bowl, mix the butter, coconut flour and eggs.
4. Sprinkle the top of the chicken and broccoli mixture evenly with the coconut flour batter.
5. Place the dish in the air fryer.
6. Cook for 30 minutes at 160°C.

354. Broccoli and Cheese Rice Casserole

Servings: 4
Cooking time: 28 minutes
Ingredients:
- 1 can (280 grams) chicken chunks, drained
- 1 cup uncooked instant rice
- 1 cup of water
- 1/2 can (300 g) condensed cream of chicken soup
- 1/2 can (300 grams) condensed cream of mushroom soup
- 1/2 cup milk
- 1/2 small white onion, chopped
- 1/2 pound processed cheese
- 2 tablespoons butter
- Frozen chopped broccoli 225 grams

Addresses:
1. Lightly grease the air fryer tray with cooking spray. Add water and bring to a boil at 200°C. Add rice and cook for 3 minutes.
2. Stir in the melted cheese, onion, broccoli, milk, butter, chicken stock, mushroom soup and chicken. Mix well.
3. Cook for 15 minutes, fluff the mixture and continue cooking for another 10 minutes until the top is golden brown.
4. Serve and enjoy.

355. Chicken Parmesan and Dill

Servings: 6
Cooking time: 20 minutes
Ingredients:
- 500 grams of chicken breast, skinned and boneless
- 140 grams of pork rinds
- 85 grams grated Parmesan cheese
- 3 beaten eggs
- 1 teaspoon chilli flakes
- 1 teaspoon ground paprika
- 2 tablespoons avocado oil
- 1 teaspoon Erythritol
- ¼ teaspoon onion powder
- 1 teaspoon cayenne pepper
- 1 chopped chilli

- ½ teaspoon dried dill

Addresses:
1. In a shallow bowl mix the chilli flakes, ground paprika, erythritol. In addition, stir in onion powder and cayenne pepper.
2. Add the dried dill and stir the mixture gently. Next, rub the chicken breast with the spice mixture. Then rub the chicken with the chopped chilli.
3. Dip the chicken breast in the beaten eggs. Then dredge it in the Parmesan and dip it in the eggs again.
4. Dredge the chicken in the pork rinds and drizzle with avocado oil.
5. Preheat the fryer to 190°C.
6. Place the chicken breast in the air fryer and cook for minutes. Then turn the chicken breast on the other side and cook for 4 more minutes.

356. Mixed Vegetable Breakfast Frittata

Servings: 6
Cooking time: 45 minutes
Ingredients:
- 225 grams of breakfast sausage
- 1 cup shredded cheddar cheese
- 1 teaspoon kosher salt
- 1/2 cup milk or cream
- 1/2 teaspoon black pepper
- 6 eggs
- 225 grams of mixed vegetables for freezing (peppers, broccoli, etc.), thawed

Addresses:
1. Lightly grease the air fryer tray with cooking spray.
2. Cook the breakfast sausage for a few minutes at 180°C and crumble it. Halfway through the cooking time, crumble the sausage a little more until it resembles ground meat. When the cooking is finished, discard the excess fat.
3. Stir in the thawed mixed vegetables and cook for 7 minutes or until heated through, stirring halfway through cooking.
4. Meanwhile, in a bowl, whisk together the eggs, cream, salt and pepper.
5. Remove the basket, spread the vegetable mixture evenly and pour in the egg mixture. Cover the pan with aluminium foil.
6. Cook for a further 1 minute, remove the foil and continue cooking for a further 5-10 minutes or until the eggs are cooked to the desired doneness.
7. Serve and enjoy.

357. Turkey and Coconut Broccoli

Servings: 4
Cooking time: 25 minutes
Ingredients:
- 450 grams of ground turkey meat
- 2 cloves garlic, minced
- 1 teaspoon grated ginger
- 2 teaspoons coconut aminos
- 3 tablespoons olive oil
- 2 heads of broccoli, florets separated and halved
- Pinch of salt and black pepper
- 1 teaspoon chilli paste

Addresses:
1. Heat a frying pan that fits the air fryer with the oil over medium heat, add the meat and brown for 5 minutes.
2. Add the rest of the ingredients, stir, put the pan in the fryer and cook at 190°C for 20 minutes.
3. Divide between the plates and serve.

358. Chicken wings with cheese

Servings: 2
Cooking time: 25 minutes
Ingredients:
- 450 grams of chicken wings
- 1 clove garlic, minced
- 2 tablespoons butter
- 2 tablespoons grated Parmesan cheese
- 1/8 teaspoon paprika
- 1/2 teaspoon oregano
- 1/2 teaspoon rosemary
- 1/4 teaspoon salt

Addresses:
1. Preheat the air fryer to 200°C.
2. Add the chicken wings to the basket of the air fryer and cook for a few minutes. Shake the basket 2-3 times during cooking.
3. Meanwhile, for the sauce, melt the butter in a frying pan over medium heat. Add the garlic and sauté for a few seconds.
4. Mix the herbs and spices and add them to the pan.
5. Add the chicken wings to the sauce in the pan and toss to coat with cheese.
6. Serve and enjoy.

359. Maple Glazed Chicken Special

Servings: 4
Cooking time: 20 minutes
Ingredients:
- 2 ½ tablespoons maple syrup
- 1 tablespoon of tamari soy sauce
- 1 tablespoon oyster sauce
- 1 teaspoon fresh lemon juice
- 1 teaspoon chopped fresh ginger
- 1 teaspoon garlic puree
- Seasoned salt and freshly ground pepper, to taste
- 2 boneless and skinless chicken breasts

Addresses:
1. In a bowl, combine the maple syrup, tamari sauce, oyster sauce, lemon juice, fresh ginger and garlic puree. This is your marinade.

2. Sprinkle the chicken breasts with salt and pepper.
3. Coat the chicken breasts with the marinade. Place some aluminium foil over the dish and refrigerate for hours, or overnight if possible.
4. Remove the chicken from the marinade. Place in the Air Fryer and fry for 15 minutes at 185°C turning each one once or twice lengthwise.
5. Meanwhile, add the remaining marinade to a frying pan over medium heat. Allow the marinade to simmer for 3 minutes until it has reduced by half.
6. Pour over the cooked chicken and serve.

360. Chinese duck

Servings: 6
Cooking time: 30 minutes + marinating time
Ingredients:
- 900 grams of duck breast, boneless
- 2 green onions, chopped
- 1 tablespoon light soy sauce
- 1 teaspoon of 5 Chinese spice powder
- 1 teaspoon Szechuan peppercorns
- 3 tablespoons Shaoxing rice wine
- 1 teaspoon coarse salt
- 1/2 teaspoon ground black pepper

For the enamel you need:
- 1/4 cup molasses
- 3 tablespoons orange juice
- 1 tablespoon soy sauce

Addresses:
1. In a ceramic bowl, place the duck breasts, green onions, light soy sauce, Chinese 5-spice powder, Szechuan peppercorns and Shaoxing rice wine. Marinate for one hour in the refrigerator.
2. Preheat your Air Fryer to 200°C for 5 minutes.
3. Now, discard the marinade and season the duck breasts with salt and pepper. Cook the duck breasts for 12 to 15 minutes or until golden brown. Repeat with the remaining ingredients.
4. Meanwhile, add the reserved marinade to the preheated pan over medium-high heat. Add molasses, orange juice and 1 tablespoon soy sauce.
5. Bring to a simmer and then whisk constantly until it becomes syrupy.
6. Brush the surface of the duck breasts with the glaze so that they are completely covered.
7. Place the duck breasts back in the basket of the Air Fryer, cook for 5 more minutes, enjoy!

Beef, pork and lamb recipes

361. Veal cubes with vegetables

Servings: 4
Cooking time: 20 minutes + marinating time
Ingredients:
- 450 grams top round steak, cut into cubes
- 2 tablespoons olive oil
- 1 tablespoon apple cider vinegar
- 1 teaspoon fine sea salt
- 1/2 teaspoon ground black pepper
- 1 teaspoon shallot powder
- 3/4 teaspoon smoked cayenne pepper
- 1/2 teaspoon garlic powder
- 1/4 teaspoon ground cumin
- 115 grams of broccoli, cut into florets
- 115 grams of mushrooms, cut into slices
- 1 teaspoon basil, dried
- 1 teaspoon celery seeds

Addresses:
1. First, marinate the meat with olive oil, vinegar, salt, black pepper, shallot powder, cayenne pepper, garlic powder and cumin. Toss to coat well and leave to rest for at least 3 hours.
2. Place the meat cubes in the cooking basket of the Air Fryer, cook at 185°C for 1 minute. Pause the machine, check the cubes for doneness and transfer to a platter.
3. Now clean the cooking basket and place the vegetables in it, sprinkle with basil and celery seeds, toss to coat.
4. Transfer to the air fryer and cook for 5 to 6 minutes or until the vegetables are heated through.
5. Serve with the reserved meat cubes - bon appetit!

362. Smoked brisket with dill pickles

Servings: 6
Cooking time: 1 hour
Ingredients:
- ¼ teaspoon liquid smoke
- 1 cup dill pickles
- 1,360 of flat cut breast
- Salt and pepper to taste

Addresses:
1. Preheat the fryer to 200°C.
2. Place the grill pan attachment on the air fryer.
3. Season the brisket with liquid smoke, salt and pepper.
4. Place on the grill pan and cook for 30 minutes per batch.
5. Turn the meat over halfway through the cooking time so that it cooks evenly.
6. Serve with dill pickles.

363. Kansas City Pork Ribs Recipe

Servings: 2

Cooking time: 50 minutes
Ingredients:
- ¼ cup apple cider vinegar
- ¼ cup molasses
- ¼ teaspoon cayenne pepper
- 1 cup ketchup
- 1 tablespoon brown sugar
- 1 tbsp. liquid smoke flavouring, hickory
- 1 tablespoon Worcestershire sauce
- 1 teaspoon dry mustard
- Pork ribs 450 grams, small
- 2 cloves garlic
- Salt and pepper to taste

Addresses:
1. Place all ingredients in a Ziploc bag and marinate in the refrigerator for at least 2 hours.
2. Preheat the fryer to 200°C.
3. Place the grill pan attachment on the air fryer.
4. Roast the meat for 25 minutes per batch.
5. Turn the meat over halfway through cooking.
6. Pour the marinade into a saucepan and simmer until the sauce thickens.
7. Pour the glaze over the meat before serving.

364. Pepper lamb with rhubarb

Servings: 4
Cooking time: 30 minutes
Ingredients:
- 680 grams of lamb ribs
- Pinch of salt and black pepper
- 1 tablespoon ground black peppercorns
- 1 tablespoon ground white peppercorns
- 1 tablespoon of ground fennel seeds
- 1 tablespoon ground coriander seeds
- 4 stalks of rhubarb, chopped
- ¼ cup balsamic vinegar
- 2 tablespoons olive oil

Addresses:
1. Heat a frying pan that fits your air fryer with the oil over medium heat, add the lamb and brown for 2 minutes.
2. Add the rest of the ingredients, stir, simmer for 2 minutes and remove from the heat.
3. Place the pan in the fryer and cook at 190°C for 25 minutes.
4. Divide into bowls and serve.

365. Beef with mixed mushrooms and ghee

Servings: 4
Cooking time: 25 minutes
Ingredients:
- 4 beef fillets
- 1 tablespoon of olive oil
- Pinch of salt and black pepper
- 2 tablespoons melted ghee
- 2 cloves garlic, minced
- 5 cups of sliced wild mushrooms
- 1 tablespoon chopped parsley

Addresses:
1. Heat a frying pan suitable for a deep fryer with the oil over medium-high heat, add the fillets and brown them for 2 minutes on each side.
2. Add the rest of the ingredients, stir, transfer the pan to your air fryer and cook at 190°C for 20 minutes.
3. Divide between the plates and serve.

366. Pork and garlic sauce

Servings: 4
Cooking time: 25 minutes
Ingredients:
- 450 grams of pork tenderloin, sliced
- Pinch of salt and black pepper
- 4 tablespoons melted butter
- 2 teaspoons minced garlic
- 1 teaspoon sweet paprika

Addresses:
1. Heat a frying pan that fits the air fryer with the butter over medium heat, add all the ingredients in it except the pork medallions, whisk well and cook over low heat for 4-5 minutes.
2. Add the pork, mix, place the pan in your air fryer and cook at 190°C for 20 minutes.
3. Divide between plates and serve with a side salad.

367. Tasty pork chops with peanut sauce

Servings: 4
Cooking time: 12 minutes
Ingredients:
- 450 grams pork chops, cut into 2.5 centimetre cubes
- 1 shallot, finely chopped
- ¾ cup of ground peanuts
- ¾ cup coconut milk

For the pig you need:
- 1 teaspoon chopped fresh ginger
- 1 clove garlic, minced
- 2 tablespoons soy sauce
- 1 tablespoon of olive oil
- 1 teaspoon hot pepper sauce

For the peanut sauce you will need:
- 1 tablespoon of olive oil
- 1 clove garlic, minced
- 1 teaspoon ground coriander
- 1 tablespoon of olive oil
- 1 teaspoon hot pepper sauce

Addresses:
1. Preheat the fryer to 200°C and grease one fryer basket.

Steps to prepare the pork:
2. Mix all ingredients in a bowl and set aside for a few minutes.

98

3. Place the cutlets in the fryer basket and cook for about 12 minutes, turning once in between.

Steps to prepare the peanut sauce:
4. Heat the olive oil in a frying pan over medium heat and add the shallot and garlic.
5. Sauté for about 3 minutes and add the coriander.
6. Sauté for 1 minute and add the rest of the ingredients.
7. Cook for about 5 minutes and pour over the pork chops to serve.

368. Meatball and Mushroom Casserole with Cheese

Servings: 4
Cooking time: 41 minutes
Ingredients:
- 2 tablespoons Italian breadcrumbs
- 280 grams lean ground pork
- 1 ½ cup mushrooms, sliced
- 3 carrots, peeled and grated
- 1 teaspoon saffron
- 2 teaspoons of fennel seeds
- 1/3 cup Monterey Jack cheese, preferably freshly grated
- 1/3 cup cream
- 2 medium leeks, finely chopped
- 1/teaspoon dried dill
- 2 small eggs
- 1/2 teaspoon cumin
- ½ teaspoon fine sea salt
- Freshly ground black pepper, to taste

Addresses:
1. Start by preheating the fryer to 200°C.
2. In a bowl, mix the ingredients for the meatballs. Form the mixture into mini meatballs.
3. In an ovenproof frying dish, mix the carrots and mushrooms with the cream, cook for 2 minutes in the preheated fryer.
4. Pause the machine and place the reserved meatballs in a single layer on top of the carrot and mushroom mixture.
5. Top with grated Monterey Jack cheese, bake for 9 minutes more. Serve hot.

369. Za'atar lamb loin chops

Servings: 4
Cooking time: 30 minutes
Ingredients:
- 8 lamb loin chops on the bone, trimmed
- 3 crushed garlic cloves
- 1 tablespoon fresh lemon juice
- 1 teaspoon olive oil
- 1 tablespoon Za'atar
- Salt and black pepper to taste

Addresses:
1. Preheat the fryer to 200°C and grease the fryer basket.
2. Mix the garlic, lemon juice, oil, Za'atar, salt and black pepper in a large bowl.
3. Coat the chops generously with the herb mixture and place them in the fryer basket.
4. Cook for about 15 minutes, turning twice in between and serve the lamb chops hot.

370. Grilled sirloin steak

Servings: 4
Cooking time: 20 minutes
Ingredients:
- 1 cup mayonnaise
- 1 tablespoon fresh rosemary, finely chopped
- 2 tablespoons Worcestershire sauce
- Sea salt, to taste
- 1/2 teaspoon ground black pepper
- 1 teaspoon smoked paprika
- 1 teaspoon chopped garlic
- 680 grams of sirloin steak

Addresses:
1. Combine mayonnaise, rosemary, Worcestershire sauce, salt, pepper, paprika and garlic, stir to combine.
2. Now, spread the mayonnaise mixture on both sides of the steak. Lower the steak onto the grill pan.
3. Grill in the preheated Air Fryer at 200°C for 8 minutes. Turn the fillets over and grill for a further 7 minutes.
4. Check the doneness with a meat thermometer. Serve hot and enjoy.

371. Meat with hot paprika

Servings: 4
Cooking time: 20 minutes
Ingredients:
- 1 tbsp hot paprika
- 4 beef fillets
- Salt and black pepper to taste
- 1 tablespoon melted butter

Addresses:
1. In a bowl, mix the meat with the rest of the ingredients and rub well.
2. Transfer the fillets to the basket of your air fryer and cook at 200°C for about 10 minutes on each side.
3. Divide the fillets between plates and serve with a side salad.

372. Garlic and Ginger Sauce

Servings: 4
Cooking time: 35 minutes
Ingredients:
- 450 grams of pork loin, cut into strips
- 1 clove garlic, minced
- Pinch of salt and black pepper
- 1 tablespoon grated ginger
- 3 tablespoons coconut aminos
- 2 tbsp. melted coconut oil

Addresses:

1. Heat a frying pan suitable for a deep fryer with the oil over medium-high heat, add the meat and brown for 3 minutes.
2. Add the rest of the ingredients, cook for a further 2 minutes, place the pan in the fryer and cook at 190°C for 30 minutes.
3. Divide between plates and serve with a side salad.

373. Max's Meatloaf

Servings: 4
Cooking time: 35 minutes
Ingredients:
- 1 large onion, peeled and diced
- 2 kilograms of minced meat
- 1 teaspoon Worcester sauce
- 3 tablespoons tomato ketchup
- 1 tablespoon basil
- 1 tablespoon oregano
- 1 tablespoon mixed herbs
- 1 tablespoon of quality breadcrumbs
- Salt and pepper to taste

Addresses:
1. In a large bowl, combine the minced beef with the herbs, Worcester sauce, onion and tomato ketchup, incorporating each component well.
2. Pour in the breadcrumbs and stir again.
3. Transfer the mixture to a small plate and cook for 25 minutes in the air fryer at 200°C.

374. Wine marinated sirloin steak

Servings: 4
Cooking time: 20 minutes + marinating time
Ingredients:
- 680 grams of flank steak
- 1/2 cup red wine
- 1/2 cup apple cider vinegar
- 2 tablespoons soy sauce
- Salt, to taste
- 1/2 teaspoon ground black pepper
- 1/2 teaspoon crushed red pepper flakes
- 1/2 teaspoon dried basil
- 1 teaspoon thyme

Addresses:
1. Add all ingredients to a large ceramic bowl. Cover and marinate for 3 hours in your fridge.
2. Transfer the steak to the basket of the Air Fryer previously greased with non-stick cooking oil.
3. Cook in the preheated air fryer at 200°C for 12 minutes, turning halfway through the cooking time. Bon appetit!

375. Pork roulade

Servings: 2
Cooking time: 17 minutes
Ingredients:
- 2 pork chops
- 1 teaspoon German mustard
- 1 teaspoon chopped chives
- 1 pickled cucumber, diced
- 1 teaspoon almond butter
- ½ teaspoon ground black pepper
- 1 teaspoon olive oil

Addresses:
1. Tap the pork chops gently with the kitchen hammer and place them on the chopping board overlapping.
2. Then rub the meat with ground black pepper and German mustard. Top with spring onions, diced pickled cucumber and almond butter.
3. Roll the meat in the roulade and secure with kitchen string. Then drizzle the roulade with olive oil.
4. Preheat the air fryer to 200°C.
5. Place the roulade in the air fryer and cook for a few minutes. Cut the cooked roulade into slices.

376. Pork loin with potatoes

Portions: 5
Cooking time: 25 minutes
Ingredients:
- 900 grams of pork loin
- 1 teaspoon chopped fresh parsley
- 3 large red potatoes, chopped
- 3 tablespoons of olive oil, divided
- salt and ground black pepper, as needed
- ½ teaspoon garlic powder
- ½ teaspoon crushed red pepper flakes

Addresses:
1. Preheat the fryer to 160°C and grease a frying pan.
2. Rub the pork loin evenly with 1 ½ tablespoons of olive oil, parsley, salt and black pepper.
3. Mix the potatoes, remaining oil, garlic powder, red pepper flakes, salt and black pepper in a bowl.
4. Place the pork loin in the basket of the air fryer and place the potato pieces on the sides.
5. Cook for about 2 minutes and serve in a serving dish.
6. Cut into slices of the desired size and serve with the potatoes.

377. Simple beef patties

Servings: 6
Cooking time: 12 minutes
Ingredients:
- 900 grams of ground beef
- 12 slices of cheddar cheese
- 12 dinner rolls
- 6 tablespoons tomato ketchup
- Salt and black pepper, to taste

Addresses:

1. Preheat the fryer to 200°C and grease one fryer basket.
2. Mix the meat, salt and black pepper in a bowl.
3. Make small patties of the same size with the meat mixture and place half of the patties in the fryer basket.
4. Cook for about 12 minutes and top each burger with 1 slice of cheese.
5. Place the burgers between the buns and drizzle with ketchup.
6. Repeat with the rest of the batch and plate to serve hot.

378. Salami Rolls with Homemade Mustard Spread

Servings: 4
Cooking time: 10 minutes
Ingredients:
- 200 grams of grated Manchego cheese
- 300 grams of pork salami, chopped
- 200 grams of canned crescent rolls

For the mustard paste you need:
- 1 tablespoon sour cream
- 1/3 teaspoon garlic powder
- 1/3 cup mayonnaise
- 2 ½ tablespoons spicy brown mustard
- Salt, to taste

Addresses:
1. Start by preheating your air fryer to 160°C. Now, form the crescent rolls into "sheets".
2. Place the chopped manchego and pork salami in the centre of each sheet of dough.
3. Form the dough into rolls, bake the rolls for 8 minutes.
4. Then lower the temperature of the air fryer and bake at 140°C for a further 5 minutes.
5. In the meantime, mix all the ingredients for the mustard spread. Place the warm rolls on a platter and serve with the mustard spread on the side - enjoy!

379. Beef jerky

Servings: 3
Cooking time: 1 hour
Ingredients:
- 450 grams of round beef, cut into thin strips
- ½ cup brown sugar
- ½ cup soy sauce
- ¼ cup Worcestershire sauce
- 1 tablespoon chilli sauce
- 1 tablespoon of liquid hickory smoke
- 1 teaspoon garlic powder
- 1 teaspoon onion powder
- 1 teaspoon cayenne pepper
- ½ teaspoon smoked paprika
- ½ teaspoon ground black pepper

Addresses:
1. Preheat the fryer to 200°C and grease the fryer basket.
2. Mix brown sugar, all sauces, liquid smoke and spices in a bowl.
3. Coat the meat strips generously with this marinade and leave to marinate overnight.
4. Place half of the meat strips in the fryer basket in a single layer.
5. Install a cooking rack over the strips and place the remaining strips of meat.
6. Cook for about 1 hour and serve.

380. Sirloin steak with butter

Servings: 2
Cooking time: 12 minutes
Ingredients:
- 2 (200 grams) tenderloin steak
- 1½ tablespoons softened butter
- Salt and black pepper, to taste

Addresses:
1. Preheat the fryer to 200°C and grease one fryer basket.
2. Rub the fillet generously with salt and black pepper and coat with butter.
3. Place the fillet in the fryer basket and cook for about 12 minutes, turning once in between.
4. Serve the steak and cut into slices of the desired serving size.

381. Roast beef with garlic and celery with butter

Servings: 8
Cooking time: 1 hour
Ingredients:
- 1 garlic bulb, peeled and crushed
- 1 tablespoon butter
- 2 medium onions, chopped
- 900 grams of beef
- 2 celery sticks, cut into slices
- 3 tablespoons olive oil
- A bunch of fresh herbs of your choice
- Salt and pepper to taste

Addresses:
1. Preheat the air fryer for 5 minutes.
2. In an ovenproof dish that will fit in the air fryer, place all the ingredients and stir well.
3. Place the dish in the air fryer and bake for 1 hour at 200°C.

382. Top roast with mustard, rosemary and thyme mixture.

Portions: 10
Cooking time: 1 hour
Ingredients:
- 1 teaspoon dry mustard
- 2 teaspoons dried rosemary
- 3 tablespoons olive oil
- 1,800 kilograms of roast veal
- 4 teaspoons dried oregano
- 4 teaspoons dried thyme
- Salt and pepper to taste

Addresses:

1. Preheat the air fryer for 5 minutes.
2. Place all ingredients in a baking dish that will fit in the air fryer.
3. Place the dish in the air fryer and cook for 1 hour at 200°C.

383. Smoked pork

Portions: 5
Cooking time: 20 minutes
Ingredients:
- Pork shoulder 450 grams
- 1 tablespoon liquid smoke
- 1 tablespoon of olive oil
- 1 teaspoon salt

Addresses:
1. Mix the liquid smoke, salt and olive oil in the shallow bowl.
2. Then carefully brush the pork shoulder with the liquid smoke mixture on each side.
3. Make small cuts in the meat.
4. Preheat the air fryer to 200°C.
5. Place the pork shoulder in the basket of the air fryer and cook the meat for minutes. After this, turn the meat over on the other side and cook for a further 10 minutes.
6. Leave the cooked pork shoulder to rest for 10-15 minutes. Shred with the help of 2 forks.

384. Meat, lettuce and cabbage salad

Servings: 4
Cooking time: 25 minutes
Ingredients:
- 450 grams of beef, cut into cubes
- ¼ cup coconut aminos
- 1 tbsp melted coconut oil
- 170 grams iceberg lettuce, shredded
- 2 tablespoons chopped coriander
- 2 tablespoons chopped chives
- 1 grated courgette
- ½ head of green cabbage, shredded
- 2 tablespoons sliced almonds
- 1 tablespoon sesame seeds
- ½ tablespoon white vinegar
- Pinch of salt and black pepper

Addresses:
1. Heat a frying pan suitable for a deep fryer with the oil over medium-high heat, add the meat and brown for 5 minutes.
2. Add the aminos, courgette, cabbage, salt and pepper, mix, put the pan in the fryer and cook at 185°C for 20 minutes.
3. Cool the mixture, transfer it to a salad bowl, add the rest of the ingredients, mix well and serve.

385. Lamb kebabs with caraway, sichuan and cumin

Servings: 3
Cooking time: 1 hour
Ingredients:
- 680 grams of lamb shoulder, boned and cut into chunks
- 1 tbsp Sichuan peppercorns
- 1 teaspoon sugar
- 2 tablespoons roasted cumin seeds
- 2 teaspoons roasted caraway seeds
- 2 teaspoons crushed red pepper flakes
- Salt and pepper to taste

Addresses:
1. Put all the ingredients in a bowl and marinate the meat in the refrigerator for at least 2 hours.
2. Preheat the fryer to 200°C.
3. Place the grill pan attachment on the air fryer.
4. Roast the meat for 15 minutes per batch.
5. Turn the meat every 8 minutes to roast evenly.

386. Veal schnitzel

Servings: 1
Cooking time: 30 minutes
Ingredients:
- 1 egg
- 1 thin veal schnitzel
- 3 tablespoons of quality breadcrumbs
- 2 tablespoons olive oil
- 1 chopped parsley
- ½ lemon, cut into wedges

Addresses:
1. Preheat your Air Fryer to 180°C.
2. In a bowl, combine the breadcrumbs and olive oil to form a loose, crumbly mixture.
3. Beat the egg with a mixer.
4. Dredge the schnitzel first in the egg and then in the breadcrumbs, making sure to coat it completely.
5. Place the schnitzel in the Air Fryer and cook for 12 - 14 minutes. Garnish the schnitzel with the lemon wedges and parsley before serving.

387. Pork Chops and Sage Sauce Recipe

Servings: 2
Cooking time: 25 minutes
Ingredients:
- 2 pork chops
- 1 shallot, sliced
- 1 handful of chopped sage
- Salt and black pepper to taste
- 1 tablespoon of olive oil
- 2 tablespoons butter
- 1 teaspoon lemon juice

Addresses:
1. Season the pork chops with salt and pepper, rub them with the oil, put them in your air fryer and cook them at 190°C for a few minutes, turning them over halfway through.

2. Meanwhile, heat the frying pan with the butter over medium heat, add the shallot, stir and cook for a few minutes.
3. Add the sage and lemon juice, stir well, cook for a few more minutes and remove from the heat.
4. Divide the pork chops among the plates, drizzle the sage sauce on top and serve.

388. Sausage meatballs

Servings: 4
Cooking time: 15 minutes
Ingredients:
- 100 grams of sausage, casing removed
- ½ medium onion, finely chopped
- 1 teaspoon fresh sage, finely chopped
- 3 tablespoons Italian breadcrumbs
- ½ teaspoon minced garlic
- Salt and black pepper, to taste

Addresses:
1. Preheat the fryer to 180°C and grease the fryer basket.
2. Mix all ingredients in a bowl until well combined.
3. Form the mixture into balls of the same size and place them in the fryer basket.
4. Cook for about 15 minutes and serve hot.

389. Veal brisket with cumin and paprika

Portions: 12
Cooking time: 2 hours
Ingredients:
- ¼ teaspoon cayenne pepper
- 1 ½ tablespoons paprika
- 1 teaspoon garlic powder
- 1 teaspoon ground cumin
- 1 teaspoon onion powder
- 2 teaspoons dry mustard
- 2 teaspoons ground black pepper
- 2 teaspoons salt
- 2,260 kilograms of roast brisket
- 5 tablespoons olive oil

Addresses:
1. Place all ingredients in a Ziploc bag and marinate in the refrigerator for at least 2 hours.
2. Preheat the air fryer for 5 minutes.
3. Place the meat in an ovenproof dish that will fit in the air fryer.
4. Transfer to the air fryer and cook for 2 hours at 180°C.

390. Stuffed peppers

Servings: 4
Cooking time: 25 minutes
Ingredients:
- 4 peppers, cut off the top part of the pepper
- 1,170 kilograms of ground meat
- 2/3 cup grated cheese
- ½ cup cooked rice
- 1 teaspoon basil, dried
- ½ teaspoon chilli powder
- 1 teaspoon black pepper
- 1 teaspoon garlic salt
- 2 teaspoons Worcestershire sauce
- 225 grams of tomato sauce
- 2 cloves garlic, minced
- 1 small onion, chopped

Addresses:
1. Grease a frying pan with cooking spray and fry the onion and garlic over medium heat.
2. Add the meat, basil, chilli powder, black pepper and garlic salt, combining well. Allow to cook until the meat is well browned, before removing the pan from the heat.
3. Add half the cheese, rice, Worcestershire sauce and tomato sauce and stir to combine.
4. Spoon equal amounts of the meat mixture into the four peppers, filling them completely.
5. Preheat the Air Fryer to 200°C.
6. Spray the Air Fryer basket with cooking spray.
7. Place the stuffed peppers in the basket and cook for 11 minutes.
8. Add the remaining cheese on top of each pepper with the remaining cheese and cook for 2 more minutes. When the cheese has melted and the peppers are heated through, serve immediately.

391. Monterey Jack'n Sausage Brekky Casserole

Servings: 2
Cooking time: 20 minutes
Ingredients:
- ½ cup shredded Cheddar-Monterey Jack cheese
- 1 chopped green onion
- 1 pinch of cayenne pepper
- 115 grams of breakfast sausage
- 2 tablespoons chopped red pepper
- 4 eggs

Addresses:
1. Lightly grease the air fryer tray with cooking spray.
2. Add the sausage and cook at 200°C for 8 minutes. Halfway through, crumble the sausage and stir well.
3. Meanwhile, beat the eggs in a bowl and add the pepper, green onion and cayenne.
4. Remove the basket and stir the mixture a little. Spread the cheese evenly and pour the eggs on top.
5. Cook for a further 12 minutes at 165°C or until the eggs are set.
6. Serve and enjoy.

392. Fig wrapped in grilled prosciutto

Servings: 2
Cooking time: 8 minutes
Ingredients:
- 2 whole figs, cut into quarters
- 8 slices of Serrano ham
- Pepper and salt to taste

Addresses:
1. Wrap a slice of prosciutto around a slice and then thread it onto the skewer. Repeat the process with the rest of the ingredients. Place them on the skewer rack of the fryer.
2. Cook at 200°C for 8 minutes. Halfway through the cooking time, turn the skewers over.
3. Serve and enjoy.

393. Pork with coconut and green beans

Servings: 4
Cooking time: 25 minutes
Ingredients:
- 4 pork chops
- 2 tbsp. melted coconut oil
- 2 cloves garlic, minced
- Pinch of salt and black pepper
- 225 grams of green beans, trimmed and cut in halves
- 2 tablespoons of keto tomato sauce

Addresses:
1. Heat a frying pan that fits the air fryer with the oil over medium heat, add the pork chops and brown for 5 minutes.
2. Add the rest of the ingredients, put the pan in the machine and cook at 200°C for 20 minutes.
3. Divide between plates and serve

394. Pepper jacket potato with smoked bacon

Servings: 2
Cooking time: 15 minutes
Ingredients:
- 5 small peaks of smoked bacon
- 1/3 teaspoon garlic powder
- 1 teaspoon sea salt
- 2 teaspoons paprika
- 1/3 teaspoon ground black pepper
- 1 pepper, seeded and cut into slices
- 1 teaspoon mustard
- 2 habanero chillies, halved

Addresses:
1. Just mix all the ingredients in a bowl.
2. Then transfer them to the basket of the air fryer.
3. Air fry at 190°C for 10 minutes. Serve hot.

395. Steak with rattlesnake and garlic sauce

Servings: 4
Cooking time: 20 minutes
Ingredients:
- 2 teaspoons brown mustard
- 2 tablespoons mayonnaise
- 680 g beef flank steak, cubed
- 2 teaspoons of chopped rattlesnakes
- ½ cup spring onions, finely chopped
- 1/3 cup Crème fraîche
- 2 teaspoons cumin seeds
- 3 crushed garlic cloves
- Pink peppercorns, freshly cracked, to taste
- 1 teaspoon fine table salt
- 1/3 teaspoon of black pepper, preferably freshly ground

Addresses:
1. First, fry the cumin seeds for just one minute or until they pop.
2. Next, season the beef arrachera with fine table salt, black pepper and the fried cumin seeds, arrange the seasoned beef cubes in the bottom of the baking dish that fits in the air fryer.
3. Add the chopped rattlesnake, garlic and spring onions, fry in the open air for about 8 minutes at 200°C.
4. Once the veal cubes start to become tender, add your favourite mayonnaise, Crème fraîche, freshly ground pink peppercorns and mustard, air fry for a further 7 minutes. Serve over hot wild rice. Bon appetit!

396. Simple meatballs with garlic and herbs

Servings: 4
Cooking time: 20 minutes
Ingredients:
- 1 clove garlic, minced
- 1 beaten egg
- 1 tbsp. breadcrumbs or flour
- 1 teaspoon dried mixed herbs
- 450 grams of lean ground beef

Addresses:
1. Put all the ingredients in a bowl and mix with your hands.
2. Form small balls with your hands and set aside in the fridge to set.
3. Preheat the air fryer to 200°C.
4. Place the meatballs in the basket of the air fryer and cook for 20 minutes.
5. Halfway through the cooking time, shake the meatballs so that they cook evenly.

397. Moroccan beef kebab

Servings: 4
Cooking time: 30 minutes
Ingredients:
- 1/2 cup chopped leeks
- 2 cloves garlic, crushed
- 900 grams of veal minced meat
- Salt, to taste
- 1/4 teaspoon ground black pepper, or more to taste
- 1 teaspoon of cayenne pepper
- 1/2 teaspoon ground sumac

- 3 saffron threads
- 2 tablespoons fresh continental parsley leaves, loosely packed
- 4 tablespoons tahini sauce
- 115 grams of small rocket
- 1 tomato, sliced

Addresses:
1. In a bowl, mix the chopped leeks, garlic, minced meat and spices, knead with your hands until everything is well incorporated.
2. Now, pile the meat mixture around a wooden skewer to form a pointed sausage.
3. Cook in the preheated air fryer at 200°C for 25 minutes.
4. Serve your kebab with the tahini sauce, rocket and tomato. Enjoy.

398. Pork with raspberry jam and balsamic glaze

Servings: 4
Cooking time: 30 minutes
Ingredients:
- ¼ cup all-purpose flour
- ¼ cup milk
- 1 cup chopped walnuts
- 1 cup of panko breadcrumbs
- 2 large eggs, beaten
- 2 tablespoons raspberry jam
- 2 tablespoons sugar
- 2/3 cup balsamic vinegar
- 4 smoked pork chops
- Salt and pepper to taste

Addresses:
1. Preheat the fryer to 150°C.
2. Season the pork chops with salt and pepper to taste.
3. In a small bowl, whisk together the eggs and milk. Set aside.
4. Dredge the pork chops in flour and then in the egg mixture before dredging them in the panko mixed with the walnuts.
5. Place in the air fryer and cook for 30 minutes.
6. Meanwhile, prepare the sauce by adding the remaining ingredients to the pan. Season with salt and pepper.
7. Drizzle the cooked pork chops with the sauce.

399. Filet Mignon with herb crust

Servings: 4
Cooking time: 20 minutes
Ingredients:
- 450 grams of filet mignon
- Sea salt and ground black pepper, to taste
- 1/2 teaspoon cayenne pepper
- 1 teaspoon basil, dried
- 1 teaspoon dried rosemary
- 1 teaspoon dried thyme
- 1 tablespoon sesame oil
- 1 small egg, well beaten
- 1/2 cup grated Parmesan cheese

Addresses:
1. Season the filet mignon with salt, black pepper, cayenne pepper, basil, rosemary and thyme. Brush with sesame oil.
2. Place the egg in a shallow dish. Now, place the Parmesan cheese on another plate.
3. Coat the filet mignon with the egg, then dip it in the Parmesan cheese. Set your Air Fryer to cook at 200°C.
4. Cook for 10 to 13 minutes or until golden brown. Serve with mixed salad leaves and enjoy.

400. Rare lamb chops

Servings: 4
Cooking time: 8 minutes
Ingredients:
- 2 tablespoons fresh mint leaves, chopped
- 4 (170 grams) lamb chops
- 2 carrots, peeled and cut into cubes
- 1 parsnip, peeled and cut into cubes
- 1 fennel bulb, diced
- 1 clove garlic, minced
- 2 tablespoons dried rosemary
- 3 tablespoons olive oil
- Salt and black pepper, to taste

Addresses:
1. Preheat the fryer to 200°C and grease one fryer basket.
2. Mix the herbs, garlic and oil in a large bowl and coat the cutlets generously with this mixture.
3. Leave to marinate in the fridge for a few hours.
4. Soak the vegetables in a large pan of water for about 15 minutes.
5. Place the cutlets in the fryer basket and cook for about 2 minutes.
6. Remove the cutlets and place the vegetables in the fryer basket.
7. Place the cutlets on top and cook for about 6 minutes.
8. Serve hot.

401. Grandma's famous pork chops

Servings: 4
Cooking time: 1 hour and 12 minutes
Ingredients:
- 3 eggs, well beaten
- 1 ½ cup crushed butter biscuits
- 2 teaspoons of mustard powder
- 1 ½ tablespoons olive oil
- 1/2 tablespoon soy sauce
- 2 tablespoons Worcestershire sauce
- ½ teaspoon dried rosemary
- 4 large pork chops
- ½ teaspoon dried thyme
- 2 teaspoons of fennel seeds
- Salt and freshly ground black pepper, to taste

- 1 teaspoon crushed red pepper flakes

Addresses:
1. Add the pork chops along with the olive oil, soy sauce, Worcestershire sauce and seasonings to a resealable plastic bag.
2. Allow the pork chops to marinate for 50 minutes in your refrigerator.
3. The next step is to dip the pork chops in the beaten eggs, then coat the pork chops with the butter biscuits on both sides.
4. Cook in the air fryer for 18 minutes at 200°C, turning once - bon appetit!

402. Easy corn dog chews

Servings: 2
Cooking time: 10 minutes
Ingredients:
- ½ cup plain flour
- 1 ½ cup cornflakes, crushed
- 2 large veal sausages, cut in half cross-wise
- 2 large eggs, beaten
- Salt and pepper to taste

Addresses:
1. Preheat the fryer to 150°C.
2. Thread the hot dogs with the metal skewers included in the double-layer grid accessory.
3. In a bowl, mix the flour and eggs to form a dough. Season with salt and pepper to taste. Add water if it is too dry.
4. Dip the hot dog skewers into the batter and roll them in the cornflakes.
5. Place on the double-layer grid accessory and cook for 10 minutes.

403. Smoked beef burgers

Servings: 4
Cooking time: 20 minutes
Ingredients:
- 1 ¼ pounds lean ground beef
- 1 tablespoon soy sauce
- 1 teaspoon Dijon mustard
- A pinch of liquid smoke
- 1 teaspoon shallot powder
- 1 clove garlic, minced
- 1/2 teaspoon cumin powder
- 1/4 cup chopped onions
- 1/3 teaspoon of flaked sea salt
- 1/3 teaspoon freshly ground mixed peppercorns
- 1 teaspoon celery seeds
- 1 teaspoon parsley flakes

Addresses:
1. Mix all the above ingredients in a bowl, knead until everything is well incorporated.
2. Form the mixture into four patties. Then make a shallow indentation in the centre of each patty to prevent them from puffing up during frying.
3. Spray the burgers on all sides with non-stick cooking spray. Cook for approximately 12 minutes at 200°C.
4. Check the cooking level: an instant-read thermometer should read 70°C. Enjoy your meal!

404. Spicy and saucy veal fingers

Servings: 4
Cooking time: 20 minutes + marinating time
Ingredients:
- 680 grams of sirloin steak
- 1/4 cup red wine
- 1/4 cup fresh lime juice
- 1 teaspoon garlic powder
- 1 teaspoon shallot powder
- 1 teaspoon celery seeds
- 1 teaspoon mustard seeds
- Coarse sea salt and ground black pepper, to taste
- 1 teaspoon red pepper flakes
- 2 eggs, lightly beaten
- 1 cup Parmesan cheese
- 1 teaspoon paprika

Addresses:
1. Place the steak, red wine, lime juice, garlic powder, shallot powder, celery seeds, mustard seeds, salt, black pepper and red pepper in a large ceramic bowl, marinate for 3 hours.
2. Soften the steak into cubes by pounding with a mallet, cut into 2.5 centimetre strips.
3. In a shallow bowl, beat the eggs. In another bowl, mix the Parmesan cheese and paprika.
4. Dip the pieces of meat into the beaten eggs and coat them on all sides. Then coat the veal pieces in the parmesan mixture.
5. Cook at 200°C for 14 minutes, turning halfway through the cooking time.
6. Meanwhile, prepare the sauce by heating the reserved marinade in a saucepan over medium heat, simmering until heated through. Serve the steak fingers with the sauce on the side. Enjoy.

405. Veal fillets with lemon sauce

Servings: 2
Cooking time: 25 minutes
Ingredients:
- 450 grams of beef fillets
- 4 tablespoons of white wine
- 2 teaspoons crushed coriander seeds
- ½ teaspoon fennel seeds
- 1/3 cup beef broth
- 2 tablespoons lemon zest
- 2 tablespoons canola oil
- 1/2 lemon, cut into wedges
- Salt and freshly ground black pepper flakes, to taste

Addresses:
1. Heat the oil in a saucepan over moderate heat. Then cook the garlic for one minute, or until fragrant.
2. Remove the pan from the heat, add the beef stock, wine, lemon zest, coriander seeds, fennel, salt flakes and freshly ground black. Pour the mixture into a baking dish.
3. Add the veal fillets to the baking dish, tossing them to coat them well. Now, place the lemon wedges between the beef fillets.
4. Bake for 18 minutes at 170°C. Serve hot.

406. Pork tail with herb and garlic sauce

Servings: 4
Cooking time: 35 minutes + marinating time
Ingredients:
- 450 grams of pork butt, cut into 5-centimetre long pieces
- 1 teaspoon golden flaxseed meal
- 1 egg white, well beaten
- Salt and ground black pepper to taste
- 1 tablespoon of olive oil
- 1 tablespoon coconut aminos
- 1 teaspoon lemon juice, preferably freshly squeezed

For the coriander and garlic sauce you will need:
- 3 peeled garlic cloves
- 1/3 cup fresh parsley leaves
- 1/3 cup fresh coriander leaves
- 1/2 tablespoon salt
- 1 teaspoon lemon juice
- 1/3 cup extra virgin olive oil

Addresses:
1. Combine the pork strips with the flaxseed meal, egg white, salt, pepper, olive oil, coconut aminos and lemon juice. Cover and refrigerate for 30 to 45 minutes.
2. Then spray the pork strips with non-stick cooking spray.
3. Set your Air Fryer to cook at 200°C. Press the power button and air fry for 15 minutes, pause the machine, shake the basket and cook for a further 15 minutes.
4. Meanwhile, puree the garlic in a food processor until finely chopped. Now puree the parsley, coriander, salt and lemon juice. With the machine running, carefully pour in the olive oil.
5. Serve the pork with the sauce well chilled and enjoy.

407. Lamb steak with garlic and lemon

Servings: 4
Cooking time: 1 hour and 30 minutes
Ingredients:
- ¼ cup extra virgin olive oil
- ½ cup dry white wine
- 1 tablespoon brown sugar
- 900 grams of lamb meat, minced
- 2 tablespoons lemon juice
- 3 tablespoons ancho chili powder
- 8 cloves of garlic, minced
- Salt and pepper to taste

Addresses:
1. Put all the ingredients in a bowl and marinate the meat in the refrigerator for at least 2 hours.
2. Preheat the fryer to 200°C.
3. Place the grill pan attachment on the air fryer.
4. Roast the meat for 20 minutes per batch.
5. Meanwhile, pour the marinade into a saucepan and simmer for 10 minutes until the sauce thickens.

408. Eggs and Bacon with Brekky's Biscuit

Servings: 4
Cooking time: 28 minutes
Ingredients:
- ¼ cup milk
- ½ of 1,170 gram refrigerated breakfast biscuits
- 1 cup shredded extra sharp cheddar cheese
- 4 onions, chopped
- 5 eggs
- 8 slices of cooked bacon cut down the middle

Addresses:
1. On a baking sheet, cook the bacon for 8 minutes at 180°C or until crisp. Remove the bacon and discard the excess fat.
2. Spread the biscuits evenly on the bottom. Cook at the same temperature for 5 minutes.
3. Meanwhile, whisk together the eggs, milk and spring onions.
4. Remove the basket, place an even layer of bacon on the biscuit, sprinkle the cheese on top and pour in the eggs.
5. Cook for a further 1 minute or until the eggs are set.
6. Serve and enjoy.

409. Southwestern meatloaf

Servings: 6
Cooking time: 45 minutes
Ingredients:
- 1 can of tomatoes, diced, undrained
- 1 cup shredded Monterey Jack cheese
- 1 cup uncooked macaroni, cooked according to manufacturer's instructions
- 1 jalapeño pepper, seeded and chopped
- 1 large onion, chopped
- 1 teaspoon chilli powder
- 1 teaspoon salt
- 1/2 can (1,170 grams) kidney beans, rinsed and drained
- 1/2 can (115 g) chopped green chillies, drained

- 1/2 can (170 grams) tomato paste
- 1/2 teaspoon ground cumin
- 1/2 teaspoon pepper
- 450 grams of ground beef
- 2 cloves garlic, minced

Addresses:
1. Lightly grease air fryer pan with cooking spray. Add ground beef, onion and garlic.
2. Cook at 180°C. Halfway through the cooking time, stir and shred the meat.
3. Combine chopped tomatoes, kidney beans, tomato paste, green chillies, salt, chilli powder, cumin and pepper. Mix well. Cook for another 10 minutes.
4. Stir in macaroni and mix well. Top with jalapeños and cheese.
5. Cover the pan with aluminium foil.
6. Cook for 1 minute at 200°C, remove the foil and continue cooking for another 10 minutes until the top is lightly browned.
7. Serve and enjoy.

410. Lamb with mustard, chives and basil

Servings: 4
Cooking time: 30 minutes
Ingredients:
- 8 lamb chops
- Pinch of salt and black pepper
- A drizzle of olive oil
- 2 cloves garlic, minced
- ¼ cup mustard
- 1 tablespoon chopped chives
- 1 tablespoon basil, chopped
- 1 tablespoon chopped oregano
- 1 tablespoon chopped mint

Addresses:
1. In a bowl, mix the lamb with the rest of the ingredients and rub well.
2. Place the chops in the basket of your air fryer and cook at 190°C on each side.
3. Divide among plates and serve with a side salad.

411. Grilled coriander lamb chops

Servings: 6
Cooking time: 24 minutes
Ingredients:
- 12 lamb chops
- Pinch of salt and black pepper
- ½ cup chopped coriander
- 1 chopped green chilli
- 1 clove garlic, minced
- Juice of 1 lime
- 3 tablespoons olive oil

Addresses:
1. In a bowl, mix the lamb chops with the rest of the ingredients and rub well.
2. Place the chops in the basket of your air fryer and cook at 200°C for minutes on each side.
3. Divide between the plates and serve.

412. Sausage and cauliflower frittata

Servings: 3
Cooking time: 27 minutes
Ingredients:
- 450 grams of hot pork sausage, diced
- ½ cup grated Cheddar cheese
- 1 teaspoon salt
- ½ cup milk
- 1 small cauliflower, shredded
- 3 large eggs
- 1/2 package (850 grams) frozen potatoes, thawed
- 1/2 teaspoon ground black pepper

Addresses:
1. Lightly grease the air fryer tray with cooking spray. And add the diced sausage and cook for minutes at 180°C.
2. Add the fried potatoes and the cauliflower pieces. Cook for another 5 minutes.
3. In the meantime, beat the eggs, salt, pepper and milk well.
4. Remove the basket and stir the mixture a little. Spread the cheese evenly and pour in the eggs.
5. Cook for another 12 minutes or until set.
6. Serve and enjoy.

413. Grilled fillet steak with tomato and olive salad

Portions: 5
Cooking time: 50 minutes
Ingredients:
- ¼ cup extra virgin olive oil
- ¼ teaspoon cayenne pepper
- ½ cup green olives, pitted and sliced
- 1 cup chopped red onion
- 1 tablespoon of oil
- 1 teaspoon paprika
- 1,130 kilograms of skirt
- 900 grams of cherry tomatoes, halved
- 2 tablespoons of sherry vinegar
- Salt and pepper to taste

Addresses:
1. Preheat the fryer to 200°C.
2. Place the grill pan attachment on the air fryer.
3. Season steak with salt, pepper, paprika and cayenne pepper. Brush with oil.
4. Place on the grill and cook for 50 minutes.
5. In the meantime, prepare the salad by mixing the rest of the ingredients.
6. Serve the meat with salad.

414. Classic Keto Cheeseburgers

Servings: 4
Cooking time: 15 minutes
Ingredients:
- 680 grams of minced veal
- 1 packet of onion soup
- Kosher salt and freshly ground black pepper, to taste
- 1 teaspoon paprika

- 4 slices Monterey-Jack cheese

Addresses:
1. In a mixing bowl, thoroughly mix the minced meat, onion soup mix, salt, black pepper and paprika.
2. Next, set your Air Fryer to cook at 195°C. Form the mixture into 4 patties. Air fry them for 10 minutes.
3. The next step is to place the cheese slices on top of the hot burgers. Air fry for another minute.
4. Serve with mustard and pickle salad of your choice, enjoy!

415. Filet Mignon with butter

Servings: 4
Cooking time: 14 minutes
Ingredients:
- 2 mignon fillets
- 1 tablespoon softened butter
- Salt and black pepper, to taste

Addresses:
1. Preheat the fryer to 200°C and grease one fryer basket.
2. Rub the fillet generously with salt and black pepper and coat with butter.
3. Place the fillets in the fryer basket and cook for about 14 minutes.
4. Serve the fillets and cut them into slices of the desired size.

416. Veal and kale omelette

Servings: 4
Cooking time: 20 minutes
Ingredients:
- Cooking spray
- 225 grams of leftover beef, coarsely minced
- 2 cloves garlic, pressed
- 1 cup of kale, chopped and wilted
- 1 chopped tomato
- ¼ teaspoon sugar
- 4 beaten eggs
- 4 tablespoons of cream
- ½ teaspoon turmeric powder
- Salt and ground black pepper to taste
- 1/8 teaspoon ground allspice

Addresses:
1. Grease four ramekins with cooking spray.
2. Place equal amounts of each ingredient in each ramekin and mix well.
3. Air fry for 16 minutes, or longer if necessary. Serve immediately.

417. Classic flank steak strips with vegetables

Servings: 4
Cooking time: 17 minutes
Ingredients:
- 1 flank steak (340 grams), cut into thin strips
- 225 grams of fresh mushrooms, cut into quarters
- Snow peas 170 grams
- 1 onion, cut in half rings
- ¼ cup olive oil, divided
- 2 tablespoons soy sauce
- 2 tablespoons honey
- Salt and black pepper, to taste

Addresses:
1. Preheat the fryer to 200°C and grease one fryer basket.
2. Mix tablespoons of oil, soy sauce and honey in a bowl and coat the steak strips with this marinade.
3. Put the vegetables, remaining oil, salt and black pepper in another bowl and mix well.
4. Place the steak strips and vegetables in the fryer basket and cook for about 17 minutes.
5. Serve hot.

418. Rack of lamb breaded with herbs

Portions: 5
Cooking time: 30 minutes
Ingredients:
- 1 tablespoon melted butter
- 1 clove garlic, finely minced
- 790 grams of rack of lamb
- salt and ground black pepper, as needed
- 1 egg
- ½ cup panko breadcrumbs
- 1 tablespoon chopped fresh thyme
- 1 tablespoon chopped fresh rosemary

Addresses:
1. In a bowl, combine the butter, garlic, salt and black pepper.
2. Coat the rack of lamb evenly with the garlic mixture.
3. In a shallow dish, beat the egg.
4. In another dish, mix the breadcrumbs and herbs.
5. Dip the rack of lamb in the beaten egg and then in the breadcrumb mixture.
6. Set the temperature of the air fryer to 100°C. Grease the air fryer basket.
7. Place the rack of lamb in the prepared fryer basket.
8. Air fry for about 25 minutes and then 5 more minutes at 200°C.
9. Remove from the fryer and place the rack of lamb on a cutting board for about 5 minutes.
10. With a sharp knife, cut the rack of lamb into individual chops and serve.

419. Winter veal with garlic mayonnaise sauce

Servings: 4
Cooking time: 1 hour and 22 minutes
Ingredients:
- 680 grams of beef, cut into cubes

109

- ½ cup whole sour cream
- 1/2 cup white wine
- 2 teaspoons dried rosemary
- 1½ tablespoons herb vinegar
- 1 teaspoon sweet paprika
- 3 cloves garlic, minced
- 2 tablespoons extra virgin olive oil
- 2 teaspoons basil, dried
- 1 tablespoon of mayonnaise
- Salt and ground black pepper to taste

Addresses:
1. In a large bowl, whisk together the oil, wine and meat. Then add the seasoning and herb vinegar. Cover and marinate for at least 50 minutes.
2. Then preheat your Air Fryer to 190°C. Grill the marinated meat for about 18 minutes, turning halfway through.
3. Meanwhile, make the sauce by mixing the sour cream with the mayonnaise and garlic. Serve the meat hot with the garlic sauce and enjoy.

420. Beef and courgette stir-fry

Servings: 4
Cooking time: 25 minutes
Ingredients:
- 450 grams of beef, cut into thin strips
- 1 courgette, diced
- 2 tablespoons coconut aminos
- 2 cloves garlic, minced
- ¼ cup chopped coriander
- 2 tablespoons avocado oil

Addresses:
1. Add the oil to a frying pan sized to fit the air fryer.
2. Take it to the cooker and heat it over medium heat.
3. Add the meat and brown for 5 minutes. Then add the rest of the ingredients and stir.
4. Place the frying pan in the deep fryer and cook at 190°C for 20 minutes. Divide into bowls and serve.

421. Steak frites with gravy

Servings: 2
Cooking time: 25 minutes
Ingredients:
- 1 cup flour
- 1 cup panko breadcrumbs
- 1 teaspoon garlic powder
- 1 teaspoon onion powder
- 2 cups of milk
- 2 tablespoons flour
- 3 beaten eggs
- 170 grams ground sausage meat
- 170 grams sirloin steak, finely pounded
- Salt and pepper to taste

Addresses:
1. Preheat the fryer to 150°C.
2. Season the steak with salt and pepper to taste.
3. Dredge the fillet in the egg and the flour mixture (consisting of flour, breadcrumbs, onion powder and garlic powder).
4. Place in the air fryer and cook for 25 minutes.
5. Meanwhile, place the sausage meat in a saucepan and allow the fat to melt. Stir in the flour to form a roux and add the milk. Season with salt and pepper to taste. Continue stirring until the sauce thickens.
6. Serve the steak with the milk sauce.

422. Spring meat and onions

Servings: 2
Cooking time: 15 minutes
Ingredients:
- 2 cups corned beef, cooked and shredded
- 2 cloves garlic, minced
- 450 grams of radishes, cut into quarters
- 2 spring onions, chopped
- Pinch of salt and black pepper

Addresses:
1. In a frying pan that fits your air fryer, mix the meat with the rest of the ingredients and stir.
2. Place the frying pan in the deep fryer and cook at 200°C.
3. Divide into bowls and serve.

423. Roast loin of pork with herbs de Provence

Servings: 4
Cooking time: 35 minutes
Ingredients:
- 1,800 kilograms of pork loin
- A pinch of garlic salt
- A pinch of herbes de Provence

Addresses:
1. Preheat the fryer to 150°C.
2. Season the pork with the garlic salt and herbs,
3. Place in the frying pan of the air fryer.
4. Cook for 30 to 35 minutes.

424. Lemon Osso Bucco

Servings: 4
Cooking time: 40 minutes
Ingredients:
- 3 chopped spring onions
- 1 clove garlic, minced
- 30 grams of chopped celery
- 450 grams of veal shank, boneless, minced
- ½ teaspoon salt
- ½ teaspoon ground black pepper
- 1 tablespoon ghee
- 1 tablespoon keto tomato sauce
- 2 tablespoons of water
- ½ teaspoon dried thyme
- 1 teaspoon lemon juice
- 1 teaspoon sunflower oil

Addresses:
1. Preheat the fryer to 190°C.
2. In the bowl of a blender, combine the spring onions, garlic, celery, salt, ground black pepper, ghee, tomato sauce, water, dried thyme, lemon juice and sunflower oil.
3. Add the veal shank and mix the ingredients carefully. Then cover the mixture with aluminium foil and place it in the fryer. Cook the Osso Bucco for 40 minutes.
4. Allow the preparation to cool to room temperature.

425. Sweet pork belly

Servings: 6
Cooking time: 55 minutes
Ingredients:
- 450 grams of pork belly
- 1 teaspoon Splenda
- 1 teaspoon salt
- 1 teaspoon white pepper
- 1 teaspoon softened butter
- ½ teaspoon onion powder

Addresses:
1. Sprinkle the pork belly with salt, white pepper and onion powder.
2. Then preheat the air fryer to 195°C.
3. Place the pork belly in the air fryer and cook for 45 minutes.
4. Then turn the pork belly over on the other side and baste it with butter.
5. After this, coat the pork belly with Splenda and cook at 200°C for minutes.

426. Perfect Thai Meatballs

Servings: 4
Cooking time: 20 minutes
Ingredients:
- 450 grams of minced meat
- 1 teaspoon Thai red curry paste
- 1/2 lime, zest and juice
- 1 teaspoon Chinese spices
- 2 teaspoons lemongrass, finely minced
- 1 tablespoon sesame oil

Addresses:
1. Combine all ingredients well in a mixing bowl.
2. Form meatballs and place them in the cooking basket of the Air Fryer.
3. Cook at 190°C for 10 minutes, pause the machine and cook for a further 5 minutes, or until cooked through.
4. Serve with the dipping sauce and enjoy!

427. Orange roast beef

Servings: 4
Cooking time: 14 minutes
Ingredients:
- 2 tablespoons orange juice
- 1 teaspoon dried coriander
- 1 chopped chilli
- 1 tablespoon sesame oil
- 1 tablespoon apple cider vinegar
- ½ teaspoon chilli paste
- ½ teaspoon ground cumin
- ½ teaspoon salt
- Beef flank steak 450 grams

Addresses:
1. Chop the lime into chunks and place in a blender. Add the orange juice, dried coriander, chilli, sesame oil, apple cider vinegar, chilli paste, ground cumin and salt.
2. Blend the mixture until smooth. Cut the flank steak into 4 portions. Then brush each fillet with the lime mixture and marinate for a few minutes.
3. Meanwhile, preheat the air fryer to 200°C.
4. Place the fillets in the air fryer in one layer and cook for 7 minutes.
5. Turn the meat on the other side and cook for a further 7 minutes.

428. Meatballs with Cheese and Honey Mustard

Servings: 8
Cooking time: 15 minutes
Ingredients:
- 2 onions, chopped
- 450 grams of minced meat
- 4 tablespoons of chopped fresh basil
- 2 tablespoons grated cheddar cheese
- 2 teaspoons garlic paste
- 2 teaspoons honey
- Salt and black pepper, to taste
- 2 teaspoons mustard

Addresses:
1. Preheat the fryer to 195°C and grease the fryer basket.
2. Mix all ingredients in a bowl until well combined.
3. Carefully form the mixture into equal-sized balls and place the meatballs in the fryer basket.
4. Cook for about 15 minutes and serve hot.

429. Sweet and sour pork chops

Servings: 4
Cooking time: 16 minutes
Ingredients:
- 6 pork loin chops
- Salt and black pepper, to taste
- 2 cloves garlic, minced
- 2 tablespoons honey
- 2 tablespoons soy sauce
- 1 tablespoon balsamic vinegar
- ¼ teaspoon ground ginger

Addresses:
1. Preheat the fryer to 180°C and grease a baking tray.
2. Season the chops with a little salt and black pepper.

3. Mix the rest of the ingredients in a large bowl and add the cutlets.
4. Cover generously with the marinade and cover to refrigerate for about 8 hours.
5. Place the cutlets on a baking tray and transfer them to the fryer.
6. Cook for about 1 minute, turning once in between and remove to serve hot.

430. Nutmeg pork chops

Servings: 3
Cooking time: 11 minutes
Ingredients:
- 3 pork chops (85 grams each)
- 55 grams of grated Parmesan cheese
- 1 tablespoon almond flour
- ½ teaspoon chilli powder
- ¼ teaspoon ground nutmeg
- 1 teaspoon sesame oil
- 1 teaspoon lemon juice
- 1 beaten egg

Addresses:
1. In the bowl of a blender, mix the Parmesan, almond flour, chilli powder and ground nutmeg.
2. In another bowl, mix together the lemon juice and egg. Next, dip the pork chops in the egg mixture and then dredge them in the Parmesan mixture.
3. Drizzle each coated cutlet with sesame oil.
4. Preheat the air fryer to 200°C.
5. Place the pork chops in the fryer basket and cook for 6 minutes. Then carefully turn them over on the other side and cook for a further 5 minutes.

431. Plain meat

Servings: 1
Cooking time: 25 minutes
Ingredients:
- 1 thin veal schnitzel
- 1 beaten egg
- ½ cup quality breadcrumbs
- 2 tablespoons olive oil
- Pepper and salt to taste

Addresses:
1. Preheat the Air Fryer to 180°C.
2. In a shallow dish, mix the breadcrumbs, oil, pepper and salt.
3. In a second shallow dish, place the beaten egg.
4. Dip the schnitzel in the egg before dipping in the breadcrumbs.
5. Place the coated schnitzel in the fryer basket and air fry for 12 minutes.

432. Favourite Beef Stroganoff

Servings: 4
Cooking time: 20 minutes + marinating time
Ingredients:
- 560 g beef tenderloin, cut into small strips
- 1/4 cup balsamic vinegar
- 1 tablespoon brown mustard
- 1 tablespoon butter
- 1 cup beef broth
- 1 cup chopped leek
- 2 cloves garlic, crushed
- 1 teaspoon cayenne pepper
- Sea salt and crushed red pepper flakes, to taste
- 1 cup sour cream
- 2 ½ tablespoons tomato paste

Addresses:
1. Place the meat together with the balsamic vinegar and mustard in a bowl, cover and marinate in the refrigerator for about an hour.
2. Butter the inside of a baking dish and place the meat in the dish.
3. Add the stock, leeks and garlic. Cook at 200°C for 8 minutes. Pause the machine and add the cayenne pepper, salt, red pepper, sour cream and tomato paste, cook for a further 7 minutes, bon appetit!

433. Lamb sausages

Servings: 4
Cooking time: 10 minutes
Ingredients:
- 4 sausage links
- 340 grams of ground lamb
- 1 teaspoon chopped garlic
- ½ teaspoon onion powder
- 1 teaspoon dried parsley
- ½ teaspoon salt
- 1 teaspoon ghee
- ½ teaspoon ground ginger
- 1 tablespoon sesame oil

Addresses:
1. In the bowl of a blender, combine the ground lamb, minced garlic, onion powder, dried parsley, salt and ground ginger.
2. Then stuff the sausages with the ground lamb mixture. Secure the ends of the sausages.
3. Coat the basket of the air fryer with sesame oil from the inside and place the sausages in it.
4. Drizzle the sausages with ghee. Cook the lamb sausages for minutes at 200°C. Turn them over on the other side after 5 minutes of cooking.

434. Chinese-style creamed veal

Servings: 4
Cooking time: 19 minutes
Ingredients:
- Cooked rice noodles
- 150 grams of beef tenderloin, cut into strips
- 1/2 teaspoon balsamic vinegar
- ½ cup corn flour mix

- 1 cup buttermilk
- 1/3 teaspoon ground black pepper, or to taste
- 1½ cup plain flour
- Seven spice powder
- 1/2 teaspoon ground cinnamon
- 1 teaspoon hot paprika
- 1/3 teaspoon salt

Addresses:
1. Take three mixing bowls.
2. Combine the cornmeal mixture, 3/4 cup flour and the seven-spice powder in the first bowl.
3. Whisk the buttermilk and balsamic vinegar in the second bowl.
4. Add the remaining 3/4 cup of flour to the third bowl, which should be shallow.
5. Sprinkle the meat strips with black pepper, salt, ground cinnamon and paprika. Dredge each strip in the remaining flour, then dip in the buttermilk mixture, then coat in the spiced cornmeal mixture.
6. Cook in the air fryer pan for about 12 minutes at 185°C or until done. Serve over hot rice noodles - bon appetit!

435. Glazed ham

Servings: 4
Cooking time: 40 minutes
Ingredients:
- 450 grams of ham
- ¾ cup whisky
- 2 tablespoons French mustard
- 2 tablespoons honey

Addresses:
1. Preheat the fryer to 160°C and grease a frying pan.
2. Mix all the ingredients in a bowl, except the ham.
3. Keep the ham for a few minutes at room temperature and place it in the frying pan of the deep fryer.
4. Cover with half of the whisky mixture and transfer to the fryer.
5. Cook for about 1 minute and turn to the side.
6. Cover with the rest of the whisky mixture and cook for about 25 minutes.
7. Place on a platter and serve hot.

436. Lamb chops with sesame seeds

Servings: 6
Cooking time: 11 minutes
Ingredients:
- 6 lamb chops (85 grams each)
- 1 tablespoon sesame oil
- 1 tablespoon za'atar seasoning

Addresses:
1. Rub the lamb chops with za'atar seasoning and drizzle with sesame oil.
2. Preheat the air fryer to 200°C.
3. Then place the lamb chops in the air fryer in one layer and cook for 5 minutes.
4. Turn the cutlets on the other side and cook for a further 6 minutes.

437. Leg of lamb with herbs

Portions: 5
Cooking time: 75 minutes
Ingredients:
- 900 grams of bone-in leg of lamb
- 2 tablespoons olive oil
- salt and ground black pepper, as needed
- 2 sprigs of fresh rosemary
- 2 sprigs of fresh thyme

Addresses:
1. Brush the leg of lamb with oil and sprinkle with salt and black pepper.
2. Wrap the leg of lamb with sprigs of herbs.
3. Set the temperature of the air fryer to 200°C. Grease the air fryer basket.
4. Place the leg of lamb in the prepared fryer basket.
5. Fry in the open air for about 7 minutes.
6. Remove from the fryer and transfer the leg of lamb to a serving dish.
7. Using a piece of aluminium foil, cover the leg of lamb for about 10 minutes before slicing.
8. Cut the leg of lamb into desired size pieces and serve.

438. Sirloin steak with yoghurt and curry paprika

Servings: 3
Cooking time: 25 minutes
Ingredients:
- ¼ cup chopped mint
- ½ cup low-fat yoghurt
- 680 grams of boneless top sirloin steak
- 2 teaspoons curry powder
- 2 teaspoons paprika
- 3 tablespoons lemon juice
- 6 cloves garlic, minced
- Salt and pepper to taste

Addresses:
1. Place all ingredients except green onions in a Ziploc bag and marinate in the refrigerator for at least 2 hours.
2. Preheat the fryer to 200°C.
3. Place the grill pan attachment on the air fryer.
4. Roast for 25 to 30 minutes.
5. Turn the fillets halfway through the cooking time to cook evenly.

439. Wet Stuffed Pork Rolls

Servings: 4
Cooking time: 15 minutes
Ingredients:
- 1 chopped spring onion
- ¼ cup sundried tomatoes, finely chopped
- 2 tablespoons fresh parsley, chopped

- 4 (170 grams) pork chops, lightly pounded
- Salt and black pepper, to taste
- 2 teaspoons paprika
- ½ tablespoon olive oil

Addresses:
1. Preheat the fryer to 200°C and grease one fryer basket.
2. Mix the spring onion, tomatoes, parsley, salt and black pepper in a large bowl.
3. Coat the cutlets with the tomato mixture and roll each cutlet.
4. Secure the chops with cocktail sticks and rub with paprika, salt and black pepper.
5. Coat evenly with oil and transfer to the fryer basket.
6. Cook for about 15 minutes, turning once in between and remove to serve hot.

440. Pig and cabbage

Servings: 6
Cooking time: 35 minutes
Ingredients:
- 1,350 kilograms of pork for stewing, cut into cubes
- 2 teaspoons olive oil
- 2 bay leaves
- 3 cloves garlic, minced
- 4 carrots, chopped
- 1 head red cabbage, shredded
- Salt and black pepper to taste
- ½ cup tomato sauce

Addresses:
1. Heat a frying pan that fits your fryer with the oil over medium-high heat, add the meat and brown for 5 minutes.
2. Add all the remaining ingredients and mix.
3. Place the pan in the fryer and cook at 200°C for 30 minutes.
4. Divide the mixture among the plates and serve.

441. Teriyaki Steak with Fresh Herbs

Servings: 4
Cooking time: 40 minutes
Ingredients:
- 2 heaped tablespoons fresh parsley, coarsely chopped
- 450 grams of rump steak
- 2 heaped tablespoons fresh chives, coarsely chopped
- Salt and black pepper (or mixture of peppercorns), to taste

For the sauce you need:
- 1/4 cup rice vinegar
- 1 tablespoon grated fresh ginger
- 1 ½ tablespoons mirin
- 3 cloves garlic, minced
- 2 tablespoons rice bran oil
- 1/3 cup soy sauce
- A few drops of liquid Stevia

Addresses:

1. First steam the rump steaks for 8 minutes (use your preferred steaming method). Season the meat with salt and black pepper, sprinkle the chopped parsley and chives on top.
2. Grill the rump steaks in a basket of the Air Fryer for minutes at 175°C, turning them halfway through.
3. While the meat is cooking, combine the teriyaki sauce ingredients in a frying pan. Then simmer until it has thickened.
4. Toss the meat with the teriyaki sauce until well coated and serve. Enjoy.

442. Beef with marinade and oregano

Servings: 4
Cooking time: 30 minutes
Ingredients:
- 450 grams of roast beef, trimmed
- ½ teaspoon dried oregano
- ¼ teaspoon garlic powder
- Pinch of salt and black pepper
- ½ teaspoon turmeric powder
- 1 tablespoon of olive oil

Addresses:
1. In a bowl, mix the roast beef with the rest of the ingredients and rub well.
2. Place the roast in the basket of the air fryer and cook at 200°C for 30 minutes.
3. Cut the roast into slices, divide between plates and serve with a side salad.

443. Lamb with mint and rosemary

Servings: 2
Cooking time: 35 minutes
Ingredients:
- 340 grams of leg of lamb, boneless
- 1 teaspoon dried rosemary
- ½ teaspoon dried mint
- 1 clove garlic, minced
- ½ teaspoon salt
- ¼ teaspoon ground black pepper
- 1 teaspoon apple cider vinegar
- 1 tablespoon of olive oil

Addresses:
1. In the bowl, mix the dried rosemary, mint, minced garlic, salt, ground black pepper, apple cider vinegar and olive oil.
2. Then rub the leg of lamb with the spice mixture and marinate for 2 hours.
3. Preheat the air fryer to 200°C.
4. Place the leg of lamb in the air fryer and sprinkle with all the remaining spice mixture.
5. Cook the meat for 25 minutes. Then turn the meat on the other side and cook for a few more minutes.

444. Fried pork with sweet and sour glaze

Servings: 4
Cooking time: 30 minutes
Ingredients:

- ¼ cup rice wine vinegar
- ¼ teaspoon Chinese five spice powder
- 1 cup potato starch
- 1 chopped green onion
- 2 large eggs, beaten
- 900 grams of pork chops cut into chunks
- 2 tablespoons cornstarch + 3 tablespoons water
- 5 tablespoons brown sugar
- Salt and pepper to taste

Addresses:
1. Preheat the fryer to 200°C.
2. Season the pork chops with salt and pepper to taste.
3. Dip the pork chops in the egg. Set aside.
4. In a bowl, combine the potato starch and Chinese five-spice powder.
5. Dredge the pork chops in the flour mixture.
6. Place on the double-layer rack and cook for 30 minutes.
7. Meanwhile, place the vinegar and brown sugar in a saucepan. Season with salt and pepper to taste. Add the cornstarch mixture and simmer until thickened.
8. Serve the pork chops with the sauce and garnish with green onions.

445. Pork with chilli and tomato

Servings: 3
Cooking time: 15 minutes
Ingredients:
- 340 grams of pork loin
- 1 tablespoon mustard seeds
- 1 tablespoon swerve
- 1 tablespoon keto tomato sauce
- 1 teaspoon ground chilli pepper
- ¼ teaspoon garlic powder
- 1 tablespoon of olive oil

Addresses:
1. In the bowl of a blender, combine the mustard seeds, swerve, tomato sauce, chilli, garlic powder and olive oil.
2. Rub the pork loin generously with the mustard mixture and marinate for 5 minutes.
3. Meanwhile, preheat the air fryer to 190°C.
4. Place the marinated pork tenderloin on the fryer's baking tray.
5. Then place the pan in the preheated air fryer and cook the meat for 15 minutes.
6. Cool the cooked meat to room temperature and cut into portions.

446. Coriander and English mustard veal chops

Servings: 3
Cooking time: 35 minutes
Ingredients:
- 1 ½ teaspoon of English mustard
- 3 boneless veal chops
- 1/3 teaspoon of garlic pepper
- 2 teaspoons dried oregano
- 2 tablespoons vegetable oil
- 1 ½ tablespoons chopped fresh coriander
- 1/2 teaspoon onion powder
- 1/2 teaspoon dried basil
- Zest of 1/2 small lime
- 1/2 teaspoon fine sea salt

Addresses:
1. First, make the dressing for the veal cutlets by mixing all the ingredients except the cutlets and the new potatoes.
2. Now spread the veal cutlets evenly with the English mustard rub.
3. Then place the new potatoes in the bottom of the fryer's cooking basket. Place the prepared veal cutlets on top.
4. Roast for about 27 minutes at 185°C, turning halfway through. Serve on individual plates with a keto salad on the side, if desired.

447. Meat and tofu mixture

Servings: 6
Cooking time: 30 minutes
Ingredients:
- 1 cup beef broth
- 900 grams of steak, cut into thin strips and browned
- Salt and black pepper to taste
- 1 yellow onion, thinly sliced
- 340 grams extra firm tofu, cut into cubes
- 1 chilli, sliced
- 1 chopped spring onion

Addresses:
1. Combine all ingredients in a pan that fits your air fryer, mix well.
2. Place the pan in the fryer and cook at 190°C for 30 minutes.
3. Divide among the plates and serve.

448. Sausage and semolina pie with southern cheese

Servings: 4
Cooking time: 30 minutes
Ingredients:
- 1/2 cup uncooked semolina
- 115 grams of ground pork sausage
- 1 or ½ cups of water
- 2 tablespoons butter, divided
- 2 tablespoons milk
- 3 eggs
- 3/4 cup shredded Cheddar cheese, shredded, divided
- Salt and pepper to taste

Addresses:
1. In a large saucepan, bring water to a boil. Add the grits and simmer until the liquid is absorbed, about 5 minutes.
2. Now, add ¼ cup of cheese and a tablespoon of butter. Mix well until fully incorporated.

3. Lightly grease the air fryer tray with cooking spray. Add the pork sausage and cook at 180°C for 5 minutes. Crumble the sausage and discard excess fat.
4. Transfer the semolina to the sausage pan.
5. Whisk the milk and eggs together in a bowl and pour them into the pan. Mix well.
6. Spread the top with butter and sprinkle with cheese. Season with pepper and salt.
7. Cook until the top is golden brown, about 20 minutes.
8. Serve and enjoy.

449. Honey-mustard marinated pork chops

Servings: 4
Cooking time: 25 minutes
Ingredients:
- 2 tablespoons honey
- 2 tablespoons minced garlic
- 4 pork chops
- 4 tablespoons mustard
- Salt and pepper to taste

Addresses:
1. Preheat the fryer to 150°C.
2. Position the basket of the air fryer.
3. Season the pork chops with the rest of the ingredients.
4. Place inside the basket.
5. Cook for 20 minutes until golden brown.

450. Lamb loin chops in lemon sauce

Servings: 4
Cooking time: 30 minutes
Ingredients:
- 2 tablespoons Dijon mustard
- 1 tablespoon fresh lemon juice
- ½ teaspoon olive oil
- 1 teaspoon dried tarragon
- salt and ground black pepper, as needed
- 8 lamb loin chops (about 115 grams each)

Addresses:
1. In a large bowl, combine the mustard, lemon juice, oil, tarragon, salt and black pepper.
2. Add the cutlets and coat them generously with the mixture.
3. Set the temperature of the air fryer to 200°C. Grease the air fryer basket.
4. Place the cutlets in the prepared air fryer basket in a single layer in 2 batches.
5. Air fry for about 1 minute, turning halfway through.
6. Remove the cutlets from the fryer and place them on plates.
7. Serve hot.

451. Meat and vegetable kebabs

Servings: 4
Cooking time: 12 minutes
Ingredients:
- ¼ cup soy sauce
- ¼ cup olive oil
- 1 tablespoon chopped garlic
- 1 teaspoon brown sugar
- ½ teaspoon ground cumin
- salt and ground black pepper, as needed
- 450 grams sirloin steak, cut into 2.5 centimetre pieces
- 225 grams of baby Bella mushrooms, stems removed
- 1 large pepper, seeded and cut into 2.5-centimetre pieces
- 1 red onion, cut into approximately 2.5 centimetre pieces

Addresses:
1. In a bowl, mix together the soy sauce, oil, garlic, brown sugar, cumin, salt and black pepper.
2. Add the meat cubes and cover generously with the marinade.
3. Refrigerate to marinate for a few minutes.
4. Thread the steak cubes, mushrooms, pepper and onion onto the metal skewers.
5. Set the temperature of the Air Fryer to 200°C. Grease the basket of the Air Fryer.
6. Place the skewers in the prepared fryer basket.
7. Fry in the open air for about 10-12 minutes, turning once halfway through.
8. Remove from the Air Fryer and transfer the skewers to a tray.
9. Serve hot.

452. Tomato riblets

Servings: 4
Cooking time: 40 minutes
Ingredients:
- 450 grams of pork ribs
- 2 tablespoons erythritol
- ½ teaspoon ground paprika
- ½ teaspoon chilli powder
- 1 teaspoon yellow mustard
- 2 tablespoons apple cider vinegar
- 1 teaspoon keto tomato sauce
- ¼ cup water
- 1 teaspoon salt

Addresses:
1. In the bowl of a blender, combine the erythritol, ground paprika, chilli powder, yellow mustard, apple cider vinegar, ketchup and water. Add the salt.
2. Whisk the mixture until homogenous. Then put the pork fillets into the homogeneous mixture and mix well. Leave the meat for 20 minutes in this sauce.
3. After this, preheat the fryer to 180°C.
4. Place the pork ribs in the air fryer and cook for 40 minutes. Turn the pork ribs over on the other side after 20 minutes of cooking.

453. Rack of lamb in saffron sauce

Servings: 4

Cooking time: 1 hour and 10 minutes
Ingredients:
- ½ teaspoon crumbled saffron strands
- 1 cup plain Greek yoghurt
- 1 teaspoon lemon zest
- 2 cloves garlic, minced
- 2 rack of lamb, rib bones separated
- 2 tablespoons olive oil
- Salt and pepper to taste

Addresses:
1. Preheat the fryer to 200°C.
2. Place the grill pan attachment on the air fryer.
3. Season the lamb meat with salt and pepper to taste. Set aside.
4. In a bowl, combine the rest of the ingredients.
5. Brush the mixture over the lamb.
6. Place on the grill and cook for 1 hour and 10 minutes.

454. Creamy pork schnitzel

Servings: 2
Cooking time: 10 minutes
Ingredients:
- 225 grams of pork chops (about 115 grams per chop)
- 1 teaspoon sunflower oil
- 1 beaten egg
- 1 tablespoon of cream
- ½ cup coconut flour
- ½ teaspoon ground black pepper
- ½ teaspoon salt

Addresses:
1. Beat the pork chops with a kitchen hammer and sprinkle with ground black pepper and salt.
2. Next, mix the egg and cream together. Dip the pork chops in the egg mixture and then dredge them in the coconut flour. Repeat the same steps once more.
3. Preheat the air fryer to 200°C.
4. Drizzle the pork chops with sunflower oil and place them in the air fryer.
5. Cook the cutlets for 5 minutes on each side.

455. Meatballs with Mexican chilli

Servings: 4
Cooking time: 25 minutes
Ingredients:
- 1 cup green onion, finely chopped
- 1/2 teaspoon parsley flakes
- 2 teaspoons of onion flakes
- 450 grams of chili sausage, shredded
- 2 tablespoons flaxseed meal
- 3 cloves garlic, finely chopped
- 1 teaspoon of Mexican oregano
- 1 tablespoon of chopped poblano chili pepper
- Fine sea salt and ground black pepper, to taste
- ½ tablespoon chopped fresh sage

Addresses:
1. Mix all ingredients in a bowl until the mixture has a uniform consistency.
2. Roll into bite-sized balls and transfer to a baking dish.
3. Cook in the preheated Air Fryer for 18 minutes.
4. Serve on wooden sticks and enjoy.

456. Wrapped pork

Servings: 2
Cooking time: 16 minutes
Ingredients:
- 225 grams of pork loin
- 4 slices of bacon
- ½ teaspoon salt
- 1 teaspoon olive oil
- ½ teaspoon chilli powder

Addresses:
1. Sprinkle the pork loin with salt and chilli powder.
2. Then wrap it in the bacon slices and drizzle with olive oil. Secure the bacon with toothpicks if necessary.
3. After this, preheat the air fryer to 190°C.
4. Place the wrapped pork loin in the air fryer and cook for 7 minutes.
5. Carefully turn the meat on the other side and cook for a further 9 minutes.
6. When the meat is cooked, remove the toothpicks (if used) and cut into slices.

457. Mint lamb mix

Servings: 4
Cooking time: 24 minutes
Ingredients:
- 8 lamb chops
- Pinch of salt and black pepper
- 1 cup chopped mint
- 1 clove garlic, minced
- Juice of 1 lemon
- 2 tablespoons olive oil

Addresses:
1. In a blender, combine all ingredients except the lamb and pulse well.
2. Brush the lamb chops with the mint sauce, place them in the basket of your air fryer and cook at 200°C for minutes on each side.
3. Divide between the plates and serve.

458. Peach purée on ribs

Servings: 2
Cooking time: 45 minutes
Ingredients:
- ¼ cup balsamic vinegar
- 1 cup peach puree
- 1 tablespoon paprika

- 1 teaspoon thyme
- T-bone steak 450 grams
- 2 teaspoons lemon pepper seasoning
- Salt and pepper to taste

Addresses:
1. Place all ingredients in a Ziploc bag and marinate in the refrigerator for at least 2 hours.
2. Preheat the fryer to 200°C.
3. Place the grill pan attachment on the air fryer.
4. Roast for 20 minutes and turn the meat halfway through cooking.

459. Irish whiskey fillet

Servings: 6
Cooking time: 25 minutes + marinating time
Ingredients:
- 900 grams of sirloin steaks
- 1 ½ tablespoons tamari sauce
- 1/3 teaspoon of cayenne pepper
- 1/3 teaspoon ground ginger
- 2 cloves garlic, thinly sliced
- 2 tablespoons Irish whiskey
- 2 tablespoons olive oil
- Fine sea salt, to taste

Addresses:
1. First, add all the ingredients, except the olive oil and the fillet, to a resealable plastic bag.
2. Toss the sirloin steak and leave to marinate for a couple of hours. Then drizzle the sirloin steaks with tablespoons of olive oil.
3. Roast for approximately 22 minutes, turning halfway through the roasting time. Bon appetit!

460. Asian beef patties

Servings: 4
Cooking time: 20 minutes
Ingredients:
- 340 grams of lean minced meat
- 1 tablespoon soy sauce
- 1 teaspoon Dijon mustard
- A pinch of liquid smoke
- 1 teaspoon shallot powder
- 1 clove garlic, minced
- ½ teaspoon cumin powder
- ¼ cup chopped onions
- ⅓ teaspoon sea salt flakes
- ⅓ teaspoon freshly ground mixed peppercorns
- 1 teaspoon celery seeds
- 1 teaspoon parsley flakes

Addresses:
1. Mix all the ingredients in a bowl with your hands, combining everything well.
2. Take four equal amounts of the mixture and mould each into a hamburger shape.
3. Use the back of a spoon to create a shallow indentation in the centre of each patty. This will prevent them from puffing up during the cooking process.
4. Lightly coat all sides of the patties with cooking spray.
5. Place each in the Air Fryer and cook for approximately 12 minutes at 180°C.
6. Test with a meat thermometer - the burgers are ready when they have reached 70°C.
7. Serve them on buttered rolls with sauces and toppings of your choice.

Fish and seafood recipes

461. Grilled tilapia

Servings: 4
Cooking time: 10 minutes
Ingredients:
- 450 grams of tilapia fillets
- ½ teaspoon lemon pepper
- Salt to taste

Addresses:
1. Spray the basket of the Air Fryer with a little cooking spray.
2. Place the tilapia fillets in the basket and sprinkle with lemon pepper and salt.
3. Cook at 200°C for 7 minutes.
4. Serve with a side dish of vegetables.

462. Salmon with tarragon and spring onions

Servings: 4
Cooking time: 15 minutes
Ingredients:
- Salmon fillet 340 grams
- 2 spring onions, chopped
- 1 tablespoon melted ghee
- 1 teaspoon peppercorns
- ½ teaspoon salt
- ½ teaspoon ground black pepper
- 1 teaspoon tarragon
- ½ teaspoon dried coriander

Addresses:
1. Cut the salmon fillet into 4 portions.
2. Then make the parchment pockets and place the fish fillets in them.
3. Sprinkle the salmon with salt, ground black pepper, tarragon and dried coriander.
4. Top the fish with spring onions, peppercorns and ghee.
5. Preheat the air fryer to 195°C.
6. Place the salmon pockets in the air fryer in a single layer and cook.

463. Fillet of cod in beer sauce

Servings: 2
Cooking time: 15 minutes

Ingredients:
- ½ cup plain flour
- ¾ teaspoon baking powder
- 1 ¼ cup lager beer
- 2 cod fillets
- 2 beaten eggs
- Salt and pepper to taste

Addresses:
1. Preheat the fryer to 200°C.
2. Dry the fish fillets and set aside.
3. In a bowl, combine the rest of the ingredients to create a dough.
4. Dip the fillets in the batter and place them on the double-layer grid.
5. Cooking.

464. Salted fish fillets

Servings: 4
Cooking time: 15 minutes
Ingredients:
- 1 cup crushed crackers
- ¼ cup extra virgin olive oil
- 1 teaspoon garlic powder
- ½ teaspoon shallot powder
- 1 egg, well beaten
- 4 white fish fillets
- Salt and ground black pepper to taste
- Fresh Italian parsley to serve

Addresses:
1. In a shallow bowl, combine the crushed crackers and olive oil.
2. In a separate bowl, mix together the garlic powder, shallot powder and beaten egg.
3. Sprinkle a good amount of salt and pepper over the fish, before dipping each fillet into the egg mixture.
4. Coat the fillets with the crumb mixture.
5. Fry the fish in the open air at 190°C for 10 - 12 minutes.
6. Serve with fresh parsley.

465. Cod with basil and paprika

Servings: 4
Cooking time: 15 minutes
Ingredients:
- 4 fillets of cod, boneless
- 1 teaspoon red pepper flakes
- ½ teaspoon hot paprika
- 2 tablespoons olive oil
- 1 teaspoon basil, dried
- Salt and black pepper to taste

Addresses:
1. In a bowl, combine the cod with all the other ingredients and mix.
2. Place the fish in the basket of your air fryer and cook at 190°C for minutes.
3. Divide the cod between the plates and serve.

466. Hot tilapia

Servings: 2
Cooking time: 9 minutes
Ingredients:
- 1 chopped chilli
- 1 teaspoon chilli flakes
- 1 tablespoon sesame oil
- ½ teaspoon salt
- Tilapia fillet 280 grams
- ¼ teaspoon onion powder

Addresses:
1. In a shallow bowl, combine chilli, chilli flakes, salt and onion powder. Gently whisk the mixture and add sesame oil.
2. Next, cut the tilapia fillet and sprinkle it with the chilli mixture. Massage the fish gently with your fingertips and leave to marinate for a few minutes.
3. Preheat the air fryer to 200°C.
4. Place the tilapia fillets in the basket of the air fryer and cook for 5 minutes. Then turn the fish over on the other side and cook for a further 4 minutes.

467. Cajun fish cakes with cheese

Servings: 4
Cooking time: 30 minutes
Ingredients:
- 2 catfish fillets
- 1 cup all-purpose flour
- 85 grams of butter
- 1 teaspoon baking powder
- 1 teaspoon bicarbonate of soda
- 1/2 cup buttermilk
- 1 teaspoon Cajun seasoning
- 1 cup grated Swiss cheese

Addresses:
1. Bring a pan of salted water to the boil. Boil the fish fillets for 5 minutes or until opaque. Flake the fish into small pieces.
2. Mix the rest of the ingredients in a bowl, add the fish and mix until well combined. Form the fish mixture into patty shapes.
3. Bake in the preheated Air Fryer at 200°C for 15 minutes. Work in batches. Enjoy.

468. Rice Flour Coated Shrimp

Servings: 3
Cooking time: 20 minutes
Ingredients:
- 3 tablespoons rice flour
- 450 grams of shrimps, peeled and deveined
- 2 tablespoons olive oil
- 1 teaspoon icing sugar
- Salt and black pepper, as needed

Addresses:
1. Preheat the fryer to 160°C and grease the fryer basket.
2. Mix the rice flour, olive oil, sugar, salt and black pepper in a bowl.
3. Stir in the prawns and transfer half of the prawns to the fryer basket.

4. Cook for about 10 minutes, turning once in between.
5. Divide the mixture among serving plates and repeat with the rest of the mixture.

469. Salmon and garlic sauce

Servings: 4
Cooking time: 15 minutes
Ingredients:
- 3 tablespoons chopped parsley
- 4 salmon fillets, boneless
- ¼ cup ghee, melted
- 2 cloves garlic, minced
- 4 chopped shallots
- Salt and black pepper to taste

Addresses:
1. Heat a frying pan that fits the air fryer with the ghee over medium-high heat, add the garlic, shallots, salt, pepper and parsley, stir and cook for 5 minutes.
2. Add the salmon fillets, stir gently, place the pan in the air fryer and cook at 190°C for a few minutes.
3. Divide among the plates and serve.

470. Golden cod nuggets

Servings: 4
Cooking time: 20 minutes
Ingredients:
- 2 tablespoons olive oil
- 2 beaten eggs
- 1 cup breadcrumbs
- A pinch of salt
- 1 cup flour

Addresses:
1. Preheat the fryer to 200°C.
2. Mix the breadcrumbs, olive oil and salt in a bowl until combined. In another bowl, place the eggs, and the flour in a third bowl.
3. Dredge the cod fillets in the flour, eggs and breadcrumb mixture.
4. Place the fillets in the fryer basket and cook for 9 minutes. After 5 minutes, quickly turn the chicken nuggets over.
5. Once done, remove to a serving plate.

471. Fish with Garam Masala sauce

Servings: 2
Cooking time: 25 minutes
Ingredients:
- 2 teaspoons olive oil
- 1/4 cup coconut milk
- 1/2 teaspoon cayenne pepper
- 1 teaspoon Garam masala
- 1/4 teaspoon Kala namak (Indian black salt)
- 1/2 teaspoon grated fresh ginger
- 1 clove garlic, minced
- 2 catfish fillets
- 1/4 cup coriander, coarsely chopped

Addresses:
1. Preheat your Air Fryer to 200°C.
2. Then, spray the baking sheet with non-stick cooking spray.
3. In a bowl, whisk together the olive oil, milk, cayenne pepper, Garam masala, Kala namak, ginger and garlic.
4. Coat the catfish fillets with the Garam masala mixture. Cook the catfish fillets in the preheated air fryer for approximately 18 minutes, turning them over halfway through cooking.
5. Garnish with fresh coriander and serve over hot noodles if desired.

472. Tasty crab croquettes

Servings: 4
Cooking time: 30 minutes
Ingredients:
- 1,350 kilograms of crab meat
- 3 beaten egg whites
- ⅓ cup sour cream
- ⅓ cup mayonnaise
- 1 ½ tablespoons olive oil
- 1 red pepper, finely chopped
- ⅓ cup chopped red onion
- 2 ½ tablespoons chopped celery
- ½ teaspoon chopped tarragon
- ½ teaspoon of chopped chives
- 1 teaspoon of chopped parsley
- 1 teaspoon cayenne pepper

For breading you need:
- 1 ½ cup breadcrumbs
- 2 teaspoons olive oil
- 1 cup flour
- 4 beaten eggs
- Salt to taste

Addresses:
1. Place a skillet over medium heat on the cooker, add ½ tablespoon of olive oil, the red pepper, onion and celery. Sauté for 5 minutes or until sweaty and translucent.
2. Turn off the heat. Add the breadcrumbs, remaining olive oil and salt to a food processor. Blend evenly and set aside. In 2 separate bowls, add the flour and the 4 eggs respectively, set aside.
3. In a separate bowl, add the crabmeat, mayonnaise, egg whites, sour cream, tarragon, chives, parsley, cayenne pepper and sautéed celery and mix evenly. Form the mixture into bite-sized balls and place on a plate.
4. Preheat the fryer to 200°C.
5. Dip each crab meatball (croquettes) into the egg mixture and press them into the breadcrumb mixture.
6. Place the croquettes in the fryer basket, avoiding overcrowding.

7. Close the fryer and cook for 10 minutes or until golden brown. Remove and plate them.
8. Serve the crab croquettes with tomato sauce and a side of chips.

473. Trout salad with cream

Servings: 2
Cooking time: 20 minutes
Ingredients:
- 225 grams skinless trout fillets
- 2 tablespoons prepared and drained horseradish
- 1/4 cup mayonnaise
- 1 tablespoon fresh lemon juice
- 1 teaspoon mustard
- Salt and ground white pepper to taste
- 170 grams of chickpeas, canned and drained
- 1 red onion, thinly sliced
- 1 cup Iceberg lettuce, cut into pieces

Addresses:
1. Spray the Air Fryer basket with cooking spray.
2. Cook the trout fillets in the preheated Air Fryer at 200°C for 10 minutes or until opaque. Be sure to turn them over halfway through the cooking time.
3. Cut the fish into bite-sized pieces and place in the refrigerator to cool. Mix the fish with the rest of the ingredients - bon appetit!

474. Tilapia Ham

Servings: 4
Cooking time: 10 minutes
Ingredients:
- Tilapia fillet of 1,170 kilograms
- 4 slices of ham
- 1 teaspoon sunflower oil
- ½ teaspoon salt
- 1 teaspoon dried rosemary

Addresses:
1. Cut the tilapia into 4 portions. Sprinkle each portion of fish with salt, dried rosemary and sunflower oil.
2. Then carefully wrap the fish fillets in the ham slices and secure them with toothpicks.
3. Preheat the air fryer to 200°C.
4. Place the wrapped tilapia in the basket of the air fryer in a single layer and cook for minutes. Gently turn the fish over onto the other side after 5 minutes of cooking.

475. Creamy salmon

Servings: 2
Cooking time: 20 minutes
Ingredients:
- 340 grams salmon, cut into 6 pieces
- ¼ cup yogurt
- 1 tablespoon of olive oil
- 1 tablespoon chopped dill
- 3 tablespoons sour cream
- Salt to taste

Addresses:
1. Sprinkle a little salt over the salmon.
2. Place the salmon slices in the basket of the Air Fryer and add a drizzle of olive oil.
3. Air fry the salmon at 140°C for 10 minutes.
4. Meanwhile, mix together the cream, dill, yoghurt and salt.
5. Serve the salmon on a plate and pour the creamy sauce on top. Serve hot.

476. Pistachio-crusted salmon

Servings: 1
Cooking time: 15 minutes
Ingredients:
- 1 teaspoon mustard
- 3 tablespoons pistachios
- A pinch of sea salt
- A pinch of garlic powder
- Pinch of black pepper
- 1 teaspoon lemon juice
- 1 teaspoon grated Parmesan cheese
- 1 teaspoon olive oil

Addresses:
1. Preheat the fryer to 180°C, and whisk in the mustard and lemon juice.
2. Season the salmon with salt, pepper and garlic powder. Brush olive oil on all sides. Spread salmon with mustard mixture.
3. Finely chop the pistachios and combine with the Parmesan cheese, sprinkle over the salmon.
4. Place the salmon in the fryer basket, skin side down. Cook for 1 minute, or as desired.

477. Salmon with prawns and pasta

Servings: 4
Cooking time: 18 minutes
Ingredients:
- 1,115 kilograms of pasta
- 4 tablespoons pesto, divided
- 4 (115 grams) salmon fillets
- 2 tablespoons olive oil
- 225 grams chopped cherry tomatoes
- 8 large prawns, peeled and deveined
- 2 tablespoons fresh lemon juice
- 2 tablespoons chopped fresh thyme

Addresses:
1. In a large saucepan of boiling salted water, add the pasta and cook for about 8 minutes or until desired doneness.
2. Meanwhile, in the bottom of a baking dish, spread 1 tablespoon of pesto.
3. Place the salmon fillets and tomatoes on top of the pesto in a single layer and drizzle evenly with the oil.
4. Now add the prawns on top in a single layer.

5. Drizzle with lemon juice and sprinkle with thyme.
6. Set the temperature of the air fryer to 200°C.
7. Place the baking dish in the air fryer and fry for about 8 minutes.
8. Once done, remove the salmon mixture from the air fryer.
9. Drain the pasta and transfer it to a large bowl.
10. Add the rest of the pesto and mix to coat well.
11. Add the pasta evenly on each plate and top with the salmon mixture.
12. Serve immediately.

478. Cajun Spiced Vegetable and Shrimp Cake

Servings: 4
Cooking time: 20 minutes
Ingredients:
- 1 bag of frozen mixed vegetables
- 1 tablespoon gluten-free Cajun seasoning
- Olive oil spray
- Season with salt and pepper
- Peeled and deveined small prawns (normal size bag of about 50-80 small prawns)

Addresses:
1. Lightly grease the air fryer pan with cooking spray. Add all ingredients and toss well to coat. Season generously with pepper and salt.
2. Cook at 165°C for 10 minutes. Halfway through the cooking time, stir.
3. Cook for 10 minutes at 0oF.
4. Serve and enjoy.

479. Old bay and dijon seasoned crab cakes

Servings: 2
Cooking time: 10 minutes
Ingredients:
- ¼ cup chopped green onion
- ½ cup panko
- 1 ½ teaspoon old bay seasoning
- 1 teaspoon Dijon mustard
- 1 teaspoon Worcestershire sauce
- 450 grams of crab meat
- 2 large eggs
- Salt and pepper to taste

Addresses:
1. Preheat the fryer to 200°C.
2. Place the grill pan attachment on the air fryer.
3. In a bowl, combine all ingredients until well incorporated.
4. Use your hands to form small crab patties.
5. Place on the grill pan and cook for 10 minutes.
6. Turn the crab cakes halfway through cooking so that they brown evenly.

480. Salmon with lemon and chilli

Servings: 4
Cooking time: 17 minutes
Ingredients:
- 900 grams salmon fillet, skinned and boned
- 2 lemon juice
- 1 orange juice
- 1 tablespoon of olive oil
- 1 bunch fresh dill
- 1 chilli, sliced
- Pepper
- Salt

Addresses:
1. Preheat the air fryer to 160°C.
2. Place the salmon fillets in the pan of the air fryer and drizzle with olive oil, lemon juice and orange juice.
3. Sprinkle the chilli slices over the salmon and season with pepper and salt.
4. Place the pan in the air fryer and cook for 15-17 minutes.
5. Garnish with dill and serve.

481. Curried halibut fillets

Servings: 4
Cooking time: 20 minutes
Ingredients:
- 2 medium halibut fillets
- 1 teaspoon curry powder
- 1/2 teaspoon ground coriander
- Kosher salt and freshly ground mixed peppercorns, to taste
- 1 ½ tablespoons olive oil
- 1/2 cup grated Parmesan cheese
- 2 eggs
- 1/2 teaspoon hot paprika
- A few drops of Tabasco sauce

Addresses:
1. Set your Air Fryer to cook at 185°C.
2. Next, take two mixing bowls. In the first bowl, combine the Parmesan cheese with the olive oil.
3. In another shallow bowl, beat the egg well. Then sprinkle the halibut fillets with the Tabasco sauce, add the paprika, curry, coriander, salt and peppercorns.
4. Dip each fish fillet in the beaten egg, now dip it in the parmesan mixture.
5. Place in a single layer in the cooking basket of the Air Fryer. Cook for 10 minutes, working in batches. Serve over cream salad if desired - bon appetit!

482. Tuna stuffed potato sticks

Servings: 4
Cooking time: 16 minutes
Ingredients:
- 4 starchy potatoes, soaked for approx. 30 minutes and drained
- 1 can (170 g) tuna, drained

- 2 tablespoons plain Greek yoghurt
- 1 spring onion, chopped and divided
- 1 tablespoon capers
- ½ tablespoon olive oil
- 1 teaspoon red chilli powder
- Salt and black pepper, to taste

Addresses:
1. Preheat the fryer to 180°C and grease the fryer basket.
2. Place the potatoes in the fryer basket and cook for about 30 minutes.
3. Meanwhile, combine the tuna, yoghurt, red chilli powder, salt, black pepper and half the spring onion in a bowl and mash the mixture well.
4. Remove the potatoes from the air fryer and carefully cut them in half lengthwise.
5. Fill the potatoes with the tuna mixture and top with the capers and the remaining spring onion.
6. Place on a platter and serve immediately.

483. Spicy prawn kebab

Servings: 4
Cooking time: 25 minutes
Ingredients:
- 680 grams jumbo shrimps, cleaned, peeled and deveined
- 450 grams of cherry tomatoes
- 2 tablespoons melted butter
- 1 tablespoon Sriracha sauce
- Sea salt and ground black pepper, to taste
- 1/2 teaspoon dried oregano
- 1/2 teaspoon dried basil
- 1 teaspoon dried parsley flakes
- 1/2 teaspoon marjoram
- 1/2 teaspoon of mustard seeds

Addresses:
1. Mix all the ingredients in a bowl until the prawns and tomatoes are coated on all sides.
2. Soak the wooden skewers in water for 15 minutes.
3. Thread the jumbo prawns and cherry tomatoes onto the skewers.
4. Cook in the preheated Air Fryer at 200°C for 5 minutes, working in batches. Enjoy!

484. Trout and shallots

Servings: 4
Cooking time: 12 minutes
Ingredients:
- 4 fillets of trout, boneless
- Juice of 1 lime
- ½ cup melted butter
- ½ cup olive oil
- 3 cloves garlic, minced
- 6 chopped shallots
- Pinch of salt and black pepper

Addresses:
1. In a frying pan that fits the air fryer, combine the fish with the shallots and the rest of the ingredients, mix gently.
2. Place the pan in the machine and cook at 200°C, turning the fish halfway through.
3. Divide among plates and serve with a side salad.

485. Smoked halibut and eggs on brioche

Servings: 4
Cooking time: 25 minutes
Ingredients:
- 4 brioche buns
- 450 grams of smoked halibut, minced
- 4 eggs
- 1 teaspoon dried thyme
- 1 teaspoon basil, dried
- Salt and black pepper, to taste

Addresses:
1. Cut off the top of each brioche, then remove the inside to make the shells.
2. Place the prepared brioche shells in the lightly greased baking basket.
3. Drizzle with cooking oil, add the halibut. Crack an egg into each brioche shell, sprinkle with thyme, basil, salt and black pepper.
4. Bake in the preheated Air Fryer at 160°C for 20 minutes, enjoy!

486. Salmon fillets, plain

Servings: 2
Cooking time: 7 minutes
Ingredients:
- 2 salmon fillets
- 2 teaspoons olive oil
- 2 teaspoons paprika
- Pepper
- Salt

Addresses:
1. Rub the salmon fillet with oil, paprika, pepper and salt.
2. Place the salmon fillets in the basket of the air fryer and cook at 200°C for 7 minutes.
3. Serve and enjoy.

487. Grilled fish and celery burgers

Servings: 4
Cooking time: 10 minutes + cooling time
Ingredients:
- 2 tins of canned tuna
- 2 stalks celery, trimmed and finely chopped
- 1 beaten egg
- 1/2 cup grated Parmesan cheese
- 1 teaspoon wholegrain mustard
- 1/2 teaspoon sea salt
- 1/4 teaspoon of freshly ground black peppercorns
- 1 teaspoon paprika

Addresses:

1. Mix all the above ingredients in the order given, mix to combine well and shape into four cakes, chill for 50 minutes.
2. Place them in an Air Fryer pan. Spray each cake with non-stick cooking spray, coating all sides.
3. Roast for 5 minutes, then pause the machine, turn the cakes over and set the timer for a further 3 minutes. Serve over mashed potatoes.

488. Codfish pie

Servings: 4
Cooking time: 14 minutes
Ingredients:
- 450 grams cod fillets
- 1 egg
- 1/3 cup coconut, shredded and chopped
- 1 spring onion, finely chopped
- 2 tablespoons fresh parsley, chopped
- 1 teaspoon fresh lime zest, finely grated
- 1 teaspoon red chilli paste
- Salt, to taste
- 1 tablespoon fresh lime juice

Addresses:
1. Preheat the fryer to 190°C and grease the fryer basket.
2. Place the cod fillets, lime zest, egg, chilli paste, salt and lime juice in a food processor and pulse until smooth.
3. Transfer the cod mixture to a bowl and add 2 tablespoons of coconut, spring onion and parsley.
4. Make 12 round cakes of equal size with the mixture.
5. Put the remaining coconut in a shallow dish and cover the cod cakes with it.
6. Place the cakes in the fryer basket and cook for about 7 minutes.
7. Repeat with the rest of the cod cakes and serve hot.

489. Fish packages

Servings: 2
Cooking time: 15 minutes
Ingredients:
- 2 cod fillets
- 1/2 teaspoon dried tarragon
- 1/2 cup peppers, sliced
- 1/4 cup celery, julienned
- 1/2 cup julienned carrots
- 1 tablespoon of olive oil
- 1 tablespoon lemon juice
- 2 tablespoons melted butter
- Pepper
- Salt

Addresses:
1. In a bowl, combine the butter, lemon juice, tarragon and salt. Add the vegetables and mix well. Set aside.
2. Take two pieces of parchment paper to fold the vegetables and fish.
3. Spray the fish with cooking spray and season with pepper and salt.
4. Place a fish fillet on each piece of parchment paper and cover with the vegetables.
5. Fold the parchment paper around the fish and vegetables.
6. Place the vegetable fish packets in the basket of the air fryer and cook at 180°C for 15 minutes.
7. Serve and enjoy.

490. Branzino with lemon

Servings: 4
Cooking time: 8 minutes
Ingredients:
- 450 grams branzino, cut and washed
- 1 teaspoon Cajun seasoning
- 1 tablespoon sesame oil
- 1 tablespoon lemon juice
- 1 teaspoon salt

Addresses:
1. Rub the branzino with salt and Cajun seasoning carefully.
2. Then sprinkle the fish with the lemon juice and sesame oil.
3. Preheat the air fryer to 190°C.
4. Place the fish in the air fryer and cook for 8 minutes.

491. Shrimps with cheese

Servings: 4
Cooking time: 5 minutes
Ingredients:
- 395 grams of peeled prawns
- 2 beaten eggs
- ¼ cup heavy cream
- 1 teaspoon salt
- 1 teaspoon ground black pepper
- 115 grams Monterey Jack cheese, grated
- 5 tablespoons coconut flour
- 1 tablespoon lemon juice, for garnish

Addresses:
1. In the bowl of a blender, mix the cream, salt and ground black pepper. Add the eggs and beat the mixture until smooth.
2. Next, mix in the coconut flour and Monterey Jack cheese.
3. Dip the prawns in the cream mixture and dredge them in the coconut flour mixture. Then dip the prawns back into the egg mixture and dredge in the coconut flour.
4. Preheat the fryer to 200°C.
5. Place the prawns in the fryer in a single layer and cook for 5 minutes. Repeat the same step with the rest of the prawns. Drizzle the bang-bang shrimp with lemon juice.

492. Classic Parmesan Fish Fillets

Servings: 4
Cooking time: 15 minutes
Ingredients:
- 1 cup grated Parmesan
- 1 teaspoon garlic powder
- 1/2 teaspoon shallot powder
- 1 egg, well beaten
- 4 white fish fillets
- Salt and ground black pepper to taste
- Fresh Italian parsley, to serve

Addresses:
1. Place the Parmesan cheese in a shallow bowl.
2. In another bowl, combine the garlic powder, shallot powder and beaten egg.
3. Generously season the fish fillets with salt and pepper. Dip each fillet in the beaten egg.
4. Then, roll the steaks over the Parmesan mixture. Set your Air Fryer to cook at 185°C.
5. Air cool for 10 to 12 minutes.
6. Serve garnished with fresh parsley and enjoy.

493. Glazed Halibut

Servings: 3
Cooking time: 15 minutes
Ingredients:
- 1 clove garlic, minced
- ¼ teaspoon fresh ginger, finely grated
- ½ cup cooking wine
- ½ cup low-sodium soy sauce
- ¼ cup fresh orange juice
- 2 tablespoons lime juice
- ¼ cup sugar
- ¼ teaspoon crushed red pepper flakes
- 450 grams of halibut fillet

Addresses:
1. In a medium saucepan, add the garlic, ginger, wine, soy sauce, juices, sugar and red pepper flakes and bring to a boil.
2. Cook for about 3-4 minutes, stirring continuously.
3. Remove the pan of marinade from the heat and leave to cool.
4. In a small bowl, add half of the marinade and set aside in the refrigerator.
5. In a resealable bag, add the remaining marinade and halibut fillet.
6. Close the bag and shake to coat well.
7. Refrigerate for about 30 minutes.
8. Set the temperature of the air fryer to 200°C. Grease the air fryer basket.
9. Place the halibut fillet in the prepared fryer basket.
10. Fry in the open air for about 9-11 minutes.
11. Remove from the fryer and place the halibut fillet on a platter.
12. Cut the fillet into 3 equal sized pieces and coat with the remaining glaze.
13. Serve immediately.

494. Summer fish packages

Servings: 2
Cooking time: 20 minutes
Ingredients:
- 2 fillets of snapper
- 1 shallot, peeled and cut into slices
- 2 cloves garlic, halved
- 1 pepper, sliced
- 1 small serrano pepper, cut into slices
- 1 tomato, sliced
- 1 tablespoon of olive oil
- 1/4 teaspoon freshly ground black pepper
- 1/2 teaspoon paprika
- Sea salt, to taste
- 2 bay leaves

Addresses:
1. Place two sheets of parchment on a work surface. Place the fish in the centre of one side of the parchment paper.
2. Top with the shallot, garlic, peppers and tomato. Drizzle the olive oil over the fish and vegetables. Season with black pepper, paprika and salt. Add the bay leaves.
3. Fold the other half of the parchment. Now fold the paper around the edges tightly and make a crescent shape, sealing the fish inside.
4. Bake in the preheated Air Fryer at 200°C for 15 minutes. Serve hot.

495. Cod with mustard

Servings: 4
Cooking time: 14 minutes
Ingredients:
- 1 cup grated Parmesan
- 4 fillets of cod, boneless
- Salt and black pepper to taste
- 1 tablespoon mustard

Addresses:
1. In a bowl, mix the Parmesan with the salt, pepper and mustard and stir.
2. Rub this onto the cod, place the fish in the basket of the air fryer and cook at 185°C for 7 minutes on each side.
3. Divide among the plates and serve with a side salad.

496. Rosemary and garlic prawns

Servings: 2
Cooking time: 15 minutes
Ingredients:
- 3 cloves garlic, minced
- 1 sprig of rosemary, chopped
- ½ tablespoon melted butter
- Salt and pepper, to taste

Addresses:

1. Combine the garlic, butter, rosemary, salt and pepper in a bowl. Add the prawns to the bowl and toss to coat well.
2. Cover the bowl and refrigerate for one hour. Preheat the air fryer to 180°C, and cook for 6 minutes.
3. Increase the temperature to 200°C, and cook for another minute.

497. Recipe of sea bass with honey

Servings: 2
Cooking time: 20 minutes
Ingredients:
- 2 fillets of sea bass
- Zest of 1/2 orange, grated
- Juice of 1/2 orange
- 2 tablespoons mustard
- 2 teaspoons honey
- 2 tablespoons olive oil
- 225 grams of canned lentils, drained
- A small bunch of dill, chopped
- 55 grams of watercress
- 1 small bunch of parsley, chopped
- Pinch of salt and black pepper

Addresses:
1. Season the fish fillets with salt and pepper, add the zest and juice of the orange, rub with a tablespoon of oil, with the honey and mustard, rub, transfer to your air fryer and cook at 180°C, for 10 minutes, turning halfway through.
2. Meanwhile, put the lentils in a small saucepan, heat over medium heat, add the remaining oil, watercress, dill and parsley, stir well and divide among the plates. Add the fish fillets and serve immediately.

498. Hong Kong Cod Fillet Recipe

Servings: 2
Cooking time: 15 minutes
Ingredients:
- 2 cod fillets
- 250 millilitres of water
- 3 tablespoons coconut aminos
- 3 tablespoons coconut oil
- 5 slices of ginger
- A pinch of sesame oil
- Green onions for garnish

Addresses:
1. Preheat the air fryer for 5 minutes.
2. Place all the ingredients, except the green onions, in a baking dish.
3. Transfer to the air fryer and cook for 15 minutes at 200°C.
4. Garnish with green onions.

499. Catfish bites

Servings: 4
Cooking time: 10 minutes
Ingredients:
- ¼ cup coconut flakes
- 3 tablespoons coconut flour
- 1 teaspoon salt
- 3 beaten eggs
- 280 grams of catfish fillet
- Cooking spray

Addresses:
1. Cut the catfish fillet into small pieces (nuggets) and sprinkle with salt.
2. Then dip the catfish pieces in the egg and roll them in the coconut flour. Dip the fish pieces back into the egg and roll them in the coconut flakes.
3. Preheat the air fryer to 195°C.
4. Place the catfish nuggets in the fryer basket and cook for 6 minutes. Turn the nuggets on the other side and cook for a further 4 minutes.

500. Cajun lemon salmon

Servings: 1
Cooking time: 15 minutes
Ingredients:
- 1 salmon fillet
- 1 teaspoon Cajun seasoning
- Juice of ½ lemon
- ¼ teaspoon sugar
- 2 lemon wedges, to serve

Addresses:
1. Preheat the Air Fryer to 180°C.
2. Combine the lemon juice and sugar.
3. Coat the salmon with the mixture containing the sugar.
4. Coat the salmon with the Cajun seasoning.
5. Line the base of your fryer with a sheet of parchment paper.
6. Transfer the salmon to the fryer and cook for 7 minutes.

501. Fish fillets

Servings: 4
Cooking time: 25 minutes
Ingredients:
- 4 fish fillets
- 1 beaten egg
- 1 cup breadcrumbs
- 4 tablespoons olive oil
- Pepper and salt to taste

Addresses:
1. Preheat the Air Fryer to 180°C.
2. In a shallow dish, mix the breadcrumbs, oil, pepper and salt.
3. Pour the beaten egg into a second dish.
4. Dip each fish fillet in the egg before dredging in the breadcrumbs. Place them in the basket of the Air Fryer.
5. Allow to cook in the Air Fryer for 12 minutes.

502. Tuna au gratin with herbs

Servings: 4
Cooking time: 20 minutes

Ingredients:
- 1 tablespoon melted butter
- 1 medium-sized leek, thinly sliced
- 1 tablespoon chicken stock
- 1 tablespoon dry white wine
- 450 grams of tuna
- 1/2 teaspoon crushed red pepper flakes
- Sea salt and ground black pepper, to taste
- 1/2 teaspoon dried rosemary
- 1/2 teaspoon dried basil
- 1/2 teaspoon dried thyme
- 2 small ripe tomatoes, pureed
- 1 cup grated Parmesan cheese

Addresses:
1. Melt 2 tablespoons of butter in a frying pan over medium-high heat. Cook the leek and garlic until tender and aromatic. Add the stock and wine to deglaze the pan.
2. Preheat your Air Fryer to 185°C.
3. Grease a casserole dish with the remaining 1/2 tablespoon of melted butter. Place the fish in the pan. Add the seasonings. Top with the sautéed leek mixture.
4. Add the tomato puree. Cook for 10 minutes in the preheated Air Fryer. Top with grated Parmesan cheese, cook for a further 7 minutes until the crumbs are golden brown, bon appetit!

503. Herbed squid rings

Servings: 4
Cooking time: 4 minutes
Ingredients:
- 1 chopped chilli
- ¼ teaspoon salt
- 280 grams of squid
- ½ teaspoon dried coriander
- ½ teaspoon dried parsley
- 1 teaspoon apple cider vinegar
- 1 teaspoon melted butter
- ¼ teaspoon ground coriander
- 1 teaspoon sesame oil

Addresses:
1. Trim and wash the squid. Then cut into rings and sprinkle with salt, dried coriander, ground coriander and apple cider vinegar.
2. Add sesame oil and stir in the squid rings.
3. Preheat the air fryer to 200°C.
4. Place the squid rings in the basket of the air fryer and cook for 2 minutes.
5. When the time is up, shake well and cook for a further 2 minutes.
6. Transfer the squid rings into the large serving dish and drizzle with butter.

504. Fried Branzino

Servings: 4
Cooking time: 20 minutes
Ingredients:
- 4 medium-sized fillets of branzino, boneless
- 1/2 cup chopped parsley
- 2 tablespoons olive oil
- Pinch of red pepper flakes, crushed
- Zest of 1 lemon, grated
- Zest of 1 orange, grated
- Juice of 1/2 lemon
- Juice of 1/2 orange
- Salt and black pepper to taste

Addresses:
1. In a large bowl, combine the fish fillets with the lemon zest, orange zest, lemon juice, orange juice, salt, pepper, oil and pepper flakes. Stir well.
2. Transfer the fillets to your air fryer preheated to 180°C and bake, turning the fillets once.
3. Divide the fish among the plates, sprinkle with parsley and serve immediately.

505. Spicy shrimps

Servings: 2
Cooking time: 6 minutes
Ingredients:
- 225 grams of shrimps, peeled and deveined
- 1/2 teaspoon old bay seasoning
- 1 teaspoon cayenne pepper
- 1 tablespoon of olive oil
- 1/4 teaspoon paprika
- 1/8 teaspoon salt

Addresses:
1. Preheat the air fryer to 200°C.
2. Add all ingredients to the bowl and mix well.
3. Place the prawns in the fryer basket and cook for 6 minutes.
4. Serve and enjoy.

506. Delicious crab cakes

Servings: 4
Cooking time: 10 minutes
Ingredients:
- 225 grams of crab meat
- 2 tablespoons melted butter
- 2 teaspoons Dijon mustard
- 1 tablespoon of mayonnaise
- 1 egg, lightly beaten
- 1/2 teaspoon old bay seasoning
- 1 green onion, sliced
- 2 tablespoons chopped parsley
- 1/4 cup almond flour
- 1/4 teaspoon pepper
- 1/2 teaspoon salt

Addresses:
1. Add all the ingredients, except the butter, to a bowl and mix until well combined.
2. Make four equal patty shapes from the mixture and place them on a plate lined with parchment.

3. Place the dish in the refrigerator for a few minutes.
4. Spray the air fryer basket with cooking spray.
5. Spread melted butter on both sides of the crab patties.
6. Place the crab burgers in the fryer basket and cook for 10 minutes at 180°C.
7. Turn the burgers over halfway through.
8. Serve and enjoy.

507. Sunday fish with sticky sauce

Servings: 2
Cooking time: 20 minutes
Ingredients:
- 2 haddock fillets
- Salt and black pepper, to taste
- 1 tablespoon of olive oil
- 1 cup chicken stock
- 2 tablespoons light soy sauce
- 1 tablespoon brown sugar
- 2 tablespoons melted butter
- 1 teaspoon chopped fresh ginger
- 1 teaspoon chopped fresh garlic
- 2 corn tortillas

Addresses:
1. Pat the haddock fillets dry and season with salt and black pepper, sprinkle the sesame oil all over the fish fillets.
2. Preheat the Air Fryer to 190°C and cook the fish for 11 minutes. Cut into bite-sized pieces.
3. Meanwhile, prepare the sauce. Add the stock to a large saucepan and bring to the boil. Add the soy sauce, sugar, butter, ginger and garlic. Reduce the heat to simmer and cook until slightly reduced.
4. Add the fish pieces to the hot sauce, serve in corn tortillas and enjoy!

508. Easy to make garlic shrimps

Servings: 1
Cooking time: 6 minutes
Ingredients:
- 1 clove garlic, minced
- 1 cup raw prawns
- 1 lime, squeezed and zest removed
- Salt and pepper to taste

Addresses:
1. In a bowl, combine all ingredients and stir well.
2. Preheat the fryer to 200°C.
3. Thread the prawns onto the metal skewers that come with the double-layer grid accessory.
4. Place on the grid and cook for 6 minutes.

509. Squid with paprika and basil

Servings: 2
Cooking time: 4 minutes
Ingredients:
- 225 grams of squid, peeled and chopped
- 1 teaspoon melted ghee
- 1 teaspoon chopped fresh basil
- ½ teaspoon smoked paprika
- ½ teaspoon white pepper
- 1 tablespoon apple cider vinegar

Addresses:
1. In a shallow bowl, combine the melted ghee, basil, smoked paprika, white pepper and apple cider vinegar.
2. Then sprinkle the squid with the ghee mixture and marinate for a few minutes.
3. Now, cut the squid into slices.
4. Preheat the air fryer to 200°C.
5. Place the sliced squid in the air fryer and cook for 2 minutes. Shake the seafood well and cook for a further 2 minutes.

510. Swordfish with butter and paprika

Servings: 4
Cooking time: 12 minutes
Ingredients:
- 4 swordfish fillets, boneless
- 1 tablespoon of olive oil
- ¾ teaspoon sweet paprika
- 2 teaspoons basil, dried
- Juice of 1 lemon
- 2 tablespoons melted butter

Addresses:
1. In a bowl, combine the oil with the remaining ingredients, except the fish fillets, and whisk together.
2. Coat the fish with this mixture, place it in the basket of your air fryer and cook for 6 minutes on each side.
3. Divide among the plates and serve with a side salad.

511. Hearty small octopus salad

Servings: 3
Cooking time: 50 minutes
Ingredients:
- 1 ½ tablespoons olive oil
- 2 cloves garlic, minced
- 1 ½ tablespoons capers
- 1 ¼ tablespoons balsamic glaze
- 1 bunch parsley, coarsely chopped
- 1 bunch of small fennel, chopped
- 1 cup semi-dried tomatoes, chopped
- 1 red onion, sliced
- A handful of rocket
- Salt and pepper to taste
- ¼ cup of chopped roasted Halloumi
- 1 long red chilli, chopped
- 1 ½ cups of water

Addresses:
1. Pour the water into a saucepan and bring to the boil over medium heat on the cooker. Cut the octopus into bites and add to the boiling water for 45 seconds, drain the water.

2. Place the garlic, olive oil and octopus in a bowl. Cover the octopus with the garlic and olive oil. Leave to marinate for a few minutes.
3. Preheat the fryer.
4. Place the octopus in the fryer basket and grill for 5 minutes.
5. In a salad bowl, add the capers, halloumi, chilli, tomatoes, olives, parsley, red onion, fennel, octopus, rocket and balsamic glaze.
6. Season with salt and pepper and mix.
7. Serve with a side of toast.

512. Summer shrimp skewers

Servings: 4
Cooking time: 15 minutes + marinating time
Ingredients:
- 680 grams of shrimps
- 1/4 cup vermouth
- 2 cloves garlic, crushed
- Kosher salt to taste
- 1/4 teaspoon freshly ground black pepper
- 2 tablespoons olive oil
- 8 skewers soaked in water for 30 minutes
- 1 lemon, cut into wedges

Addresses:
1. Add the prawns, vermouth, garlic, salt, black pepper and olive oil in a ceramic bowl, leave to stand for one hour in the refrigerator.
2. Discard the marinade and dredge the prawns in flour. Thread onto skewers and transfer to the lightly greased cooking basket.
3. Cook at 200°C for 5 minutes, stirring halfway through.
4. Serve with lemon wedges and enjoy!

513. Grilled and herbed scallops

Servings: 3
Cooking time: 10 minutes
Ingredients:
- 450 grams of scallops, meat only
- 3 tablespoons of olive oil, divided
- 1 teaspoon dried sage
- Salt and pepper to taste
- 1 cup grape tomatoes, halved
- 1/3 cup basil leaves, grated

Addresses:
1. Preheat the air fryer to 200°C.
2. Place the grill pan attachment on the air fryer.
3. Season the scallops with half the olive oil, sage, salt and pepper.
4. Put them in the air fryer and roast them for 10 minutes.
5. Once cooked, serve with tomatoes and basil leaves.
6. Drizzle with the remaining olive oil and season with more salt and pepper to taste.

514. Herbed salmon

Servings: 4
Cooking time: 15 minutes
Ingredients:
- ½ teaspoon dried rosemary
- ½ teaspoon dried thyme
- ½ teaspoon dried basil
- ½ teaspoon ground coriander
- ½ teaspoon ground cumin
- ½ teaspoon ground paprika
- ½ teaspoon salt
- 450 grams of salmon
- 1 tablespoon of olive oil

Addresses:
1. In the bowl, mix the spices: dried rosemary, thyme, basil, coriander, cumin, paprika and salt.
2. Then gently rub the salmon with the spice mixture and drizzle with olive oil.
3. Preheat the air fryer to 190°C.
4. Line the basket of the air fryer with baking paper and place the prepared salmon inside.
5. Cook the fish for a few minutes or until it has a light crispy crust.

515. Tasty tuna empanadas

Servings: 6
Cooking time: 10 minutes
Ingredients:
- 2 cans (170 grams) tuna, drained
- ½ cup panko breadcrumbs
- 1 egg
- 2 tablespoons fresh parsley, chopped
- 2 teaspoons Dijon mustard
- A pinch of Tabasco sauce
- Salt and black pepper, to taste
- 1 tablespoon fresh lemon juice
- 1 tablespoon of olive oil

Addresses:
1. Preheat the fryer to 180°C and line a baking tray with aluminium foil.
2. Mix all ingredients in a large bowl until well combined.
3. Make equal sized patties from the mixture and refrigerate overnight.
4. Arrange the patties on the baking tray and transfer them to the fryer basket.
5. Cook for about 10 minutes and serve hot.

516. Creamy breaded shrimps

Servings: 3
Cooking time: 20 minutes
Ingredients:
- ¼ cup all-purpose flour
- 1 cup of panko breadcrumbs
- 450 grams of shrimps, peeled and deveined
- ½ cup mayonnaise
- ¼ cup sweet chili sauce
- 1 tablespoon Sriracha sauce

Addresses:
1. Preheat the fryer to 200°C and grease the fryer basket.
2. Put the flour in a shallow bowl and mix the mayonnaise, chilli sauce and Sriracha sauce in another bowl.
3. Put the breadcrumbs in a third bowl.
4. Dredge each shrimp in the flour, dip them in the mayonnaise mixture and finally dredge them in the breadcrumbs.
5. Place half of the coated prawns in the fryer basket and cook for about 10 minutes.
6. Divide the coated prawns among the serving plates and repeat with the rest of the mixture.

517. Halibut and caper mixture

Servings: 4
Cooking time: 18 minutes
Ingredients:
- 4 halibut fillets, boneless
- Pinch of salt and black pepper
- 1 chopped shallot
- 2 cloves garlic, minced
- 1 cup chopped parsley
- 1 tablespoon chopped chives
- 1 tablespoon lemon zest
- 1 tablespoon capers, drained and chopped
- 1 tablespoon lemon juice
- 1 tablespoon of olive oil
- 1 tablespoon melted butter

Addresses:
1. Heat a frying pan that fits your deep fryer with the oil over medium-high heat. Add the butter, shallot and garlic and sauté for 2 minutes.
2. Add the rest of the ingredients except the fish, stir and sauté for a further 3 minutes. Then add the fish, brown for one minute on each side, toss gently with the herb mixture.
3. Transfer the pan to the air fryer and cook at 190°C for 12 minutes.
4. Divide between the plates and serve.

518. Garlic shrimp mix

Servings: 3
Cooking time: 5 minutes
Ingredients:
- 450 grams of shrimps, peeled
- ½ teaspoon garlic powder
- ¼ teaspoon chopped garlic
- 1 teaspoon ground cumin
- ¼ teaspoon lemon zest
- ½ tablespoon avocado oil
- ½ teaspoon dried parsley

Addresses:
1. In the bowl, mix the prawns, garlic powder, minced garlic, ground cumin, lemon zest and dried parsley.
2. Then add the avocado oil and mix the shrimp well.
3. Preheat the fryer to 200°C.
4. Place the shrimp in the preheated fryer basket and cook for 5 minutes.

519. Big catfish

Servings: 4
Cooking time: 25 minutes
Ingredients:
- ¼ cup seasoned fried fish
- 1 tablespoon of olive oil
- 1 tablespoon chopped parsley

Addresses:
1. Preheat your air fryer to 200°C.
2. Add seasoned fried fish, and fillets in a large Ziploc bag, massaging well to coat.
3. Place the fillets in the cooking basket of your air fryer and cook for minutes.
4. Turn the fish over and cook for a further 2-3 minutes. Top with parsley and serve.

520. Italian shrimps

Servings: 4
Cooking time: 12 minutes
Ingredients:
- 450 grams of shrimps, peeled and deveined
- Pinch of salt and black pepper
- 1 tablespoon toasted sesame seeds
- ½ teaspoon Italian seasoning
- 1 tablespoon of olive oil

Addresses:
1. In a bowl, place the shrimp with the rest of the ingredients and mix well.
2. Place the prawns in the basket of the air fryer and cook at 185°C for a few minutes.
3. Divide into bowls and serve,

521. Pesto shrimp on the grill

Servings: 4
Cooking time: 16 minutes
Ingredients:
- 1 cup pesto
- 1/4 cup chopped fresh basil
- 450 grams extra large shrimps, peeled and deveined
- Bamboo skewers, soaked in water
- Extra virgin olive oil (for drizzling)
- Freshly ground black pepper

Addresses:
1. Thread the prawns onto the skewers and place them on the skewer rack.
2. Drizzle with oil and season with pepper and salt.
3. Cook in the air fryer at 180°C for 8 minutes. Halfway through the cooking time, turn the skewers over and spread with the pesto.
4. Serve and enjoy with a garnish of fresh basil.

522. Salmon fillet with lemon and paprika

Servings: 2
Cooking time: 15 minutes
Ingredients:
- 1 tablespoon melted butter
- 1 tablespoon of chopped fresh thyme or 1 teaspoon of dried thyme
- 1 teaspoon lemon zest
- 1/2 teaspoon salt
- 1/4 teaspoon lemon-pepper seasoning
- 1/4 teaspoon paprika
- 1-1/2 cups soft breadcrumbs
- 2 cloves garlic, minced
- 2 salmon fillets (about 170 grams each)
- 2 tablespoons fresh parsley, chopped

Addresses:
1. In a medium bowl, thoroughly mix together the breadcrumbs, fresh parsley and thyme, garlic, lemon zest, salt, lemon pepper seasoning and paprika.
2. Lightly grease the air fryer tray with cooking spray. Add salmon fillet, skin side down. Sprinkle crumbs evenly over the top of the salmon.
3. Cook in the air fryer for 10 minutes. When ready, let stand for 5 minutes, serve and enjoy.

523. Haddock coated with sesame seeds

Servings: 4
Cooking time: 14 minutes
Ingredients:
- 4 tablespoons plain flour
- 2 eggs
- ½ cup toasted sesame seeds
- ½ cup breadcrumbs
- 4 frozen haddock fillets
- 1/8 teaspoon dried rosemary, crushed
- salt and ground black pepper, as needed
- 3 tablespoons olive oil

Addresses:
1. Preheat the fryer to 200°C and grease one fryer basket.
2. Put the flour in a shallow bowl and beat the eggs in a second bowl.
3. Mix the sesame seeds, breadcrumbs, rosemary, salt, black pepper and olive oil in a third bowl until a crumbly mixture forms.
4. Dredge each fillet in flour, dip it in the beaten eggs and finally dredge it in the breadcrumb mixture.
5. Place the haddock fillets in the basket of the air fryer in a single layer and cook for about 14 minutes, turning once in between.
6. Divide the haddock fillets among the plates and serve hot.

524. Squid

Servings: 2
Cooking time: 25 minutes
Ingredients:
- 1 cup soda
- 225 grams squid tubes [or tentacles], approximately 6 millimetres wide, rinsed and dried
- ½ cup honey
- 1 - 2 tablespoons of sriracha
- 1 cup flour
- Sea salt to taste
- red pepper and black pepper to taste
- Red pepper flakes to taste

Addresses:
1. In a bowl, cover the squid rings with soda and mix well. Leave to stand for 10 minutes.
2. In a separate bowl, mix the flour, salt and red and black pepper.
3. In a third bowl, mix together the honey, pepper flakes and Sriracha to create the sauce.
4. Remove excess liquid from the squid and dredge each squid in the flour mixture.
5. Spray the fryer basket with cooking spray.
6. Place the squid in the basket, well-spaced and in a single layer.
7. Cook at 190°C for 11 minutes, shaking the basket at least twice while cooking.
8. Remove the squid from the fryer, cover with half of the sauce and return to the fryer. Cook for a further 2 minutes.
9. Plate the squid and pour the rest of the sauce on top.

525. Authentic Mediterranean Squid Salad

Servings: 3
Cooking time: 15 minutes
Ingredients:
- 450 grams of squid, cleaned, cut into rings
- 2 tablespoons sherry wine
- 1/2 teaspoon granulated garlic
- Salt to taste
- 1/2 teaspoon ground black pepper
- 1/2 teaspoon basil
- 1/2 teaspoon dried rosemary
- 1 cup grape tomatoes
- 1 small red onion, thinly sliced
- 1/3 cup Kalamata olives, pitted and sliced
- 1/2 cup mayonnaise
- 1 teaspoon of yellow mustard
- 1/2 cup fresh flat-leaf parsley leaves, coarsely chopped

Addresses:
1. Start by preheating the fryer to 200°C. Spray the fryer basket with cooking oil.
2. Mix the squid rings with the sherry wine, garlic, salt, pepper, basil and rosemary. Cook in the preheated Air Fryer for 5 minutes, shaking the basket halfway through cooking.

3. Work in batches and allow to cool to room temperature. When the squid is cool enough, add the rest of the ingredients.
4. Stir gently to combine and serve well chilled - bon appetit!

526. Lobster tails with olives and butter

Portions: 5
Cooking time: 20 minutes
Ingredients:
- 900 grams of fresh lobster tails, cleaned and cut in half, in their shells
- 2 tablespoons melted butter
- 1 teaspoon onion powder
- 1 teaspoon cayenne pepper
- Salt and ground black pepper to taste
- 2 cloves garlic, minced
- 1 cup green olives

Addresses:
1. In a sealable plastic bag, combine all ingredients well, shake to combine well.
2. Transfer the coated lobster tails to the greased cooking basket.
3. Cook for 6 to 7 minutes in the preheated Air Fryer. Shake the basket halfway through cooking. Work in batches.
4. Serve with green olives and enjoy.

527. Grilled shrimps

Servings: 4
Cooking time: 35 minutes
Ingredients:
- 18 shelled and deveined prawns
- 2 tablespoons freshly squeezed lemon juice
- ½ teaspoon hot paprika
- ½ teaspoon salt
- 1 teaspoon lemon pepper seasoning
- 2 tablespoons of extra virgin olive oil
- 2 cloves of garlic, peeled and minced
- 1 teaspoon onion powder
- ¼ teaspoon cumin powder
- ½ cup fresh parsley, coarsely chopped

Addresses:
1. Place all the ingredients in a bowl, making sure to coat the shrimp well. Refrigerate for 30 minutes.
2. Preheat the Air Fryer to 200°C.
3. Air fry the prawns for 5 minutes, making sure that the prawns turn pink.
4. Serve with pasta or rice.

528. Cod and fennel dish

Servings: 4
Cooking time: 15 minutes
Ingredients:
- Salt and pepper to taste
- 1 cup grapes, halved
- 1 small fennel bulb, cut in slices
- ½ cup walnuts
- 2 teaspoons white balsamic vinegar
- 2 tablespoons of extra virgin olive oil

Addresses:
1. Preheat the air fryer to 200°C.
2. Season the fillets with salt and pepper, drizzle oil on top. Place them in the basket of the air fryer and cook for a few minutes.
3. In a bowl, add the grapes, walnuts and fennel. Drizzle oil over the grape mixture and season with salt and pepper.
4. Add the mixture to the basket of the air fryer and cook for a further 3 minutes. Then add the balsamic vinegar and oil to the mixture, and season with salt and pepper. Pour over the fish and serve.

529. Breaded flounder

Servings: 3
Cooking time: 12 minutes
Ingredients:
- 1 egg
- 1 cup dry breadcrumbs
- 3 flounder fillets (170 grams each)
- 1 lemon, sliced
- ¼ cup vegetable oil

Addresses:
1. Preheat the fryer to 180°C and grease the fryer basket.
2. Beat the egg in a shallow bowl and mix the breadcrumbs and oil in another bowl.
3. Dip the flounder fillets in the beaten egg and coat them with the breadcrumb mixture.
4. Place the flounder fillets in the fryer basket and cook for about 12 minutes.
5. Serve the flounder fillets on plates and garnish with the lemon slices.

530. Fisherman's fish fingers

Servings: 4
Cooking time: 40 minutes
Ingredients:
- 340 grams of fish, cut into cubes
- 1 cup breadcrumbs
- 2 teaspoons mixed herbs
- ¼ teaspoon bicarbonate of soda
- 2 beaten eggs
- 3 teaspoons flour
- 2 tablespoons maida
- 1 teaspoon ginger-garlic puree
- ½ teaspoon black pepper
- 2 teaspoons garlic powder
- ½ teaspoon red chilli flakes
- ½ teaspoon turmeric powder
- 2 tablespoons lemon juice
- ½ teaspoon salt

Addresses:
1. Put the fish, ginger-garlic puree, garlic powder, red chilli flakes, turmeric powder, lemon juice, 1 teaspoon of the mixed herbs and salt in a bowl and combine well.

2. In a separate bowl, combine the flour, maida and baking soda.
3. Pour the beaten eggs into a third bowl.
4. In a fourth bowl, mix the breadcrumbs, black pepper and another teaspoon of mixed herbs.
5. Preheat the Air Fryer to 150°C.
6. Dredge the fish fingers in the flour. Dip in the egg and then in the breadcrumb mixture.
7. Place the fish fingers in the fryer basket and leave to cook for 10 minutes, making sure they are nice and crispy.

531. Tasty distress fish

Servings: 2
Cooking time: 25 minutes
Ingredients:
- ½ fennel bulb, cut into thin slices
- 4 tablespoons melted butter
- Salt and pepper to taste
- 1-2 teaspoons fresh dill
- 2 red salmon fillets
- 8 cherry tomatoes, halved
- ¼ cup fish stock

Addresses:
1. Preheat the fryer to 200°C.
2. Bring salted water to the boil over a medium heat. Add the potatoes and blanch for 2 minutes, drain.
3. Cut 2 large rectangles of parchment paper about 30 centimetres long.
4. In a large bowl, mix the potatoes, fennel, pepper and salt. Divide the mixture between the pieces of parchment paper and sprinkle with dill. Top with the fillets. Add the cherry tomatoes on top and drizzle with butter, pour the fish stock on top. Fold the squares and seal them. Cook the parcels in the air fryer for 10 minutes.

532. Frozen sesame fish fillets

Portions: 5
Cooking time: 20 minutes
Ingredients:
- 5 crumbled biscuits
- 3 tablespoons flour
- 1 beaten egg
- A pinch of salt
- Pinch of black pepper
- ¼ teaspoon rosemary
- 3 tablespoons olive oil, divided
- A handful of sesame seeds

Addresses:
1. Preheat the fryer to 200°C.
2. Combine the flour, pepper and salt in a shallow bowl. In another shallow bowl, combine the sesame seeds, crumbled crackers, oil and rosemary. Dredge the fish fillets first in the flour mixture, then in the beaten egg, then in the sesame mixture.
3. Place them in the air fryer on a sheet of aluminium foil, cook the fish for 8 minutes. Turn the fillets over and cook for a further 4 minutes. Serve and enjoy.

533. Charcoal and fennel

Servings: 4
Cooking time: 18 minutes
Ingredients:
- 4 salmon fillets, boneless
- 3 tablespoons olive oil
- 1 fennel bulb, cut with mandolin
- Pinch of salt and black pepper
- 5 cloves garlic, minced
- 1 teaspoon caraway seeds
- 2 tablespoons balsamic vinegar
- 1 tablespoon lemon juice
- 1 tablespoon grated lemon peel
- ½ cup chopped dill

Addresses:
1. In a frying pan that fits your air fryer, mix the fish with all the other ingredients and stir.
2. Place in the air fryer and cook at 200°C for minutes.
3. Divide the fish between the plates and serve with a side salad.

534. Greek style grilled fish

Servings: 3
Cooking time: 20 minutes
Ingredients:
- 2 tablespoons olive oil
- 1 red onion, sliced
- 2 cloves garlic, minced
- 1 Florina pepper, deveined and chopped
- 3 fillets of haddock, skinless
- 2 ripe tomatoes, diced
- 12 Kalamata olives, pitted and chopped
- 2 tablespoons capers
- 1 teaspoon oregano
- 1 teaspoon rosemary
- Sea salt to taste
- ½ cup white wine

Addresses:
1. Start by preheating your Air Fryer to 180°C.
2. Heat the oil in an ovenproof frying pan. Once hot, sauté the onion, garlic and pepper for 2 to 3 minutes or until fragrant.
3. Add the fish fillets to the baking tray. Top with the tomatoes, olives and capers. Sprinkle with the oregano, rosemary and salt. Pour in the white wine and transfer to the cooking basket.
4. Bake for 10 minutes. Taste for seasoning and serve on individual plates, garnished with some additional Mediterranean herbs if desired. Enjoy.

535. Shrimps with cumin, thyme and oregano

Servings: 4
Cooking time: 6 minutes
Ingredients:
- ¼ teaspoon cayenne pepper
- ¼ teaspoon red chilli flakes
- 1 teaspoon cumin
- 1 teaspoon oregano
- 1 teaspoon salt
- 1 teaspoon thyme
- 2 tablespoons coconut oil
- 2 teaspoons coriander
- 2 teaspoons onion powder
- 2 teaspoons smoked paprika
- 20 jumbo shrimp, peeled and deveined

Addresses:
1. Preheat the fryer to 200°C.
2. Season the prawns with all the ingredients.
3. Place the seasoned prawns on the double-layer grid.
4. Cook for 6 minutes.

536. Whitefish cakes

Servings: 4
Cooking time: 1 hour and 20 minutes
Ingredients:
- 1 ½ cups white fish fillets, minced
- 1 ½ cups green beans, finely chopped
- ½ cup chopped onions
- 1 chilli, deveined and chopped
- 1 tablespoon red curry paste
- 1 teaspoon sugar
- 1 tablespoon fish sauce
- 2 tablespoons apple cider vinegar
- 1 teaspoon of water
- Sea salt flakes, to taste
- ½ teaspoon ground black peppercorns
- 1 ½ teaspoons butter, at room temperature
- 1 lemon

Addresses:
1. Place all the ingredients in a bowl, following the order in which they appear in the list of ingredients.
2. Combine well with a spatula or your hands.
3. Mould the mixture into several small cakes and refrigerate for 1 hour.
4. Place a piece of aluminium foil in the baking basket and place the cakes on top.
5. Cook at 200°C for 10 minutes. Turn each fish cake over before air frying for another few minutes.
6. Serve the fish cakes with a side of cucumber sauce.

537. Delicious seafood pie

Servings: 3
Cooking time: 60 minutes
Ingredients:
- 450 grams of russet potatoes, peeled and cut into quarters
- 1 cup of water
- 1 grated carrot
- ½ small fennel head, grated
- 1 bunch of chopped dill sprigs
- 1 sprig of chopped parsley
- A handful of baby spinach
- 1 small tomato, diced
- ½ stalk celery, grated
- 2 tablespoons butter
- 1 tablespoon of milk
- ½ cup grated Cheddar cheese
- 1 small red chilli, chopped
- ½ lemon, squeezed
- Salt and pepper to taste

Addresses:
1. Put the potatoes in a saucepan, pour in the water and bring to the boil over medium heat on the cooker. Use a fork to check if they are soft and can be mashed, after a few minutes. Drain the water and use a potato masher to mash the potatoes. Add the butter, milk, salt and pepper. Mash until smooth, set aside.
2. In a bowl, add celery, carrots, cheese, chilli, fennel, parsley, lemon juice, seafood mixture, dill, tomato, spinach, salt and pepper, mix well.
3. Preheat the deep fryer. In a casserole dish, add half of the carrot mixture. Top with half of the potato mixture and level.
4. Place the dish in the air fryer and bake for 20 minutes until golden brown and the seafood is cooked through. Remove the dish and add the rest of the seafood mixture and level it.
5. Cover with the rest of the mashed potatoes and level it as well. Return the dish to the fryer and cook at 165°C for 20 minutes. Once ready, make sure it is cooked through and remove the dish. Cut the pie into slices and serve.

538. Italian mackerel

Servings: 2
Cooking time: 15 minutes
Ingredients:
- 225 grams mackerel, trimmed
- 1 tablespoon Italian seasoning
- 1 teaspoon keto tomato sauce
- 2 tablespoons melted ghee
- ½ teaspoon salt

Addresses:
1. Rub the mackerel with the Italian seasoning and tomato sauce. Then rub the fish with salt and marinate for a few minutes in the refrigerator.
2. Meanwhile, preheat the air fryer to 200°C.
3. When the marinating time is over, brush the fish with ghee and wrap it in the

baking paper. Place the wrapped fish in the air fryer and cook for 15 minutes.

539. Salmon and blackberry sauce

Servings: 2
Cooking time: 12 minutes
Ingredients:
- 2 salmon fillets, boneless
- 1 tablespoon of honey
- ½ cup blackberries
- 1 tablespoon of olive oil
- Juice of ½ lemon
- Salt and black pepper to taste

Addresses:
1. In a blender, mix the blackberries with the honey, oil, lemon juice, salt and pepper, pulse well.
2. Spread the blackberry mixture over the salmon, then place the fish in the basket of your air fryer.
3. Cook for 12 minutes, turning the fish halfway through.
4. Serve hot and enjoy.

540. Hake fillets with classic garlic sauce

Servings: 3
Cooking time: 20 minutes
Ingredients:
- 3 hake fillets
- 6 tablespoons mayonnaise
- 1 teaspoon Dijon mustard
- 1 tablespoon fresh lime juice
- 1 cup grated Parmesan cheese
- Salt to taste
- 1/4 teaspoon ground black pepper, or more to taste
- Garlic sauce
- 1/4 cup Greek yogurt
- 2 tablespoons olive oil
- 2 cloves garlic, minced
- 1/2 teaspoon tarragon leaves, chopped

Addresses:
1. Dry the hake fillets with a kitchen towel.
2. In a shallow bowl, whisk together the mayonnaise, mustard and lime juice. In another shallow bowl, thoroughly mix the Parmesan cheese with the salt and black pepper.
3. Dip the fish fillets in the mayonnaise mixture, then press them into the Parmesan mixture.
4. Spray the pan of the Air Fryer with non-stick spray. Roast in the preheated Air Fryer at 200°C for 10 minutes, turning halfway through the cooking time.
5. In the meantime, prepare the sauce by whisking all the ingredients together. Serve the fish fillets hot with the sauce on the side, enjoy!

541. Coconut prawns

Servings: 4
Cooking time: 10 minutes
Ingredients:
- 12 prawns, cleaned and deveined
- Salt and ground black pepper to taste
- ½ teaspoon cumin powder
- 1 teaspoon fresh lemon juice
- 1 medium egg, beaten
- ⅓ glass of beer
- ½ cup flour
- 1 teaspoon baking powder
- 1 tablespoon curry powder
- ½ teaspoon grated fresh ginger
- 1 cup coconut flakes

Addresses:
1. Coat the prawns in the salt, pepper, cumin powder and lemon juice.
2. In a bowl, mix together the beaten egg, beer, 1/4 cup flour, baking powder, curry powder and ginger.
3. In a second bowl, put the remaining quarter cup of flour, and in a third bowl, the flaked coconut.
4. Dredge the prawns in the flour before dredging them in the beer mixture. Finally, coat the prawns in the flaked coconut.
5. Air fry at 180°C for a few minutes. Turn them over and let them cook on the other side for another 2 to 3 minutes before serving.

542. Lemon breaded shrimps

Servings: 3
Cooking time: 14 minutes
Ingredients:
- ½ cup plain flour
- 2 egg whites
- 1 cup breadcrumbs
- 450 grams of large prawns, peeled and deveined
- salt and ground black pepper, as needed
- ¼ teaspoon lemon zest
- ¼ teaspoon cayenne pepper
- ¼ teaspoon crushed red pepper flakes
- 2 tablespoons vegetable oil

Addresses:
1. Preheat the fryer to 200°C and grease the fryer basket.
2. Mix the flour, salt and black pepper in a shallow bowl.
3. Whisk the egg whites in a second bowl and mix the breadcrumbs, lime zest and spices in a third bowl.
4. Dredge each shrimp in the flour, dip in the egg white and then in the breadcrumbs.
5. Drizzle the prawns evenly with olive oil and place half of the coated prawns in the fryer basket.
6. Cook for about 7 minutes and distribute the battered prawns on the plates.

7. Repeat with the rest of the mixture and serve hot.

543. Olives with prawns and parsley

Servings: 4
Cooking time: 12 minutes
Ingredients:
- 450 grams of shrimps, peeled and deveined
- 4 cloves garlic, minced
- 1 cup pitted, chopped black olives
- 3 tablespoons parsley
- 1 tablespoon of olive oil

Addresses:
1. In a frying pan that fits the air fryer, mix all the ingredients together.
2. Place the pan in the air fryer and cook at 190°C.
3. Divide between the plates and serve.

544. Crispy codfish sticks

Servings: 2
Cooking time: 7 minutes
Ingredients:
- 3 (115 grams) skinless cod fillets, cut into rectangular pieces
- ¾ cup flour
- 4 eggs
- 1 green chilli, finely chopped
- 2 cloves garlic, minced
- 2 teaspoons light soy sauce
- Salt and ground black pepper to taste

Addresses:
1. Preheat the fryer to 190°C and grease the fryer basket.
2. Put the flour in a shallow dish and whisk the eggs, garlic, green chilli, soy sauce, salt and black pepper in a second dish.
3. Dredge the cod fillets evenly in flour and dip them in the egg mixture.
4. Place the cod pieces in the fryer basket and cook for about 7 minutes.
5. Serve hot.

545. Cod fillets with garlic and herbs

Servings: 4
Cooking time: 15 minutes
Ingredients:
- 4 cod fillets
- 1/4 teaspoon fine sea salt
- 1/4 teaspoon ground black pepper, or more to taste
- 1 teaspoon cayenne pepper
- 1/2 cup non-dairy milk
- 1/2 cup fresh Italian parsley, coarsely chopped
- 1 teaspoon basil, dried
- 1/2 teaspoon dried oregano
- 1 Italian pepper, chopped
- 4 cloves garlic, minced

Addresses:
1. Coat the inside of a baking dish with a thin layer of vegetable oil.
2. Season the cod fillets with salt, pepper and cayenne pepper.
3. Next, puree the rest of the ingredients in your food processor. Mix the fish fillets with this mixture.
4. Set the Air Fryer to cook at 190°C. Cook for 10 to 12 minutes or until the cod flakes easily - enjoy!

546. Shrimps with cheese

Servings: 4
Cooking time: 20 minutes
Ingredients:
- ⅔ cup grated Parmesan cheese
- 900 grams of shrimps, peeled and deveined
- 4 cloves garlic, minced
- 2 tablespoons olive oil
- 1 teaspoon basil, dried
- ½ teaspoon dried oregano
- 1 teaspoon onion powder
- ½ teaspoon crushed red pepper flakes
- Ground black pepper, as needed
- 2 tablespoons fresh lemon juice

Addresses:
1. Preheat the fryer to 180°C and grease the fryer basket.
2. Mix the Parmesan cheese, garlic, olive oil, herbs and spices in a large bowl.
3. Place half of the prawns in the fryer basket in a single layer and cook for about 10 minutes.
4. Divide the prawns among the plates and sprinkle with lemon juice to serve hot.

547. Lemon salmon

Servings: 2
Cooking time: 20 minutes
Ingredients:
- Cooking spray
- Salt, to taste
- Zest of one lemon

Addresses:
1. Drizzle the fillets with olive oil and rub them with salt and lemon zest.
2. Place baking paper in the fryer basket to prevent sticking. Cook the fillets for minutes at 180°C, turning once halfway through.
3. Serve with steamed asparagus and a squeeze of lemon juice.

548. Salmon with green beans

Servings: 4
Cooking time: 12 minutes
Ingredients:
For the green beans you need:
- 5 cups green beans (can be frozen)
- 1 tablespoon avocado oil

- Salt

For salmon you need:
- 2 cloves garlic, minced
- 2 tablespoons chopped fresh dill
- 2 tablespoons fresh lemon juice
- 1 tablespoon of olive oil
- Salt
- 4 salmon fillets of about 170 grams each

Addresses:
1. Set the temperature of the air fryer to 190°C. Grease the air fryer basket.
2. In a large bowl, mix well the green beans, oil and salt.
3. Place the green beans in the prepared fryer basket.
4. Fry in the open air for about 6 minutes.
5. Meanwhile, for the salmon: in a bowl, combine the garlic, dill, lemon juice and olive oil.
6. Remove the basket from the air fryer.
7. Turn the green beans over and top with the salmon fillets.
8. Spoon the garlic mixture evenly over each salmon fillet, then sprinkle with the salt.
9. Fry in the open air for about 6 minutes.
10. Remove from the fryer and place the salmon fillets on plates.
11. Serve hot with the green beans.

549. Haddock with herbs

Servings: 2
Cooking time: 8 minutes
Ingredients:
- 2 haddock fillets weighing approximately 170 grams each
- 2 tablespoons pine nuts
- 3 tablespoons chopped fresh basil
- 1 tablespoon grated Parmesan cheese
- ½ cup extra virgin olive oil
- Salt and black pepper

Addresses:
1. Preheat the fryer to 180°C and grease the fryer basket.
2. Coat the haddock fillets evenly with olive oil and season with salt and black pepper.
3. Place the haddock fillets in the fryer basket and cook for about 8 minutes.
4. Serve the haddock fillets on plates.
5. Meanwhile, put the rest of the ingredients in a food processor and pulse until smooth.
6. Spoon this cheese sauce over the haddock fillets and serve hot.

550. Big cod fried in the open air

Servings: 4
Cooking time: 20 minutes
Ingredients:
- 4 tablespoons chopped coriander
- Salt to taste
- A handful of chopped green onions
- 1 cup of water
- 5 slices of ginger
- 5 tablespoons light soy sauce
- 3 tablespoons oil
- 1 teaspoon dark soy sauce
- 5 lumps of rock sugar

Addresses:
1. Preheat your air fryer to 180°C.
2. Coat the cod with salt and coriander, drizzle with oil.
3. Place the fish fillet in the cooking basket of your air fryer and cook for minutes.
4. Place the rest of the ingredients in a frying pan over medium heat, cook for 5 minutes.
5. Serve the fish with the sauce and enjoy.

551. Coconut crusted shrimp

Servings: 3
Cooking time: 40 minutes
Ingredients:
- 225 grams of coconut milk
- ½ cup sweetened coconut, shredded
- ½ cup panko breadcrumbs
- 450 grams of large prawns, peeled and deveined
- Salt and black pepper, to taste

Addresses:
1. Preheat the fryer to 180°C and grease the fryer basket.
2. Place the coconut milk in a shallow container.
3. Mix the coconut, breadcrumbs, salt and black pepper in another bowl.
4. Dip each shrimp in the coconut milk and then dip it in the coconut mixture.
5. Place half of the prawns in the fryer basket and cook for about 20 minutes.
6. Serve the shrimp on plates and repeat with the rest of the serving mixture.

552. Salmon with broccoli

Servings: 2
Cooking time: 12 minutes
Ingredients:
- 1½ cups small broccoli florets
- ¼ teaspoon cornstarch
- 2 salmon fillets with skin (weight approx. 170 grams)
- 1 spring onion, thinly sliced
- 2 tablespoons vegetable oil, divided
- Salt and black pepper, as needed
- 1 piece (1.25 centimetres) fresh ginger, grated
- 1 tablespoon soy sauce
- 1 teaspoon rice vinegar
- 1 teaspoon light brown sugar

Addresses:
1. Preheat the fryer to 190°C and grease the fryer basket.
2. Mix broccoli, 1 tablespoon vegetable oil, salt and black pepper.

3. Combine the ginger, soy sauce, rice vinegar, sugar and cornstarch in another bowl.
4. Rub the salmon fillets evenly with the remaining olive oil and ginger mixture.
5. Place the broccoli florets in the fryer basket and top with the salmon fillets.
6. Cook for about 12 minutes and serve on plates.

553. Salmon with pesto

Servings: 4
Cooking time: 16 minutes
Ingredients:
- 2,140 kilograms of salmon fillet
- 1 tablespoon green pesto
- 1 cup mayonnaise
- Olive oil
- 450 grams of fresh spinach
- 55 grams grated Parmesan cheese
- Pepper
- Salt

Addresses:
1. Preheat the air fryer to 190°C.
2. Spray the air fryer basket with cooking spray.
3. Season the salmon fillet with pepper and salt and place it in the fryer basket.
4. In a bowl, mix the mayonnaise, Parmesan cheese and pesto and spread over the salmon fillet.
5. Cook the salmon for 14-16 minutes.
6. Meanwhile, in a frying pan, sauté the spinach in olive oil until wilted, about 2-3 minutes. Season with pepper and salt.
7. Place the spinach in the serving dish and top with the cooked salmon.
8. Serve and enjoy.

554. Rosemary Infused Butter Scallops

Servings: 4
Cooking time: 1 hour and 10 minutes
Ingredients:
- 900 grams of scallops
- 1/2 cup beer
- 4 tablespoons butter
- 2 sprigs rosemary (leaves only)
- Sea salt and freshly ground black pepper

Addresses:
1. In a ceramic dish, mix the scallops with the beer, marinate for one hour.
2. Meanwhile, preheat your Air Fryer to 200°C.
3. Melt the butter and add the rosemary leaves. Stir for a few minutes.
4. Discard the marinade and transfer the scallops to the basket of the Air Fryer. Season with salt and black pepper.
5. Cook the scallops in the preheated Air Fryer for 7 minutes, shaking the basket halfway through cooking. Work in batches.
6. Enjoy your meal!

555. Japanese flounder with chives

Servings: 4
Cooking time: 15 minutes + marinating time
Ingredients:
- 4 flounder fillets
- Sea salt and freshly ground mixed peppercorns, to taste
- 1 ½ tablespoons dark sesame oil
- 2 tablespoons sake
- 1/4 cup soy sauce
- 1 tablespoon lemon zest
- 2 cloves garlic, minced
- 2 tablespoons chives, chopped, to serve

Addresses:
1. Place all the ingredients, without the chives, in a large bowl. Cover and marinate for about 2 hours in your fridge.
2. Remove the fish from the marinade and cook in the cooking basket of the Air Fryer at 180°C for 10 minutes, turning once during cooking.
3. Pour the remaining marinade into a preheated pan over medium-low heat, simmer, stirring continuously, until thickened.
4. Pour the prepared glaze over the flounder and serve garnished with fresh chives.

556. Filipino steak

Servings: 4
Cooking time: 10 minutes + marinating time
Ingredients:
- 2 bellies of milkfish, boned and cut into 4 portions
- ¾ teaspoon salt
- ¼ teaspoon ground black pepper
- ¼ teaspoon cumin powder
- 2 tablespoons calamansi juice
- 2 lemongrass, trimmed and cut crosswise into small pieces
- ½ cup tamari sauce
- 2 tablespoons fish sauce [Pati].
- 2 tablespoons sugar
- 1 teaspoon garlic powder
- ½ cup chicken stock
- 2 tablespoons olive oil

Addresses:
1. Pat the fish dry with kitchen paper.
2. Place the fish in a large bowl and cover with the rest of the ingredients. Leave to marinate for 3 hours in the fridge.
3. Cook the fish fillets in the grill basket of the Air Fryer for 5 minutes.
4. Turn the fillets over and cook for a few more minutes. Cook until medium brown.
5. Serve with steamed white rice.

557. Pesto sauce on fish fillets

Servings: 3

Cooking time: 20 minutes
Ingredients:
- 1 bunch fresh basil
- 1 cup olive oil
- 1 tablespoon grated Parmesan cheese
- 2 cloves garlic
- 2 tablespoons pine nuts
- 3 white fish fillets
- Salt and pepper to taste

Addresses:
1. In a food processor, combine all ingredients except fish fillets.
2. Press until smooth.
3. Place the fish in a baking dish and pour over the pesto sauce.
4. Place in the air fryer and cook for 20 minutes.

558. Flounder fillets with crust

Servings: 2
Cooking time: 20 minutes
Ingredients:
- 2 flounder fillets
- 1 egg
- 1/2 teaspoon Worcestershire sauce
- 1/4 cup coconut flour
- 1/4 cup almond flour
- 1/2 teaspoon lemon pepper
- 1/2 teaspoon coarse sea salt
- 1/4 teaspoon chilli powder

Addresses:
1. Rinse and dry the flounder fillets.
2. Whisk the egg and Worcestershire sauce in a shallow bowl. In another bowl, mix the coconut flour, almond flour, lemon pepper, salt and chili powder.
3. Then dip the fillets in the egg mixture. Finally, coat the fish fillets with the coconut flour mixture until they are coated on all sides.
4. Spray with cooking spray and transfer to the basket of the Air Fryer. Cook at 200°C for 7 minutes.
5. Turn them over, spray the other side with cooking spray and cook for another few minutes. Bon appetit!

559. Shrimp and pine nut mixture

Servings: 4
Cooking time: 12 minutes
Ingredients:
- ½ cup parsley leaves
- ½ cup basil leaves
- 2 tablespoons lemon juice
- 1/3 cup pine nuts
- ¼ cup grated Parmesan cheese
- Pinch of salt and black pepper
- ½ cup olive oil
- 1 and ½ pounds shrimp, peeled and deveined
- ¼ teaspoon lemon zest

Addresses:
1. In a blender, combine all the ingredients except the prawns and pulse well.
2. In a bowl, mix the prawns with the pesto and toss them together. Place the shrimp in the basket of your air fryer and cook at 180°C turning the shrimp halfway through.
3. Divide the shrimp into bowls and serve.

560. Shrimps with garlic and goat cheese

Servings: 2
Cooking time: 10 minutes
Ingredients:
- 1/2 tbsp. fresh parsley, coarsely chopped
- 1 ½ tablespoons balsamic vinegar
- Sea salt flakes, to taste
- 450 grams of deveined prawns
- 1 tablespoon coconut aminos
- 1 teaspoon Dijon mustard
- 1/2 teaspoon garlic powder
- 1 ½ tablespoons olive oil
- 1/2 teaspoon smoked cayenne pepper
- Salt and ground black peppercorns, to taste
- 1 cup grated goat's cheese

Addresses:
1. Set the Air Fryer to cook at 195°C.
2. In a bowl, combine all the ingredients except the cheese.
3. Pour the prawns into the cooking basket, air fry for 7 to 8 minutes, enjoy!

561. Breaded fish fillets with tarragon

Servings: 4
Cooking time: 25 minutes
Ingredients:
- 2 beaten eggs
- 1/2 teaspoon tarragon
- 4 fish fillets, cut in halves
- 2 tablespoons dry white wine
- 1/3 cup grated Parmesan cheese
- 1 teaspoon seasoned salt
- 1/3 teaspoon mixed peppercorns
- 1/2 teaspoon fennel seeds

Addresses:
1. Add the Parmesan cheese, salt, peppercorns, fennel seeds and tarragon to your food processor, blend for about 20 seconds.
2. Sprinkle the fish fillets with dry white wine. Pour the egg into a shallow dish.
3. Now, coat the fish fillets with the beaten egg on all sides, then cover them with the cracker mixture.
4. Air fry for about 17 minutes at 150°C. Bon appetit!

562. Cod and sauce

Servings: 2
Cooking time: 15 minutes
Ingredients:

- 2 cod fillets, boneless
- Salt and black pepper to taste
- 1 bunch of chopped spring onions
- 3 tablespoons melted ghee

Addresses:
1. In a frying pan that fits the air fryer, combine all ingredients, stir gently.
2. Place the pan in the air fryer and cook at 180°C for a few minutes.
3. Divide the fish and sauce between the plates and serve.

563. Flounder stuffed with crab

Servings: 3
Cooking time: 12 minutes
Ingredients:
- Flounder fillets of 255 grams
- 115 grams of crab meat, minced
- 1 tablespoon mascarpone
- ½ teaspoon ground nutmeg
- 2 spring onions, diced
- ½ teaspoon dried thyme
- 55 grams of grated Parmesan cheese
- 1 beaten egg

Addresses:
1. Line the air fryer tray with baking paper. Then cut the flounder fillet into 3 portions and place them on the baking tray in a single layer.
2. Sprinkle the fish fillets with ground nutmeg and dried thyme. Then top with the chopped crab meat, spring onions and Parmesan.
3. In the bowl of a mixer, mix the mascarpone and egg. Pour the liquid over the cheese.
4. Preheat the fryer to 195°C.
5. Place the tray with the fish in the air fryer and cook the food for minutes.

564. Haddock with chilli

Servings: 4
Cooking time: 8 minutes
Ingredients:
- 340 grams haddock fillet
- 1 beaten egg
- 1 teaspoon cream cheese
- 1 teaspoon chilli flakes
- ½ teaspoon salt
- 1 tablespoon flaxseed meal
- Cooking spray

Addresses:
1. Cut the haddock into 4 pieces and sprinkle with chilli flakes and salt.
2. Next, mix together the egg and cream cheese in a small bowl. Dip the haddock pieces into the egg mixture and sprinkle generously with linseed meal.
3. Preheat the fryer to 200°C.
4. Place the prepared haddock pieces in the air fryer in a single layer and cook for 4 minutes on each side or until golden brown.

565. Mahi Mahi with green beans

Servings: 4
Cooking time: 12 minutes
Ingredients:
- 5 cups of green beans
- 2 tablespoons chopped fresh dill
- 4 Mahi Mahi fillets
- 1 tablespoon avocado oil
- Salt, as needed
- 2 cloves garlic, minced
- 2 tablespoons fresh lemon juice
- 1 tablespoon of olive oil

Addresses:
1. Preheat the fryer to 190°C and grease the fryer basket.
2. Mix the green beans, avocado oil and salt in a large bowl.
3. Place the green beans in the fryer basket and cook for about 6 minutes.
4. Combine the garlic, dill, lemon juice, salt and olive oil in a bowl.
5. Dredge the Mahi Mahi Mahi in this garlic mixture and place it on top of the green beans.
6. Cook for a few more minutes and plate to serve hot.

566. Tilapia with Dijon mustard crust and parmesan cheese

Servings: 2
Cooking time: 15 minutes
Ingredients:
- 1 tablespoon lemon juice
- 1 teaspoon prepared horseradish
- 1/4 cup dry breadcrumbs
- 2 tablespoons grated Parmesan cheese, divided
- 2 teaspoons melted butter
- 2 teaspoons Dijon mustard
- 2 tilapia fillets (140 grams each)
- 3 tablespoons reduced-fat mayonnaise

Addresses:
1. Lightly grease air fryer tray with cooking spray. Place tilapia in a single layer.
2. In a small bowl, whisk together mayonnaise, lemon juice, mustard, 1 tablespoon cheese and horseradish. Spread over the top of the fish.
3. In a separate bowl, mix together the remaining cheese, melted butter and breadcrumbs. Sprinkle over the top of the fish.
4. Bake at 200°C for 15 minutes.
5. Serve and enjoy.

567. Prawns in butter with garlic-sriracha sauce

Servings: 2
Cooking time: 15 minutes

Ingredients:
- 1 tablespoon lime juice
- 1 tablespoon sriracha
- 450 grams of large prawns, shelled and cut lengthwise or fin-shaped
- 1 teaspoon fish sauce
- 2 tablespoons melted butter
- 2 tablespoons minced garlic
- Salt and pepper to taste

Addresses:
1. Preheat the fryer to 200°C.
2. Place the grill pan attachment on the air fryer.
3. Season the prawns with the rest of the ingredients.
4. Place on the grill and cook for 15 minutes. Be sure to turn the prawns halfway through the cooking time.

568. Grilled shrimps with butter

Servings: 4
Cooking time: 15 minutes
Ingredients:
- 6 tablespoons unsalted butter
- ½ cup chopped red onion
- 1 ½ teaspoon red pepper
- 1 teaspoon of shrimp paste or fish sauce
- 1 ½ teaspoon lime juice
- Salt and pepper to taste
- 24 large prawns, peeled and deveined

Addresses:
1. Preheat the air fryer to 200°C.
2. Place the grill pan attachment on the air fryer.
3. Transfer all ingredients to a Ziploc bag and shake well.
4. Thread the prawns onto a bamboo skewer and place on the grill
5. Cook for 1 minute.
6. Turn the prawns halfway through cooking.

569. Tuna coated with sesame seeds

Servings: 2
Cooking time: 6 minutes
Ingredients:
- ¼ cup white sesame seeds
- 1 tablespoon black sesame seeds
- 1 egg white
- 2 tuna fillets
- Salt and black pepper, as needed

Addresses:
1. Preheat the fryer to 200°C and grease the fryer basket.
2. Whisk the egg white in a shallow bowl.
3. Mix the sesame seeds, salt and black pepper in another bowl.
4. Dip the tuna fillets in the beaten egg white and roll them in the sesame seed mixture.
5. Place the tuna steaks in the basket of the air fryer in a single layer and cook for about 6 minutes, turning once in between.
6. Arrange the tuna steaks on the plates and serve hot.

570. Snapper fillets with tomato and walnut sauce

Servings: 4
Cooking time: 20 minutes
Ingredients:
- 4 snapper fillets with skin
- Sea salt and ground pepper, to taste
- 1/2 cup grated Parmesan cheese
- 2 tablespoons chopped fresh coriander
- 1/2 cup coconut flour
- 2 tablespoons flaxseed meal
- 2 medium eggs

For the almond sauce you need:
- 1/4 cup almonds
- 2 cloves garlic, pressed
- 1 cup tomato paste
- 1 teaspoon of dried dill weed
- 1/2 teaspoon salt
- 1/4 teaspoon freshly ground mixed peppercorns
- 1/4 cup olive oil

Addresses:
1. Season the fish fillets with sea salt and pepper.
2. In a shallow dish, combine the Parmesan cheese and chopped fresh coriander.
3. In another shallow dish, beat the eggs until frothy. Place the coconut flour and flaxseed meal in a third plate.
4. Dredge the fish fillets in the flour and then in the egg, then dredge them in the Parmesan mixture.
5. Set Air Fryer to cook at 200°C, air fry for 1 to 16 minutes or until crispy.
6. To make the sauce, chop the almonds in a food processor. Add the rest of the sauce ingredients, but not the olive oil.
7. Blend for 30 seconds, then slowly and gradually pour in the oil and process until smooth and even. Serve the sauce with the prepared snapper fillets, enjoy!

571. Grilled citrus Branzini

Servings: 2
Cooking time: 15 minutes
Ingredients:
- 2 branzini fillets
- Salt and pepper to taste
- 3 lemons, freshly squeezed juice
- 2 oranges, freshly squeezed juice

Addresses:
1. Place all ingredients in a Ziploc bag. Marinate in the refrigerator for 2 hours.
2. Preheat the air fryer to 200°C.
3. Place the grill pan attachment on the air fryer.
4. Transfer the fish to the grill pan and cook for 15 minutes until the fish is flaky.

572. Rice with turmeric and cauliflower

Servings: 4
Cooking time: 25 minutes
Ingredients:
- 4 salmon fillets, boneless
- Salt and black pepper to taste
- 1 cup cauliflower, mashed
- ½ cup chicken stock
- 1 teaspoon turmeric powder
- 1 tablespoon melted butter

Addresses:
1. In a frying pan that fits your air fryer, combine the cauliflower rice with the remaining ingredients, except the salmon, and mix.
2. Place the salmon fillets on the cauliflower rice, place the pan in the fryer and cook at 180°C for 25 minutes, turning the fish after a few minutes.
3. Divide between the plates and serve.

573. Famous Indian fish curry

Servings: 4
Cooking time: 25 minutes
Ingredients:
- 2 tablespoons sunflower oil
- 1/2 pound of minced fish
- 2 red chillies, chopped
- 1 tablespoon coriander powder
- 1 teaspoon curry paste
- 1 cup coconut milk
- Salt and white pepper, to taste
- 1/2 teaspoon fenugreek seeds
- 1 chopped shallot
- 1 clove garlic, minced
- 1 ripe tomato, mashed

Addresses:
1. Preheat your Air Fryer to 190°C and brush the cooking basket with a tablespoon of sunflower oil.
2. Cook the fish for 10 minutes on both sides. Transfer to the air fryer tray previously greased with the remaining tablespoon of sunflower oil.
3. Add the rest of the ingredients and reduce the temperature.
4. Continue cooking for 10 to 12 minutes more or until heated through. Enjoy.

574. Fresh tilapia fried in the open air

Servings: 4
Cooking time: 15 minutes
Ingredients:
- 1 tbsp. old bay seasoning
- 2 tablespoons canola oil
- 2 tablespoons lemon pepper
- Salt to taste
- 2-3 butter sprouts

Addresses:
1. Preheat the fryer to 200°C.
2. Drizzle the oil over the tilapia. In a bowl, mix the salt, lemon pepper, butter sprouts and seasoning, spread over the fish
3. Place the fillets in the fryer and cook for a few minutes until crispy.

575. Crab Cake Burgers

Servings: 3
Cooking time: 2 hours and 20 minutes
Ingredients:
- 2 beaten eggs
- 1 chopped shallot
- 2 cloves garlic, crushed
- 1 tablespoon of olive oil
- 1 teaspoon of yellow mustard
- 1 teaspoon chopped fresh coriander
- 280 grams of crab meat
- 1 cup tortilla chips, crushed
- 1/2 teaspoon cayenne pepper
- 1/2 teaspoon ground black pepper
- Sea salt, to taste
- 3/4 cup fresh breadcrumbs

Addresses:
1. In a bowl, combine eggs, shallot, garlic, olive oil, mustard, cilantro, crab meat, tortilla chips, cayenne pepper, black pepper and salt. Mix until well combined.
2. Form the mixture into 6 patties. Dip the crab patties in the fresh breadcrumbs, coating all sides well. Place in the refrigerator.
3. Spray the crab patties with cooking oil on both sides.
4. Cook in the preheated air fryer at 15°C for 14 minutes. Serve on buns if desired - bon appetit!

576. Trout and Almond Butter Sauce

Portions: 5
Cooking time: 15 minutes
Ingredients:
- 4 fillets of trout, boneless
- Cooking spray
- Salt and black pepper to taste

For the sauce you need:
- 1 cup almond butter
- 4 teaspoons soy sauce
- ¼ cup lemon juice
- 1 teaspoon almond oil
- ¼ cup water

Addresses:
1. Place the fish fillets in your air fryer, season with salt and pepper and grease with cooking spray.
2. Cook at 190°C for 5 minutes on each side and divide between the plates.
3. Heat a frying pan with the almond butter over medium heat, then add the soy sauce, lemon juice, almond oil and water.
4. Whisk the sauce well and cook for 2-3 minutes.

5. Drizzle the almond butter sauce over the fish and serve.

577. Fish and chips

Servings: 4
Cooking time: 25 minutes
Ingredients:
- Cooking spray
- Salt and pepper to taste
- 4 white fish fillets
- 2 tablespoons flour
- 1 beaten egg
- 1 cup breadcrumbs
- Salt and black pepper

Addresses:
1. Drizzle the slices with olive oil and season with salt and black pepper.
2. Place them in the air fryer and cook for 20 minutes at 200°C.
3. Spread flour on a plate and coat the fish.
4. Dip it in the egg, then in the crumbs and season with salt and black pepper.
5. After a few minutes, add the fish to the fryer and cook with the chips. Cook until crispy.
6. Serve with lemon slices, mayonnaise and ketchup.

578. Recipe for salted cod tapas from Portugal

Servings: 4
Cooking time: 26 minutes
Ingredients:
- 1 clove garlic, chopped, divided
- 1 yellow onion, thinly sliced
- 1/4 cup chopped fresh parsley, chopped, divided
- 1/4 cup olive oil
- 450 grams cod fillet, minced
- 2 hard-boiled eggs, chopped
- 2 tablespoons butter
- 2 Yukon Gold potatoes, peeled and diced
- 3/4 teaspoon red pepper flakes
- 5 pitted black olives
- 5 pitted green olives
- Freshly ground pepper to taste

Addresses:
1. Lightly grease the air fryer tray with cooking spray. Add and melt the butter at 180°C. Stir in onions and cook for 6 minutes until caramelised.
2. Add the black pepper, red pepper flakes, half the parsley, garlic, olive oil, diced potatoes and chopped fish.
3. Bake at 180°C for 10 minutes.
4. Halfway through the cooking time, stir well to mix.
5. Cook for a further 10 minutes until the top is lightly browned.
6. Garnish with the remaining parsley, the eggs and the black and green olives.
7. Serve and enjoy with chips.

579. Chinese garlic shrimp

Portions: 5
Cooking time: 15 minutes
Ingredients:
- Juice of 1 lemon
- 1 teaspoon sugar
- 3 tablespoons of peanut oil
- 2 tablespoons cornstarch
- 2 onions, chopped
- ¼ teaspoon Chinese powder
- Chopped chilli to taste
- Salt and black pepper to taste
- 4 cloves of garlic

Addresses:
1. Preheat the fryer to 190°C.
2. In a Ziploc bag, mix together the lemon juice, sugar, pepper, half the oil, cornstarch, cornstarch powder, Chinese powder and salt. Add the shrimp and massage to coat evenly. Let stand for a few minutes.
3. Add the remaining peanut oil, garlic, spring onions and chilli to a frying pan and fry for 5 minutes over medium heat.
4. Place the marinated prawns in the basket of your air fryer and cover them with the sauce.
5. Cook for 10 minutes, until very crispy.

580. Prawn skewers

Servings: 2
Cooking time: 10 minutes
Ingredients:
- 340 grams of shrimps, peeled and deveined
- 1 tablespoon chopped fresh coriander
- Wooden skewers, previously soaked
- 2 tablespoons fresh lemon juice
- 1 teaspoon chopped garlic
- ½ teaspoon paprika
- ½ teaspoon ground cumin
- salt and ground black pepper, as needed

Addresses:
1. Preheat the fryer to 180°C and grease the fryer basket.
2. Mix the lemon juice, garlic and spices in a bowl.
3. Add the prawns and toss to coat well.
4. Thread the prawns onto the pre-soaked wooden skewers and transfer them to the fryer basket.
5. Cook for about 10 minutes, turning once in between.
6. Divide the mixture among the plates and serve garnished with fresh coriander.

581. Haddock with Kalamata olives and capers

Servings: 3
Cooking time: 20 minutes
Ingredients:
- 2 tablespoons olive oil

- 1 red onion, sliced
- 2 cloves garlic, minced
- 1 Florina pepper, deveined and chopped
- 3 fillets of haddock, skinless
- 2 ripe tomatoes, diced
- 12 Kalamata olives, pitted and chopped
- 2 tablespoons capers
- 1 teaspoon oregano
- 1 teaspoon rosemary
- Sea salt, to taste
- 1/2 cup white wine

Addresses:
1. Start by preheating your Air Fryer to 180°C.
2. Heat the oil in a baking pan. Once the oil is hot, sauté the onion, garlic and pepper for 2 to 3 minutes or until fragrant.
3. Add the fish fillets to the baking tray. Top with the tomatoes, olives and capers. Sprinkle with the oregano, rosemary and salt. Pour in the white wine and transfer to the cooking basket.
4. Set the temperature to 180°C and bake for 10 minutes.
5. Taste for seasoning and serve on individual plates, garnished with some additional Mediterranean herbs if desired. Enjoy.

582. Mixed sea bass and olives

Servings: 2
Cooking time: 20 minutes
Ingredients:
- 2 fillets of sea bass
- 1 fennel bulb, cut into slices
- Juice of 1 lemon
- ¼ cup black olives, pitted and sliced
- 1 tablespoon of olive oil
- Pinch of salt and black pepper
- ¼ cup chopped basil

Addresses:
1. In a frying pan that fits the air fryer, combine all ingredients.
2. Place the pan in the fryer and cook at 190°C for 20 minutes, shaking the fryer halfway through cooking.
3. Divide between the plates and serve.

583. Super easy scallops

Servings: 2
Cooking time: 4 minutes
Ingredients:
- 340 grams of scallops
- 1 tablespoon melted butter
- ½ tablespoon fresh thyme, chopped
- Salt and black pepper, to taste

Addresses:
1. Preheat the fryer to 200°C and grease one fryer basket.
2. Mix all ingredients in a bowl and stir to coat well.
3. Place the scallops in the fryer basket and cook for about 4 minutes.
4. Serve hot.

584. Cajun Shrimp

Servings: 4
Cooking time: 6 minutes
Ingredients:
- 225 grams of peeled prawns
- 1 teaspoon Cajun spice
- 1 teaspoon cream cheese
- 1 beaten egg
- ½ teaspoon salt
- 1 teaspoon of avocado oil

Addresses:
1. Sprinkle the prawns with Cajun spices and salt.
2. In a bowl, mix cream cheese and egg, dip each shrimp into egg mixture.
3. Preheat the air fryer to 200°C.
4. Place shrimp in air fryer and drizzle with avocado oil.
5. Cook the shrimps for 6 minutes. Shake well after 3 minutes of cooking.

585. Grilled Halibut with lemon and tomatoes

Servings: 4
Cooking time: 15 minutes
Ingredients:
- ½ cup palm hearts, rinsed and drained
- 1 cup cherry tomatoes
- 2 tablespoons oil
- 4 halibut fillets
- Juice of 1 lemon
- Salt and pepper to taste

Addresses:
1. Preheat the fryer to 200°C.
2. Place the grill pan attachment on the air fryer.
3. Season the halibut fillets with lemon juice, salt and pepper. Brush with oil.
4. Place the fish in the grill pan.
5. Place the palm hearts and cherry tomatoes on the side and sprinkle with more salt and pepper.
6. Cook for 15 minutes.

586. Thyme catfish

Servings: 4
Cooking time: 12 minutes
Ingredients:
- 570 grams of catfish fillet
- 2 beaten eggs
- 1 teaspoon dried thyme
- ½ teaspoon salt
- 1 teaspoon apple cider vinegar
- 1 teaspoon of avocado oil
- ¼ teaspoon cayenne pepper
- 1/3 cup coconut flour

Addresses:

1. Sprinkle the catfish fillets with dried thyme, salt, apple cider vinegar, cayenne pepper and coconut flour.
2. Then, drizzle the fish fillets with avocado oil.
3. Preheat the air fryer to 195°C.
4. Place the catfish fillets in the basket of the air fryer and cook for 8 minutes.
5. Turn the fish on the other side and cook for 4 more minutes.

587. Salmon with turmeric and soy sauce

Servings: 4
Cooking time: 12 minutes
Ingredients:
- ½ tablespoon sugar
- ½ tablespoon turmeric powder
- 1 cup cherry tomatoes
- 1 salmon fillet, cut into cubes
- 1 tablespoon soy sauce
- Pinch of black pepper
- Chopped coriander for garnish

Addresses:
1. Season the salmon fillets with turmeric powder, sugar, soy sauce and black pepper. Marinate for 30 minutes in the refrigerator.
2. Preheat the fryer to 150°C.
3. Thread the salmon cubes alternately with the tomatoes.
4. Place on the double-layer grid.
5. Cook for 10 to 12 minutes.

588. Fried shrimps with sweet chilli sauce

Servings: 1
Cooking time: 6 minutes
Ingredients:
- ½ cup flour
- ½ cup sweet chilli sauce
- 225 grams of raw shrimps, peeled and deveined
- 1 beaten egg
- 1 teaspoon chilli powder
- Salt and pepper to taste

Addresses:
1. Mix the prawns and eggs in a bowl. Season with salt and pepper to taste.
2. In a separate bowl, mix together the chilli powder and flour.
3. Dredge the prawns in the flour mixture.
4. Preheat the fryer to 150°C.
5. Place the prawns on the double-layer grid.
6. Cook for minutes.
7. Serve with chilli sauce.

589. Mixed trout with herbs

Servings: 4
Cooking time: 20 minutes
Ingredients:
- 4 trout fillets, boned and skinned
- 1 tablespoon lemon juice
- 2 tablespoons olive oil
- Pinch of salt and black pepper
- 1 bunch of asparagus, trimmed
- 2 tablespoons melted ghee
- ¼ cup chive and tarragon mixture

Addresses:
1. Toss the asparagus with half the oil, salt and pepper, put them in the basket of your air fryer and cook at 190°C for 6 minutes.
2. Divide the asparagus among the plates.
3. In a bowl, toss the trout with salt, pepper, lemon juice, the remaining oil and herbs and mix, place the fillets in the basket of your air fryer and cook at 190°C for 7 minutes on each side.
4. Divide the fish among the asparagus, drizzle the melted ghee on top and serve.

590. Prawn skewers

Portions: 5
Cooking time: 5 minutes
Ingredients:
- 1 kilogram of shrimps, peeled
- 2 tablespoons chopped fresh cilantro
- 2 tablespoons apple cider vinegar
- 1 teaspoon ground coriander
- 1 tablespoon avocado oil
- Cooking spray

Addresses:
1. In the shallow bowl, mix the avocado oil, ground coriander, apple cider vinegar and fresh coriander.
2. Next, place the prawns in the large bowl and drizzle with the avocado oil mixture. Mix well and leave to marinate for a few minutes.
3. Then thread the prawns onto the skewers.
4. Preheat the fryer to 200°C.
5. Place the shrimp skewers in the air fryer and cook for 5 minutes.

591. Pesto-crusted salmon

Servings: 2
Cooking time: 15 minutes
Ingredients:
- ¼ cup pesto
- 2 salmon fillets of 115 grams
- 2 tablespoons unsalted butter, melted

Addresses:
1. Place the pesto in a bowl.
2. Transfer the salmon fillets to a round baking dish, about 15 centimetres in diameter.
3. Brush the fillets with butter and then with the pesto mixture making sure to coat both the top and bottom. Place the baking dish inside the fryer.
4. Bake for twelve minutes at 200°C.
5. The salmon is ready when it flakes easily when pierced with a fork. Serve hot.

592. Tilapia with capers and cheese sauce

Servings: 4
Cooking time: 15 minutes
Ingredients:
- 4 tilapia fillets
- 1 tablespoon of extra virgin olive oil
- Celery salt, to taste
- Freshly ground pink peppercorns, to taste

For the creamy caper sauce you need:
- 1/2 cup crème fraîche
- 2 tablespoons mayonnaise
- 1/4 cup cottage cheese, at room temperature
- 1 tablespoon capers, finely chopped

Addresses:
1. Toss tilapia fillets with olive oil, celery salt and peppercorns until well coated.
2. Place the fillets in a single layer in the bottom of the cooking basket of the Air Fryer.
3. Air fry at 180°C, turn once during cooking.
4. In the meantime, prepare the sauce by mixing the remaining elements.
5. Finally, garnish the fried tilapia fillets with the sauce and serve immediately.

593. Grilled Squid Rings with Kale and Tomatoes

Servings: 3
Cooking time: 15 minutes
Ingredients:
- 1 squid of half a kilo, cleaned and cut into rings
- Salt and pepper to taste
- 3 cloves garlic, minced
- 1 sprig of chopped rosemary
- ¼ cup red wine vinegar
- 3 pounds kale, shredded
- 3 chopped tomatoes

Addresses:
1. Preheat the air fryer to 200°C.
2. Place the grill pan attachment on the air fryer.
3. Season the squid rings with salt, pepper, garlic, rosemary and wine vinegar.
4. Roast for 15 minutes.
5. Serve the octopus on a bed of kale leaves and garnish with tomatoes on top.

594. Parsley Linguini with Grilled Tuna

Servings: 2
Cooking time: 20 minutes
Ingredients:
- 1 tablespoon chopped capers
- 1 tablespoon of olive oil
- 340 grams of linguine, cooked according to package directions
- 450 g fresh tuna fillets
- 2 cups chopped parsley leaves
- Juice of 1 lemon
- Salt and pepper to taste

Addresses:
1. Preheat the fryer to 200°C.
2. Place the grill pan attachment on the air fryer.
3. Season the tuna with salt and pepper. Brush with oil.
4. Roast for 20 minutes.
5. Once the tuna is cooked, flake it with a fork and place it on top of the cooked linguini. Add parsley and capers. Season with salt and pepper and add the lemon juice.

595. Grilled salmon with butter and wine

Servings: 4
Cooking time: 45 minutes
Ingredients:
- 2 cloves garlic, minced
- 4 tablespoons melted butter
- Sea salt and ground black pepper, to taste
- 1 teaspoon smoked paprika
- 1/2 teaspoon onion powder
- 1 tablespoon lime juice
- 1/4 cup dry white wine
- 4 salmon fillets

Addresses:
1. Place all ingredients in a large ceramic bowl. Cover and marinate for 30 minutes in the refrigerator.
2. Place the salmon fillets on the grill tray.
3. Bake at 200°C for 5 minutes, or until the salmon fillets flake easily with a fork.
4. Turn the fish fillets over, baste them with the reserved marinade and cook for another 5 minutes. Bon appetit!

596. Louisiana shrimp

Servings: 4
Cooking time: 18 minutes
Ingredients:
- 1 beaten egg
- ¼ cup flour
- ¼ cup white breadcrumbs
- 2 tablespoons Cajun seasoning
- Salt and black pepper to taste
- 1 lemon, cut into wedges

Addresses:
1. Preheat your air fryer to 200°C. Spray the air fryer basket with cooking spray.
2. Beat the eggs in a bowl and season with salt and black pepper. In another bowl, mix the white breadcrumbs with the Cajun seasoning. In a third bowl, pour the flour.
3. Dredge the prawns in the flour, then in the eggs and finally in the breadcrumb mixture. Spray with cooking spray and place in the cooking basket. Cook for 6 minutes, slide basket out of fryer and turn over, cook for a further 6 minutes. Serve with lemon wedges.

597. Sole and cauliflower fritters

Servings: 2
Cooking time: 30 minutes

Ingredients:
- 1/2 pound sole fillets
- 1/2 pound cauliflower puree
- 1 egg, well beaten
- 1/2 cup chopped red onion
- 2 cloves garlic, minced
- 2 tablespoons fresh parsley, chopped
- 1 pepper, finely chopped
- 1/2 teaspoon Bonnet scotch bonnet pepper, minced
- 1 tablespoon of olive oil
- 1 tablespoon coconut aminos
- 1/2 teaspoon paprika
- Salt and white pepper, to taste

Addresses:
1. Start by preheating your fryer to 200°C. Spray the sides and bottom of the cooking basket with cooking spray.
2. Cook the sole fillets in the preheated Air Fryer for 10 minutes, turning them halfway through cooking.
3. In a mixing bowl, mash the sole fillets into flakes. Stir in the remaining ingredients. Form fish mixture into patties.
4. Bake in the preheated Air Fryer at 200°C for 1 minute, turning them over halfway through baking. Bon appetit!

598. Rosemary shrimps

Servings: 4
Cooking time: 12 minutes
Ingredients:
- 450 grams of shrimps, peeled and deveined
- 1 cup halved cherry tomatoes
- 4 cloves garlic, minced
- Salt and black pepper to taste
- 1 tablespoon chopped rosemary
- 2 tablespoons melted ghee

Addresses:
1. In a frying pan that fits the air fryer, combine all ingredients and stir.
2. Place the pan in the fryer and cook at 190°C for a few minutes.
3. Divide into bowls and serve hot.

599. Trout and tomato mix with courgettes

Servings: 4
Cooking time: 15 minutes
Ingredients:
- 3 courgettes, cut into medium pieces
- 4 fillets of trout, boneless
- 2 tablespoons olive oil
- ¼ cup keto tomato sauce
- Salt and black pepper to taste
- 1 clove garlic, minced
- 1 tablespoon lemon juice
- ½ cup chopped coriander

Addresses:
1. In a frying pan that fits your air fryer, mix the fish with the other ingredients, stir.
2. Place in the fryer and cook at 190°C.
3. When ready, divide between the plates and serve immediately.

600. Crab cakes

Servings: 4
Cooking time: 55 minutes
Ingredients:
- ¼ cup chopped red onion
- 1 tablespoon basil, chopped
- ¼ cup chopped celery
- ¼ cup chopped red pepper
- 3 tablespoons mayonnaise
- Zest of half a lemon
- ¼ cup breadcrumbs
- 2 tablespoons chopped parsley
- Old bay seasoning, to taste
- Cooking spray

Addresses:
1. Preheat the air fryer to 200°C.
2. Place all ingredients in a large bowl and mix well.
3. Make 4 large crab cakes with the mixture and place them on a lined tray.
4. Refrigerate for 30 minutes. Coat the air basket with cooking spray and place the crab cakes in it.
5. Cook for 7 minutes on each side, until crispy.

601. Tilapia with walnut crust

Portions: 5
Cooking time: 20 minutes
Ingredients:
- 2 tablespoons ground flax seeds
- 1 teaspoon paprika
- Sea salt and white pepper, to taste
- 1 teaspoon garlic paste
- 2 tablespoons of extra virgin olive oil
- 1/2 cup ground pecans
- 5 tilapia fillets, cut in halves

Addresses:
1. Combine ground flax seeds, paprika, salt, white pepper, garlic paste, olive oil and ground walnuts in a Ziploc bag.
2. Add the fish fillets and shake to coat well.
3. Spray the Air Fryer basket with cooking spray.
4. Cook in the preheated air fryer at 200°C for 10 minutes, turn over and cook for a further 6 minutes. Work in batches.
5. Serve with lemon wedges, if desired. Enjoy.

602. Spiced coconut shrimp kebab

Servings: 6
Cooking time: 12 minutes + marinating time
Ingredients:
- 1 lime, peeled and juiced
- 1/3 cup chopped fresh cilantro
- 1/3 cup shredded coconut

- 1/4 cup olive oil
- 1/4 cup soy sauce
- 450 grams of medium-sized uncooked shrimps, peeled and deveined
- 2 cloves garlic
- 2 seeded jalapeño chillies

Addresses:
1. In food processor, process until smooth mixture of soy sauce, olive oil, coconut oil, cilantro, garlic, lime juice, lime zest and jalapeño.
2. In a shallow dish, mix well the prawns and the prepared marinade. Mix well to coat and marinate in the refrigerator for 3 hours.
3. Thread the prawns onto the skewers. Place them on the skewer rack of the fryer.
4. Cook at 180°C for 6 minutes. If necessary, cook in batches.
5. Serve and enjoy.

603. Halibut fillets

Servings: 4
Cooking time: 15 minutes
Ingredients:
- 450 grams of halibut fillets
- Salt and pepper to taste
- 1 teaspoon basil, dried
- 2 tablespoons honey
- ¼ cup vegetable oil
- 2 ½ tablespoons Worcester sauce
- 1 tablespoon freshly squeezed lemon juice
- 2 tablespoons vermouth
- 1 tablespoon of fresh parsley leaves, coarsely chopped

Addresses:
1. Place all ingredients in a large bowl. Combine and coat the fish completely with the seasoning.
2. Transfer to your Air Fryer and cook at 200°C for 5 minutes.
3. Turn the fish over and leave to cook for a further 5 minutes.
4. Make sure the fish is cooked through, leaving it in the fryer for a few more minutes if necessary.
5. Serve with a portion of potato salad.

604. Tilapia with paprika

Servings: 4
Cooking time: 20 minutes
Ingredients:
- 4 boneless tilapia fillets
- 3 tablespoons melted ghee
- Pinch of salt and black pepper
- 2 tablespoons capers
- 1 teaspoon garlic powder
- ½ teaspoon smoked paprika
- ½ teaspoon dried oregano
- 2 tablespoons lemon juice

Addresses:
1. In a bowl, combine all the ingredients except the fish and mix.
2. Place the fish in a frying pan that fits the air fryer, pour the caper mixture all over, place the pan in the air fryer and cook at 180°C for 20 minutes, shaking halfway through.
3. Divide among the plates and serve hot.

605. Jumbo shrimps

Servings: 4
Cooking time: 10 minutes
Ingredients:
- 12 jumbo shrimps
- ½ teaspoon garlic salt
- ¼ teaspoon freshly ground mixed peppercorns

For the sauce you need:
- 1 teaspoon Dijon mustard
- 4 tablespoons mayonnaise
- 1 teaspoon lemon zest
- 1 teaspoon chipotle powder
- ½ teaspoon cumin powder

Addresses:
1. Sprinkle the garlic salt over the prawns and top with the ground peppercorns.
2. Fry the prawns in the cooking basket at 200°C for 5 minutes.
3. Turn the prawns over and cook for a further 2 minutes.
4. Meanwhile, mix all the ingredients for the sauce with a whisk.
5. Serve over the prawns.

606. Cajun Cod Fillets with Avocado Sauce

Servings: 2
Cooking time: 20 minutes
Ingredients:
- 2 cod fillets
- 1 egg
- Sea salt, to taste
- 1/2 cup tortilla chips, crushed
- 2 teaspoons olive oil
- 1/2 avocado, peeled, pitted and mashed
- 1 tablespoon of mayonnaise
- 3 tablespoons sour cream
- 1/2 teaspoon yellow mustard
- 1 teaspoon lemon juice
- 1 clove garlic, minced
- 1/4 teaspoon black pepper
- 1/4 teaspoon salt
- 1/4 teaspoon hot pepper sauce

Addresses:
1. Start by preheating your fryer to 180°C. Spray the fryer basket with cooking oil.
2. Pat the fish fillets dry with a tea towel. Beat the egg in a shallow bowl.
3. In a separate bowl, thoroughly combine the salt, crushed tortilla chips and olive oil.
4. Dip the fish into the egg and then into the crumb mixture, making sure to coat well.

5. Cook in the preheated Air Fryer for approximately 12 minutes.
6. Meanwhile, prepare the avocado sauce by mixing the rest of the ingredients in a bowl. Place in your refrigerator until ready to serve.
7. Serve the fish fillets with the cold avocado sauce on the side - bon appetit!

607. Shrimp and celery salad

Servings: 4
Cooking time: 5 minutes
Ingredients:
- 85 grams of chevre
- 1 teaspoon of avocado oil
- ½ teaspoon dried oregano
- 225 grams of peeled prawns
- 1 teaspoon melted butter
- ½ teaspoon salt
- ½ teaspoon chilli flakes
- 115 grams celery stalk, chopped

Addresses:
1. Sprinkle the shrimps with dried oregano and melted butter and put them in the air fryer.
2. Cook the shellfish at 200°C for 5 minutes.
3. In the meantime, shred the chevre.
4. In a salad bowl, place the chopped celery stalk, shredded chevre, chilli flakes, salt and avocado oil.
5. Mix the salad well and top with the cooked prawns.

608. Scallops with butter

Servings: 2
Cooking time: 4 minutes
Ingredients:
- 340 grams of scallops, cleaned and very dry
- 1 tablespoon melted butter
- ½ tablespoon fresh thyme, chopped
- Salt and black pepper

Addresses:
1. Preheat the fryer to 200°C and grease one fryer basket.
2. Mix the scallops, butter, thyme, salt and black pepper in a bowl.
3. Place the scallops in the fryer basket and cook for about 4 minutes.
4. Arrange the scallops on a platter and serve hot.

609. Trout with butter and chives

Servings: 4
Cooking time: 12 minutes
Ingredients:
- 4 fillets of trout, boneless
- 4 tablespoons melted butter
- Salt and black pepper to taste
- Juice of 1 lime
- 1 tablespoon chopped chives
- 1 tablespoon chopped parsley

Addresses:
1. Mix the fish fillets with the melted butter, salt and pepper. Then rub in gently.
2. Place the fish in the basket of your air fryer and cook at 200°C for 6 minutes on each side.
3. Divide among plates and serve with lime juice drizzled over the top and parsley and chives sprinkled on top.

610. Ginger Cod

Servings: 2
Cooking time: 8 minutes
Ingredients:
- Cod fillet weighing approximately 280 grams
- ½ teaspoon cayenne pepper
- ¼ teaspoon ground coriander
- ½ teaspoon ground ginger
- ½ teaspoon ground black pepper
- 1 tablespoon sunflower oil
- ½ teaspoon salt
- ½ teaspoon dried rosemary
- ½ teaspoon ground paprika

Addresses:
1. In a shallow bowl, combine the cayenne pepper, ground coriander, ginger, ground black pepper, salt, dried rosemary and ground paprika.
2. Then rub the cod fillet with the spice mixture. Then drizzle with sunflower oil.
3. Preheat the air fryer to 200°C.
4. Place the cod fillet in the air fryer and cook for 4 minutes. Then carefully turn it over on the other side and cook for a further 4 minutes.

Vegetables and garnishes

611. Delicious ratatouille

Servings: 6
Cooking time: 15 minutes
Ingredients:
- 1 aubergine cut into cubes
- 3 cloves garlic, minced
- 1 onion, diced
- 3 diced tomatoes
- 2 diced bell peppers
- 1 tablespoon vinegar
- 1 ½ tablespoons olive oil
- 2 tablespoons Herbes de Provence
- Pepper
- Salt

Addresses:
1. Preheat the air fryer to 200°C.
2. Add all the ingredients to the bowl, mix well and transfer to the fryer's baking dish.

3. Place the dish in the air fryer and cook for 15 minutes. Remove halfway through.
4. Serve and enjoy.

612. Roasted aubergine

Servings: 1
Cooking time: 20 minutes
Ingredients:
- 1 large aubergine
- 2 tablespoons olive oil
- ¼ teaspoon salt
- ½ teaspoon garlic powder

Addresses:
1. Prepare the aubergine by cutting off the top and bottom and cutting into slices about 6 millimetres thick.
2. Apply olive oil to the slices with a brush, coating both sides. Season each side with a pinch of salt and garlic powder.
3. Place the slices in the fryer and cook at 150°C.
4. Serve immediately.

613. Green beans and tomatoes recipe

Servings: 4
Cooking time: 25 minutes
Ingredients:
- 1 pint cherry tomatoes
- 2 tablespoons olive oil
- 450 grams of green beans
- Salt and black pepper to taste

Addresses:
1. In a bowl, mix the cherry tomatoes with the green beans, olive oil, salt and pepper.
2. Mix everything very well and transfer to your air fryer.
3. Bake at 200°C.
4. Divide between plates and serve immediately.

614. Courgette latkes

Servings: 6
Cooking time: 12 minutes
Ingredients:
- 200 grams of grated courgette
- 1 beaten egg
- 1 teaspoon salt
- 2 spring onions, chopped
- 2 tablespoons almond flour
- 1 teaspoon of avocado oil
- ½ teaspoon ground black pepper

Addresses:
1. In the bowl of a blender, mix the grated courgette, egg, salt, chopped onion, almond flour and ground black pepper.
2. Use the spoon to make medium-sized latkes.
3. Preheat the air fryer to 200°C.
4. Place the latkes in the air fryer in a single layer and drizzle with avocado oil. Cook the garnish for 6 minutes on each side.

615. Summer vegetable fritters

Servings: 2
Cooking time: 20 minutes
Ingredients:
- 1 grated and squeezed courgette
- 1 cup of boiled cauliflower florets
- 4 tablespoons grated Romano cheese
- 2 tablespoons chopped fresh shallots
- 1 teaspoon chopped fresh garlic
- 1 tablespoon peanut oil
- Sea salt and ground black pepper
- 1 teaspoon cayenne pepper

Addresses:
1. In a mixing bowl, combine all ingredients well until everything is well incorporated.
2. Form the mixture into patties. Spray the basket of the Air Fryer with cooking spray.
3. Cook in the preheated Air Fryer at 180°C for 6 minutes. Turn them over and cook for another 6 minutes.
4. Serve immediately and enjoy.

616. Rainbow Cheese and Vegetable Cake

Servings: 4
Cooking time: 50 minutes
Ingredients:
- 450 grams cauliflower, cut into small florets
- 2 tablespoons olive oil
- ½ teaspoon crushed red pepper flakes
- ½ teaspoon of freshly ground black pepper
- Salt
- 3 bell peppers, thinly sliced
- 1 serrano pepper, thinly sliced
- 2 medium tomatoes, cut into slices
- 1 leek, thinly sliced
- 2 cloves garlic, minced
- 1 cup shredded Monterey cheese

Addresses:
1. Start by preheating your Air Fryer to 180°C.
2. Spray a pan with cooking oil.
3. Place the cauliflower in the pan in an even layer, drizzle 1 tablespoon of olive oil on top. Then add the red pepper, black pepper and salt.
4. Add 2 peppers and ½ leek. Then add the tomatoes and the remaining tablespoon of olive oil.
5. Add the rest of the peppers, leeks and chopped garlic. Top with the cheese.
6. Cover the pan with foil and bake for 32 minutes. Remove the foil and increase the temperature to 200°C, bake for a further 16 minutes, bon appetit!

617. Broccoli Casserole

Servings: 8
Cooking time: 30 minutes
Ingredients:
- 900 grams of broccoli florets

- 2 cups shredded cheddar cheese
- ¼ cup vegetable stock
- ½ cup heavy cream
- 2 cloves garlic, minced
- 115 grams of cream cheese
- 1 cup mozzarella cheese
- 3 tablespoons olive oil
- Pepper
- Salt

Addresses:
1. Preheat the air fryer to 190°C.
2. Layer the broccoli florets in a baking dish for frying. Drizzle with olive oil and season with pepper and salt.
3. Cook the broccoli in the air fryer for 15 minutes.
4. Meanwhile, combine heavy cream, broth, garlic, cream cheese, mozzarella cheese and 1 cup cheddar cheese in a medium saucepan over medium-low heat. Stir frequently.
5. Once the broccoli is cooked, pour the heavy cream mixture over the broccoli and stir well.
6. Sprinkle the remaining cheddar cheese on top and cook for a further 12 minutes.
7. Serve and enjoy.

618. Coconut Risotto

Servings: 4
Cooking time: 20 minutes
Ingredients:
- 2 cups cauliflower rice
- 1 cup coconut milk
- 2 tbsp. melted coconut oil
- 1 tablespoon chopped coriander
- 1 tablespoon of olive oil
- 1 teaspoon lime zest, grated
- 2 tablespoons grated Parmesan cheese

Addresses:
1. In a frying pan that fits your air fryer, combine all ingredients and stir.
2. Place in the fryer and cook at 180°C for 20 minutes.
3. Divide between plates and serve as a side dish.

619. Vegetable and egg salad

Servings: 4
Cooking time: 35 minutes
Ingredients:
- 1/3 pound of Brussels sprouts
- 1/2 cup sliced radishes
- 1/2 cup shredded mozzarella cheese
- 1 red onion, chopped
- 4 hard boiled and sliced eggs
- 1/4 cup olive oil
- 2 tablespoons champagne vinegar
- 1 teaspoon Dijon mustard
- Sea salt and ground black pepper, to taste

Addresses:
1. Start by preheating your fryer to 190°C.
2. Add the Brussels sprouts and radishes to the cooking basket.
3. Spray with cooking spray and cook for 15 minutes. Leave to cool at room temperature for about 15 minutes.
4. Mix the vegetables with the cheese and red onion.
5. Mix all the ingredients for the dressing and toss to combine well. Serve with the hard-boiled eggs and enjoy!

620. Chickpeas, fried with herbs

Servings: 4
Cooking time: 20 minutes
Ingredients:
- 2 tablespoons olive oil
- 1 teaspoon dried rosemary
- ½ teaspoon dried thyme
- ¼ teaspoon dried sage
- ¼ teaspoon salt

Addresses:
1. In a bowl, combine the chickpeas, oil, rosemary, thyme, sage and salt.
2. Transfer the preparation to the air fryer and spread into an even layer.
3. Cook at 190°C, stir once halfway through cooking.

621. Super Cabbage Canapés

Servings: 2
Cooking time: 15 minutes
Ingredients:
- 1 cube Amul cheese
- ½ carrot cut into cubes
- ¼ onion, diced
- ¼ of a pepper, diced
- Fresh basil for garnish

Addresses:
1. Preheat your fryer to 180°C.
2. In a bowl, combine the onion, carrot, pepper and cheese. Toss to coat evenly.
3. Add the cabbage rounds to the fryer cooking basket. Cover with vegetable mixture and cook for 5 minutes.
4. Serve with a garnish of fresh basil.

622. Crisp and tender Brussels sprouts

Servings: 2
Cooking time: 10 minutes
Ingredients:
- 2 cups of sliced Brussels sprouts
- 1 tablespoon balsamic vinegar
- 1 tablespoon of olive oil
- ¼ teaspoon sea salt

Addresses:
1. Add all ingredients to the large bowl and mix well.
2. Spray the air fryer basket with cooking spray.
3. Transfer the Brussels sprouts mixture to the fryer basket.

4. Cook the Brussels sprouts for 10 minutes. Shake the basket halfway through.
5. Serve and enjoy.

623. Amazing cheese sticks

Servings: 6
Cooking time: 15 minutes
Ingredients:
- 12 mozzarella cheese sticks
- ¼ cup flour
- 2 cups breadcrumbs
- 2 whole eggs
- ¼ cup grated Parmesan cheese

Addresses:
1. Preheat the fryer to 180°C.
2. Pour the breadcrumbs into a bowl.
3. Whisk the eggs in another bowl.
4. In a third bowl, mix the Parmesan and flour.
5. Dredge each cheese stick in the flour mixture, then in the eggs and finally in the breadcrumbs.
6. Place in the basket of the air fryer and cook for 7 minutes, turning once.

624. Mediterranean vegetable skewers

Servings: 4
Cooking time: 30 minutes
Ingredients:
- 2 medium courgettes cut into 2.5 centimetre chunks
- 2 red peppers cut into 2.5 centimetre pieces
- 1 green pepper cut into 2.5 centimetre pieces
- 1 red onion cut into 2.5 centimetre pieces
- 2 tablespoons olive oil
- Sea salt
- ½ teaspoon black pepper, preferably freshly ground
- ½ teaspoon red pepper flakes

Addresses:
1. Soak the wooden skewers in water for minutes.
2. Thread the vegetables onto the skewers, drizzle olive oil over all the vegetable skewers, sprinkle with the spices.
3. Cook in the preheated air fryer at 200°C for 1 minute.
4. Serve hot and enjoy.

625. Courgette mix recipe

Servings: 6
Cooking time: 24 minutes
Ingredients:
- 6 courgettes, halved and sliced
- 3 cloves garlic, minced
- 55 grams of grated Parmesan cheese
- 3/4 cup heavy cream
- Salt and black pepper to taste
- 1 tablespoon butter
- 1 teaspoon dried oregano
- 1/2 cup yellow onion, chopped

Addresses:
1. Heat a frying pan that fits your air fryer with the butter over medium-high heat, add the onion, stir and cook for 4 minutes.
2. Add the garlic, courgettes, oregano, salt, pepper and cream, mix, put in your air fryer and cook at 180°C for 10 minutes.
3. Add the Parmesan, stir, divide between the plates and serve.

626. Lemon cabbage

Servings: 4
Cooking time: 25 minutes
Ingredients:
- 1 head of green cabbage, shredded and coarsely chopped
- 2 tablespoons olive oil
- 1 tablespoon chopped coriander
- 1 tablespoon lemon juice
- Pinch of salt and black pepper

Addresses:
1. Preheat your air fryer to 185°C.
2. Add the cabbage pieces mixed with all the ingredients in the basket and cook for 25 minutes.
3. Divide between plates and serve as a side dish.

627. Mozzarella Risotto

Servings: 4
Cooking time: 20 minutes
Ingredients:
- 450 grams of white mushrooms, cut into slices
- ¼ cup shredded mozzarella cheese
- 1 head of cauliflower, florets separated and shredded
- 1 cup chicken stock
- 1 tablespoon chopped thyme
- 1 teaspoon Italian seasoning
- Pinch of salt and black pepper
- 2 tablespoons olive oil

Addresses:
1. Add the oil to a frying pan sized to fit the air fryer and heat over medium heat.
2. Add the cauliflower rice and mushrooms to the pan, stir and cook for a couple of minutes.
3. Add the rest of the ingredients to the pan except the thyme. Then mix.
4. Transfer the pan to the air fryer, set the temperature to 180°C and cook for 20 minutes.
5. Divide the risotto among the plates and serve with thyme sprinkled on top.

628. Mushroom pan with thyme

Servings: 2
Cooking time: 8 minutes

Ingredients:
- 1/2 lb. cremini mushrooms, sliced
- 1 cup coconut cream
- 1 teaspoon of avocado oil
- ¼ teaspoon chopped garlic
- ½ teaspoon dried thyme

Addresses:
1. In the frying pan of the air fryer, mix the mushrooms with the cream and the other ingredients.
2. Stir well and cook at 190°C for 8 minutes.
3. Divide into bowls and serve.

629. Fried asparagus with romesco sauce

Servings: 4
Cooking time: 30 minutes
Ingredients:
- Salt and black pepper
- ½ cup almond flour
- 450 grams of asparagus, cut and washed
- 2 eggs
- 2 chopped tomatoes
- Romesco sauce
- 2 roasted peppers, chopped
- ½ cup almond flour
- ½ teaspoon garlic powder
- 1 tablespoon vinegar
- 2 slices of toasted bread, cut into chunks
- ½ teaspoon paprika
- 1 teaspoon crushed red chilli flakes
- 1 tablespoon tomato puree
- ½ cup extra virgin olive oil

Addresses:
1. Preheat the air fryer to 200°C.
2. Grease the air fryer basket with cooking spray.
3. In a bowl, combine the panko breadcrumbs, salt and pepper. In another shallow dish, beat the eggs, season with salt and pepper. In a third plate, pour the almond flour.
4. Dredge the asparagus in the almond flour, then in the eggs and finally in the breadcrumbs.
5. Place the asparagus in the cooking basket of your air fryer and cook for 10 minutes, turning halfway through.
6. Blend all the sauce ingredients in a food processor until a good sauce is formed. Serve the asparagus with the romesco sauce.

630. Aubergine meatballs with almonds

Servings: 7
Cooking time: 8 minutes
Ingredients:
- 3 peeled and boiled aubergines
- 1 beaten egg
- 1 teaspoon chopped garlic
- 3 chopped spring onions
- ½ cup almond flour
- 1 teaspoon chives
- ½ teaspoon chilli flakes
- ½ teaspoon salt
- 1 teaspoon sesame oil

Addresses:
1. Chop the cooked aubergines and squeeze out their juice.
2. Then transfer the aubergines to the blender. Add the egg, chopped garlic, spring onion, almond flour, chives, chilli flakes and salt.
3. Mix until homogenous and smooth. Then spoon the mixture into the aubergine meatballs.
4. Preheat the air fryer to 190°C.
5. Place the aubergine meatballs in the air fryer and drizzle with sesame oil. Cook the meatballs for 8 minutes.

631. Pumpkin rice dish

Servings: 4
Cooking time: 35 minutes
Ingredients:
- 155 grams of white rice
- 4 cups chicken stock
- 170 grams of pumpkin puree
- 2 tablespoons olive oil
- 1 small yellow onion, chopped.
- 2 cloves garlic, minced
- 1/2 teaspoon nutmeg
- 1 teaspoon chopped thyme
- 1/2 teaspoon grated ginger
- 1/2 teaspoon cinnamon powder
- 1/2 teaspoon allspice
- 115 grams of milk cream

Addresses:
1. In a dish that fits your air fryer, mix the oil with the onion, garlic, rice, stock, pumpkin puree, nutmeg, thyme, ginger, cinnamon, allspice and cream.
2. Stir all ingredients well.
3. Place the preparation in the basket of your air fryer and cook at 180°C for 30 minutes.
4. Divide between plates and serve as a side dish.

632. Courgette and Parmesan crisps

Servings: 4
Cooking time: 20 minutes
Ingredients:
- 450 grams of courgettes, peeled and cut into slices
- 1 egg, lightly beaten
- 1 cup Parmesan cheese, preferably freshly grated

Addresses:
1. Dry the courgettes with a kitchen towel.
2. On a plate, mix the egg and cheese together well. Then coat the courgette slices with the breadcrumb mixture.

3. Cook in the preheated air fryer at 200°C for 9 minutes, shaking the basket halfway through the cooking time.
4. Work in batches until the potatoes are golden brown - bon appetit!

633. Spicy jacket potatoes

Servings: 2
Cooking time: 15 minutes
Ingredients:
- 4 potatoes, peeled and cut into chunks
- 2 tablespoons olive oil
- Sea salt and ground black pepper
- 1 teaspoon cayenne pepper
- ½ teaspoon ancho chili powder

Addresses:
1. Mix all the ingredients in a bowl until the potatoes are well coated.
2. Place in the basket of the Air Fryer and cook at 200°C for 6 minutes, shake the basket and cook for a further 6 minutes.
3. Serve hot with your favourite dipping sauce and enjoy!

634. Butter cabbage

Servings: 4
Cooking time: 20 minutes
Ingredients:
- 55 grams of melted butter
- 1 head of green cabbage, shredded
- 1 and ½ cups of heavy cream
- ¼ cup chopped parsley
- 1 tablespoon sweet paprika
- 1 teaspoon lemon zest

Addresses:
1. Heat a frying pan that fits the air fryer.
2. Add the butter to the pan and allow it to melt. When it does, add the cabbage and sauté for 5 minutes.
3. Then add the rest of the ingredients to the pan and mix.
4. Place the pan in the air fryer and cook at 190°C.
5. Divide between plates and serve as a side dish.

635. Japanese tempura bowl

Servings: 3
Cooking time: 20 minutes
Ingredients:
- 1 cup all-purpose flour
- Kosher salt and ground black pepper, to taste
- ½ teaspoon paprika
- 2 eggs
- 3 tablespoons sparkling water
- 1 cup panko crumbs
- 2 tablespoons olive oil
- 1 cup green beans
- 1 onion cut into rings
- 1 courgette, cut into slices
- 2 tablespoons soy sauce
- 1 tablespoon mirin
- 1 teaspoon dashi beans

Addresses:
1. In a shallow bowl, mix the flour, salt, black pepper and paprika.
2. In another bowl, whisk together the eggs and sparkling water. In a third shallow bowl, combine the panko crumbs with the olive oil.
3. Dredge the vegetables in the flour mixture, then in the egg mixture, then in the panko mixture to coat them evenly.
4. Cook in the preheated Air Fryer at 200°C for 10 minutes, shaking the basket halfway through the cooking time.
5. Work in batches until the vegetables are crisp and golden brown.
6. Next, prepare the sauce by whisking together the soy sauce, mirin and dashi granules. Enjoy!

636. Broccoli and cranberry mix

Servings: 4
Cooking time: 25 minutes
Ingredients:
- 1 head of broccoli, florets separated
- 2 chopped shallots
- Pinch of salt and black pepper
- ½ cup blueberries
- ½ cup chopped almonds
- 6 slices of bacon, cooked and crumbled
- 3 tablespoons balsamic vinegar

Addresses:
1. Look for a pan that is sized to fit your air fryer,
2. When the pan is hot, add the broccoli and the rest of the ingredients. Stir.
3. When the preparation is ready, place the pan in the air fryer and cook at 190°C for 25 minutes.
4. Divide between the plates and serve.

637. Healthy green beans

Servings: 4
Cooking time: 6 minutes
Ingredients:
- 450 grams of green beans, trimmed
- Pepper
- Salt

Addresses:
1. Spray the air fryer basket with cooking spray.
2. Preheat the air fryer to 200°C.
3. Add the green beans to the fryer basket and season with pepper and salt.
4. Cook the green beans for 6 minutes. Turn halfway through.
5. Serve and enjoy.

638. Mediterranean tomatoes with feta cheese

Servings: 2

Cooking time: 20 minutes
Ingredients:
- 3 medium-sized tomatoes, cut into four slices, patted dry
- 1 teaspoon basil, dried
- 1 teaspoon dried oregano
- ¼ teaspoon crushed red pepper flakes
- 1/2 teaspoon sea salt
- 3 slices Feta cheese

Addresses:
1. Drizzle the tomatoes with cooking oil and transfer them to the basket of the Air Fryer. Sprinkle with seasoning.
2. Cook at 180°C for approximately 8 minutes, turning them over halfway through cooking.
3. Cover with the cheese and cook for 4 more minutes, bon appetit!

639. Asparagus with paprika

Servings: 4
Cooking time: 10 minutes
Ingredients:
- 450 grams of asparagus, trimmed
- 3 tablespoons olive oil
- Pinch of salt and black pepper
- 1 tablespoon sweet paprika

Addresses:
1. In a bowl, combine the asparagus with the rest of the ingredients and mix.
2. Place the asparagus in the basket of your air fryer and cook at 200°C for minutes.
3. Divide between the plates and serve.

640. Lemon cabbage

Servings: 4
Cooking time: 15 minutes
Ingredients:
- 10 cups kale, shredded
- 2 tablespoons olive oil
- Salt and black pepper to taste
- 2 tablespoons lemon zest
- 1 tablespoon lemon juice
- 1/3 cup pine nuts

Addresses:
1. In a frying pan that fits the air fryer, combine all ingredients and mix.
2. Place the pan in the air fryer and cook at 190°C for a few minutes.
3. Divide between plates and serve as a side dish.

641. Roasted cauliflower

Servings: 4
Cooking time: 12 minutes
Ingredients:
- 1 large cauliflower head, cut into florets
- 1 lemon peel
- 3 tablespoons olive oil
- 2 teaspoons lemon juice
- 1/2 teaspoon Italian seasoning
- 1/2 teaspoon garlic powder
- 1/4 teaspoon pepper
- 1/4 teaspoon salt

Addresses:
1. Preheat the air fryer to 200°C.
2. In a bowl, combine the olive oil, lemon juice, Italian seasoning, garlic powder, lemon zest, pepper and salt.
3. Add the cauliflower florets to the bowl and mix well.
4. Add the cauliflower florets to the fryer basket and cook for 12 minutes. Shake the basket halfway through.
5. Serve and enjoy.

642. Coriander pepper mix

Servings: 4
Cooking time: 20 minutes
Ingredients:
- 225 grams of mini peppers, halved
- 1 tablespoon of olive oil
- 1 tablespoon chopped coriander
- 225 grams cream cheese, mild
- 1 cup shredded cheddar cheese
- Salt and black pepper to taste

Addresses:
1. Grease a baking dish that fits the air fryer with the oil and arrange the peppers inside.
2. In a bowl, mix all the ingredients, whisk well, spread over the peppers.
3. Place the dish in the air fryer and cook at 185°C for 20 minutes.
4. Divide the peppers between the plates and serve as a garnish.

643. Italian tomatoes with goat cheese

Servings: 4
Cooking time: 20 minutes
Ingredients:
- 170 grams of goat's cheese, sliced
- 2 shallots, thinly sliced
- 2 Pantano Romanesco tomatoes, cut into approximately 1.25 centimetre slices
- 1 ½ tablespoons of extra virgin olive oil
- 3/4 teaspoon sea salt
- Fresh parsley for garnish
- Fresh basil, chopped

Addresses:
1. Preheat your Air Fryer to 190°C.
2. Now, pat each tomato slice dry with a paper towel. Sprinkle each slice with salt and chopped basil. Top with a slice of goat cheese.
3. Top with the shallot slices, drizzle with olive oil. Add the prepared tomato and feta bites to the fryer basket.
4. Cook in the Air Fryer for about 1 minute. Finally, adjust seasoning to taste and serve garnished with fresh parsley leaves - enjoy!

644. Cauliflower with Buffalo Sauce

Servings: 4
Cooking time: 25 minutes
Ingredients:
- 3 tablespoons buffalo hot sauce
- 1 egg white
- 1 cup panko bread crumbs
- ½ teaspoon salt
- ¼ teaspoon freshly ground black pepper
- ½ head cauliflower, cut into florets
- Cooking spray

Addresses:
1. In a bowl, mix the butter, hot sauce and egg white.
2. Mix the breadcrumbs with salt and pepper in a separate bowl.
3. Place the cauliflower florets in the hot sauce mixture until well coated.
4. Stir the coated cauliflower into the crumbs until coated.
5. Then transfer the coated florets to the air fryer.
6. Spray with cooking spray.
7. Cook for 18 minutes at 170°C. If necessary, you can cook the preparation in batches.

645. Potatoes and special tomato sauce recipe

Servings: 4
Cooking time: 26 minutes
Ingredients:
- 900 grams of potatoes, diced
- 4 cloves garlic, minced
- 1 yellow onion, chopped.
- 1 cup tomato sauce
- ½ teaspoon dried oregano
- ½ teaspoon dried parsley
- 2 tablespoons basil, chopped
- 2 tablespoons olive oil

Addresses:
1. Place the oil in a frying pan that fits your air fryer and heat over medium heat.
2. When the pan is hot, add the onion, stir and cook for 2 minutes.
3. Add the garlic, potatoes, parsley, tomato sauce and oregano, stir,
4. Place the pan in your air fryer and cook at 190°C for 16 minutes.
5. Stir in the basil, divide among the plates and serve.

646. Butter fennel

Servings: 4
Cooking time: 12 minutes
Ingredients:
- 2 large fennel bulbs, cut into slices
- 2 tablespoons melted butter
- Salt and black pepper to taste
- ½ cup coconut cream

Addresses:
1. In a frying pan that fits the air fryer, combine all ingredients and stir.
2. Place the preparation in your air fryer and cook at 185°C.
3. Divide between plates and serve as a side dish.

647. Broccoli with cheese and garlic in the open air

Servings: 2
Cooking time: 25 minutes
Ingredients:
- 1 egg white
- 1 grated garlic clove
- Salt and black pepper to taste
- ½ pound broccoli florets
- ⅓ cup grated Parmesan cheese

Addresses:
1. In a bowl, whisk together the butter, egg, garlic, salt and black pepper.
2. Then add the broccoli to coat well.
3. Add the Parmesan cheese and stir to coat.
4. Place the broccoli in the air fryer until it forms a single layer (do not overfill the basket).
5. Cook for a few minutes at 180°C.
6. Remove to a plate and sprinkle with Parmesan cheese.

648. Sweet and sour vegetable mixture

Servings: 4
Cooking time: 25 minutes
Ingredients:
- 225 grams of asparagus, cut into about 3 cm pieces
- 225 grams of broccoli, cut into approximately 3 cm pieces
- 225 grams of carrots, cut into about 3 cm pieces
- 2 tablespoons peanut oil
- A little salt and white pepper
- 1/2 cup water
- 4 tablespoons of sultanas
- 2 tablespoons honey
- 2 tablespoons apple cider vinegar

Addresses:
1. Grease the basket of the air fryer and place a layer of vegetables in it.
2. When you make the vegetable layer, drizzle the peanut oil over it. Then sprinkle with salt and white pepper.
3. Cook in the air fryer for 15 minutes, shaking the basket halfway through cooking.
4. Add ½ cup of water to a saucepan and bring to a boil. At this point, add the sultanas, honey and vinegar.
5. Cook for 5 to 7 minutes or until the sauce has reduced by half.
6. Pour the sauce over the hot vegetables and serve immediately - bon appetit!

649. Vegetarian rolls

Servings: 6
Cooking time: 30 minutes

Ingredients:
- 2 mashed potatoes
- ¼ cup peas
- ¼ cup carrots, shredded
- 1 small cabbage, sliced
- ¼ of beans
- 2 tablespoons sweet corn
- 1 small onion, chopped
- 1 teaspoon capsicum
- 1 teaspoon coriander
- 2 tablespoons butter
- Ginger
- Garlic to taste
- ½ teaspoon masala powder
- ½ teaspoon chilli powder
- ½ cup breadcrumbs
- 1 packet of spring roll leaves
- ½ cup cornstarch slurry

Addresses:
1. Boil all the vegetables in water over a low heat. Rinse and leave to dry.
2. Unroll the spring roll sheets and place equal amounts of vegetables in the centre of each. Fold the spring rolls and coat each with the porridge and breadcrumbs.
3. Preheat the Air Fryer and cook the rolls for 10 minutes.
4. Serve with a side of boiled rice.

650. Broccoli and chives with almonds

Servings: 4
Cooking time: 12 minutes
Ingredients:
- 450 grams broccoli florets
- 3 cloves garlic, minced
- Pinch of salt and black pepper
- 3 tbsp. melted coconut oil
- ½ cup chopped almonds
- 1 tablespoon chopped chives
- 2 tablespoons red vinegar

Addresses:
1. In a bowl, combine the broccoli with the garlic, salt, pepper, vinegar and oil and mix.
2. Place the broccoli in the basket of your air fryer and cook at 190°C.
3. Divide the broccoli among the plates and serve with the almonds and chives sprinkled on top.

651. Leeks and spring onions

Servings: 4
Cooking time: 6 minutes
Ingredients:
- 1 cup chopped spring onions
- 3 leeks, cut into slices
- 55 grams of grated Parmesan cheese
- 1 beaten egg
- ½ teaspoon ground black pepper
- 1 teaspoon dried parsley

Addresses:
1. Preheat the air fryer to 200°C.
2. Combine all ingredients inside and cook for 6 minutes.
3. Divide among the plates and serve.

652. Asparagus with bacon

Servings: 4
Cooking time: 25 minutes
Ingredients:
- 4 slices of bacon
- 20 asparagus
- 1 tablespoon of olive oil
- 1 tablespoon sesame oil
- 1 tablespoon brown sugar
- 1 crushed garlic clove

Addresses:
1. Preheat your fryer to 190°C.
2. In a bowl, mix the oils, sugar and crushed garlic.
3. Separate the asparagus into 4 bundles (5 asparagus spears per bundle) and wrap each bundle with a slice of bacon.
4. Coat the bunches with the sugar-oil mixture.
5. Place the bundles in the cooking basket of your air fryer and cook for 8 minutes.

653. Balsamic Mustard Greens

Servings: 4
Cooking time: 12 minutes
Ingredients:
- 1 bunch of mustard greens, trimmed
- 2 tablespoons olive oil
- ½ cup chicken stock
- 2 tablespoons tomato puree
- 3 cloves garlic, minced
- Salt and black pepper to taste
- 1 tablespoon balsamic vinegar

Addresses:
1. Combine all ingredients in a pan that fits your air fryer and mix well.
2. Place the pan in the fryer and cook for 12 minutes.
3. Divide between the plates, serve and enjoy.

654. Crispy cauliflower bites

Servings: 4
Cooking time: 20 minutes
Ingredients:
- 1 cup flour
- 1 cup of milk
- 1 beaten egg
- 1 head of cauliflower, cut into florets

Addresses:
1. Preheat the air fryer to 200°C.
2. Grease air fryer basket with cooking spray. In a bowl, mix together flour, milk, egg and Italian seasoning. Dredge cauliflower in mixture and drain excess liquid.

3. Place the florets in the cooking basket of the air fryer, spray with cooking spray and cook for 7 minutes, shake and continue cooking for another 5 minutes. Allow to cool before serving.

655. Nutmeg and Dill Ravioli

Servings: 6
Cooking time: 8 minutes
Ingredients:
- 4 tablespoons almond flour
- 2 tablespoons coconut flour
- 1 tablespoon xanthan gum
- ½ teaspoon baking powder
- 1 beaten egg
- 1 tablespoon of water
- 1 teaspoon apple cider vinegar
- 4 tablespoons ricotta cheese
- ½ teaspoon minced garlic
- ¼ teaspoon ground nutmeg
- ½ teaspoon dried dill
- 1 beaten egg yolk
- Cooking spray

Addresses:
To make the dough:
1. Mix together the almond flour, coconut flour, xanthan gum, baking powder, egg, water and apple cider vinegar.
2. Then knead the dough with your fingertips until it is smooth and non-sticky. Roll out the dough and cut it into ravioli squares.

To prepare the ravioli filling:
3. Mix the dry flour, ground nutmeg, chopped garlic and ricotta cheese.
4. Next, fill the dough squares with ricotta cheese. Cover the cheese with other ravioli dough squares. Secure the edges. Brush the ravioli with egg yolk.
5. Preheat the air fryer to 190°C.
6. Spray the basket of the air fryer with cooking spray and place the ravioli inside in a single layer.
7. Cook for 4 minutes on each side or until lightly browned.

656. Crispy rosemary potatoes

Servings: 4
Cooking time: 35 minutes
Ingredients:
- 2 tablespoons olive oil
- 3 grated garlic cloves
- 1 tablespoon chopped fresh rosemary
- 1 teaspoon salt
- ¼ teaspoon freshly ground black pepper

Addresses:
1. In a bowl, mix the potatoes, olive oil, garlic, rosemary, salt and pepper until well coated.
2. Place the potatoes in the air fryer and cook at 180°C for 25 minutes, stirring twice during cooking.
3. Cook until crispy on the outside and tender on the inside.

657. Broccoli puree

Servings: 4
Cooking time: 20 minutes
Ingredients:
- 570 grams broccoli florets
- A dash of olive oil
- 4 tablespoons chopped basil
- 85 grams of melted butter
- 1 clove garlic, minced
- Pinch of salt and black pepper

Addresses:
1. In a bowl, combine the broccoli with the oil, salt and pepper, mix and transfer to the basket of your air fryer.
2. Cook at 190°C for 20 minutes, cool the broccoli and place in a blender.
3. Add the rest of the ingredients, pulse, divide the puree between the plates and serve as a garnish.

658. Courgette and rocket mixture

Servings: 4
Cooking time: 20 minutes
Ingredients:
- 450 grams of courgettes, sliced
- 1 tablespoon of olive oil
- Salt and white pepper to taste
- 115 grams of rocket leaves
- ¼ cup chopped chives
- 1 cup chopped walnuts

Addresses:
1. In a frying pan that fits the air fryer, combine all ingredients except arugula and walnuts, toss.
2. Place the pan in the machine and cook at 180°C for 20 minutes.
3. Transfer to a salad bowl, add the rocket and walnuts, toss and serve as a side salad.

659. Crunchy pickles

Servings: 4
Cooking time: 6 minutes
Ingredients:
- 16 dill pickles, cut into slices
- 1 egg, lightly beaten
- 1/2 cup almond flour
- 3 tablespoons grated parmesan cheese
- 1/2 cup pork rind, shredded

Addresses:
1. Take three bowls. Mix the pork rinds and cheese in the first bowl.
2. In a second bowl, add the egg.
3. In the last bowl, add the almond flour.
4. Dredge each gherkin slice in almond flour, then in egg and finally in the pork and cheese mixture.
5. Spray the air fryer basket with cooking spray.

6. Place the coated gherkins in the fryer basket. Cook the gherkins for 6 minutes.
7. Serve and enjoy.

660. Cauliflower parmesan risotto

Servings: 4
Cooking time: 18 minutes
Ingredients:
- 1 cup shredded cauliflower
- 115 grams of cremini mushrooms, sliced
- 55 grams of grated Parmesan cheese
- 1 teaspoon ground black pepper
- 1 tablespoon of cream
- ¼ teaspoon garlic powder
- 3 spring onions, diced
- 1 tablespoon of olive oil
- ½ teaspoon Italian seasoning

Addresses:
1. Preheat the air fryer to 200°C.
2. Next, spray the basket of the air fryer with olive oil.
3. Place the mushrooms inside and sprinkle with ground black pepper.
4. Cook at 200°C for 4 minutes.
5. Then stir well and add the spring onion. Cook the vegetables for a further 4 minutes. Stir well and sprinkle with garlic powder and Italian seasoning.
6. Mix well and transfer into the air fryer mould. Add the crème fraîche and the grated cauliflower.
7. Add the Parmesan and mix. Place the pan in the air fryer and cook for a few minutes at 190°C.
8. Then mix the risotto and transfer to serving plates.

661. Open-air jacket potatoes

Servings: 4
Cooking time: 45 minutes
Ingredients:
- 2 tablespoons olive oil
- Salt and ground black pepper to taste

Addresses:
1. Rub the potatoes with half a tablespoon of olive oil. Season with salt and pepper, and place in the air fryer.
2. Bake for 40 minutes at 200°C.
3. Let them cool slightly and then cut a slit in the top.
4. Use a fork to fluff the inside of the potatoes.
5. Fill the potato with cheese or garlic mayonnaise.

662. Pumpkin noodles

Servings: 2
Cooking time: 17 minutes
Ingredients:
- 1 medium-sized pumpkin, peeled and spiralised
- 3 tablespoons cream
- 1/4 cup Parmesan cheese
- 1 teaspoon chopped thyme
- 1 tablespoon chopped sage
- 1 teaspoon garlic powder
- 2 tablespoons cream cheese

Addresses:
1. Preheat the air fryer to 190°C.
2. In a bowl, combine cream cheese, Parmesan, thyme, sage, cream and garlic powder.
3. Add the noodles to the air fryer tray.
4. Place the pan in the air fryer and cook for 15 minutes.
5. Spread the cream cheese mixture over the noodles and cook for a further 2-3 minutes.
6. Serve and enjoy.

663. Cheese and bacon fries

Servings: 4
Cooking time: 25 minutes
Ingredients:
- 5 slices of chopped bacon
- 2 tablespoons vegetable oil
- 2 ½ cups shredded Cheddar cheese
- 85 grams of melted cream cheese
- Salt and pepper to taste
- ¼ cup chopped onions

Addresses:
1. Preheat your air fryer to 200°C.
2. Add the bacon to the basket of the air fryer and cook for 4 minutes and shake the basket once during cooking. When the preparation is ready, set aside.
3. Add the potatoes to the basket of the air fryer and drizzle the oil over the top to coat them.
4. Cook for minutes, shaking the basket every 5 minutes. Season with salt and pepper.
5. In a bowl, mix the cheddar cheese and cream cheese. Pour over the potatoes and cook for a further 5 minutes.
6. Sprinkle the chopped spring onions on top and serve.

664. Endive and rice mix

Servings: 4
Cooking time: 20 minutes
Ingredients:
- 2 onions, chopped
- 3 cloves garlic, minced
- 1 tablespoon of olive oil
- Salt and black pepper to taste
- ½ cup white rice
- 1 cup vegetable stock
- 1 teaspoon chilli sauce
- 4 endives, trimmed and shredded

Addresses:
1. Take the oil and grease a frying pan that fits your air fryer.
2. Add all the other ingredients and mix.

3. Place the pan in the air fryer and cook for 20 minutes.
4. Divide between the plates and serve as a garnish.

665. Fennel with lemon

Servings: 4
Cooking time: 15 minutes
Ingredients:
- 450 grams of fennel, cut into small pieces
- Pinch of salt and black pepper
- 3 tablespoons olive oil
- Salt and black pepper to taste
- Juice of ½ lemon
- 2 tablespoons sunflower seeds

Addresses:
1. In a bowl, mix the fennel pieces with all the ingredients except the sunflower seeds.
2. Place the preparation in the basket of your air fryer and cook them at 200°.
3. Divide the fennel between the plates, sprinkle the sunflower seeds on top and serve as a garnish.

666. Green celery puree

Servings: 6
Cooking time: 6 minutes
Ingredients:
- 450 grams celery stalks, chopped
- ½ cup chopped spinach
- 55 grams of grated Parmesan cheese
- ¼ cup chicken broth
- ½ teaspoon cayenne pepper

Addresses:
1. In the pan of the air fryer, toss the celery stalk with the chopped spinach, chicken stock and cayenne pepper.
2. Whisk the mixture until smooth. Then top the puree with Parmesan.
3. Preheat the air fryer to 200°C.
4. Place the pan with the puree in the basket of the air fryer and cook the food for 6 minutes.

667. Tamarind Glazed Sweet Potatoes

Servings: 4
Cooking time: 24 minutes
Ingredients:
- ⅓ teaspoon of white pepper
- 1 tablespoon melted butter
- ½ teaspoon turmeric powder
- 5 garnet sweet potatoes, peeled and diced
- A few drops of liquid Stevia
- 2 teaspoons tamarind paste
- 1 ½ tablespoons fresh lime juice
- 1 ½ teaspoon ground allspice

Addresses:
1. In a bowl, mix all the ingredients together until the sweet potatoes are well coated.
2. Air fry at 170°C.
3. Pause the Air Fryer and stir again.
4. Increase the temperature to 200°C and cook for a further 10 minutes.
5. Eat hot, enjoy!

668. Cauliflower puree

Servings: 4
Cooking time: 20 minutes
Ingredients:
- 900 grams of cauliflower florets
- 1 teaspoon olive oil
- 85 grams grated Parmesan cheese
- 115 grams of softened butter
- Juice of ½ lemon
- zest of ½ lemon
- Salt and black pepper to taste

Addresses:
1. Preheat your air fryer to 190°C.
2. In the fryer basket, add the cauliflower and oil. Mix well and cook for 20 minutes.
3. When the preparation is ready, transfer the cauliflower to a bowl, mash well and add the rest of the ingredients. Stir.
4. Divide among the plates and serve as a garnish.

669. Brussels sprouts chips

Servings: 1
Cooking time: 15 minutes
Ingredients:
- 450 grams of Brussels sprouts
- 1 tbsp melted coconut oil
- 1 tablespoon unsalted butter, melted

Addresses:
1. Prepare the Brussels sprouts by cutting them in half and discarding the loose leaves.
2. Combine with the melted coconut oil and transfer to your air fryer.
3. Cook at 200°C in the air fryer for 10 minutes giving the basket a good shake during the cooking time to brown them if desired.
4. The sprouts are ready when they are partially caramelised. Remove from the fryer and serve with a coating of melted butter before serving.

670. Courgette nests

Servings: 6
Cooking time: 6 minutes
Ingredients:
- 280 grams of grated courgette
- 4 quail eggs
- 1 tablespoon coconut flour
- 30 grams of grated Parmesan cheese
- ¼ teaspoon cayenne pepper
- 1 teaspoon melted butter

Addresses:
1. Grease the muffin tins with butter.
2. Then mix in the cayenne pepper and grated courgette.

3. Spoon the vegetable mixture into the muffin tins and flatten into nests.
4. Crack the quail eggs into the nests and sprinkle with grated Parmesan.
5. Preheat the fryer to 200°C.
6. Place the muffin tins with the nests in the basket of the air fryer and cook for 6 minutes.

671. Potato casserole dish

Servings: 4
Cooking time: 55 minutes
Ingredients:
- 1,360 kilograms of sweet potatoes, washed
- 1/4 cup milk
- 2 tablespoons white flour
- 1/4 teaspoon ground allspice
- 1/2 teaspoon ground nutmeg
- Salt

For coverage you need:
- 1/2 cup almond flour
- 1/2 cup walnuts, soaked, drained and ground
- 1/4 cup sugar
- 1 teaspoon cinnamon powder
- 5 tablespoons butter
- 1/4 cup pecans, soaked, drained and chopped
- 1/4 cup shredded coconut
- 1 tablespoon chia seeds

Addresses:
1. Place the potatoes in the basket of your air fryer, pierce with a fork and cook at 180°C for 30 minutes.
2. Meanwhile, in a bowl, combine the almond flour with the walnuts, 1/4 cup coconut, 1/4 cup sugar, chia seeds, 1 teaspoon cinnamon and butter and stir together.
3. Transfer the potatoes to a cutting board, cool, peel and place on a baking tray that fits your air fryer.
4. Add the milk, flour, salt, nutmeg and allspice and stir.
5. Add the crumble mixture you made earlier on top, place the dish in the basket of your air fryer and cook at 200°C for 8 minutes.
6. Divide among the plates and serve with a garnish.

672. Scrambled eggs

Servings: 2
Cooking time: 15 minutes
Ingredients:
- 2 tablespoons melted olive oil
- 4 beaten eggs
- 140 grams of chopped fresh spinach
- 1 medium-sized tomato, chopped
- 1 teaspoon fresh lemon juice
- ½ teaspoon coarse salt
- ½ teaspoon ground black pepper
- ½ cup fresh basil, coarsely chopped

Addresses:
1. Grease the tray of the Air Fryer with the oil, tilting it to distribute the oil.
2. Preheat the fryer to 140°C.
3. Mix in the rest of the ingredients, apart from the basil leaves, beating well until everything is completely combined.
4. Cook in the fryer for 8 - 12 minutes.
5. Top with fresh basil leaves before serving with a dollop of sour cream if desired.

673. Mushroom melt with cheese simple

Servings: 2
Cooking time: 20 minutes
Ingredients:
- Salt and pepper
- 10 mushromm button caps
- 2 cups chopped mozzarella cheese
- 2 cups chopped cheddar cheese
- 3 tablespoons Italian herb mixture

Addresses:
1. Preheat the fryer to 170°C.
2. In a bowl, mix the oil, salt, pepper and herbs to form a marinade. Add the mushrooms to the marinade and stir to coat well.
3. In a separate bowl, mix the two types of cheese. Stuff the mushrooms with the cheese mixture.
4. Place the preparation in the cooking basket of the air fryer and cook for a few minutes.

674. Cauliflower fritters Mexican style

Servings: 6
Cooking time: 48 minutes
Ingredients:
- 2 teaspoons chilli powder
- 1 ½ teaspoon kosher salt
- 1 teaspoon dried marjoram, crushed
- 2 ½ cups cauliflower, cut into florets
- 1 ⅓ cup tortilla crumbs
- ½ teaspoon crushed red pepper flakes
- 3 eggs, beaten
- 1 ½ cups of crumbled Cotija cheese

Addresses:
1. Puree the cauliflower florets in your food processor until they are shredded (about the size of rice). Then combine the cauliflower "rice" with the other elements.
2. Now roll the cauliflower mixture into small balls, refrigerate for 30 minutes.
3. Preheat your Air Fryer to 180°C and set the timer for 14 minutes.
4. Cook until the balls are golden brown and serve immediately.

675. Lime and mozzarella aubergines

Servings: 4
Cooking time: 15 minutes
Ingredients:
- 2 tablespoons olive oil

- 2 aubergines, diced
- 225 grams of grated mozzarella cheese
- 3 chopped spring onions
- Juice of 1 lime
- 2 tablespoons melted butter
- 4 beaten eggs

Addresses:
1. Heat a frying pan that fits the fryer over medium-high heat. Then add the oil and butter.
2. Then add the spring onions and aubergines, stir and cook for 5 minutes.
3. Stir in the eggs and lime juice and stir well.
4. Sprinkle the cheese on top, place the frying pan in the deep fryer and cook at 190°C.
5. Divide among the plates and serve as a garnish.

676. Veal meatballs

Servings: 3
Cooking time: 25 minutes
Ingredients:
- 1 small finger of ginger, crushed
- 1 tablespoon hot sauce
- 3 tablespoons vinegar
- 1 ½ teaspoon lemon juice
- ½ cup tomato ketchup, reduced sugar
- 2 tablespoons sugar
- ¼ teaspoon dry mustard
- Salt and pepper to taste, if necessary

Addresses:
1. In a bowl, add the meat, ginger, hot sauce, vinegar, lemon juice, tomato ketchup, sugar, mustard, pepper and salt.
2. Mix well with a spoon. Shape into 5 centimetre sized balls with your hands.
3. Add the balls to the fryer without overfilling and cook at 190°C stirring once during cooking. Serve with tomato sauce.

677. Sauteed artichokes

Servings: 4
Cooking time: 10 minutes
Ingredients:
- 4 artichoke hearts, chopped
- 4 teaspoons lemon juice
- 2 teaspoons avocado oil
- ¼ teaspoon lemon zest

Addresses:
1. Preheat the fryer to 180°C.
2. Meanwhile, drizzle the chopped artichoke hearts with lemon juice, avocado oil and lemon zest.
3. Shake all ingredients well and leave to marinate for a few minutes.
4. Then place the artichoke hearts in the preheated air fryer and cook for 8 minutes.
5. Stir well and cook for a further 2 minutes.

678. Barbecue chicken pizza

Servings: 1
Cooking time: 15 minutes
Ingredients:
- Cooking spray
- ¼ cup barbecue sauce
- ¼ cup shredded mozzarella cheese
- ¼ cup shredded Monterey Jack cheese
- 2 tbsp red onion, thinly sliced
- ½ chicken sausage with herbs
- Chopped coriander or parsley (for garnish)

Addresses:
1. Spray the bottom of the naan bread with cooking spray and place in the air fryer.
2. Spread well with barbecue sauce, sprinkle mozzarella cheese, Monterey Jack cheese and red onion on top.
3. Cover with the sausage and spray the crust with cooking spray.
4. Cook for 8 minutes in the air fryer preheated to 200°C.

679. Balsamic cabbage mix

Servings: 4
Cooking time: 15 minutes
Ingredients:
- 6 cups shredded green cabbage
- 6 radishes, sliced
- ½ cup chopped celery leaves
- ¼ cup chopped green onions
- 2 tablespoons balsamic vinegar
- 1 teaspoon lemon juice
- 3 tablespoons olive oil
- ½ teaspoon hot paprika

Addresses:
1. In the pan of your air fryer, combine all ingredients and mix well.
2. Place the pan in the fryer and cook at 190°C for 15 minutes.
3. Divide between the plates and serve as a side dish.

680. Fried agnolotti

Servings: 6
Cooking time: 25 minutes
Ingredients:
- 1 cup flour
- Salt and black pepper
- 4 beaten eggs
- 2 cups breadcrumbs
- Cooking spray

Addresses:
1. Mix the flour with the salt and pepper.
2. Dredge the dough in the flour, then in the egg and finally in the breadcrumbs.
3. Drizzle oil on the batter and place it in the basket of the air fryer in an even layer.
4. Set the air fryer to 200°C and cook the preparation, turning it once halfway through cooking.
5. Cook until golden brown. Serve with goat cheese.

681. Mung bean mix

Servings: 3
Cooking time: 16 minutes
Ingredients:
- 1 cup mung beans
- ½ teaspoon olive oil
- 1 teaspoon ground coriander
- ½ teaspoon turmeric powder
- 1 cup vegetable stock
- ½ cup chopped red onion
- ½ teaspoon cumin seeds
- 3 chopped tomatoes
- ½ teaspoon garam masala
- Salt and black pepper
- 1 tablespoon lemon juice
- 4 cloves garlic, minced

Addresses:
1. Place all the ingredients in a pan that fits your air fryer and mix them together.
2. Place the pan in the fryer and cook at 185°C for 16 minutes.
3. Divide the mixture between the plates and serve as a garnish.

682. Rice pilaf with cremini mushrooms

Servings: 6
Cooking time: 30 minutes
Ingredients:
- 4 cups of heated vegetable broth
- 2 cups long grain rice
- 1 onion, chopped
- 2 cloves garlic, minced
- 2 cups of chopped cremini mushrooms
- Salt and ground black pepper
- 1 tablespoon chopped fresh parsley

Addresses:
1. Preheat your air fryer to 200°C.
2. Place a frying pan over medium heat and add the oil, onion, garlic and rice. Cook for 5 minutes.
3. Pour in the vegetable stock and mushrooms and whisk well. Season with salt and pepper to taste.
4. Transfer the ingredients to the basket of your air fryer and cook.
5. Serve sprinkled with chopped fresh parsley.

683. Portobello mushroom recipe

Servings: 4
Cooking time: 22 minutes
Ingredients:
- 4 Portobello mushrooms, stems removed and chopped.
- 10 basil leaves
- 1 cup baby spinach
- 3 cloves garlic, minced
- 1 cup almonds, coarsely chopped.
- 1 tablespoon parsley
- ¼ cup olive oil
- 8 cherry tomatoes, halved
- Salt and black pepper to taste

Addresses:
1. In your food processor, combine the basil with the spinach, garlic, almonds, parsley, oil, oil, salt, black pepper to taste and mushroom stems and mix well.
2. Stuff each mushroom with this mixture, place them in your air fryer and cook at 180°C.
3. Divide the mushrooms among the plates and serve.

684. Turmeric and kale mixture

Servings: 2
Cooking time: 12 minutes
Ingredients:
- 3 tablespoons melted butter
- 2 cups kale leaves
- Salt and black pepper
- ½ cup chopped yellow onion
- 2 teaspoons turmeric powder

Addresses:
1. Place all ingredients in a pan that fits your air fryer and mix well.
2. Place the pan in the fryer and cook for 12 minutes.
3. Divide among the plates and serve.

685. Tomato bites with creamy parmesan sauce

Servings: 4
Cooking time: 20 minutes
Ingredients:
For the sauce you need:
- ½ cup grated Parmigiano-Reggiano cheese
- 4 tablespoons chopped walnuts
- 1 teaspoon garlic puree
- ½ teaspoon fine sea salt
- ⅓ cup extra virgin olive oil

For the tomato bites you will need:
- 2 large roma tomatoes, thinly sliced and patted dry
- 225 grams Halloumi cheese, thinly sliced
- ⅓ cup sliced onions
- 1 teaspoon basil, dried
- ¼ teaspoon crushed red pepper flakes
- ⅛ teaspoon sea salt

Addresses:
1. Start by preheating your fryer to 195°C.
2. Make the sauce by blending all the ingredients, except the extra virgin olive oil, in your food processor.
3. While the machine is running, slowly and gradually pour in the olive oil, mashing until everything is well blended.
4. Now, spread a teaspoon of the sauce on each tomato slice. Place a slice of Halloumi cheese on top of each tomato slice.
5. Top with onion slices. Sprinkle with basil, red pepper and sea salt.
6. Transfer the assembled bites to the cooking basket of the Air Fryer. Spray with

non-stick cooking spray and cook for approximately 13 minutes.
7. Place these bites on a nice serving platter, garnish with the remaining sauce and serve at room temperature. Enjoy!

686. Grilled cheese

Servings: 2
Cooking time: 25 minutes
Ingredients:
- 4 slices of bread
- ½ cup sharp cheddar cheese
- ¼ cup melted butter

Addresses:
1. Preheat the Air Fryer to 180°C.
2. Put the cheese and butter in separate bowls.
3. Apply the butter to each side of the bread slices with a brush.
4. Spread cheese on two of the slices of bread and make two sandwiches. Transfer both to the fryer.
5. Cook until a golden colour is achieved and the cheese is melted.

687. Cold chicken croquettes

Servings: 4
Cooking time: 20 minutes
Ingredients:
- 1 beaten egg
- Salt and pepper
- 1 cup oatmeal, crumbled
- ½ teaspoon garlic powder
- 1 tablespoon parsley

Addresses:
1. Preheat the fryer to 180°C.
2. Rub the chicken with garlic, parsley, salt and pepper.
3. In one bowl, add the beaten egg. In another bowl, add the crumbled oats.
4. Form the chicken mixture into croquettes and dip into the egg and oatmeal until coated.
5. Place the croquettes in the basket of your fryer.
6. Cook for minutes, stirring once.

688. Sweet potato and chickpea tacos

Servings: 4
Cooking time: 15 minutes
Ingredients:
- 2 cups sweet potato puree
- 2 tablespoons melted butter
- 1.115 kilograms of canned chickpeas, rinsed
- 1 cup Colby cheese, grated
- 1 teaspoon garlic powder
- 1 teaspoon onion powder
- Salt and freshly ground black pepper
- 8 corn tortillas
- ¼ cup Pico de gallo
- 2 tablespoons chopped fresh coriander

Addresses:
1. Mix the sweet potatoes with the butter, chickpeas, cheese, garlic powder, onion powder, salt and black pepper.
2. Divide the sweet potato mixture between the tortillas. Bake in the preheated Air Fryer at 200°C for 7 minutes.
3. Garnish with Pico de gallo and cilantro - bon appetit!

689. Macadamia Rice and Cauliflower

Servings: 4
Cooking time: 8 minutes
Ingredients:
- 255 grams of cauliflower
- 1 tablespoon butter
- 30 grams of ground macadamia nuts
- 3 tablespoons chicken stock

Addresses:
1. Cut the cauliflower into florets and grate.
2. Grease the frying pan of the deep fryer with butter and put the cauliflower rice in it.
3. Add the ground macadamia nuts and chicken stock. Gently stir the vegetable mixture.
4. Cook the cauliflower rice at 185°C for 8 minutes. Stir the vegetables after 4 minutes of cooking.

690. Smoked BBQ Toast S

Servings: 1
Cooking time: 10 minutes
Ingredients:
- 2 teaspoons coconut oil, melted
- ¼ teaspoon smoked paprika
- 1 teaspoon chilli powder
- ¼ teaspoon cumin
- 1 cup of s

Addresses:
1. Mix the melted coconut oil with the paprika, chilli powder and cumin. Place the s in a large bowl and pour the coconut oil over them, stirring to coat evenly.
2. Place the s in the basket of your fryer and distribute them around the base.
3. Cook for six minutes at 200°C and shake the fryer basket from time to time to make sure everything cooks evenly.
4. Leave to cool and serve.

691. Coconut crusted shrimp

Portions: 5
Cooking time: 30 minutes
Ingredients:
- ¾ cup shredded coconut
- 1 tablespoon maple syrup
- ½ cup breadcrumbs
- ⅓ cup corn starch
- ½ cup milk

Addresses:
1. Pour the cornflour and prawns into a zip-top bag and shake vigorously to coat. Mix the syrup and milk in a bowl and set aside. In another bowl, mix together the breadcrumbs and shredded coconut. Open the zip-top bag and take out the prawns while shaking out the excess starch.
2. Dip the prawns into the milk mixture and then into the crumb mixture.
3. Place in the fryer and cook at 180°C, turning once halfway through. Cook until golden brown. Serve with a coconut-based sauce.

692. Mixed courgettes and pumpkins

Servings: 4
Cooking time: 12 minutes
Ingredients:
- 280 grams of Kabocha pumpkin
- ½ chopped courgette
- 3 chopped spring onions
- 1 teaspoon dried thyme
- 2 teaspoons ghee
- 1 teaspoon salt
- 1 teaspoon ground turmeric

Addresses:
1. Cut the pumpkin into small cubes and sprinkle with salt and ground turmeric.
2. Put the pumpkin in the bowl, add the courgette, spring onion, dried thyme and ghee. Gently shake the vegetables.
3. Preheat the air fryer to 200°C.
4. Place the vegetable mixture in the air fryer and cook for minutes. Shake the vegetables after 6 minutes of cooking to prevent them from burning.

693. Green beans fried with Pecorino Romano

Servings: 3
Cooking time: 15 minutes
Ingredients:
- 2 tablespoons buttermilk
- 1 egg
- 4 tablespoons maize flour
- 4 tablespoons crushed tortilla chips
- 4 tablespoons Pecorino Romano cheese, finely grated
- Coarse salt and ground black pepper, to taste
- 1 teaspoon smoked paprika
- 340 grams of green beans, trimmed

Addresses:
1. In a shallow bowl, whisk together the buttermilk and egg.
2. In a separate bowl, combine the corn flour, tortilla chips, Pecorino Romano cheese, salt, black pepper and paprika.
3. Dip the green beans into the egg mixture and then into the cornflour and cheese mixture. Place the green beans in the lightly greased baking basket.
4. Cook in the preheated Air Fryer at 200°C for minutes. Shake the basket and cook for another 3 minutes.
5. Taste, adjust seasoning and serve with dipping sauce if desired - bon appetit!

694. Harissa Broccoli Spread

Servings: 4
Cooking time: 6 minutes
Ingredients:
- 2 cups broccoli, chopped
- 1 teaspoon tahini
- 2 tablespoons sesame oil
- 1 teaspoon salt
- 1 clove of garlic
- 1 tsp melted coconut oil
- 1 teaspoon harissa

Addresses:
1. Preheat the air fryer to 200°C.
2. Place the broccoli and garlic clove in the basket of the air fryer and drizzle with a teaspoon of sesame oil.
3. Cook the vegetables for 6 minutes.
4. Then transfer the cooked broccoli and garlic to the food processor and grind to a smooth texture.
5. Add the salt, all the remaining sesame oil, coconut oil and harissa. Then add the tahini and whisk the mixture for a further 30 seconds.
6. Put the cooked hummus in the bowl.

695. Cabbages and sprouts

Servings: 8
Cooking time: 15 minutes
Ingredients:
- 450 grams Brussels sprouts, trimmed
- 2 cups kale, shredded
- 1 tablespoon of olive oil
- Salt and black pepper to taste
- 85 grams of mozzarella cheese, grated

Addresses:
1. In a frying pan that fits the air fryer, combine all ingredients except the mozzarella and mix.
2. Place the pan in the air fryer and cook at 190°C for minutes.
3. Divide among the plates, sprinkle the cheese on top and serve.

696. Pumpkin wedges

Servings: 3
Cooking time: 30 minutes
Ingredients:
- 1 tablespoon paprika
- 1 whole lime, squeezed
- 1 cup paleo dressing
- 1 tablespoon balsamic vinegar
- Salt and pepper to taste

- 1 teaspoon turmeric

Addresses:
1. Preheat your air fryer to 180°C.
2. Add the pumpkin chunks to the cooking basket of your air fryer, and cook for 20 minutes.
3. In a bowl, mix the lime juice, vinegar, turmeric, salt, pepper and paprika to form a marinade.
4. Pour the marinade over the pumpkin and cook for a further 5 minutes.

697. Mushrooms stuffed with butter and mint

Servings: 3
Cooking time: 19 minutes
Ingredients:
- 3 cloves garlic, minced
- 1 teaspoon ground black pepper
- ⅓ cup seasoned bread crumbs
- 1½ tablespoons chopped fresh mint
- 1 teaspoon salt, or more to taste
- 1½ tablespoons melted butter
- 14 medium-sized mushrooms, cleaned and stalks removed

Addresses:
1. Mix all the above ingredients, except the mushrooms, in a bowl to prepare the stuffing.
2. Then fill the mushrooms with the prepared stuffing.
3. Fry the stuffed mushrooms in the air fryer at 180°C for about 12 minutes.
4. Taste for doneness and serve at room temperature as a vegetarian appetizer.

698. Broccoli Empanadas

Servings: 4
Cooking time: 8 minutes
Ingredients:
- ½ teaspoon onion powder
- 1 cup broccoli, shredded
- ½ teaspoon salt
- ½ teaspoon chilli flakes
- 1 teaspoon ground paprika
- 1 beaten egg
- ¼ cup coconut flour
- 1 teaspoon chopped chives

Addresses:
1. In the bowl of a blender, combine the onion powder, shredded broccoli, salt, chilli flakes, ground paprika and chives.
2. Then add the egg and stir the mixture with a spoon. Also add the coconut flour and stir well again.
3. Make patties with your fingertips.
4. Preheat the fryer to 195°C and place the patties in the fryer basket.
5. Cook for 4 minutes on each side.

699. Perfect crispy tofu

Servings: 4
Cooking time: 20 minutes
Ingredients:
- 1 block of firm tofu, pressed and cut into approximately 2.5 centimetre cubes
- 1 tablespoon arrowroot flour
- 2 teaspoons sesame oil
- 1 teaspoon vinegar
- 2 tablespoons soy sauce

Addresses:
1. In a bowl, mix the tofu with the oil, vinegar and soy sauce and let it sit for a few minutes.
2. Mix the marinated tofu with the arrowroot flour.
3. Spray the air fryer basket with cooking spray.
4. Add the tofu to the basket of the air fryer and cook for 20 minutes at 190°C. Shake the basket halfway through cooking.
5. Serve and enjoy.

700. Roasted almond delight

Portions: 12
Cooking time: 20 minutes
Ingredients:
- 3 tablespoons liquid smoke
- 2 teaspoons salt
- 2 tablespoons molasses

Addresses:
1. Preheat your fryer to 180°C.
2. In a bowl, add the salt, liquid, molasses and cashew nuts, toss to coat.
3. Place the preparation in the cooking basket of your air fryer and cook for minutes, shaking the basket every 5 minutes.

701. Green beans with spices

Servings: 2
Cooking time: 10 minutes
Ingredients:
- 2 cups green beans
- 1/8 teaspoon cayenne pepper
- 1/8 teaspoon ground allspice
- 1/4 teaspoon ground cinnamon
- 1/2 teaspoon dried oregano
- 2 tablespoons olive oil
- 1/4 teaspoon ground coriander
- 1/4 teaspoon ground cumin
- 1/2 teaspoon salt

Addresses:
1. Add all ingredients to the large bowl and mix well.
2. Spray the fryer basket with cooking spray.
3. Add the mixture from the bowl to the fryer basket.
4. Bake at 190°C for 10 minutes. Shake the basket halfway through
5. Serve and enjoy.

702. Kabocha crisps

Servings: 2
Cooking time: 11 minutes
Ingredients:
- 170 grams Kabocha pumpkin, peeled
- ½ teaspoon olive oil
- ½ teaspoon salt

Addresses:
1. Slice the Kabocha squash into chips and drizzle with olive oil.
2. Preheat the air fryer to 200°C.
3. Place the Kabocha pumpkin chips in the basket of the air fryer and cook for 5 minutes.
4. Then shake well and cook for a further 6 minutes.
5. Sprinkle the cooked Kabocha chips with salt and mix well.

703. Coconut cabbage and parmesan

Servings: 4
Cooking time: 15 minutes
Ingredients:
- 900 grams of kale, shredded
- Pinch of salt and black pepper
- 2 tablespoons olive oil
- 2 cloves garlic, minced
- 1 and ½ cups of coconut cream
- ½ teaspoon ground nutmeg
- ½ cup grated Parmesan

Addresses:
1. In a frying pan sized to fit the air fryer, mix the kale with the rest of the ingredients.
2. After stirring the ingredients well, place the frying pan in the deep fryer and cook at 200°C.
3. Divide between the plates and serve.

704. Roasted beetroot salad

Servings: 2
Cooking time: 20 minutes + cooling time
Ingredients:
- 2 medium beetroots, peeled and cut into chunks
- 2 tablespoons of extra virgin olive oil
- 1 tablespoon balsamic vinegar
- 1 teaspoon of yellow mustard
- 1 clove garlic, minced
- 1/4 teaspoon cumin powder
- Coarse sea salt and ground black pepper, to taste
- 1 tablespoon fresh parsley leaves, coarsely chopped

Addresses:
1. Place the beets in a single layer in the lightly greased baking basket.
2. Cook at 185°C for 13 minutes, shaking the basket halfway through cooking.
3. Allow to cool to room temperature, mix the beetroot with the rest of the ingredients. Serve well chilled. Enjoy.

705. Fried green olives stuffed with peppers

Servings: 4
Cooking time: 15 minutes
Ingredients:
- ¼ cup flour
- ¼ cup Parmesan cheese
- Salt and black pepper
- ½ cup panko breadcrumbs
- 1 beaten egg
- 1 teaspoon cayenne pepper

Addresses:
1. Preheat the air fryer to 200°C.
2. Grease the air fryer basket with cooking spray.
3. In a bowl, combine the flour, cayenne pepper, salt and black pepper.
4. In another bowl, add the beaten egg.
5. In a third bowl, place the panko breadcrumbs with the Parmesan cheese.
6. Drain and dry the olives with a paper towel. Dredge the olives in flour, then in egg and finally in breadcrumbs.
7. Place the olives in the cooking basket of the air fryer, spray with cooking spray and cook for 5 minutes, shake and continue cooking for another few minutes.
8. Allow to cool before serving.

706. Low Carbohydrate Pita Crisps

Servings: 1
Cooking time: 15 minutes
Ingredients:
- 1 cup grated mozzarella cheese
- 1 egg
- ¼ cup finely ground, blanched flour
- 15 grams of finely ground pork rind

Addresses:
1. Melt the mozzarella in the microwave. Add the egg, flour and pork rind and combine to form a smooth paste. Reheat the cheese in the microwave if it starts to curdle.
2. Place the dough between two sheets of parchment paper and use a rolling pin to flatten it into a rectangle. The thickness is up to you. Using a sharp knife, cut the dough to form triangles. It may be necessary to complete this step in several batches.
3. Place the fries in the fryer and cook for five minutes. Turn them over and cook on the other side for another five minutes, or until the potatoes are golden brown and firm.
4. Allow the chips to cool and harden further. They can be stored in an airtight container.

707. Cabbage wedges

Servings: 6
Cooking time: 14 minutes
Ingredients:
- 1 small head of cabbage, cut into pieces

- 3 tablespoons olive oil
- 1/4 teaspoon red chilli flakes
- 1/2 teaspoon fennel seeds
- 1 teaspoon garlic powder
- 1 teaspoon onion powder
- Pepper
- Salt

Addresses:
1. Spray the air fryer basket with cooking spray.
2. In a small bowl, combine garlic powder, red chilli flakes, fennel seeds, onion powder, pepper and salt.
3. Rub the cabbage wedges with oil and rub them with the garlic powder mixture.
4. Place the cabbage wedges in the basket of the air fryer and cook for 8 minutes.
5. Turn the cabbage wedges to the other side and cook for a further 6 minutes.
6. Serve and enjoy.

708. Rainbow vegetables and parmesan croquettes

Servings: 4
Cooking time: 40 minutes
Ingredients:
- 450 grams of peeled potatoes
- 4 tablespoons milk
- 2 tablespoons butter
- Salt and black pepper to taste
- 1/2 teaspoon cayenne pepper
- 1/2 cup chopped mushrooms
- 1/4 cup broccoli, chopped
- 1 grated carrot
- 1 clove garlic, minced
- 3 tablespoons chopped onions
- 2 tablespoons olive oil
- 1/2 cup all-purpose flour
- 2 eggs
- 1/2 cup panko breadcrumbs
- 1/2 cup grated Parmesan cheese

Addresses:
1. In a large saucepan, boil the potatoes for 20 minutes. Drain the potatoes and mash them with the milk, butter, salt, black pepper and cayenne pepper.
2. Add the mushrooms, broccoli, carrots, garlic, spring onions and olive oil, stir to combine well. Form the mixture into patties.
3. In a shallow bowl, place the flour, beat the eggs in another bowl, in a third bowl, combine the breadcrumbs with the Parmesan cheese.
4. Dredge each patty in the flour, then in the eggs and finally in the breadcrumb mixture, pressing to adhere.
5. Cook in the preheated air fryer at 190°C for 16 minutes, stirring halfway through the cooking time. Enjoy!

709. Cabbage puree

Servings: 4
Cooking time: 20 minutes
Ingredients:
- 1 head of cauliflower, florets separated
- 4 teaspoons melted butter
- 4 cloves garlic, minced
- 3 cups chopped kale
- 2 onions, chopped
- Pinch of salt and black pepper
- 1/3 cup coconut cream
- 1 tablespoon chopped parsley

Addresses:
1. In a frying pan that will fit in the air fryer, combine the cauliflower with the butter, garlic, spring onions, salt, pepper and cream. Mix together.
2. Place the pan in the air fryer and cook at 190°C for 20 minutes.
3. Mash the mixture well, add the rest of the ingredients, whisk, divide among the plates and serve.

710. Sweet corn fritters with avocado

Servings: 3
Cooking time: 20 minutes
Ingredients:
- 2 cups of sweet corn kernels
- 1 small onion, chopped
- 1 clove garlic, minced
- 2 beaten eggs
- 1 teaspoon baking powder
- 2 tablespoons chopped fresh coriander
- Sea salt and ground black pepper, to taste
- 1 avocado, peeled, pitted and diced
- 2 tablespoons sweet chilli sauce

Addresses:
1. In a mixing bowl, thoroughly combine the corn, onion, garlic, eggs, baking powder, coriander, salt and black pepper.
2. Form the corn mixture into 6 patties and transfer them to the lightly greased air fryer basket.
3. Cook in the preheated Air Fryer at 200°C for 8 minutes, turn them over and cook for a further 7 minutes.
4. Serve the fritters with the avocado and chilli sauce.

711. Rosemary olive mix

Servings: 4
Cooking time: 15 minutes
Ingredients:
- 2 cups of black olives, pitted and halved
- A handful of chopped basil
- 2 sprigs of rosemary, chopped
- 2 red peppers, sliced
- 340 grams of chopped tomatoes
- 4 cloves garlic, minced
- 2 tablespoons olive oil

Addresses:

1. In a frying pan that fits the air fryer, combine the olives with the rest of the ingredients and mix.
2. Place the frying pan in the deep fryer and cook at 190°C.
3. Divide between the plates and serve.

712. Crunchy wax beans with almonds and blue cheese

Servings: 3
Cooking time: 15 minutes
Ingredients:
- 450 grams of wax beans, cleaned
- 2 tablespoons peanut oil
- 4 tablespoons seasoned bread crumbs
- Sea salt and ground black pepper, to taste
- 1/2 teaspoon crushed red pepper flakes
- 2 tablespoons sliced almonds
- 1/3 cup blue cheese, shredded

Addresses:
1. Mix the beans with the peanut oil, breadcrumbs, salt, black pepper and red pepper.
2. Place the beans in the lightly greased cooking basket.
3. Cook in the preheated Air Fryer at 200°C for 5 minutes. Shake the basket once or twice.
4. Add the almonds and cook for a further 3 minutes or until lightly toasted. Serve with the blue cheese and enjoy.

713. Almond Brussels sprouts

Servings: 4
Cooking time: 15 minutes
Ingredients:
- 225 grams of Brussels sprouts
- 2 tablespoons ground almonds
- 1 teaspoon coconut flakes
- 2 egg whites
- ½ teaspoon salt
- ½ teaspoon white pepper
- Cooking spray

Addresses:
1. Beat the egg whites and add salt and white pepper.
2. Then cut the Brussels sprouts into halves and put the egg white mixture on them.
3. Whisk the vegetables well and then cover them with the ground almonds and coconut flakes.
4. Preheat the air fryer to 190°C.
5. Place Brussels sprouts in the basket of the air fryer and cook for minutes. Shake the vegetables after 8 minutes of cooking.

714. Shredded beans

Servings: 4
Cooking time: 10 minutes
Ingredients:
- ½ cup flour
- 1 teaspoon smoked chipotle powder
- ½ teaspoon ground black pepper
- 1 tsp sea salt flakes
- 2 beaten eggs
- ½ cup crushed crackers
- 280 grams of wax beans

Addresses:
1. Combine the flour, chipotle powder, black pepper and salt in a bowl. Put the eggs in a second bowl. Put the crushed crackers in the third bowl.
2. Wash the beans in cold water and discard the tough strings.
3. Dredge the beans in the flour mixture before dipping them in the beaten egg. Finally, cover them with the crushed crackers.
4. Spray the beans with a cooking spray.
5. Air fry at 180°C for 4 minutes. Shake the cooking basket well and continue cooking for 3 minutes. Serve hot.

715. Asparagus Parmesan

Servings: 4
Cooking time: 5 minutes
Ingredients:
- 450 grams of asparagus, with the tips cut off
- 1/2 cup grated Parmesan cheese
- 1 tablespoon fresh lemon juice
- 1 teaspoon garlic powder
- 1 tablespoon of olive oil
- 1/4 teaspoon pepper
- 1/2 teaspoon sea salt

Addresses:
1. Preheat the air fryer to 200°C.
2. In a large bowl, add the asparagus.
3. In a small bowl, whisk together the olive oil, garlic powder, pepper and salt.
4. Pour the oil mixture over the asparagus and mix well.
5. Place the asparagus in the fryer basket and cook for a few minutes.
6. Pour the lemon juice over the cooked asparagus and sprinkle with grated cheese.
7. Serve and enjoy.

716. Cream of broccoli and cauliflower soup

Servings: 4
Cooking time: 20 minutes
Ingredients:
- 425 grams of broccoli florets
- 280 grams of cauliflower florets
- 1 chopped leek
- 2 spring onions, chopped
- Salt and black pepper
- 55 grams of melted butter
- 2 tablespoons mustard
- 1 cup sour cream
- 140 grams of grated mozzarella cheese

Addresses:
1. In a baking dish that fits the size of the air fryer, add the butter and spread it well.
2. Add the broccoli, cauliflower and the rest of the ingredients, except the mozzarella, and mix.
3. Sprinkle the cheese on top.
4. Place the pan in the air fryer and cook at 190°C for 20 minutes.
5. Divide among the plates and serve as a garnish.

717. Fennel with Shirataki noodles

Servings: 3
Cooking time: 20 minutes + cooling time
Ingredients:
- 1 fennel bulb, cut in quarters
- Salt and white pepper, to taste
- 1 clove garlic, finely chopped
- 1 green onion, thinly sliced
- 1 cup shredded Chinese cabbage
- 2 tablespoons rice wine vinegar
- 2 tablespoons sesame oil
- 1 teaspoon freshly grated ginger
- 1 tablespoon soy sauce
- 1 ⅓ cups Shirataki noodles, boiled

Addresses:
1. Start by preheating your fryer to 185°C.
2. Now cook the fennel bulb in the lightly greased cooking basket for 15 minutes, shaking the basket once or twice.
3. Allow to cool completely and mix with the rest of the ingredients. Serve well chilled.

718. Cranberry salad

Servings: 6
Cooking time: 15 minutes
Ingredients:
- 6 cloves garlic, minced
- 2 ½ cups canned cranberry beans, drained
- 1 yellow onion, chopped
- 2 chopped celery ribs
- ½ teaspoon smoked paprika
- ½ teaspoon red pepper flakes
- 3 teaspoons basil, chopped
- Salt and black pepper to taste
- 700 grams of canned tomatoes, drained and chopped
- 280 grams kale, shredded

Addresses:
1. In a frying pan that fits your air fryer, add all the ingredients and mix them together.
2. Place the pan in the fryer and cook at 185°C for 15 minutes.
3. Divide between the plates and serve as a side salad.

719. Greek Roasted Tomatoes with Feta

Servings: 2
Cooking time: 20 minutes
Ingredients:
- 3 medium-sized tomatoes, cut into four slices, patted dry
- 1 teaspoon basil, dried
- 1 teaspoon dried oregano
- 1/4 teaspoon crushed red pepper flakes
- 1/2 teaspoon sea salt
- 3 slices Feta cheese

Addresses:
1. Drizzle the tomatoes with cooking oil and transfer them to the basket of the Air Fryer. Sprinkle with seasoning.
2. Cook at 180°C for approximately 8 minutes, turning them halfway through cooking.
3. Cover with the cheese and cook for 4 more minutes, bon appetit!

720. American-style Brussels sprouts salad

Servings: 4
Cooking time: 35 minutes
Ingredients:
- 450 grams of Brussels sprouts
- 1 apple, cored and diced
- 1/2 cup shredded mozzarella cheese
- 1/2 cup pomegranate seeds
- 1 small red onion, chopped
- 4 hard boiled and sliced eggs
- 1/4 cup olive oil
- 2 tablespoons champagne vinegar
- 1 teaspoon Dijon mustard
- 1 teaspoon honey
- Sea salt and ground black pepper, to taste

Addresses:
1. Start by preheating your fryer to 190°C.
2. Add the Brussels sprouts to the cooking basket. Spray with cooking spray and cook for 15 minutes. Allow to cool at room temperature for about 15 minutes.
3. Mix the Brussels sprouts with the apple, cheese, pomegranate seeds and red onion.
4. Add all the ingredients for the dressing and mix to combine well. Serve with the hard-boiled eggs and enjoy!

721. Crispy asparagus with parmesan cheese

Servings: 4
Cooking time: 20 minutes
Ingredients:
- 2 eggs
- 1 teaspoon Dijon mustard
- 1 cup grated Parmesan cheese
- 1 cup breadcrumbs
- Sea salt and ground black pepper, to taste
- 18 asparagus spears, trimmed
- 1/2 cup sour cream

Addresses:
1. Start by preheating your fryer to 200°C.
2. In a shallow bowl, whisk together the eggs and mustard. In another shallow bowl, combine the Parmesan cheese, breadcrumbs, salt and black pepper.

3. Dip the asparagus into the egg mixture and then into the Parmesan mixture, pressing to adhere.
4. Cook for 5 minutes, working in three batches. Serve with sour cream on the side. Enjoy.

722. Roasted vegetables

Servings: 6
Cooking time: 30 minutes
Ingredients:
- 1 ⅓ cup small parsnips
- 1 ⅓ cup celery [3 or 4 stalks].
- 2 red onions
- 1 ⅓ cup small pumpkin
- 1 tbsp. fresh thyme needles
- 1 tablespoon of olive oil
- Salt and pepper

Addresses:
1. Preheat the Air Fryer to 200°C.
2. Peel the parsnips and onions and cut them into centimetre-sized cubes. Cut the onions into wedges.
3. Do not peel the pumpkin. Cut in half, scoop out the seeds and cut into cubes.
4. Combine the chopped vegetables with the thyme, olive oil, salt and pepper.
5. Place the vegetables in the basket and transfer the basket to the Air Fryer.
6. Cook for 20 minutes, stirring once during cooking, until the vegetables are well browned and cooked.

723. Sweetcorn fritters

Servings: 4
Cooking time: 20 minutes
Ingredients:
- 1 medium carrot, grated
- 1 yellow onion, finely chopped
- 115 grams canned sweetcorn kernels, drained
- 1 teaspoon flaked sea salt
- 1 heaped tablespoon of chopped fresh coriander
- 1 medium egg, beaten
- 2 tablespoons of regular milk
- 1 cup grated Parmesan cheese
- ¼ cup flour
- ⅓ teaspoon baking powder
- ⅓ teaspoon sugar

Addresses:
1. Place the grated carrot in a colander and press to squeeze out excess moisture. Pat dry with a paper towel.
2. Combine the carrots with the rest of the ingredients.
3. Mould 1 tablespoon of the mixture into a ball and press it with your hand or a spoon to flatten it. Repeat until the rest of the mixture is used up.
4. Spray the balls with cooking spray.
5. Place them in the basket of your Air Fryer, taking care not to overlap any balls.
6. Bake at 150°C for 8 to 11 minutes or until firm.
7. Serve hot.

724. Fried asparagus with goat cheese

Servings: 3
Cooking time: 15 minutes
Ingredients:
- 1 bunch of asparagus, trimmed
- 1 tablespoon of olive oil
- 1/2 teaspoon kosher salt
- 1/4 teaspoon ground black pepper, to taste
- 1/2 teaspoon dried dill weed
- 1/2 cup crumbled goat's cheese

Addresses:
1. Place the asparagus in the lightly greased cooking basket. Toss the asparagus with the olive oil, salt, black pepper and dill.
2. Cook in the preheated Air Fryer at 200°C for 9 minutes.
3. Serve garnished with goat's cheese and enjoy!

725. Mushroom pies

Servings: 4
Cooking time: 8 minutes
Ingredients:
- 255 grams of mushrooms, finely chopped
- ¼ cup coconut flour
- 1 teaspoon salt
- 1 beaten egg
- 85 grams of Cheddar cheese, grated
- 1 teaspoon dried parsley
- ½ teaspoon ground black pepper
- 1 teaspoon sesame oil
- 30 grams of chopped spring onion

Addresses:
1. In the bowl of a blender, mix the chopped mushrooms, coconut flour, salt, egg, dried parsley, ground black pepper and chopped onion.
2. Stir the mixture until smooth and add the Cheddar cheese. Stir with a fork.
3. Preheat the air fryer to 195°C and line the air fryer tray with baking paper.
4. With the help of a spoon, make medium-sized patties and place them in the frying pan.
5. Drizzle the patties with sesame oil and cook for 4 minutes on each side.

726. Simple green beans with butter

Servings: 4
Cooking time: 12 minutes
Ingredients:
- 350 grams of green beans, cleaned
- 1 tablespoon balsamic vinegar
- 1/4 teaspoon kosher salt

- 1/2 teaspoon mixed peppercorns, freshly ground
- 1 tablespoon butter
- 2 tablespoons sesame seeds, toasted, to serve

Addresses:
1. Set your Air Fryer to cook at 200°C.
2. Mix the green beans with all the above ingredients except the sesame seeds. Set the timer for 10 minutes.
3. Meanwhile, toast the sesame seeds in a small non-stick frying pan, making sure to stir continuously.
4. Serve the sautéed green beans in a nice serving dish sprinkled with toasted sesame seeds. Enjoy!

727. Dill corn

Servings: 4
Cooking time: 6 minutes
Ingredients:
- 4 ears of corn
- Salt and black pepper
- 2 tablespoons melted butter
- 2 tablespoons chopped dill

Addresses:
1. In a bowl, combine the salt, pepper and butter.
2. Rub the corn with the butter mixture, then place it in your air fryer.
3. Cook at 200°C for 6 minutes.
4. Divide the corn among the plates, sprinkle the dill on top and serve.

728. Smoked asparagus

Servings: 4
Cooking time: 20 minutes
Ingredients:
- 450 grams of asparagus stalks
- Salt and black pepper
- Olive oil (¼ cup + 1 teaspoon)
- 1 tablespoon smoked paprika
- 2 tablespoons balsamic vinegar
- 1 tablespoon lime juice

Addresses:
1. In a bowl, toss the asparagus with salt, pepper and a teaspoon of oil. Mix together.
2. Transfer the ingredients to the basket of your air fryer and cook at 185°C for 20 minutes.
3. Meanwhile, in a bowl, combine all the other ingredients and whisk well.
4. Divide the asparagus among the plates, drizzle the balsamic vinaigrette on top and serve as a garnish.

729. Greek-style vegetable pie

Servings: 4
Cooking time: 35 minutes
Ingredients:
- 1 aubergine, peeled and cut into slices
- 2 red bell peppers, seeded and sliced
- 1 red onion, sliced
- 1 teaspoon chopped fresh garlic
- 4 tablespoons olive oil
- 1 teaspoon mustard
- 1 teaspoon dried oregano
- 1 teaspoon smoked paprika
- Salt and ground black pepper
- 1 tomato, sliced
- 170 grams of halloumi cheese, cut lengthwise

Addresses:
1. Start by preheating your fryer to 185°C.
2. Spray a baking sheet with non-stick spray.
3. Place the aubergine, peppers, onion and garlic in the bottom of the baking dish. Add the olive oil, mustard and spices.
4. Transfer to the cooking basket and cook for 14 minutes.
5. Top with the tomatoes and cheese, increase the temperature to 200°C and cook for a further 5 minutes until bubbling.
6. Leave to cool on a cooling rack for 10 minutes before serving.
7. Enjoy your meal!

730. Coconut mushroom mix

Servings: 4
Cooking time: 15 minutes
Ingredients:
- 450 grams of brown mushrooms, cut into slices
- 450 grams kale, shredded
- Salt and black pepper to taste
- 2 tablespoons olive oil
- 1,115 kilograms of coconut milk

Addresses:
1. In a frying pan that fits your air fryer, combine the kale with the rest of the ingredients and stir.
2. Place frying pan in deep fryer, cook at 190°C.
3. Divide between the plates and serve.

731. Avocados wrapped in bacon

Servings: 6
Cooking time: 40 minutes
Ingredients:
- 3 large avocados, sliced
- ⅓ teaspoon salt
- ⅓ teaspoon chilli powder
- ⅓ teaspoon of cumin powder

Addresses:
1. Stretch the bacon strips to lengthen them and cut them in half to make 24 pieces.
2. Wrap each piece of bacon around a slice of avocado.
3. Tuck the bacon end into the wrapper. Season with salt, chilli and cumin.

4. Place the wrapped pieces in the air fryer and cook at 180°C for 8 minutes, turning halfway through cooking to cook evenly.
5. Transfer to a grid and repeat the process with the remaining avocado pieces.

732. Veggie Tots for children

Servings: 4
Cooking time: 20 minutes
Ingredients:
- 1 grated courgette
- 1 grated parsnip
- 1 grated carrot
- 1 onion, chopped
- 1 clove garlic, minced
- 2 tablespoons ground flax seeds
- 2 beaten eggs
- 1/2 cup tortilla chips, crushed
- 1/4 cup pork rinds
- Sea salt and ground black pepper

Addresses:
1. Start by preheating your fryer to 200°C.
2. Then, in a bowl, mix all the ingredients well until everything is well combined. Shape the mixture into a tot and place in the lightly greased baking basket.
3. Bake for 9 to 12 minutes, turning halfway through, until the edges are golden brown. Enjoy!

733. Indian Malai Kofta

Servings: 4
Cooking time: 40 minutes
Ingredients:
For the vegetable dumplings you need:
- 450 grams of potatoes, peeled and diced
- 1/2 lb cauliflower, cut into small florets
- 2 tablespoons olive oil
- 2 cloves garlic, minced
- 1 tbsp Garam masala
- 1 cup chickpea flour
- Himalayan pink salt and ground black pepper

For the sauce you need:
- 1 tablespoon sesame oil
- 1/2 teaspoon cumin seeds
- 2 cloves garlic, coarsely chopped
- 1 onion, chopped
- 1 Kashmiri chilli, seeded and minced
- 1 piece of ginger (about 2.5 centimetres)
- 1 teaspoon paprika
- 1 teaspoon turmeric powder
- 2 ripe tomatoes, mashed
- 1/2 cup vegetable stock
- 1/4 of whole coconut milk

Addresses:
1. Start by preheating your Air Fryer to 200°C.
2. Place the potato and cauliflower in a lightly greased baking basket.
3. Cook for 15 minutes, shaking the basket halfway through cooking.
4. Mash the cauliflower and potatoes in a bowl.
5. Add the rest of the ingredients for the vegetable dumplings and stir to combine well.
6. Form the vegetable mixture into small balls and place them in the cooking basket.
7. Cook in the preheated Air Fryer at 180°C for 15 minutes or until cooked through and crispy.
8. Repeat the process until you run out of ingredients.
9. Heat the sesame oil in a saucepan over medium heat and add the cumin seeds. Once the cumin seeds are browned, add the garlic, onion, chilli and ginger.
10. Sauté for 2 to 3 minutes.
11. Add the paprika, turmeric powder, tomatoes and stock. Put the lid on and simmer for 4-5 minutes, stirring occasionally.
12. Add the coconut milk. Then turn off the heat, add the vegetable balls and stir gently to combine, enjoy!

734. Smoked fish balls

Servings: 6
Cooking time: 45 minutes
Ingredients:
- 2 cups cooked rice
- 2 eggs, lightly beaten
- 1 cup grated Grana Padano cheese
- ¼ cup finely chopped thyme
- Salt and pepper
- 1 cup panko crumbs
- Cooking spray

Addresses:
1. In a bowl, add the fish, rice, eggs, Grana Padano cheese, thyme, salt and pepper.
2. Stir until well combined.
3. Use the mixture to form balls of uniform size.
4. Roll the balls in breadcrumbs and sprinkle with oil.
5. Place the balls in the fryer and cook for 16 minutes at 200°C or until crispy.

735. Cheese stuffed mushrooms

Portions: 10
Cooking time: 30 minutes
Ingredients:
- Olive oil to brush on the mushrooms
- 1 cup cooked brown rice
- 1 cup grated Grana Padano cheese
- 1 tsp dried mixed herbs
- Salt and black pepper

Addresses:
1. Brush each mushroom with oil and set aside.

2. In a bowl, mix the rice, cheese, herbs, salt and pepper.
3. Then fill the mushrooms with the mixture.
4. Place the mushrooms in the air fryer and cook them for minutes at 180°C.
5. Make sure the mushrooms are cooked until golden brown and the cheese has melted. When ready, serve with herbs.

736. Pumpkin Parm

Servings: 4
Cooking time: 25 minutes
Ingredients:
- 1 medium spaghetti squash
- 55 grams of grated mozzarella cheese
- 30 grams of grated Parmesan cheese
- 1 teaspoon of avocado oil
- ½ teaspoon dried oregano
- ½ teaspoon dried coriander
- ½ teaspoon ground nutmeg
- 2 teaspoons butter

Addresses:
1. Cut the spaghetti into halves and remove the seeds. Then sprinkle with avocado oil, dried oregano, dried coriander and ground nutmeg.
2. Put a teaspoon of butter on each spaghetti squash half and transfer the vegetables into the air fryer.
3. Cook for 15 minutes at 185°C.
4. After this, fill the pumpkin with mozzarella and Parmesan and cook for 10 more minutes at the same temperature.

737. Roasted broccoli

Servings: 4
Cooking time: 7 minutes
Ingredients:
- 4 cups broccoli florets
- 1/4 cup water
- 1 tablespoon of olive oil
- 1/4 teaspoon pepper
- 1/8 teaspoon kosher salt

Addresses:
1. Add the broccoli, oil, pepper and salt to a bowl and stir well.
2. Add ¼ cup of water to the bottom of the fryer (under the basket).
3. Transfer the broccoli to the basket of the air fryer and cook for 7 minutes at 200°C.
4. Serve and enjoy.

738. Spinach and cheese

Servings: 4
Cooking time: 10 minutes
Ingredients:
- 1.115 kilograms of spinach
- 1 tablespoon of olive oil
- 2 beaten eggs
- 2 tablespoons milk
- 85 grams of cottage cheese
- Salt and black pepper to taste
- 1 yellow onion, chopped

Addresses:
1. In a frying pan that fits your air fryer, heat the oil over medium heat, add the onions, stir and sauté for 2 minutes.
2. Add all the other ingredients and mix.
3. Place the pan in the air fryer and cook at 200°C for 8 minutes.
4. Divide the spinach among the plates and serve as a garnish.

739. Celery and coconut sprouts

Servings: 4
Cooking time: 12 minutes
Ingredients:
- 1 stalk celery, coarsely chopped
- 1 cup coconut cream
- Salt and black pepper to taste
- 1 tablespoon chopped parsley
- 1 tbsp melted coconut oil
- ½ pound Brussels sprouts, cut in half

Addresses:
1. Heat a frying pan that fits the air fryer with the oil over medium heat.
2. When the oil is hot, add the sprouts and celery, stir and cook for 2 minutes.
3. Then add the cream and the rest of the ingredients, stir.
4. Place the pan in the air fryer and cook at 190°C for minutes. Transfer to bowls and serve.

740. Pepper stuffed with cheese and broccoli

Servings: 4
Cooking time: 20 minutes
Ingredients:
- 4 eggs
- 2 medium-sized peppers, halved and cored
- 1 teaspoon dried sage
- 70 grams grated cheddar cheese
- 200 grams of almond milk
- 1/4 cup broccoli florets
- 1/4 cup cherry tomatoes
- Pepper
- Salt

Addresses:
1. Preheat the air fryer to 190°C.
2. In a bowl, whisk together the eggs, milk, broccoli, cherry tomatoes, sage, pepper and salt.
3. Spray the air fryer basket with cooking spray.
4. Place the pepper halves in the fryer basket.
5. Pour the egg mixture into the pepper halves.
6. Sprinkle the cheese over the pepper and cook for 20 minutes.
7. Serve and enjoy.

741. Cheese Sticks with Sweet Thai Sauce

Servings: 4
Cooking time: 20 minutes + freezing time
Ingredients:
- 2 cups breadcrumbs
- 3 eggs
- 1 cup Thai sweet sauce
- 4 tablespoons skimmed milk

Addresses:
1. Pour the breadcrumbs into a bowl.
2. Beat the eggs in another bowl with milk.
3. One after the other, dip the sticks into the egg mixture, into the crumbs, then into the egg mixture again and into the crumbs again.
4. Freeze for one hour.
5. Preheat the fryer to 190°C.
6. Place the sticks in the fryer and cook for 5 minutes, turning them halfway through cooking so that they brown evenly.
7. Cook in batches and serve with a sweet Thai sauce.

742. Easy vegetable fried dumplings

Servings: 3
Cooking time: 30 minutes
Ingredients:
- 225 grams of grated sweet potatoes
- 1 cup carrots
- 1 cup maize
- 2 cloves garlic, minced
- 1 chopped shallot
- Sea salt and ground black pepper
- 2 tablespoons fresh parsley, chopped
- 1 egg, well beaten
- ½ cup wheat flour
- ½ cup grated Romano cheese
- ½ cup dried bread flakes
- 1 tablespoon of olive oil

Addresses:
1. Mix the vegetables, spices, egg, flour and Romano cheese until well incorporated.
2. Take 1 tablespoon of the vegetable mixture and roll into balls. Roll the balls in the dry bread flakes. Brush the vegetable balls with olive oil on all sides.
3. Cook in the preheated Air Fryer at 200°C for 15 minutes or until cooked through and crispy.
4. Repeat the process until you run out of ingredients - bon appetit!

743. Parmesan artichoke hearts

Servings: 4
Cooking time: 15 minutes
Ingredients:
- 1 egg
- ¼ cup flour
- ¼ of grated Parmesan cheese
- ⅓ cup panko breadcrumbs
- 1 teaspoon garlic powder
- Salt and black pepper

Addresses:
1. Preheat the air fryer to 200°C.
2. Grease the air fryer basket with cooking spray.
3. Dry the artichokes with kitchen paper and cut them into pieces. In a bowl, beat the egg white with the salt.
4. In another bowl, mix the Parmesan cheese, breadcrumbs and garlic powder. In a third pour the flour, mix with salt and pepper.
5. Dredge the artichokes in the flour, then in the egg and finally in the breadcrumb mixture.
6. Place them in the cooking basket of your air fryer and cook for 10 minutes, turning once. Allow to cool before serving.

744. Winter vegetable stew

Servings: 2
Cooking time: 25 minutes
Ingredients:
- 4 potatoes, peeled and cut into 2.5 centimetre pieces
- 1 celery root, peeled and cut into 2.5 centimetre pieces
- 1 cup winter squash
- 2 tablespoons unsalted butter, melted
- 1/2 cup chicken stock
- 1/4 cup tomato sauce
- 1 teaspoon parsley
- 1 teaspoon rosemary
- 1 teaspoon thyme

Addresses:
1. Start by preheating your Air Fryer to 185°C.
2. Add all ingredients to a lightly greased saucepan. Stir to combine well.
3. Bake in the preheated air fryer for 10 minutes.
4. Gently stir the vegetables with a large spoon and increase the temperature to 200°C, cook for a further 10 minutes.
5. Serve in individual bowls with a squeeze of lemon juice and enjoy!

745. Rutabaga Chili

Servings: 4
Cooking time: 20 minutes
Ingredients:
- 425 grams rutabagas, cut into fries
- 4 tablespoons olive oil
- 1 teaspoon chilli powder
- Pinch of salt and black pepper

Addresses:
1. In a bowl, mix the fried turnips with all the other ingredients, stir and place in the basket of your air fryer.
2. Bake at 200°C for 20 minutes
3. Divide between plates and serve as a side dish.

746. Mushrooms stuffed with garlic

Servings: 4
Cooking time: 25 minutes
Ingredients:
- 6 small mushrooms
- 30 g. onion, peeled and diced
- 1 tablespoon of quality breadcrumbs
- 1 tablespoon of olive oil
- 1 teaspoon crushed garlic
- 1 teaspoon parsley
- Salt and pepper

Addresses:
1. Mix the breadcrumbs, oil, onion, parsley, salt, pepper and garlic in a bowl.
2. Cut the stems off the mushrooms and stuff each cap with the breadcrumb mixture.
3. Cook in the Air Fryer for 10 minutes at 180°C.
4. Serve with a garnish of mayonnaise sauce.

747. Leeks with paprika

Servings: 3
Cooking time: 8 minutes
Ingredients:
- 2 large leeks, cut into slices
- 1 beaten egg
- ½ teaspoon ground paprika
- ½ teaspoon salt
- ½ teaspoon ground turmeric
- 2 tablespoons almond flour
- Cooking spray

Addresses:
1. Sprinkle the leek slices with ground paprika, salt and ground turmeric.
2. Then dip each leek slice in the egg and dredge it in the almond flour.
3. Preheat the air fryer to 200°C.
4. Place the leek pieces inside the fryer and spray them with cooking spray.
5. Cook for 8 minutes and shake after 4 minutes of cooking.

748. Plum and bacon pumps

Portions: 10
Cooking time: 25 minutes
Ingredients:
- 2 tablespoons fresh rosemary, finely chopped
- 1 cup chopped almonds in small pieces
- Salt and black pepper
- 15 chopped dried plums
- 15 slices of bacon

Addresses:
1. Line the fryer basket with baking paper.
2. In a bowl, add the cheese, rosemary, almonds, salt, pepper and plums, stir well.
3. Form into balls and wrap in a slice of bacon.
4. Place the bombs in the fryer and cook them for a few minutes at 200°C.
5. Leave to cool before removing from the fryer. Serve with chopsticks.

749. Balsamic radishes

Servings: 4
Cooking time: 15 minutes
Ingredients:
- 2 bunches of red radishes, cut in halves
- 1 tablespoon of olive oil
- 2 tablespoons balsamic vinegar
- 2 tablespoons chopped parsley
- Salt and black pepper

Addresses:
1. In a bowl, combine the radishes with the rest of the ingredients, except the parsley, and mix.
2. Transfer the preparation to the basket of the air fryer and cook at 200°C.
3. Divide among the plates, sprinkle the parsley on top and serve as a garnish.

750. Jalapeño clouds

Servings: 4
Cooking time: 4 minutes
Ingredients:
- 2 egg whites
- 1 jalapeño pepper
- 1 teaspoon almond flour
- 30 grams Jarlsberg cheese, grated

Addresses:
1. Beat the egg whites until stiff peaks form.
2. Then carefully mix in the peaks of the egg whites, the almond flour and the Jarlsberg cheese.
3. Cut the jalapeño chilli into 4 slices.
4. Preheat the air fryer to 195°C.
5. Line the basket of the air fryer with baking paper. With the help of the spoon make the egg white clouds on the baking paper.
6. Top the clouds with the sliced jalapeños.
7. Cook for 4 minutes or until the clouds are lightly browned.

751. Asparagus and mozzarella mixture

Servings: 4
Cooking time: 10 minutes
Ingredients:
- 450 grams of asparagus, trimmed
- 2 tablespoons olive oil
- Pinch of salt and black pepper
- 2 cups shredded mozzarella cheese
- ½ cup balsamic vinegar
- 2 cups halved cherry tomatoes

Addresses:
1. In a frying pan that fits your air fryer, combine the asparagus with the rest of the ingredients, except the mozzarella, and mix.
2. Place the pan in the air fryer and cook at 200°C.
3. Divide among the plates and serve.

752. Simple tomato and pepper sauce recipe

Servings: 4
Cooking time: 25 minutes
Ingredients:
- 2 red peppers, chopped
- 2 cloves garlic, minced
- 2 tablespoons olive oil
- 1 tablespoon balsamic vinegar
- 450 grams of halved cherry tomatoes
- 1 teaspoon dried rosemary
- 3 bay leaves
- Salt and black pepper to taste

Addresses:
1. In a bowl, combine the tomatoes with the garlic, salt, black pepper, rosemary, bay leaves, half the oil and half the vinegar, stir to coat.
2. Place the preparation in your air fryer and roast it at 160°C.
3. Meanwhile, in your food processor, combine the peppers with a pinch of sea salt, black pepper, the rest of the oil and the rest of the vinegar and blend very well.
4. Divide the roasted tomatoes among the plates, drizzle the pepper sauce on top and serve.

753. Easy sweet potato pie

Servings: 3
Cooking time: 35 minutes
Ingredients:
- 1 stick of melted butter
- 450 grams of mashed sweet potatoes
- 2 tablespoons honey
- 2 beaten eggs
- 1/3 cup coconut milk
- 1/4 cup flour
- 1/2 cup fresh breadcrumbs

Addresses:
1. Start by preheating your fryer to 160°C.
2. Spray a casserole dish with cooking oil.
3. In a bowl, mix all the ingredients except the breadcrumbs and 1 tablespoon of butter. Pour the mixture into the prepared casserole dish.
4. Coat with the breadcrumbs and brush the top with the remaining tablespoon of butter.
5. Bake in the preheated Air Fryer for 30 minutes, enjoy!

754. Roast red potatoes with duck fat

Servings: 4
Cooking time: 15 minutes
Ingredients:
- 1 tablespoon garlic powder
- Salt and black pepper
- 2 tablespoons chopped thyme
- 3 tablespoons of melted duck fat

Addresses:
1. Preheat the fryer to 190°C.
2. In a bowl, combine the duck fat, garlic powder, salt and pepper. Add the potatoes and toss to coat.
3. Place them in the cooking basket of the air fryer and cook for a few minutes, then shake and continue cooking for another 10 minutes.
4. Serve hot, sprinkled with thyme.

755. Air fried onions and peppers

Servings: 3
Cooking time: 25 minutes
Ingredients:
- 6 sliced peppers
- 1 tablespoon Italian seasoning
- 1 tablespoon of olive oil
- 1 onion, sliced

Addresses:
1. Add all ingredients to the large bowl and mix well.
2. Preheat the air fryer to 150°C.
3. Transfer the pepper and onion mixture to the basket of the air fryer and cook for 15 minutes.
4. Mix well and cook for a further 10 minutes.
5. Serve and enjoy.

756. Breaded mushrooms

Servings: 4
Cooking time: 55 minutes
Ingredients:
- 2 cups breadcrumbs
- 2 beaten eggs
- Salt and pepper to taste
- 2 cups grated Parmigiano Reggiano cheese

Addresses:
1. Preheat the fryer to 180°C.
2. Pour the breadcrumbs into a bowl, add salt and pepper and mix well. Then add the cheese in a separate bowl.
3. Dip each mushroom in the eggs, then in the breadcrumbs and then in the cheese.
4. Cook 6 mushrooms in the basket of the air fryer and cook for 20 minutes.
5. Serve with the cheese sauce.

757. Spicy ricotta stuffed mushrooms

Servings: 4
Cooking time: 35 minutes
Ingredients:
- 225 grams of small white mushrooms
- Sea salt and ground black pepper
- 2 tablespoons ricotta cheese
- 1/2 teaspoon ancho chili powder
- 1 teaspoon paprika
- 4 tablespoons plain flour
- 1 egg
- 1/2 cup fresh breadcrumbs

Addresses:
1. Remove the stems from the mushroom caps and chop the mushrooms, mix the

chopped mushroom vapours with the salt, black pepper, cheese, chilli powder and paprika.
2. Fill the mushroom caps with the cheese filling.
3. Put the flour in a shallow bowl and beat the egg in another bowl. Put the breadcrumbs in a third shallow bowl.
4. Dredge the mushrooms in the flour, then in the egg mixture and finally dredge them in the breadcrumbs and press them to adhere. Spray the stuffed mushrooms with cooking spray.
5. Cook in the preheated air fryer at 180°C for 18 minutes, enjoy!

758. Vegetable gratin with the family

Servings: 4
Cooking time: 35 minutes
Ingredients:
- 450 grams of Chinese cabbage, coarsely chopped
- 2 sweet red peppers, seeded and sliced
- 1 jalapeño pepper, seeded and sliced
- 1 onion, thickly sliced
- 2 cloves garlic, cut into slices
- 1/2 stick of butter
- 4 tablespoons plain flour
- 1 cup of milk
- 1 cup cream cheese
- Sea salt and freshly ground black pepper
- 1/2 teaspoon cayenne pepper
- 1 cup Monterey Jack cheese, shredded

Addresses:
1. Heat a pan of salted water and bring to the boil. Cook the Chinese cabbage for 2 to 3 minutes.
2. Transfer the Chinese cabbage to cold water to stop the cooking process.
3. Place the Chinese cabbage in a lightly greased casserole dish. Add the peppers, onion and garlic.
4. Next, melt the butter in a saucepan over moderate heat. Gradually add the flour and cook for 2 minutes to form a paste.
5. Slowly pour in the milk, stirring continuously until a thick sauce forms. Add the cream cheese. Season with the salt, black pepper and cayenne pepper. Add the mixture to the casserole dish.
6. Top with grated Monterey Jack cheese and bake in the air fryer preheated to 200°C. Serve hot.

759. Garnished with lemon artichokes

Servings: 4
Cooking time: 25 minutes
Ingredients:
- 2 medium artichokes, trimmed and halved
- 2 tablespoons lemon juice
- Cooking spray
- Salt and black pepper to taste

Addresses:
1. Grease your air fryer with cooking spray.
2. Add the artichokes, drizzle with lemon juice and sprinkle with salt and black pepper and cook at 190°C.
3. Divide between plates and serve as a side dish.

760. Lemongrass rice mixture

Servings: 4
Cooking time: 10 minutes
Ingredients:
- ½ cup broccoli, shredded
- ½ cup shredded cauliflower
- ¼ teaspoon lemongrass
- 1 teaspoon ground turmeric
- ¼ cup beef broth
- 1 teaspoon butter
- ½ teaspoon salt
- 85 grams of Cheddar cheese, grated

Addresses:
1. In the bowl of a blender, mix the shredded broccoli and cauliflower. Add the lemongrass, turmeric and salt.
2. Then transfer the mixture to the air fryer pan and add the meat stock.
3. Add the butter and top the keto rice with Cheddar cheese.
4. Preheat the air fryer to 185°C.
5. Place the pan with the "rice" in the air fryer and cook it.

Vegan and vegetarian recipes

761. Vegetarian rice

Servings: 2
Cooking time: 18 minutes
Ingredients:
- 2 cups cooked white rice
- 1 large egg, lightly beaten
- ½ cup frozen peas, thawed
- ½ cup frozen carrots, thawed
- ½ teaspoon toasted sesame seeds
- 1 tablespoon vegetable oil
- 2 teaspoons toasted and divided sesame oil
- 1 tablespoon of water
- Salt and ground white pepper
- 1 teaspoon soy sauce
- 1 teaspoon Sriracha sauce

Addresses:
1. Preheat the fryer to 190°C and grease a frying pan.
2. Mix the rice, vegetable oil, 1 teaspoon sesame oil, water, salt and white pepper in a bowl.

3. Transfer the rice mixture to the fryer basket and cook for about 12 minutes.
4. Pour the beaten egg over the rice and cook for a few minutes.
5. Stir in the peas and carrots and cook for a further 2 minutes.
6. Meanwhile, mix the soy sauce, Sriracha sauce, sesame seeds and remaining sesame oil in a bowl.
7. Divide the potato cubes among the serving plates and drizzle with the serving sauce.

762. Mushrooms stuffed with vegetables

Servings: 3
Cooking time: 15 minutes
Ingredients:
- 1 tomato, diced
- 1 small red onion, diced
- 1 green pepper, diced
- ½ cup grated mozzarella cheese
- ½ teaspoon garlic powder
- ¼ teaspoon pepper
- ¼ teaspoon salt

Addresses:
1. Preheat the fryer to 165°C.
2. Wash the mushrooms, remove the stems and pat dry. Drizzle them with the olive oil.
3. Combine all remaining ingredients, except mozzarella, in a bowl.
4. Divide the filling between the mushrooms and top the mushrooms with mozzarella.
5. Place the preparation in the fryer and cook for 8 minutes.

763. Carrot and courgette with butter and mayonnaise

Servings: 4
Cooking time: 25 minutes
Ingredients:
- 1 tablespoon grated onion
- 2 tablespoons melted butter
- 225 grams carrots, cut into slices
- 1 or 2 courgettes cut in slices
- 1/4 cup water
- 1/4 cup mayonnaise
- 1/4 teaspoon prepared horseradish
- 1/4 teaspoon salt
- 1/4 teaspoon ground black pepper
- 1/4 cup Italian breadcrumbs

Addresses:
1. Lightly grease the air fryer tray with cooking spray. Add carrots.
2. Cook at 180°C for 8 minutes.
3. Add the courgettes and continue cooking for a further 5 minutes.
4. Meanwhile, in a bowl, whisk together the pepper, salt, horseradish, onion, mayonnaise and water. Pour into the pan of vegetables. Toss well to coat.
5. In a small bowl, mix melted butter and breadcrumbs. Sprinkle over the vegetables.
6. Bake for 10 minutes at 200°C until the top is lightly browned.
7. Serve and enjoy.

764. Baked Portobello, Pasta 'n Cheese

Servings: 4
Cooking time: 30 minutes
Ingredients:
- 1 cup of milk
- 1 cup grated mozzarella cheese
- 1 large garlic clove, minced
- 1 tablespoon vegetable oil
- 1/4 cup margarine
- 1/4 teaspoon dried basil
- 115 grams of portobello mushrooms, thinly sliced
- 2 tablespoons plain flour
- 2 tablespoons soy sauce
- 115 g penne pasta, cooked according to the manufacturer's cooking instructions
- 140 grams frozen chopped spinach, thawed

Addresses:
1. Lightly grease the air fryer tray with oil. Heat for 2 minutes at 180°C.
2. Add the mushrooms and cook for one minute. Transfer to a plate.
3. In the same pan, melt the margarine for one minute. Stir in the basil, garlic and flour. Cook for 3 minutes. Stir and cook for another minute.
4. Add half of the milk slowly while whisking continuously. Cook for another 2 minutes. Mix well. Cook for another 2 minutes.
5. Add the rest of the milk and cook for another 3 minutes. Then add the cheese and mix well.
6. Stir in the soy sauce, spinach, mushrooms and pasta. Mix well. Top with remaining cheese.
7. Cook for 1 minute at 200°C until the top is lightly browned.
8. Serve and enjoy.

765. Simply stunning vegetables

Servings: 4
Cooking time: 35 minutes
Ingredients:
- 225 grams of carrots, peeled and cut into slices
- 450 grams of yellow pumpkin, sliced
- 450 grams courgettes, cut into slices
- 1 tablespoon chopped tarragon leaves
- 6 teaspoons of olive oil, divided
- 1 teaspoon kosher salt
- ½ teaspoon ground white pepper

Addresses:

1. Preheat the fryer to 200°C and grease the fryer basket.
2. Mix the teaspoons of olive oil and the carrots in a bowl until combined.
3. Transfer to the fryer basket and cook for about 5 minutes.
4. Meanwhile, combine the remaining teaspoons of olive oil, yellow squash, courgette, salt and white pepper in a large bowl.
5. Transfer this vegetable mixture to the fryer basket with the carrots.
6. Cook for about 30 minutes and serve in a serving dish.
7. Top with tarragon leaves and mix well to serve.

766. Crispy asparagus dipped in paprika and garlic

Portions: 5
Cooking time: 15 minutes
Ingredients:
- ¼ cup almond flour
- ½ teaspoon garlic powder
- ½ teaspoon smoked paprika
- 10 medium-sized asparagus spears, trimmed
- 2 large eggs, beaten
- 2 tablespoons chopped parsley
- Salt and pepper to taste

Addresses:
1. Preheat the air fryer for 5 minutes.
2. In a bowl, combine the parsley, garlic powder, almond flour and smoked paprika. Season with salt and pepper to taste.
3. Dip the asparagus in the beaten eggs and dredge in the almond flour mixture.
4. Place in the fryer basket and close to cook at 180°C.

767. Vegetable pie with cheese and olives

Servings: 3
Cooking time: 25 minutes
Ingredients:
- 225 grams of cauliflower, cut into 2.5 cm florets
- 115 grams of courgette, cut into 2.5 centimetre pieces
- 1 red onion, sliced
- 2 bell peppers, cut into 2.5 centimetre pieces
- 2 tablespoons of extra virgin olive oil
- 1 cup dry white wine
- 1 teaspoon dried rosemary
- Sea salt and freshly ground black pepper
- 1/2 teaspoon dried basil
- 1/2 cup crushed tomato
- 1/2 cup shredded cheddar cheese
- 30 grams of Kalamata olives, stoned and halved

Addresses:
1. Toss the vegetables with the olive oil, wine, rosemary, salt, black pepper and basil until well coated.
2. Add the tomato puree to a lightly greased baking dish, spread to cover the bottom of the dish.
3. Add the vegetables and top with grated cheese. Sprinkle the Kalamata olives on top.
4. Bake in the preheated Air Fryer at 200°C for 20 minutes, turning the dish halfway through the cooking time. Serve hot and enjoy.

768. Fresh green beans from the garden

Servings: 4
Cooking time: 12 minutes
Ingredients:
- 450 grams of green beans, washed and trimmed
- 1 teaspoon melted butter
- 1 tablespoon fresh lemon juice
- ¼ teaspoon garlic powder
- Salt and freshly ground pepper

Addresses:
1. Preheat the fryer to 200°C and grease the fryer basket.
2. Place all ingredients in a large bowl and transfer to the fryer basket.
3. Cook for about 8 minutes and serve in a serving dish to keep warm.

769. Aubergines stuffed with spices

Servings: 4
Cooking time: 12 minutes
Ingredients:
- 8 small aubergines
- 4 teaspoons of olive oil, divided
- ¾ teaspoon dried mango powder
- ¾ tbsp ground coriander
- ½ teaspoon ground cumin
- ½ teaspoon ground turmeric
- ½ teaspoon garlic powder
- Salt

Addresses:
1. Preheat the fryer to 190°C and grease the fryer basket.
2. Make cuts from the bottom of each aubergine leaving the stems intact.
3. Mix a teaspoon of oil and spices in a bowl and fill each indentation of the aubergines with this mixture.
4. Brush the outside of each aubergine with the remaining oil and place in the fryer basket.
5. Cook for about 12 minutes and plate to serve hot.

770. Easy glazed carrots

Servings: 4
Cooking time: 12 minutes
Ingredients:

- 3 cups carrots, peeled and coarsely chopped
- 1 tablespoon of olive oil
- 1 tablespoon of honey
- Salt and black pepper

Addresses:
1. Preheat the fryer to 200°C and grease one fryer basket.
2. Mix all ingredients in a bowl and stir to coat well.
3. Transfer to the fryer basket and cook for about 12 minutes.
4. Serve hot.

771. Vegetable frittata with two cheeses

Servings: 2
Cooking time: 35 minutes
Ingredients:
- ⅓ cup sliced mushrooms
- 1 large courgette, cut to 2.5 cm thickness
- 1 small red onion, sliced
- ¼ cup chopped chives
- 225 grams of asparagus, trimmed and cut into thin slices
- 2 teaspoons olive oil
- 4 cracked eggs in a bowl
- ⅓ cup of milk
- Salt and pepper
- ⅓ cup grated Cheddar cheese
- ⅓ cup crumbled feta cheese

Addresses:
1. Preheat the fryer to 190°C.
2. Line a baking dish with parchment paper and set aside.
3. In the bowl of eggs, add the milk, salt and pepper, whisk evenly. Place a frying pan over medium heat on the cooker, and heat the olive oil.
4. Add the asparagus, courgette, onion, mushrooms and baby spinach, sauté for 5 minutes.
5. Pour the vegetables into the baking dish and cover with the egg mixture.
6. Sprinkle the feta and cheddar cheese on top and place in the fryer.
7. Cook for 15 minutes. Remove the baking dish from the oven and garnish with fresh chives.

772. Potato, aubergine and courgette chips

Servings: 4
Cooking time: 45 minutes
Ingredients:
- 5 potatoes cut into strips
- 3 courgettes cut into strips
- ½ cup corn starch
- ½ cup water
- ½ cup olive oil
- Salt for seasoning

Addresses:
1. Preheat the air fryer to 200°C.
2. In a bowl, mix together the cornflour, water, salt, pepper, oil, aubergines, courgette and potatoes.
3. Place one third of the vegetable strips in the fryer basket and cook for a few minutes, shaking once.
4. When ready, transfer to a serving platter. Serve hot.

773. Drizzle Onion Blossoming

Servings: 4
Cooking time: 20 minutes
Ingredients:
- Olive oil
- 1 teaspoon cayenne pepper
- 1 teaspoon garlic powder
- 2 cups flour
- 1 tablespoon pepper
- 1 tablespoon paprika
- 1 tablespoon salt
- ¼ cup mayonnaise
- 1 tablespoon ketchup
- ¼ cup mayonnaise
- ¼ cup sour cream

Addresses:
1. In a bowl, mix the salt, pepper, paprika, flour, garlic powder and cayenne pepper.
2. Add the mayonnaise, ketchup and sour cream to the mixture and stir.
3. Coat the onions with the prepared mixture and drizzle with oil.
4. Preheat your air fryer to 180°C. Add the coated onions to the basket and cook for minutes.

774. Parsnip and potato pie

Servings: 8
Cooking time: 30 minutes
Ingredients:
- 3 tablespoons pine nuts
- 790 grams chopped parsnips
- 40 grams of coarsely chopped Parmesan cheese
- 190 grams of crème fraiche
- 1 slice of bread
- 2 tablespoons sage
- 4 tablespoons butter
- 4 teaspoons mustard

Addresses:
1. Preheat the fryer to 180°C.
2. Put salted water in a saucepan over medium heat. Add the potatoes and parsnips. Bring to the boil.
3. In a bowl, mix the mustard, crème fraiche, sage, salt and pepper. Drain the potatoes and parsnips and mash them with butter using a potato masher.
4. Add the mustard mixture, bread, cheese and walnuts to the puree and mix.

5. Add the batter to the basket of your air fryer and cook for 15 minutes stirring once. Serve.

775. Ultimate Vegan Calzone

Servings: 1
Cooking time: 25 minutes
Ingredients:
- 1 teaspoon olive oil
- 1/2 small onion, chopped
- 2 sweet peppers, seeded and sliced
- Sea salt
- 1/4 teaspoon ground black pepper
- 1/4 teaspoon dried oregano
- 115 grams of prepared Italian pizza dough
- 1/4 cup marinara sauce
- 55 grams of vegetable Mozzarella cheese, grated

Addresses:
1. Heat the olive oil in a non-stick frying pan. Once hot, cook the onion and peppers until tender and fragrant, about 5 minutes. Add salt, black pepper and oregano.
2. Sprinkle a little flour on the kitchen worktop and roll out the pizza dough.
3. Pour the marinara sauce over half of the dough, add the sautéed mixture and sprinkle with the vegan cheese. Now gently fold the dough over to create a pocket, making sure to seal the edges.
4. Use a fork to prick the dough in some places. Add a few drops of olive oil and place in the lightly greased baking basket.
5. Bake in the preheated Air Fryer at 165°C for 12 minutes, turning the calzones halfway through baking. Bon appetit!

776. Cornish Vegetarian Herbed Cornish Pies

Servings: 4
Cooking time: 30 minutes
Ingredients:
- ¼ cup chopped mushrooms
- ¾ cup cold coconut oil
- 1 ½ cups plain flour
- 1 medium carrot, chopped
- 1 medium potato, diced
- 1 onion, sliced
- 1 stalk celery, chopped
- 1 tablespoon nutritional yeast
- 1 tablespoon of olive oil
- 1 teaspoon oregano
- A pinch of salt
- Cold water for mixing the dough
- Salt and pepper to taste

Addresses:
1. Preheat the air fryer to 200°C.
2. Prepare the dough by mixing the flour, coconut oil and salt in a bowl. Use a fork and press down on the flour to combine everything.
3. Gradually add a drop of water to the dough until a stiff dough consistency is achieved.
4. Cover the dough with cling film and leave to rest for 30 minutes in the fridge.
5. Roll out the dough and cut into squares. Set aside.
6. Heat the olive oil over medium heat and sauté the onions for 2 minutes.
7. Add the celery, carrots and potatoes. Continue stirring for 3 to 5 minutes before adding the mushrooms and oregano.
8. Season with salt and pepper to taste. Add the nutritional yeast last. Leave to cool and set aside.
9. Drop a spoonful of the vegetable mixture onto the dough and seal the edges of the dough with water.
10. Place inside the basket of the air fryer and cook for 20 minutes or until the batter is crispy.

777. Tofu Italian style

Servings: 2
Cooking time: 30 minutes
Ingredients:
- Black pepper
- 1 tablespoon vegetable stock
- 1 tablespoon soy sauce
- ⅓ teaspoon dried oregano
- ⅓ teaspoon garlic powder
- ⅓ teaspoon dried basil
- ⅓ teaspoon of onion powder

Addresses:
1. Place the tofu on a cutting board and cut into 3 lengthwise slices with a knife.
2. Line one side of a cutting board with kitchen paper, place the tofu on it and cover it with kitchen paper.
3. Use your hands to press the tofu gently until as much liquid as possible has been extracted.
4. Remove the kitchen paper and use a knife to cut the tofu into 8 cubes, set aside.
5. In another bowl, add the soy sauce, vegetable stock, oregano, basil, garlic powder, onion powder and black pepper, mix well with a spoon.
6. Pour the spice mixture over the tofu, toss the tofu until well coated, leave to marinate for 10 minutes.
7. Preheat the fryer to 150°C.
8. Place the tofu in the fryer basket, in a single layer, cook for 10 minutes, turning after 6 minutes. Remove to a plate and serve with green salad.

778. Tofu in sweet and spicy sauce

Servings: 3
Cooking time: 23 minutes
Ingredients:
For tofu it is needed:

182

- 1 block of firm tofu, pressed and cut in cubes
- ½ cup arrowroot flour
- ½ teaspoon sesame oil

For the sauce it is needed:
- 4 tablespoons low sodium soy sauce
- 1½ tablespoons rice vinegar
- 1½ tablespoons chilli sauce
- 1 tablespoon agave nectar
- 2 large garlic cloves, minced
- 1 teaspoon fresh ginger, peeled and grated
- 2 spring onions (chopped green part)

Addresses:
1. In a bowl, mix the tofu, arrowroot flour and sesame oil.
2. Set the temperature of the air fryer to 180°C.
3. Generously grease one basket of the air fryer.
4. Place the tofu pieces in the prepared air fryer basket in a single layer.
5. Fry in the open air for about 20 minutes, stirring once halfway through.
6. Meanwhile, to prepare the sauce use a bowl, add all the ingredients except the spring onions and whisk until well combined.
7. Remove from the air fryer and transfer the tofu to a frying pan with sauce over medium heat and cook for about 3 minutes, stirring occasionally.
8. Garnish with spring onions and serve hot.

779. Crispy Pumpkin Crisps

Servings: 4
Cooking time: 25 minutes
Ingredients:
- 1 cup all-purpose flour
- Salt and ground black pepper
- 3 tablespoons of nutritional yeast flakes
- ½ cup almond milk
- ½ cup almond flour
- ½ cup breadcrumbs
- 1 tablespoon herbs (oregano, basil, rosemary, chopped)
- 450 grams of pumpkin, peeled and cut into crisp shapes

Addresses:
1. In a shallow bowl, combine the flour, salt and black pepper.
2. In another shallow bowl, mix the nutritional yeast flakes with the almond milk until well combined.
3. Mix the almond flour, breadcrumbs and herbs in a third shallow dish.
4. Dredge the pumpkin in the flour mixture, shaking off the excess. Then dredge in the milk mixture and finally dredge in the breadcrumb mixture.
5. Drizzle the pumpkin chips with cooking oil on all sides.
6. Cook in the preheated Air Fryer at 180°C for approximately 12 minutes, turning them over halfway through cooking.
7. Serve with your favourite dipping sauce and enjoy!

780. Honey-glazed carrots

Servings: 4
Cooking time: 12 minutes
Ingredients:
- 3 cups carrots, peeled and coarsely chopped
- 1 tablespoon of olive oil
- 1 tablespoon of honey
- 1 tablespoon fresh thyme, finely chopped
- Salt and ground black pepper

Addresses:
1. Set the air fryer temperature to 200°C and grease the air fryer basket.
2. In a bowl, mix well the carrot, oil, honey, thyme, salt and black pepper.
3. Place the carrot pieces in the prepared fryer basket in a single layer.
4. Fry in the open air for about 12 minutes.
5. Remove from the fryer and transfer the carrot pieces to serving plates.
6. Serve hot.

781. Cheese rolls

Servings: 3
Cooking time: 8 minutes
Ingredients:
- 1 cup cheddar cheese, smoked and grated
- 1 mashed avocado
- ¼ cup ranch-style salad dressing
- 1 cup alfalfa sprouts
- 1 chopped tomato
- 1 sweet onion, chopped
- ¼ cup toasted sesame seeds

Addresses:
1. Place the open buns in the fryer basket.
2. Spread the avocado puree on each muffin half.
3. Place the halves next to each other. Top the rolls with the sprouts, tomatoes, onion, dressing, sesame seeds and cheese.
4. Bake for 7-8 minutes at 180°C.

782. Vegetarian Tandoori Spiced Grill Recipe

Servings: 6
Cooking time: 20 minutes
Ingredients:
- ½ head cauliflower, cut into florets
- ½ cup yoghurt
- 1 carrot, peeled and cut to about 5 millimetres thick
- 1 cup of young cobs
- 1 handful of sugar snap peas
- 1 small courgette, thickly sliced
- 1 sweet yellow pepper, seeded and chopped

- 2 small onions, cut into pieces
- 2 tablespoons canola oil
- Fresh ginger chopped to about 5 centimetres
- 3 tablespoons Tandoori spice blend
- 6 cloves garlic, minced

Addresses:
1. Preheat the fryer to 150°C.
2. Place the grill pan attachment on the air fryer.
3. In a Ziploc bag, put all the ingredients and shake to season all the vegetables.
4. Put all the ingredients in the grill pan and cook for 20 minutes.
5. Be sure to shake the vegetables halfway through the cooking time.

783. Ultra crispy tofu

Servings: 4
Cooking time: 30 minutes
Ingredients:
- 1 teaspoon chicken bouillon granules
- 340 grams of extra-strong tofu, drained and cut into 2.5 cm cubes
- 1 teaspoon butter
- 2 tablespoons low sodium soy sauce
- 2 tablespoons fish sauce
- 1 teaspoon sesame oil

Addresses:
1. Preheat the fryer to 180°C and grease the fryer basket.
2. Combine the soy sauce, fish sauce, sesame oil and chicken granules in a bowl and stir to coat well.
3. Stir in the tofu cubes and mix until well combined.
4. Leave to marinate for about 30 minutes and then transfer to the fryer basket.
5. Cook for about 30 minutes, turning every 10 minutes and serve hot.

784. Baked Aubergines with cheese and marinara

Servings: 3
Cooking time: 45 minutes
Ingredients:
- 1 clove of garlic, sliced and minced
- 1 large aubergine
- 1 tablespoon of olive oil
- 1 tablespoon of olive oil
- ½ pinch of salt or as needed
- Dried breadcrumbs (¼ cup + 2 tablespoons)
- ¼ cup and 2 tablespoons ricotta cheese
- ¼ cup grated Parmesan cheese
- ¼ cup grated Parmesan cheese
- ¼ cup water, plus as needed
- ¼ teaspoon red pepper flakes
- 1 to 2 cups prepared marinara sauce
- 1 or 2 teaspoons olive oil
- 2 tablespoons grated pepper jack cheese
- Salt and freshly ground black pepper

Addresses:
1. Cut the aubergine crosswise into 5 pieces.
2. Peel and cut two pieces into cubes of approximately 1.25 centimetres.
3. Lightly grease the air fryer tray with 1 tablespoon of olive oil.
4. Heat the oil to 200°C for 5 minutes. Then add half of the aubergine strips and cook for a few minutes on each side. Transfer to a plate.
5. Add 1 ½ teaspoon of olive oil and add the garlic. Cook for one minute. Add the chopped aubergines.
6. Season with pepper flakes and salt.
7. Cook for 4 minutes. When this time is up, reduce the heat to 150°C and continue cooking the aubergines until soft, about 8 minutes more.
8. Add water and marinara sauce. Cook for 7 minutes until heated through. Stir occasionally. Transfer to a bowl.
9. In a bowl, whisk together the pepper, salt, pepper jack cheese, Parmesan cheese and ricotta. Spread the cheeses evenly over the aubergine strips and then fold them in half.
10. Place the folded aubergines on the baking tray. Pour the marinara sauce over the top.
11. In a small bowl, whisk together the olive oil and breadcrumbs. Sprinkle over the sauce.
12. Bake for 15 minutes at 200°C until the top is lightly browned.
13. Serve and enjoy.

785. Mexican Baked Courgettes recipe

Servings: 4
Cooking time: 30 minutes
Ingredients:
- 1 tablespoon of olive oil
- 900 grams courgettes, diced
- ½ cup chopped onion
- ½ teaspoon garlic salt
- ½ teaspoon paprika
- ½ teaspoon dried oregano
- ½ teaspoon cayenne pepper
- ½ cup cooked long grain rice
- ½ cup cooked pinto beans
- 1 cup sauce
- ¾ cup shredded Cheddar cheese

Addresses:
1. Lightly grease the air fryer tray with olive oil.
2. Add the onions and courgettes and cook at 180°C for a few minutes.
3. Halfway through the cooking time, stir.
4. Season with cayenne, oregano, paprika and garlic salt. Mix well.
5. Add the sauce, beans and rice. Cook for 5 minutes.
6. Stir in the cheddar cheese and mix well.
7. Cover the pan with aluminium foil.

8. Cook for 15 minutes at 200°C until bubbling.
9. Serve and enjoy.

786. Ribs with pineapple appetizer

Servings: 4
Cooking time: 30 minutes
Ingredients:
- 200 grams of salad dressing
- 140 g can of pineapple juice
- 2 cups of water
- Garlic salt
- Salt and black pepper

Addresses:
1. Sprinkle the ribs with salt and pepper and place them in a casserole dish.
2. Pour in water and cook the ribs for a few minutes over high heat.
3. Drain the ribs and place them in the fryer, sprinkle with garlic salt.
4. Cook for 15 minutes at 200°C.
5. Prepare sauce by combining salad dressing and pineapple juice. Serve the ribs drizzled with the sauce.

787. Roasted mushrooms in herb and garlic oil

Servings: 4
Cooking time: 25 minutes
Ingredients:
- ½ teaspoon minced garlic
- 900 grams of mushrooms
- 2 teaspoons Herbes de Provence
- 3 tablespoons coconut oil
- Salt and pepper to taste

Addresses:
1. Preheat the air fryer for 5 minutes.
2. Place all ingredients in a baking dish that will fit in the air fryer.
3. Mix to combine.
4. Place the baking dish in the air fryer.
5. Cook for 2 minutes at 180°C.

788. Hoisin-glazed Bok Choy

Servings: 4
Cooking time: 10 minutes
Ingredients:
- 450 grams of baby Bok choy, bottom removed and leaves separated
- 2 cloves garlic, minced
- 1 teaspoon onion powder
- ½ teaspoon sage
- 2 tablespoons hoisin sauce
- 2 tablespoons sesame oil
- 1 tablespoon of plain flour

Addresses:
1. Place the bok choy, garlic, onion powder and sage in the lightly greased basket of the Air Fryer.
2. Cook in the preheated Air Fryer at 180°C for 3 minutes.
3. In a small dish, whisk together the hoisin sauce, sesame oil and flour. Drizzle the sauce over the bok choy. Cook for a few more minutes and enjoy!

789. Air-fried plain ravioli

Servings: 6
Cooking time: 15 minutes
Ingredients:
- 2 cups Italian breadcrumbs
- ¼ cup Parmesan cheese
- 1 cup buttermilk
- 1 teaspoon olive oil
- ¼ teaspoon garlic powder

Addresses:
1. Preheat the fryer to 200°C.
2. In a small bowl, combine the breadcrumbs, Parmesan cheese, garlic powder and olive oil.
3. Dip the ravioli in the buttermilk and then dredge them in the breadcrumb mixture.
4. Line a baking tray with parchment paper and arrange the ravioli on it.
5. Place them in the air fryer and cook for 5 minutes.
6. Serve the air-fried ravioli with marinara jar sauce.

790. Brussels sprouts with cheese

Servings: 3
Cooking time: 10 minutes
Ingredients:
- 450 grams of Brussels sprouts, cut and halved
- ¼ cup wholemeal breadcrumbs
- ¼ cup grated Parmesan cheese
- 1 tablespoon balsamic vinegar
- 1 tablespoon of extra virgin olive oil
- Salt and black pepper

Addresses:
1. Preheat the fryer to 200°C and grease the fryer basket.
2. Combine the Brussels sprouts, vinegar, oil, salt and black pepper in a bowl and toss to coat well.
3. Place the Brussels sprouts in the fryer basket and cook for about 5 minutes.
4. Sprinkle with the breadcrumbs and cheese and cook for a further 5 minutes.
5. Serve hot.

791. Fried halloumi with vegetables

Servings: 2
Cooking time: 15 minutes
Ingredients:
- 2 courgettes, cut into uniform pieces
- 1 large carrot, cut into chunks
- 1 large aubergine, peeled and cut into chunks
- 2 teaspoons olive oil
- 1 tsp dried mixed herbs

- Salt and black pepper

Addresses:
1. In a bowl, add the halloumi, courgette, carrot, aubergine, olive oil, herbs, salt and pepper.
2. Sprinkle with oil, salt and pepper.
3. Place the halloumi and vegetables in the basket of the air fryer and drizzle with olive oil.
4. Cook for minutes at 170°C, stirring once.
5. Sprinkle with herb mixture to serve.

792. Delicious asparagus and mushroom fritters

Servings: 4
Cooking time: 15 minutes
Ingredients:
- 450 grams of asparagus
- 1 tablespoon canola oil
- 1 teaspoon paprika
- Sea salt and freshly ground black pepper, to taste
- 1 teaspoon garlic powder
- 3 tablespoons chopped spring onions
- 1 cup mushrooms, chopped
- ½ cup fresh breadcrumbs
- 1 tablespoon flaxseed, soaked in 2 tablespoons water
- 4 tablespoons sun-dried tomato hummus

Addresses:
1. Place the asparagus in the lightly greased cooking basket. Toss the asparagus with the canola oil, paprika, salt and black pepper.
2. Cook in the preheated Air Fryer at 200°C for 5 minutes.
3. Chop the asparagus and add the garlic powder, spring onions, mushrooms, breadcrumbs and vegan "egg".
4. Mix until well incorporated and form the asparagus mixture into patties.
5. Cook in the preheated Air Fryer for 5 minutes, turning halfway through cooking.
6. Serve with sundried tomato hummus and enjoy!

793. Mint green beans with shallots

Servings: 6
Cooking time: 25 minutes
Ingredients:
- 1 tablespoon chopped fresh mint
- 1 tablespoon toasted sesame seeds
- 1 tablespoon vegetable oil
- 1 teaspoon soy sauce
- 450 grams of fresh green beans, trimmed
- 2 large shallots, cut into slices
- 2 tablespoons of chopped fresh basil
- 2 tablespoons pine nuts

Addresses:
1. Preheat the fryer to 150°C.
2. Place the grill pan attachment on the air fryer.
3. In a bowl, combine the green beans, shallots, vegetable oil and soy sauce.
4. Place in the air fryer and cook for 25 minutes.
5. Once cooked, garnish with basil, mint, sesame seeds and pine nuts.

794. Tortilla layer cake

Servings: 6
Cooking time: 30 minutes
Ingredients:
- 1 can (425 grams) of black beans, rinsed and drained
- 1 cup sauce
- 1 cup sauce, divided
- 1/2 cup chopped tomatoes
- 1/2 cup sour cream
- 2 cans (425 grams each) of pinto beans, drained and rinsed
- 2 cloves garlic, minced
- 2 cups shredded reduced-fat cheddar cheese
- 2 tablespoons chopped fresh coriander
- 7 flour tortillas

Addresses:
1. Mash the pinto beans in a large bowl and mix with the garlic and sauce.
2. In another bowl, whisk together tomatoes, black beans, cilantro and ¼ cup salsa.
3. Lightly grease the air fryer tray with cooking spray.
4. Spread 1 tortilla, spread ¾ cup pinto bean mixture evenly up to 1.25 centimetres from edge of tortilla. Then top with ¼ cup of cheese.
5. Top with another tortilla, sprinkle with black bean mixture and ¼ cup cheese.
6. Repeat the layering process twice. Top with the last tortilla, cover with the pinto bean mixture and then with the cheese.
7. Cover the pan with aluminium foil.
8. Cook for 2 minutes at 200°C, remove the foil and cook for 5 minutes or until the top is lightly browned.
9. Serve and enjoy.

795. Refreshing and spicy broccoli

Servings: 4
Cooking time: 15 minutes
Ingredients:
- 1 tablespoon butter
- 1 large head of broccoli, cut into bite-size pieces
- 1 tablespoon white sesame seeds
- 2 tablespoons vegetable stock
- 1 tablespoon fresh lemon juice
- 3 cloves garlic, minced
- ½ teaspoon finely grated grated fresh lemon zest
- ½ teaspoon crushed red pepper flakes

Addresses:

1. Preheat the fryer to 180°C and grease a frying pan.
2. Mix the butter, vegetable stock and lemon juice in the frying pan of the deep fryer.
3. Transfer to the air fryer and cook for about 2 minutes.
4. Stir in the garlic and broccoli and cook for 1 minute.
5. Add the sesame seeds, lemon zest and red pepper flakes and cook for a few minutes.
6. Serve hot.

796. Cauliflower in the open air

Servings: 4
Cooking time: 20 minutes
Ingredients:
- 2 tablespoons olive oil
- ½ teaspoon salt
- ¼ teaspoon freshly ground black pepper

Addresses:
1. In a bowl, mix the cauliflower, oil, salt and black pepper until the florets are well coated.
2. Place the florets in the fryer and cook for 8 minutes at 180°C, working in batches if necessary.
3. Serve crispy cauliflower in lettuce wraps with chicken, cheese or mushrooms.

797. Vegetable Fingers with Monterey Jack Cheese

Servings: 4
Cooking time: 20 minutes
Ingredients:
- 280 grams of cauliflower
- 1/4 cup almond flour
- 1 ½ teaspoons soy sauce
- Salt and freshly ground black pepper to taste
- 1 teaspoon cayenne pepper
- 1 cup grated Parmesan cheese
- 3/4 teaspoon dried dill weed
- 1 tablespoon of olive oil

Addresses:
1. First, pulse the cauliflower in your food processor, transfer to a bowl and add 4 cups of almond flour, soy sauce, salt, black pepper and cayenne pepper.
2. Roll the mixture into vegetable fingers. In another bowl, place the grated Parmesan cheese and the dried dill.
3. Now, coat the vegetable fingers with the parmesan mixture, covering them completely. Drizzle the vegetable fingers with olive oil.
4. Air fry for 15 minutes at 180°C, turning once or twice during the cooking time. Eat them with your favourite sauce. Enjoy.

798. Marinated Tofu Bowl with Pearled Onions

Servings: 4
Cooking time: 1 hour and 20 minutes
Ingredients:
- 450 grams of firm tofu, pressed and cut into approximately 2.5 centimetre pieces
- 2 tbsp. vegan Worcestershire sauce
- 1 tablespoon apple cider vinegar
- 1 tablespoon maple syrup
- 1/2 teaspoon shallot powder
- 1/2 teaspoon boletus powder
- 1/2 teaspoon garlic powder
- 2 tablespoons peanut oil
- 1 cup pearled onions, peeled

Addresses:
1. Place the tofu, Worcestershire sauce, vinegar, maple syrup, shallot powder, boletus powder and garlic powder in a ceramic dish. Marinate in your refrigerator for one hour.
2. Place the tofu in the lightly greased fryer basket. Add the peanut oil and pearl onions, stir to combine.
3. Cook the tofu with the pearl onions in the preheated Air Fryer at 180°C for 6 minutes, pause and brush with the reserved marinade, cook for a further 5 minutes.
4. Serve immediately and enjoy!

799. Tofu in sweet and sour sauce

Servings: 3
Cooking time: 25 minutes
Ingredients:
- 2 tablespoons Shoyu sauce
- 450 grams extra-strong tofu, drained, pressed and cut into cubes
- 1/2 cup water
- 1/4 cup pineapple juice
- 2 cloves garlic, minced
- 1/2 teaspoon grated fresh ginger
- 1 teaspoon cayenne pepper
- 1/4 teaspoon ground black pepper
- 1/2 teaspoon salt
- 1 teaspoon honey
- 1 tablespoon arrowroot powder

Addresses:
1. Drizzle the Shoyu sauce over the tofu cubes.
2. Cook in the preheated Air Fryer at 190°C for 6 minutes, shake the basket and cook for a further 5 minutes.
3. Meanwhile, cook the rest of the ingredients in a heavy frying pan over medium heat for 10 minutes, until the sauce has thickened slightly.
4. Stir the fried tofu into the sauce and continue to cook for a further 4 minutes or until the tofu is heated through.
5. Serve hot and enjoy.

800. Peppers stuffed with oatmeal

Servings: 2
Cooking time: 16 minutes
Ingredients:

- 2 large red peppers, cut in half lengthwise and seeded
- 2 cups cooked oatmeal
- 4 tablespoons canned red kidney beans, rinsed and drained
- 4 tablespoons coconut yoghurt
- ¼ teaspoon ground cumin
- ¼ teaspoon smoked paprika
- Salt and ground black pepper

Addresses:
1. Set the temperature of the air fryer to 180°C. Grease the basket of the air fryer.
2. Place the peppers in the prepared air fryer basket, cut side down.
3. Fry in the open air for about 8 minutes.
4. Remove from the fryer and leave to cool.
5. Meanwhile, in a bowl, mix well the oats, beans, coconut yoghurt and spices.
6. Stuff each pepper half with the oat mixture.
7. Now, set the air fryer to 180°C.
8. Place the peppers in the fryer basket and fry for a few minutes.
9. Remove from the fryer and transfer the peppers to a serving dish.
10. Allow to cool slightly.
11. Serve hot.

801. Roasted and glazed strawberries

Servings: 2
Cooking time: 20 minutes
Ingredients:
- 1 tablespoon of honey
- 1 teaspoon lemon zest
- 450 grams of large strawberries
- 3 tablespoons melted butter
- Lemon wedges
- A pinch of kosher salt

Addresses:
1. Thread the strawberries on 4 skewers.
2. In a small bowl, mix the remaining ingredients well, except for the lemon wedges. Brush over strawberries.
3. Place the skewer on the fryer rack.
4. Cook at 180°C for 10 minutes. Halfway through the cooking time, brush with the honey mixture and turn the skewer over.
5. Serve and enjoy with a squeeze of lemon.

802. Aubergine caviar

Servings: 3
Cooking time: 20 minutes
Ingredients:
- ½ red onion, chopped and blended
- 2 tablespoons balsamic vinegar
- 1 tablespoon of olive oil
- Salt

Addresses:
1. Place the aubergines in the basket and cook them for a few minutes at 190°C. Remove and leave to cool.
2. Then cut the aubergines in half lengthways and scoop out the inside with a spoon.
3. Grind the onion in a blender. Put the inside of the aubergines in the blender and process everything.
4. Add the vinegar, olive oil and salt, and blend again.
5. Serve cold with bread and tomato sauce or ketchup.

803. Sweet and sour Brussels sprouts

Servings: 2
Cooking time: 10 minutes
Ingredients:
- 2 cups Brussels sprouts, chopped and halved lengthwise
- 1 tablespoon balsamic vinegar
- 1 tablespoon maple syrup
- Salt

Addresses:
1. Preheat the fryer to 200°C and grease the fryer basket.
2. Mix all ingredients in a bowl and stir to coat well.
3. Place the Brussels sprouts in the fryer basket and cook for about 10 minutes, shaking once halfway through.
4. Place on a platter and serve hot.

804. Asian-style cauliflower

Servings: 4
Cooking time: 25 minutes
Ingredients:
- 2 cups shredded cauliflower
- 1 onion, peeled and finely chopped
- 1 tablespoon sesame oil
- 1 tablespoon tamari sauce
- 1 tablespoon of sake
- 2 cloves garlic, peeled and crushed
- 1 tablespoon freshly grated ginger
- 1 tablespoon fresh parsley, finely chopped
- 1/4 cup lime juice
- 2 tablespoons sesame seeds

Addresses:
1. Combine cauliflower, onion, sesame oil, tamari sauce, sake, garlic and ginger in a bowl, stir until well incorporated.
2. Air fry at 200°C for 1 minute.
3. Pause the Air Fryer. Add the parsley and lemon juice. Turn the machine to cook for a further 10 minutes.
4. Meanwhile, toast the sesame seeds in a non-stick frying pan, stirring constantly over medium-low heat.
5. Sprinkle the seeds over the prepared cauliflower and serve hot.

805. Shallots and almonds in green beans

Servings: 4
Cooking time: 10 minutes
Ingredients:

- ¼ cup slivered almonds, toasted
- 225 grams of shallots, peeled and cut into quarters
- ½ teaspoon ground white pepper
- 680 grams French green beans, stalks removed and blanched
- 1 tablespoon salt
- 2 tablespoons olive oil

Addresses:
1. Preheat the air fryer to 200°C.
2. Place all ingredients in a bowl and mix until well combined.
3. Transfer the mixture to the fryer basket and cook for 10 minutes or until lightly browned.

806. Rosemary potatoes au gratin

Servings: 4
Cooking time: 45 minutes
Ingredients:
- 900 grams of potatoes
- 1/4 cup sunflower kernels, soaked overnight
- 1/2 cup of almonds, soaked overnight
- 1 cup unsweetened almond milk
- 2 tablespoons nutritional yeast
- 1 teaspoon shallot powder
- 2 cloves fresh garlic, minced
- 1/2 cup water
- Kosher salt and ground black pepper
- 1 teaspoon cayenne pepper
- 1 tablespoon fresh rosemary

Addresses:
1. Bring a large pan of water to the boil. Boil the potatoes whole for about 20 minutes. Drain the potatoes and leave to stand until cool enough to handle.
2. Peel the potatoes and cut them into slices of about half a centimetre.
3. Add the sunflower kernels, almonds, almond milk, nutritional yeast, shallot powder and garlic to your food processor, blend until smooth and creamy. Add the water and blend for a few more seconds.
4. Place ½ of the potatoes in a single layer on top of each other in the lightly greased casserole dish. Spoon 1/2 of the sauce on top of the potatoes. Repeat the layers, finishing with the sauce.
5. Top with salt, black pepper, cayenne pepper and fresh rosemary. Bake in preheated air fryer at 160°C for 20 minutes. Serve hot.

807. Seasoned Creole vegetables

Portions: 5
Cooking time: 15 minutes
Ingredients:
- ¼ cup honey
- ¼ cup yellow mustard
- 1 large red pepper, cut into slices
- 1 teaspoon black pepper
- 1 teaspoon salt
- 2 large yellow pumpkins, cut into 1.25 centimetre-thick slices
- 2 medium courgettes, cut into 1.25 centimetre-thick slices
- 2 teaspoons Creole seasoning
- 2 teaspoons smoked paprika
- 3 tablespoons olive oil

Addresses:
1. Preheat the fryer to 150°C.
2. Place the grill pan attachment on the air fryer.
3. In a Ziploc bag, place the courgette, squash, red pepper, olive oil, salt and pepper. Give a shake to season all the vegetables.
4. Place on the grill pan and cook for 15 minutes.
5. Meanwhile, prepare the sauce by combining the mustard, honey, paprika and Creole seasoning. Season with salt to taste.
6. Serve the vegetables with the sauce.

808. Tomato sandwiches with feta and pesto

Servings: 2
Cooking time: 60 minutes
Ingredients:
- 1 block of Feta cheese
- 1 small red onion, thinly sliced
- 1 clove of garlic
- Salt
- Olive oil (2 teaspoons + ¼ cup)
- 1 ½ tablespoons toasted pine nuts
- ¼ cup chopped parsley
- ¼ cup grated Parmesan cheese
- ¼ cup chopped basil

Addresses:
1. Add the basil, pine nuts, garlic and salt to a food processor. Process while gradually adding the ¼ cup olive oil.
2. Once the oil is finished, pour the basil pesto into a bowl and refrigerate for 30 minutes.
3. Preheat the air fryer to 200°C.
4. Cut the feta cheese and tomato into 1.25 cm circular slices.
5. Use a kitchen towel to dry the tomatoes. Remove the pesto from the fridge and use a spoonful to spread a little pesto on each tomato slice.
6. Top with a slice of feta cheese. Add the onion and remaining olive oil to a bowl and mix. Place on top of the feta cheese.
7. Place the tomato in the fryer basket and cook for 12 minutes. Remove to a serving platter, sprinkle lightly with salt and top with the remaining pesto. Serve with a side of rice or lean meat.

809. Pepper stuffed with oatmeal

Servings: 2
Cooking time: 16 minutes
Ingredients:
- 1 large red pepper, cut in half and seeded
- 1 cup cooked oatmeal
- 2 tablespoons canned red kidney beans
- 2 tablespoons plain yoghurt
- ⅛ teaspoon of ground cumin
- ⅛ teaspoon smoked paprika
- Salt and black pepper

Addresses:
1. Preheat the fryer to 180°C and grease a frying pan.
2. Place the peppers in the frying pan of the deep fryer and cook for about 8 minutes.
3. Meanwhile, mix the oat flour with the rest of the ingredients in a bowl.
4. Stuff the oat mixture into each pepper half and cook for about 8 minutes.
5. Place on a platter and serve hot.

810. Carrots in abundance

Servings: 4
Cooking time: 25 minutes
Ingredients:
- 2 chopped shallots
- 3 carrots, cut into slices
- Salt
- ¼ cup yogurt
- 2 cloves garlic, minced
- 3 tablespoons chopped parsley

Addresses:
1. Preheat the fryer to 190°C.
2. In a bowl, mix carrots, salt, garlic, shallots, parsley and yoghurt. Drizzle with oil.
3. Place the vegetables in the basket of the air fryer and cook.
4. Serve with basil and garlic mayonnaise.

811. Barbecued Tofu with Green Beans

Servings: 3
Cooking time: 1 hour
Ingredients:
- 340 grams super firm tofu, pressed and cubed
- 1/4 cup ketchup
- 1 tablespoon white vinegar
- 1 tablespoon coconut sugar
- 1 tablespoon mustard
- 1/4 teaspoon ground black pepper
- 1/2 teaspoon sea salt
- 1/4 teaspoon smoked paprika
- 1/2 teaspoon grated fresh ginger
- 2 cloves garlic, minced
- 2 tablespoons olive oil
- 450 grams of green beans

Addresses:
1. Mix the tofu with the ketchup, white vinegar, coconut sugar, mustard, black pepper, sea salt, paprika, ginger, garlic and olive oil.
2. Leave to marinate for 30 minutes.
3. Cook at 180°C for 10 minutes, turn over and cook for 1 minute more. Set aside.
4. Place the green beans in the lightly greased basket of the Air Fryer.
5. Roast at 200°C for 5 minutes, enjoy!

812. Thai spicy vegetables recipe

Servings: 4
Cooking time: 15 minutes
Ingredients:
- 1 ½ cups packed coriander leaves
- 1 tablespoon black pepper
- 1 tbsp chili garlic sauce
- ⅓ cup vegetable oil
- 900 grams of vegetables of your choice, cut into cubes
- 2 tablespoons fish sauce
- 8 cloves of garlic, minced

Addresses:
1. Preheat the fryer to 150°C.
2. Place the grill pan attachment on the air fryer.
3. Put all the ingredients in a bowl and stir to coat.
4. Place on the grill and cook for 15 minutes.

813. The best falafel ever

Servings: 2
Cooking time: 20 minutes
Ingredients:
- 1 cup of dried chickpeas, soaked overnight
- 1 small onion, chopped
- 2 cloves garlic, minced
- 2 tablespoons fresh coriander leaves, chopped
- 1 tablespoon flour
- ½ teaspoon baking powder
- 1 teaspoon cumin powder
- Pinch of ground cardamom
- Sea salt and ground black pepper

Addresses:
1. Pulse all ingredients in your food processor until the chickpeas are ground.
2. Form the falafel mixture into balls and place them in the lightly greased basket of the Air Fryer.
3. Cook for about 15 minutes, shaking the basket occasionally to ensure even cooking.
4. Serve in pita bread with toppings of your choice. Enjoy.

814. Courgette crisps for children

Servings: 4
Cooking time: 20 minutes
Ingredients:
- 2 tablespoons olive oil
- 1/2 teaspoon smoked cayenne pepper

- 1 large courgette, peeled and cut into slices about 5 millimetres in length
- 1/2 teaspoon shallot powder
- 1/3 teaspoon freshly ground black pepper, or more to taste
- 3/4 teaspoon garlic salt

Addresses:
1. First, preheat your Air Fryer to 180°C.
2. Then add the courgettes to a mixing bowl, mix with the other ingredients.
3. Cook the fried courgettes for approximately 14 minutes.
4. Serve with a dipping sauce of your choice.

815. Roasted vegetables restaurant style

Servings: 4
Cooking time: 25 minutes
Ingredients:
- 1 red pepper, seeded and cut into 1 centimetre pieces
- 1 yellow pepper, seeded and cut into 1 centimetre pieces
- 1 yellow onion, cut into quarters
- 1 green pepper, seeded and cut into 1 centimetre pieces
- 1 cup broccoli, broken into 1-centimetre florets
- 1/2 cup parsnips, trimmed and cut into 1-centimetre pieces
- 2 cloves garlic, minced
- Himalayan pink salt and ground black pepper
- 1/2 teaspoon marjoram
- 1/2 teaspoon dried oregano
- 1/4 cup dry white wine
- 1/4 cup vegetable stock
- 1/2 cup Kalamata olives, pitted and sliced

Addresses:
1. Arrange the vegetables in a single layer in the baking dish in the order of the rainbow (red, orange, yellow and green). Sprinkle the chopped garlic around the vegetables.
2. Season with salt, black pepper, marjoram and oregano. Drizzle the white wine and vegetable stock over the vegetables.
3. Roast in the preheated Air Fryer at 180°C for 15 minutes, turning the pan once or twice.
4. Sprinkle the Kalamata olives over the vegetables and serve hot - bon appetit!

816. Crunchy battered onion rings with almond flour

Servings: 3
Cooking time: 15 minutes
Ingredients:
- ½ cup almond flour
- ¾ cup coconut milk
- 1 large white onion, sliced into rings
- 1 beaten egg
- 1 tablespoon baking powder
- 1 tablespoon smoked paprika
- Salt and pepper to taste

Addresses:
1. Preheat the air fryer for 5 minutes.
2. In a bowl, mix together the almond flour, baking powder, smoked paprika, salt and pepper.
3. In a separate bowl, combine the eggs and coconut milk.
4. Dip the onion slices into the egg mixture.
5. Dredge the onion slices in the almond flour mixture.
6. Place in the basket of the air fryer.
7. Close and cook for 15 minutes at 160°C.
8. Halfway through the cooking time, shake the fryer basket to ensure even cooking.

817. Crunchy aubergine rounds

Servings: 4
Cooking time: 45 minutes
Ingredients:
- 1 aubergine (450 grams), sliced
- 1/2 cup flaxseed meal
- 1/2 cup rice flour
- Coarse sea salt and ground black pepper, to taste
- 1 teaspoon paprika
- 1 cup of water
- 1 cup cornbread crumbs, crushed
- 1/2 cup vegan parmesan

Addresses:
1. Mix the aubergine with a tablespoon of salt and leave to stand for 30 minutes. Drain and rinse well.
2. Combine the flax flour, rice flour, salt, black pepper and paprika in a bowl. Then pour in the water and whisk to combine well.
3. In another shallow bowl, mix together the cornbread crumbs and vegan parmesan.
4. Dip the aubergine slices into the flour mixture and then into the crumb mixture, pressing to coat all sides. Transfer to the lightly greased Air Fryer basket.
5. Cook at 185°C for 6 minutes. Turn each slice over and cook for a further minute.
6. Serve garnished with spicy ketchup if desired - bon appetit!

818. Crispy ham rolls

Servings: 3
Cooking time: 17 minutes
Ingredients:
- 3 packets of Pepperidge farm rolls
- 1 tablespoon softened butter
- 1 teaspoon mustard seeds
- 1 teaspoon poppy seeds
- 1 small onion, chopped

Addresses:
1. Mix the butter, mustard, onion and poppy seeds.

2. Spread the mixture on the rolls, cover with the chopped ham and roll up.
3. Place them in the basket of the air fryer and cook at 180°C.

819. Tofu in rice flour crust

Servings: 3
Cooking time: 28 minutes
Ingredients:
- 1 block of firm tofu, pressed and cut into 1.25 centimeter cubes
- 2 tablespoons cornstarch
- ¼ cup rice flour
- Salt and ground black pepper
- 2 tablespoons olive oil

Addresses:
1. In a bowl, mix together the cornflour, rice flour, salt and black pepper.
2. Coat the tofu evenly with the flour mixture.
3. Drizzle the tofu with oil.
4. Set the temperature of the air fryer to 180°C. Grease the basket of the air fryer.
5. Place the tofu cubes in the prepared air fryer basket in a single layer.
6. Air fry for about 14 minutes per side.
7. Remove from the fryer and transfer the tofu to serving plates.
8. Serve hot.

820. Swiss cheese and aubergine crispies

Servings: 4
Cooking time: 45 minutes
Ingredients:
- 225 grams of aubergine, cut into slices
- 1/4 cup almond flour
- 2 tablespoons flaxseed meal
- Coarse sea salt and ground black pepper
- 1 teaspoon paprika
- 1 cup freshly grated Parmesan cheese

Addresses:
1. Mix the aubergine with a tablespoon of salt and leave to stand for 30 minutes. Drain and rinse well.
2. Place the almond flour, flaxseed meal, salt, black pepper and paprika in a bowl. Then pour in the water and whisk to combine well.
3. Then transfer the Parmesan into another shallow bowl.
4. Dip the aubergine slices in the almond flour mixture and then in the Parmesan, pressing to coat all sides. Transfer to the lightly greased Air Fryer basket.
5. Cook at 185°C for 6 minutes. Turn each slice over and cook for a further minute.
6. Serve garnished with spicy ketchup if desired - bon appetit!

821. Open vegan flatbread

Servings: 4
Cooking time: 25 minutes
Ingredients:
- 1 can chickpeas, drained and rinsed
- 1 medium sized head of cauliflower, cut into florets
- 1 tablespoon of extra virgin olive oil
- 2 ripe avocados, mashed
- 2 tablespoons lemon juice
- 4 toasted flatbreads
- Salt and pepper

Addresses:
1. Preheat the fryer to 220°C.
2. In a bowl, mix the cauliflower, chickpeas, olive oil and lemon juice. Season with salt and pepper to taste.
3. Place inside the basket of the air fryer and cook for 25 minutes.
4. Once cooked, place on half of the flatbread and add the mashed avocado.
5. Season with more salt and pepper to taste.
6. Serve with hot sauce.

822. Cheese Pizza with Broccoli Crust

Servings: 1
Cooking time: 30 minutes
Ingredients:
- 3 cups broccoli rice, steamed
- ½ cup grated Parmesan cheese
- 1 egg
- 3 tablespoons low-carbohydrate Alfredo sauce
- ½ cup grated Parmesan cheese

Addresses:
1. Drain the broccoli rice and combine it with the Parmesan cheese and egg in a bowl, mixing well.
2. Cut a piece of parchment paper about the size of the base of the fryer basket. Place four equal amounts of the broccoli mixture on the paper and press each portion into the shape of a pizza crust. You may need to complete this part in two batches. Transfer the parchment to the fryer.
3. Bake at 200°C for five minutes. When the crust is firm, turn over and cook for a further two minutes.
4. Add the Alfredo sauce and mozzarella cheese over the crusts and cook for a further seven minutes. Crusts are ready when sauce and cheese have melted. Serve hot.

823. Chewy glazed parsnips

Servings: 6
Cooking time: 44 minutes
Ingredients:
- 900 grams of parsnips, peeled and cut into 2.5 centimetre pieces
- 1 tablespoon melted butter
- 2 tablespoons maple syrup
- 1 tablespoon dried parsley flakes, crushed
- ¼ teaspoon crushed red pepper flakes

Addresses:

1. Preheat the fryer to 180°C and grease the fryer basket.
2. Combine the parsnips and butter in a bowl and toss to coat well.
3. Place the parsnips in the fryer basket and cook for about 40 minutes.
4. Meanwhile, mix the rest of the ingredients in a large bowl.
5. Transfer this mixture to the fryer basket and cook for about 4 minutes more.
6. Serve hot.

824. Egg and cauliflower rice casserole

Servings: 4
Cooking time: 15 minutes
Ingredients:
- 2 cups olive oil
- 1 yellow pepper, chopped
- 1 cup chopped okra
- ½ cup chopped onion
- Salt and black pepper
- 1 tablespoon soy sauce
- 2 beaten eggs

Addresses:
1. Preheat the fryer to 190°C. Grease a baking dish with cooking spray.
2. Pulse the cauliflower in your food processor until it turns into small rice granules.
3. Add the rice to the baking dish and mix with the pepper, okra, onion, soy sauce, salt and pepper.
4. Pour over the beaten eggs and drizzle with olive oil.
5. Place in the fryer and cook. Serve hot.

825. Easy roasted winter vegetable delight

Servings: 2
Cooking time: 30 minutes
Ingredients:
- 1 cup chopped pumpkin
- 2 small red onions, cut into chunks
- 1 cup chopped celery
- 1 tablespoon chopped fresh thyme
- Salt and pepper
- 2 teaspoons olive oil

Addresses:
1. Preheat the air fryer to 200 F.
2. In a bowl, add the turnip, pumpkin, red onions, celery, thyme, pepper, salt and olive oil, mix well.
3. Pour the vegetables into the fryer basket and cook for minutes, stirring once halfway through cooking.

826. Sautéed spinach

Servings: 2
Cooking time: 9 minutes
Ingredients:
- 1 small onion, chopped
- 170 grams of fresh spinach
- 2 tablespoons olive oil
- 1 teaspoon chopped ginger
- Salt and black pepper

Addresses:
1. Preheat the fryer to 180°C and grease a frying pan.
2. Put the olive oil, onions and ginger in the frying pan and place in the fryer basket.
3. Cook for about 4 minutes and add the spinach, salt and black pepper.
4. Cook for a few more minutes and serve on a platter.

827. Sweet and sour Brussels sprouts

Servings: 2
Cooking time: 10 minutes
Ingredients:
- 2 cups Brussels sprouts, chopped and halved lengthwise
- 1 tablespoon balsamic vinegar
- 1 tablespoon maple syrup
- Salt

Addresses:
1. Set the temperature of the air fryer to 200°C. Grease the air fryer basket.
2. In a bowl, add all the ingredients and stir to coat well.
3. Place the Brussels sprouts in the prepared fryer basket in a single layer.
4. Fry in the open air for about 8-10 minutes, stirring once halfway through.
5. Remove from the fryer and transfer the Brussels sprouts to serving plates.
6. Serve hot.

828. Mushrooms stuffed with cream cheese-pesto sauce

Portions: 5
Cooking time: 15 minutes
Ingredients:
- ¼ cup olive oil
- ½ cup cream cheese
- ½ cup pine nuts
- 1 cup basil leaves
- 1 tablespoon freshly squeezed lemon juice
- 450 grams cremini mushrooms, stalks removed
- Salt

Addresses:
1. Place all the ingredients, except the mushrooms, in a food processor.
2. Press until fine.
3. The mixture is collected and placed on the side where the stalks have been removed.
4. Place the mushrooms in the fryer basket.
5. Close and cook for 1 minute in a preheated 180°C air fryer.

829. Stuffed aubergine

Servings: 2
Cooking time: 35 minutes
Ingredients:

- Large aubergine
- ¼ medium yellow onion, chopped
- 2 tablespoons chopped red pepper
- 1 cup spinach
- ¼ cup chopped artichoke hearts

Addresses:
1. Cut the aubergine lengthwise into slices and scoop out the flesh with a spoon, leaving a peel about half a centimetre thick. Chop and set aside.
2. Place a frying pan over medium heat and spray with cooking spray. Cook the onions for three to five minutes to soften. Then add the pepper, spinach, artichokes and aubergine flesh. Fry for another five minutes and remove from the heat.
3. Pour this mixture in equal parts into the aubergine shells and place each in the fryer.
4. Cook for twenty minutes at 320°F until the aubergine shells are soft. Serve hot.

830. Roasted broccoli with salted garlic

Servings: 6
Cooking time: 15 minutes
Ingredients:
- ½ teaspoon black pepper
- ½ teaspoon lemon juice
- 1 clove garlic, minced
- 1 teaspoon salt
- 2 heads of broccoli, cut into florets
- 2 teaspoons extra virgin olive oil

Addresses:
1. Line the fryer basket with aluminium foil and coat it with oil.
2. Preheat the fryer to 190°C.
3. Combine all ingredients except lemon juice in a bowl and place in the fryer basket.
4. Cook for 15 minutes.
5. Serve with lemon juice.

831. Brussels sprouts chips with paprika

Servings: 2
Cooking time: 20 minutes
Ingredients:
- 10 Brussels sprouts
- 1 teaspoon canola oil
- 1 teaspoon coarse sea salt
- 1 teaspoon paprika

Addresses:
1. Place all ingredients in the lightly greased fryer basket.
2. Bake at 190°C for 15 minutes, shaking the basket halfway through the baking time to ensure even baking.
3. Serve and enjoy.

832. Spicy cooked vegetables

Servings: 4
Cooking time: 25 minutes
Ingredients:
- 1 large courgette, cut into slices
- 1 serrano pepper, deveined and cut into thin slices
- 2 bell peppers, deveined and thinly sliced
- 1 stalk celery, cut into sticks
- 1/4 cup olive oil
- 1/2 teaspoon boletus powder
- 1/4 teaspoon mustard powder
- 1/2 teaspoon fennel seeds
- 1 tablespoon garlic powder
- 1/2 teaspoon fine sea salt
- 1/4 teaspoon ground black pepper
- 1/2 cup tomato puree

Addresses:
1. Place the sweet potatoes, courgette, peppers and carrot in the cooking basket of the Air Fryer.
2. Drizzle with olive oil and toss to coat, cook in preheated air fryer at 180°C for 15 minutes.
3. While the vegetables are cooking, prepare the sauce by whisking the remaining ingredients well, minus the tomato ketchup. Lightly grease a baking dish that will fit in your machine.
4. Transfer the cooked vegetables to the prepared baking dish, add the sauce and toss to coat well.
5. Set the Air Fryer to 200°C and cook the vegetables for more minutes, enjoy!

833. Corn skewers in the air fryer

Servings: 2
Cooking time: 25 minutes
Ingredients:
- 450 grams of apricots, halved
- 2 ears of corn
- 2 medium green peppers, coarsely chopped
- 2 teaspoons prepared mustard
- Salt and pepper

Addresses:
1. Preheat the fryer to 150°C.
2. Place the grill pan attachment on the air fryer.
3. Thread the corn, green peppers and apricot onto the double-layer grid with the skewer attachments. Season with salt and pepper to taste.
4. Place the corn skewers on the double-layer grid and cook for 25 minutes.
5. Once cooked, brush with the prepared mustard.

834. Tomatoes stuffed with cheese

Servings: 2
Cooking time: 15 minutes
Ingredients:
- 2 large tomatoes
- ½ cup broccoli, finely chopped
- ½ cup grated cheddar cheese

- 1 tablespoon unsalted butter, melted
- ½ teaspoon dried thyme, crushed

Addresses:
1. Cut off the top of each tomato and scoop out the flesh and seeds.
2. In a bowl, mix the chopped broccoli and cheese.
3. Fill each tomato evenly with the broccoli mixture.
4. Set the temperature of the air fryer to 180°C. Grease the basket of the air fryer.
5. Place the tomatoes in the prepared fryer basket.
6. Drizzle evenly with butter.
7. Fry in the open air for about 12-15 minutes.
8. Remove from the fryer and transfer the tomatoes to a serving dish.
9. Allow to cool slightly.
10. Garnish with thyme and serve.

835. Courgette with Mediterranean Dill Sauce

Servings: 4
Cooking time: 1 hour
Ingredients:
- 450 grams of courgettes, peeled and diced
- 2 tablespoons melted butter
- 1 tsp sea salt flakes
- 1 sprig of rosemary, leaves only, crushed
- 2 sprigs of thyme, leaves only, crushed
- 1/2 teaspoon freshly ground black peppercorns

For the Mediterranean sauce you need:
- 1/2 cup mascarpone cheese
- 1/3 cup yogurt
- 1 tbsp chopped fresh dill
- 1 tablespoon of olive oil

Addresses:
1. First of all, set your Air Fryer to cook at 180°C. Now add the potato cubes to the bowl of cold water and soak for approximately 35 minutes.
2. Then dry the potato cubes with a paper towel.
3. In a bowl, whisk together the melted butter with the sea salt flakes, rosemary, thyme and freshly ground peppercorns.
4. Rub the potato cubes with this butter and spice mixture.
5. Fry the potato cubes in the cooking basket for 18-20 minutes or until cooked through, making sure to shake the potatoes so that they cook evenly.
6. Meanwhile, prepare the Mediterranean dipping sauce by mixing the rest of the ingredients together. Serve the hot potatoes with the Mediterranean dipping sauce and enjoy!

836. Salad of roasted peppers with goat's cheese

Servings: 4
Cooking time: 20 minutes + cooling time
Ingredients:
- 1 yellow pepper
- 1 red pepper
- 1 serrano pepper
- 4 tablespoons olive oil
- 2 tablespoons cider vinegar
- 2 cloves garlic, peeled and crushed
- 1 teaspoon cayenne pepper
- Sea salt
- 1/2 teaspoon mixed peppercorns, freshly crushed
- 1/2 cup of goat cheese, cubed
- 2 tablespoons fresh Italian parsley leaves, coarsely chopped

Addresses:
1. Start by preheating your fryer to 200°C. Grease the fryer basket with cooking oil.
2. Then roast the peppers for 5 minutes. Turn the peppers halfway around, return them to the cooking basket and roast for a further 5 minutes.
3. Turn once more and roast until the skin is charred and soft or 5 minutes more. Peel the peppers and let them cool to room temperature.
4. In a small bowl, whisk together the olive oil, vinegar, garlic, cayenne pepper, salt and crushed peppercorns. Dress the salad and set aside.
5. Sprinkle the goat's cheese over the peppers and garnish with parsley. Bon appetit!

837. Vegetables au gratin with rosemary

Servings: 4
Cooking time: 45 minutes
Ingredients:
- 350 grams of steamed cauliflower
- 1 onion, sliced
- 2 cloves garlic, minced
- 1 pepper, deveined and cut into slices
- 2 beaten eggs
- 1 cup sour cream
- Kosher salt and ground black pepper
- 1 teaspoon cayenne pepper
- 1 tablespoon fresh rosemary

Addresses:
1. Place the vegetables in the lightly greased casserole dish. In a mixing bowl, combine remaining ingredients well.
2. Spoon the cream mixture over the vegetables.
3. Bake in the preheated Air Fryer at 180°C for 20 minutes. Serve hot.

838. Crunchy and healthy avocado fingers

Servings: 4
Cooking time: 10 minutes
Ingredients:
- ½ cup panko breadcrumbs

- ½ teaspoon salt
- 1 pitted, peeled and sliced Haas avocado
- Liquid from 1 can of white beans or aquafaba beans

Addresses:
1. Preheat the air fryer to 180°C.
2. In a shallow bowl, mix the breadcrumbs and salt until well combined.
3. Dip the avocado slices first in the aquafaba and then in the breadcrumb mixture.
4. Place the avocado slices in a single layer inside the fryer basket.
5. Cook for 10 minutes and stir halfway through cooking.

839. Air-fried vegetable sushi

Servings: 4
Cooking time: 60 minutes
Ingredients:
- 4 sheets of nori
- 1 carrot, cut lengthwise
- 1 red pepper, seeded, cut in slices
- 1 avocado, sliced
- 1 tablespoon of olive oil
- 1 tablespoon rice wine vinegar
- 1 cup panko crumbs
- 2 tablespoons sesame seeds
- Soy sauce, wasabi and pickled ginger to serve

Addresses:
1. Prepare a clean work surface, a small bowl of warm water and a sushi mat.
2. Wet your hands and place a sheet of nori on the sushi mat and spread half a cup of sushi rice, leaving about 1.5 centimetres of nori free, so you can seal the roll.
3. Place the carrot, pepper and avocado on the side of the rice.
4. Roll the sushi tightly and rub hot water along the cleaned nori strip to seal it.
5. In a bowl, mix the oil and rice vinegar. In another bowl, mix the crumbs and sesame seeds.
6. Dip each sushi log in the vinegar mixture and then directly into the sesame bowl to coat.
7. Transfer the sushi to the air fryer and cook for 14 minutes at 180°C, turning once.
8. Slice and serve with soy sauce, pickled ginger and wasabi.

840. Tofu with cauliflower

Servings: 2
Cooking time: 15 minutes
Ingredients:
- ½ block of firm tofu, pressed and cut into cubes
- ½ small head of cauliflower, cut into florets
- 1 tablespoon canola oil
- 1 tablespoon nutritional yeast
- ¼ teaspoon dried parsley
- 1 teaspoon ground turmeric
- ¼ teaspoon paprika
- Salt and ground black pepper

Addresses:
1. In a bowl, mix well the tofu, cauliflower and the rest of the ingredients.
2. Set the temperature of the air fryer to 200°C. Grease the air fryer basket.
3. Place the tofu mixture in the prepared fryer basket in a single layer.
4. Fry in the open air for about 12-15 minutes, stirring once halfway through.
5. Remove from the fryer and transfer the tofu to serving plates.
6. Serve hot.

841. Courgette pie with garlic and sour cream

Portions: 5
Cooking time: 20 minutes
Ingredients:
- 1 package (225 grams) cream cheese, softened
- 1 cup sour cream
- 1 large courgette, cut lengthwise and then cut in half
- 1 tablespoon chopped garlic
- 1/4 cup grated Parmesan cheese
- Paprika to taste

Addresses:
1. Lightly grease the air fryer tray with cooking spray.
2. Place the courgette slices in a single layer in the pan.
3. In a bowl, whisk together the remaining ingredients except the paprika. Spread over the courgette slices. Sprinkle with paprika.
4. Cover the pan with aluminium foil.
5. Cook at 200°C for 10 minutes.
6. Remove the foil and cook for 10 minutes at 165°C.
7. Serve and enjoy.

842. The best crispy tofu

Servings: 4
Cooking time: 55 minutes
Ingredients:
- 450 grams of firm tofu, pressed and cut into cubes
- 1 tablespoon vegan oyster sauce
- 1 tablespoon tamari sauce
- 1 teaspoon cider vinegar
- 1 teaspoon pure maple syrup
- 1 teaspoon sriracha
- 1/2 teaspoon shallot powder
- 1/2 teaspoon boletus powder
- 1 teaspoon garlic powder
- 1 tablespoon sesame oil
- 5 tablespoons cornstarch

Addresses:

1. Mix the tofu with the oyster sauce, tamari sauce, vinegar, maple syrup, sriracha, shallot powder, mushroom powder, garlic powder and sesame oil.
2. Leave to marinate for 30 minutes.
3. Mix the marinated tofu with the cornflour.
4. Cook at 200°C for 10 minutes, turn over and cook for a further 12 minutes, enjoy!

843. Roasted peppers with Greek mayonnaise sauce

Servings: 4
Cooking time: 35 minutes
Ingredients:
- 2 bell peppers, cut into strips
- 1 teaspoon of avocado oil
- 1/2 teaspoon celery salt
- 1/4 teaspoon crushed red pepper flakes
- 1/2 cup mayonnaise
- 1 clove garlic, minced
- 1 teaspoon lemon juice

Addresses:
1. Toss the peppers with the avocado oil, celery salt and red pepper flakes.
2. Air fry at 190°C for 10 minutes. Shake the cooking basket and cook for another few minutes.
3. Meanwhile, mix the mayonnaise, garlic and lemon juice together well.
4. When the peppers come out of the Air Fryer, check that they are ready.
5. Serve with cold mayonnaise sauce and enjoy.

844. Stuffed peppers Greek style

Servings: 4
Cooking time: 20 minutes
Ingredients:
- 2 cups cooked rice
- 1 onion, chopped
- 1 tablespoon Greek seasoning
- ¼ cup sliced kalamata olives
- ¾ cup tomato sauce
- Salt and black pepper
- 1 cup crumbled feta cheese
- 2 tablespoons chopped fresh dill

Addresses:
1. Preheat the fryer to 180°C.
2. Heat the peppers in the microwave for 2 minutes until soft.
3. In a bowl, combine the rice, onion, Greek seasoning, feta cheese, olives, tomato sauce, salt and pepper.
4. Divide the mixture between the peppers and place them in a greased baking dish.
5. Transfer to the air fryer and cook for 15 minutes.
6. When ready, remove to a plate, sprinkle with dill and serve.

845. Bread rolls with butter

Portions: 12
Cooking time: 30 minutes
Ingredients:
- 1 cup of milk
- 1 tablespoon coconut oil
- 1 tablespoon of olive oil
- 3 cups plain flour
- 7½ tablespoons unsalted butter
- 1 teaspoon of yeast
- Salt and ground black pepper

Addresses:
1. In a frying pan, add the milk, coconut oil and olive oil and cook until lukewarm.
2. Remove from the heat and stir well.
3. In a large bowl, add the flour, butter, yeast, salt, black pepper and milk mixture and mix until a dough forms.
4. Knead with your hands for about 5 minutes.
5. Cover the dough with a damp cloth and leave it in a warm place for a few minutes.
6. Again, with your hands, knead the dough for about 4-5 minutes.
7. Cover the dough with a damp cloth and leave it in a warm place for about 30 minutes.
8. Place the dough on a lightly floured surface.
9. Divide the dough into 12 equal pieces and form each into a ball.
10. Set the temperature of the air fryer to 180°C. Grease the basket of the air fryer.
11. Place the rolls in the prepared air fryer basket in 2 batches in a single layer.
12. Fry in the open air for about 15 minutes.
13. Remove from the fryer and serve hot.

846. Perfectly roasted mushrooms

Servings: 4
Cooking time: 32 minutes
Ingredients:
- 1 tablespoon butter
- 900 grams of mushrooms, cut into quarters
- 2 tablespoons white vermouth
- 2 teaspoons Herbes de Provence
- ½ teaspoon garlic powder

Addresses:
1. Preheat the fryer to 160°C and grease a frying pan.
2. Mix the herbs de Provence, garlic powder and butter in the frying pan and transfer to the fryer basket.
3. Cook for about 2 minutes and add the mushrooms.
4. Cook for about 25 minutes and add the white vermouth. Cook for a few more minutes and plate to serve hot.

847. Cheese stuffed mushrooms

Servings: 4
Cooking time: 8 minutes

Ingredients:
- 4 large fresh mushrooms, stalk and gills removed
- 115 grams cream cheese, softened
- ¼ cup grated Parmesan cheese
- 2 tablespoons grated white cheddar cheese
- 2 tablespoons sharp cheddar cheese, grated
- 1 teaspoon Worcestershire sauce
- 2 cloves garlic, minced
- Salt and ground black pepper

Addresses:
1. In a bowl, mix together cream cheese, Parmesan, cheddar cheeses, Worcestershire sauce, garlic, salt and black pepper.
2. Set the temperature of the air fryer to 185°C. Grease the air fryer basket.
3. Stuff each mushroom with the cheese mixture.
4. Place the stuffed mushrooms in the prepared fryer basket.
5. Fry in the open air for about 8 minutes.
6. Remove from the fryer and transfer the mushrooms to a serving dish.
7. Allow to cool slightly before serving.

848. Radish salad

Servings: 4
Cooking time: 30 minutes
Ingredients:
- 680 grams of radishes, sliced and halved
- 225 grams of fresh mozzarella cheese, sliced
- 6 cups of fresh salad greens
- 3 tablespoons olive oil
- 1 teaspoon honey
- 1 tablespoon balsamic vinegar
- Salt and black pepper,

Addresses:
1. Preheat the fryer to 180°C and grease the fryer basket.
2. Combine the radishes, salt, black pepper and olive oil in a bowl and toss to coat well.
3. Place the radishes in the fryer basket and cook for a few minutes, turning them twice.
4. Serve the radishes in a bowl and set aside to cool.
5. Add the mozzarella cheese and the vegetables and mix well.
6. Mix the honey, oil, vinegar, salt and black pepper in a bowl and pour over the salad.
7. Now mix again until everything is well coated. Serve immediately.

849. Onion rings with spicy ketchup

Servings: 2
Cooking time: 30 minutes
Ingredients:
- 1 onion, cut into rings
- 1/3 cup plain flour
- 1/2 cup oat milk
- 1 teaspoon curry powder
- 1 teaspoon cayenne pepper
- Salt and ground black pepper
- 1/2 cup maize flour
- 4 tablespoons vegan parmesan
- 1/4 cup spicy ketchup

Addresses:
1. Put the onion rings in the bowl with cold water, soak for about 20 minutes, drain the onion rings and dry them with a kitchen towel.
2. In a shallow bowl, combine the flour, milk, curry powder, cayenne pepper, salt and black pepper. Mix to combine well.
3. Mix the cornflour and vegan parmesan in another shallow bowl. Dip the onion rings in the flour and milk mixture, then roll them in the cornflour mixture.
4. Spray the Air Fryer basket with cooking spray, place the breaded onion rings in the Air Fryer basket.
5. Cook in the air fryer preheated to 200°C for 4 minutes, turning them over halfway through cooking. Serve with spicy ketchup - bon appetit!

850. Spinach quiche without eggs

Servings: 4
Cooking time: 30 minutes
Ingredients:
- ½ cup cold coconut oil
- ½ tablespoon dried dill
- ¾ cup wholemeal flour
- 1 onion, chopped
- 1 packet firm tofu, pressed to remove excess water and shredded
- 450 grams of spinach, washed and chopped
- 2 tablespoons of cold water
- 2 tablespoons nutritional yeast
- 2 tablespoons olive oil
- 115 grams of mushrooms, cut into slices
- A pinch of salt
- A sprig of chopped fresh parsley
- Salt and pepper

Addresses:
1. Preheat the fryer to 190°C.
2. Create the dough by sifting the flour and salt together. Add the coconut oil until the flour crumbles. Gradually add water to bind the dough or until it forms a stiff dough. Wrap in cling film and leave to rest in the fridge for 30 minutes.
3. Heat the olive oil in a frying pan over medium heat and sauté the onion for 1 minute. Add the mushroom and tofu. Add the spinach, dried dill and nutritional

yeast. Season with salt and pepper to taste. Finally add the parsley. Set aside.
4. Roll the dough on a floured surface until it forms a thin dough. Place the dough in a greased baking dish that will fit into the air fryer.
5. Pour in the tofu mixture and cook for 30 minutes or until the batter is crispy.

851. Classic baked banana

Servings: 2
Cooking time: 20 minutes
Ingredients:
- 2 freshly ripe bananas
- 2 teaspoons lime juice
- 2 tablespoons honey
- 1/4 teaspoon grated nutmeg
- 1/2 teaspoon ground cinnamon
- A pinch of salt

Addresses:
1. Mix the banana with all the ingredients until well coated.
2. Transfer your bananas to the parchment-lined cooking basket.
3. Bake in preheated air fryer at 185°C for 1 minute, turning them over halfway through cooking. Enjoy.

852. Vegetables flavoured with garlic and wine

Servings: 4
Cooking time: 15 minutes
Ingredients:
- ¼ cup chopped fresh basil
- 1 ½ tablespoons honey
- 1 teaspoon Dijon mustard
- 1 cup small Portobello mushrooms, chopped
- 1 packet of frozen chopped vegetables
- 1 red onion, sliced
- 1/3 cup olive oil
- 3 tablespoons of red wine vinegar
- 4 cloves garlic, minced
- Salt and pepper to taste

Addresses:
1. Preheat the fryer to 150°C.
2. Place the grill pan attachment on the air fryer.
3. In a Ziploc bag, combine the vegetables and season with salt, pepper and garlic. Give a good shake to combine everything.
4. Place on the grill pan and cook for 15 minutes.
5. Meanwhile, combine the rest of the ingredients in the bowl and season with more salt and pepper.
6. Drizzle the roasted vegetables with the sauce.

853. Indian Aloo Tikka

Servings: 2
Cooking time: 20 minutes
Ingredients:
- 3 tablespoons lemon juice
- 1 pepper, sliced
- Salt and pepper
- 2 onions, chopped
- 4 tablespoons fennel
- 5 tablespoons flour
- 2 tablespoons ginger-garlic paste
- ½ cup chopped mint leaves
- 2 cups chopped coriander

Addresses:
1. Preheat your air fryer to 180°C.
2. In a bowl, mix the coriander, mint, fennel, ginger-garlic paste, flour, salt and lemon juice.
3. Mix to a paste and add the potato.
4. In another bowl, combine the pepper, onion and fennel mixture. Mix until a thick mixture is formed.
5. Divide the mixture evenly into 5-6 cakes.
6. Add the prepared potato cakes to the air fryer and cook for 15 minutes. Serve with ketchup.

854. Baked oatmeal with berries

Servings: 4
Cooking time: 30 minutes
Ingredients:
- 1 cup fresh strawberries
- ½ cup dried cranberries
- 1 ½ cups oat flakes
- ½ teaspoon baking powder
- A pinch of sea salt
- A pinch of grated nutmeg
- ½ teaspoon ground cinnamon
- ½ teaspoon vanilla extract
- 4 tablespoons agave syrup
- 1 ½ cups coconut milk

Addresses:
1. Spray a baking dish with cooking spray.
2. Put 1 cup of strawberries in the bottom of the pan, place the blueberries on top.
3. In a bowl, thoroughly combine the rolled oats, baking powder, salt, nutmeg, cinnamon, vanilla, agave syrup and milk.
4. Pour the oat mixture over the fruit and let stand for 15 minutes. Top with the rest of the fruit.
5. Bake at 165°C for 12 minutes. Serve warm or at room temperature. Enjoy.

855. Mushroom and cheese pizza

Servings: 2
Cooking time: 6 minutes
Ingredients:
- 2 Portobello mushroom caps, stalk removed
- 2 tablespoons olive oil
- 1/8 tsp dried Italian seasoning
- Salt
- 2 tablespoons canned tomatoes, chopped

- 2 tablespoons of grated mozzarella cheese
- 2 Kalamata olives, pitted and sliced
- 2 tablespoons freshly grated Parmesan cheese
- 1 teaspoon crushed red pepper flakes

Addresses:
1. Set the air fryer temperature to 160°C and grease the air fryer basket.
2. Using a spoon, scoop out the centre of each mushroom cap.
3. Brush each mushroom cap with oil on both sides.
4. Sprinkle the inside of the lids with Italian seasoning and salt.
5. Place the canned tomato evenly over both lids, followed by the olives and mozzarella cheese.
6. Transfer the mushroom caps to the prepared fryer basket and cook for 5 to 6 minutes.
7. When the recommended time is up, remove the mushrooms from the fryer and immediately sprinkle with the Parmesan cheese and red pepper flakes.
8. Serves.

856. Crunchy tofu with paprika

Servings: 4
Cooking time: 15 minutes
Ingredients:
- ¼ cup corn starch
- 1 block of extra firm tofu, pressed to remove excess water and cut into cubes
- 1 tablespoon smoked paprika
- Salt and pepper

Addresses:
1. Line the fryer basket with aluminium foil and coat it with oil.
2. Preheat the fryer to 190°C.
3. Combine all ingredients in a bowl. Mix to combine.
4. Place in the fryer basket and cook for 12 minutes.

857. Broccoli Shawarma Crispy

Servings: 4
Cooking time: 25 minutes
Ingredients:
- 450 grams of broccoli, steamed and drained
- 2 tablespoons canola oil
- 1 teaspoon cayenne pepper
- 1 teaspoon sea salt
- 1 tablespoon Shawarma spice blend

Addresses:
1. Mix all ingredients in a bowl.
2. Roast in the preheated Air Fryer at 190°C for 10 minutes, shaking the basket halfway through the cooking time.
3. Work in batches - bon appetit!

858. Aubergines stuffed with sauce

Servings: 2
Cooking time: 25 minutes
Ingredients:
- 1 large aubergine
- 8 cherry tomatoes, quartered
- ½ tablespoon fresh parsley
- 2 teaspoons of olive oil, divided
- 2 teaspoons fresh lemon juice, divided
- 2 tablespoons tomato sauce
- Salt and black pepper

Addresses:
1. Preheat the fryer to 200°C and grease one fryer basket.
2. Place the aubergines in the fryer basket and cook for about 15 minutes.
3. Cut the aubergines in half lengthwise and drizzle evenly with a teaspoon of oil.
4. Set the fryer to 180°C and place the aubergines in the fryer basket, cut side up.
5. Cook for another 10 minutes and serve in a serving dish.
6. Scoop out the flesh from the aubergine and transfer to a bowl.
7. Stir in the tomatoes, sauce, parsley, salt, black pepper, remaining oil and lemon juice.
8. Squeeze the lemon juice over the aubergine halves and fill with the sauce mixture to serve.

859. Delicious potato pancakes

Servings: 4
Cooking time: 15 minutes
Ingredients:
- 1 medium onion, chopped
- 1 beaten egg
- ¼ cup milk
- 2 tablespoons unsalted butter
- ½ teaspoon garlic powder
- ¼ teaspoon salt
- ¼ teaspoon pepper
- 3 tablespoons flour
- Black pepper

Addresses:
1. Preheat your air fryer to 200°C.
2. In a medium bowl, combine egg, potatoes, onion, milk, butter, pepper, garlic powder and salt.
3. Stir in flour and form dough. Make cakes with about ¼ cup of dough.
4. Place the cakes in the fryer cooking basket and cook for minutes. Serve and enjoy.

860. Vegetable kebabs with simple peanut sauce

Servings: 4
Cooking time: 30 minutes
Ingredients:
- 8 small whole potatoes, cut into 2.5-centimetre pieces

- 2 bell peppers, cut into 2.5-centimetre pieces
- 8 pearl onions, halved
- 8 small mushrooms, cleaned
- 2 tablespoons extra virgin olive oil
- Sea salt and ground black pepper
- 1 teaspoon crushed red pepper flakes
- 1 teaspoon dried rosemary, crushed
- 1/3 teaspoon of granulated garlic

For the peanut sauce you will need:
- 2 tablespoons of peanut butter
- 1 tablespoon balsamic vinegar
- 1 tablespoon soy sauce
- 1/2 teaspoon garlic salt

Addresses:
1. Soak the wooden skewers in water for minutes.
2. Thread the vegetables onto the skewers, drizzle the olive oil all over the vegetable skewers, sprinkle with the spices.
3. Cook in the preheated air fryer at 200°C for 1 minute.
4. Meanwhile, in a small dish, whisk the peanut butter with the balsamic vinegar, soy sauce and garlic salt. Serve the skewers with the peanut sauce on the side. Enjoy.

861. Vegetable fritters for children

Servings: 4
Cooking time: 20 minutes
Ingredients:
- 450 grams broccoli florets
- 1 tablespoon ground flax seeds
- 1 yellow onion, finely chopped
- 1 sweet pepper, seeded and minced
- 1 grated carrot
- 2 cloves garlic, pressed
- 1 teaspoon turmeric powder
- 1/2 teaspoon ground cumin
- 1/2 cup all-purpose flour
- 1/2 cup maize flour
- Salt and ground black pepper
- 2 tablespoons olive oil

Addresses:
1. Blanch the broccoli in boiling salted water until al dente, about 3-4 minutes.
2. Drain well and transfer to a bowl, mash the broccoli florets with the rest of the ingredients.
3. Form the mixture into patties and place them in the lightly greased fryer basket.
4. Cook at 200°C for 6 minutes, turning halfway through cooking, working in batches.
5. Serve hot with your favourite Vegenaise. Enjoy.

862. Almond-apple deal

Servings: 4
Cooking time: 15 minutes
Ingredients:
- Apples
- 40 grams of almonds
- 20 grams of sultanas
- 2 tablespoons sugar

Addresses:
1. Preheat the fryer to 180°C.
2. In a bowl, combine the sugar, almonds and sultanas. Beat the mixture with a hand mixer.
3. Fill the apples with the almond mixture.
4. Place in the basket of the air fryer and cook for minutes. Serve.

863. Mushrooms with cheese

Servings: 4
Cooking time: 8 minutes
Ingredients:
- Button mushrooms, 170 grams, without stalk
- 2 tablespoons of grated mozzarella cheese
- 2 tablespoons grated cheddar cheese
- 2 tablespoons olive oil
- 2 tablespoons mixed dried Italian herbs
- Salt and freshly ground black pepper
- 1 teaspoon dried dill

Addresses:
1. Preheat the fryer to 180°C and grease the fryer basket.
2. Combine the mushrooms, dried Italian herbs, oil, salt and black pepper in a bowl and stir to coat well.
3. Place mushrooms in the fryer basket and top with mozzarella and cheddar cheese.
4. Cook for about 8 minutes and sprinkle with dried dill to serve.

864. Deliciously healthy crisps

Servings: 2
Cooking time: 10 minutes
Ingredients:
- 1 bunch of kale
- 1 teaspoon garlic powder
- 2 tablespoons almond flour
- 2 tablespoons olive oil
- Salt and pepper to taste

Addresses:
1. Preheat the air fryer for 5 minutes.
2. In a bowl, combine all ingredients until the kale leaves are coated with the other ingredients.
3. Place in the fryer basket and cook for 10 minutes until crispy.

865. Mixed fresh vegetables from the garden

Servings: 4
Cooking time: 15 minutes
Ingredients:
- 2 yellow peppers, seeded and chopped
- 1 aubergine, chopped
- 1 courgette, chopped

- 3 chopped tomatoes
- 2 small onions, chopped
- 2 cloves garlic, minced
- 2 tablespoons Herbes de Provence
- 1 tablespoon of olive oil
- 1 tablespoon balsamic vinegar
- Salt and black pepper

Addresses:
1. Preheat the fryer to 180°C and grease the fryer basket.
2. Mix all ingredients in a bowl and stir to coat well.
3. Transfer to the fryer basket and cook for about 15 minutes.
4. Keep in the fryer for about 5 minutes and remove to serve hot.

866. Curry and Coriander Spiced Bread Rolls

Portions: 5
Cooking time: 15 minutes
Ingredients:
- ½ teaspoon of mustard seeds
- ½ teaspoon turmeric
- 1 bunch chopped coriander
- 1 tablespoon of olive oil
- 2 green chillies, seeded and chopped
- 2 small onions, chopped
- 2 sprigs of curry leaves
- 5 large potatoes, cooked
- 8 slices of vegan wheat bread, brown sides removed
- Salt and pepper to taste

Addresses:
1. In a bowl, mash the potatoes and season to taste. Set aside.
2. Heat the olive oil in a frying pan over medium-low heat and add the mustard seeds. Stir until the seeds sizzle.
3. Then add the onions and fry until translucent. Add the turmeric powder and curry leaves.
4. Continue cooking for more minutes until the aroma is felt.
5. Remove from the heat and add the potatoes. Stir in the green chillies and coriander. This will be the filling.
6. Wet the bread and remove excess water.
7. Place a spoonful of the potato mixture in the centre of the bread and gently roll it up so that the potato filling is completely sealed inside the bread.
8. Coat with oil and place inside the air fryer.
9. Cook in a preheated air fryer at 200°C for 15 minutes.
10. Be sure to gently shake the fryer basket halfway through the cooking time for even cooking.

867. Coloured vegetable croquettes

Servings: 4
Cooking time: 40 minutes
Ingredients:
- 225 grams of broccoli
- 4 tablespoons milk
- 2 tablespoons butter
- Salt and black pepper
- 1/2 teaspoon cayenne pepper
- 1/2 cup chopped mushrooms
- 1 pepper, chopped
- 1 clove garlic, minced
- 3 tablespoons chopped onions
- 2 tablespoons olive oil
- 1/2 cup almond flour
- 1/4 cup coconut flour
- 2 eggs
- 1/2 cup grated Parmesan cheese

Addresses:
1. In a large saucepan, boil the broccoli for 20 minutes. Drain the broccoli and mash it with the milk, butter, salt, black pepper and cayenne pepper.
2. Add the mushrooms, pepper, garlic, garlic, spring onions and olive oil, stir to combine well. Form the mixture into patties.
3. In a shallow bowl, place the flour, beat the eggs in another bowl, in a third bowl, place the Parmesan cheese.
4. Dredge each patty in the flour, then in the eggs and finally in the parmesan cheese, pressing to adhere.
5. Cook in the preheated air fryer at 190°C for 16 minutes, stirring halfway through the cooking time. Enjoy!

868. Croissant rolls

Servings: 8
Cooking time: 6 minutes
Ingredients:
- 1 tin (225 grams) of croissant rolls
- 4 tablespoons melted butter

Addresses:
1. Set the temperature of the air fryer to 160°C.
2. Grease the air fryer basket.
3. Place the croissant rolls in the prepared air fryer basket.
4. Fry in the open air for about 4 minutes.
5. Turn over on the side and air fry for a further 1 to 2 minutes.
6. Remove from the fryer and transfer to a serving dish.
7. Drizzle with the melted butter and serve hot.

869. Barbecued roasted almonds

Servings: 6
Cooking time: 20 minutes
Ingredients:
- 1 ½ cups of raw almonds
- Sea salt and ground black pepper
- 1/4 teaspoon garlic powder
- 1/4 teaspoon mustard powder

- 1/2 teaspoon cumin powder
- 1/4 teaspoon smoked paprika
- 1 tablespoon of olive oil

Addresses:
1. Mix all ingredients in a bowl.
2. Line the basket of the Air Fryer with baking paper. Spread the coated almonds in a single layer in the basket.
3. Roast for 6 to 8 minutes, shaking the basket once or twice. Work in batches. Enjoy.

870. Bacon sautéed with spinach

Servings: 2
Cooking time: 9 minutes
Ingredients:
- 3 slices of meatless bacon, chopped
- 1 onion, chopped
- 115 grams of fresh spinach
- 2 tablespoons olive oil
- 1 clove garlic, minced

Addresses:
1. Preheat the fryer to 170°C and grease a frying pan.
2. Place the olive oil and garlic in the frying pan of the fryer and place it in the fryer basket.
3. Cook for about 2 minutes and add the bacon and onions.
4. Cook for about 3 minutes and add the spinach. Cook for a further 4 minutes and serve in a serving dish.

871. Thai sweet potato dumplings

Servings: 4
Cooking time: 50 minutes
Ingredients:
- 450 grams of sweet potatoes
- 1 cup brown sugar
- 1 tablespoon orange juice
- 2 teaspoons grated orange zest
- 1/2 teaspoon ground cinnamon
- 1/4 teaspoon ground cloves
- 1/2 cup almond flour
- 1 teaspoon baking powder
- 1 cup coconut flakes

Addresses:
1. Bake the sweet potatoes at 190°C for 30-35 minutes until tender, peel and mash them.
2. Add the brown sugar, orange juice, orange zest, ground cinnamon, cloves, almond flour and baking powder, mix to combine well.
3. Roll the balls in the coconut flakes.
4. Bake in the preheated air fryer at 180°C for 15 minutes or until cooked through and crispy.
5. Repeat the process until you run out of ingredients - bon appetit!

872. Italian easy to season pasta sheets

Servings: 2
Cooking time: 10 minutes
Ingredients:
- ½ teaspoon salt
- 1 ½ teaspoon Italian seasoning blend
- 1 tablespoon nutritional yeast
- 1 tablespoon of olive oil
- 2 cups of wholemeal bow tie pasta

Addresses:
1. Place the baking attachment in the air fryer.
2. Give a good stir.
3. Close the air fryer and cook for 10 minutes at 200°C.

873. Spicy tofu

Servings: 3
Cooking time: 13 minutes
Ingredients:
- 1 block of extra firm tofu, pressed and cut into cubes of about 2 centimetres.
- 3 teaspoons cornstarch
- 1½ tablespoons avocado oil
- 1½ teaspoons paprika
- 1 teaspoon onion powder
- 1 teaspoon garlic powder
- Salt and black pepper

Addresses:
1. Preheat the fryer to 200°C and grease one fryer basket.
2. Combine the tofu, oil, cornstarch and spices in a bowl and stir to coat well.
3. Place the tofu pieces in the fryer basket and cook for about 1 minute, stirring twice in between.
4. Divide the tofu among plates and serve hot.

874. Cheese balls with mushrooms and cauliflower

Servings: 4
Cooking time: 50 minutes
Ingredients:
- 3 tablespoons olive oil
- 1 small red onion, chopped
- 3 cloves garlic, minced
- 3 cups chopped cauliflower
- 2 tablespoons chicken stock
- 1 cup breadcrumbs
- 1 cup Grana Padano cheese
- ¼ cup coconut oil
- 2 sprigs of chopped fresh thyme
- Salt and pepper

Addresses:
1. Place a frying pan over medium heat.
2. Add the olive oil, once hot, sauté the garlic and onion, until translucent.
3. Now add the mushrooms and cauliflower and sauté for 5 minutes. Pour in the stock, thyme and simmer until the cauliflower

has absorbed the stock. Add the Grana Padano cheese, pepper and salt.
4. Allow the mixture to cool and roll the mixture into bite-sized balls. Refrigerate for 30 minutes to harden.
5. Preheat the air fryer to 180°C.
6. In a bowl, add the breadcrumbs and coconut oil and mix well. Remove the mushroom balls from the fridge, stir the breadcrumb mixture again and roll the balls in the breadcrumb mixture.
7. Place the balls in the basket of the air fryer without overfilling and cook for 15 minutes, stirring every 5 minutes for even cooking. Serve with stir-fried noodles and tomato sauce.

875. Almond Flour Battered Wings

Servings: 4
Cooking time: 25 minutes
Ingredients:
- ¼ cup melted butter
- ¾ cup almond flour
- 16 pieces of chicken wings
- 2 tablespoons stevia powder
- 4 tablespoons minced garlic
- Salt and pepper to taste

Addresses:
1. Preheat the air fryer for 5 minutes.
2. In a bowl, combine the chicken wings, almond flour, stevia powder and garlic. Season with salt and pepper to taste.
3. Place in the basket of the air fryer and cook for 25 minutes at 200°C.
4. Halfway through the cooking time, be sure to shake the fryer basket.
5. Once cooked, place in a bowl and drizzle with melted butter. Toss to coat.

876. Open-air Falafel

Servings: 6
Cooking time: 25 minutes
Ingredients:
- ½ cup chickpea flour
- 1 cup chopped fresh parsley
- Juice of 1 lemon
- 4 cloves garlic, minced
- 1 onion, chopped
- 2 teaspoons ground cumin
- 2 teaspoons ground coriander
- 1 teaspoon chilli powder
- Salt and black pepper

Addresses:
1. In a blender, add the chickpeas, flour, parsley, lemon juice, garlic, onion, cumin, cumin, coriander, chilli, turmeric, salt and pepper, and blend until well combined, but not too blended - there should be some lumps.
2. Form the mixture into balls and press them with your hands, making sure that they are all around.
3. Spray with oil and arrange them in a paper-lined air fryer basket, working in batches if necessary.
4. Bake at 180°C for 14 minutes, turning them once halfway through. They should be crisp and golden brown.

877. Aubergines stuffed with vegetables

Portions: 5
Cooking time: 14 minutes
Ingredients:
- 10 small aubergines, halved lengthwise
- 1 onion, chopped
- 1 chopped tomato
- ¼ cup chopped cottage cheese
- ½ green pepper, seeded and chopped
- 1 tablespoon fresh lime juice
- 1 tablespoon vegetable oil
- ½ teaspoon minced garlic
- Salt and ground black pepper
- 2 tablespoons tomato paste

Addresses:
1. Preheat the fryer to 160°C and grease the fryer basket.
2. Cut a slice from one side of each aubergine lengthwise and scoop out the flesh into a bowl.
3. Drizzle the aubergines with lime juice and place them in the fryer basket.
4. Cook for a few minutes and remove from the fryer.
5. Heat the vegetable oil in a frying pan over medium heat and add the garlic and onion.
6. Sauté for about 2 minutes and add the aubergine flesh, tomato, salt and black pepper.
7. Sauté for about 3 minutes and add the cheese, pepper, tomato paste and coriander.
8. Cook for about 1 minute and stuff the aubergines with this mixture.
9. Close each aubergine with its cut side and set the fryer to 180°C.
10. Place them in the fryer basket and cook for about 5 minutes.
11. Place on a plate and serve hot.

878. Mushroom and pepper pizza

Portions: 10
Cooking time: 10 minutes
Ingredients:
- ¼ red pepper, chopped
- 1 cup oyster mushrooms, chopped
- 1 chopped shallot
- 1 vegan pizza dough
- 2 tablespoons parsley
- Salt and pepper

Addresses:

1. Preheat the air fryer to 200°C.
2. Cut the pizza dough into squares. Set aside.
3. In a bowl, mix the mushrooms, shallot, pepper and parsley.
4. Season with salt and pepper to taste.
5. Place the topping on the pizza squares.
6. Place in the air fryer and cook for 10 minutes.

879. Twice-fried cauliflower tater tots

Portions: 12
Cooking time: 16 minutes
Ingredients:
- ½ cup breadcrumbs
- ½ cup nutritional yeast
- 1 flax egg
- 3 tablespoons of desiccated coconut
- 1 onion, chopped
- 1 teaspoon chopped chives
- 1 teaspoon chopped garlic
- 1 teaspoon oregano, chopped
- 1 teaspoon chopped parsley
- 450 g cauliflower, steamed and chopped
- 3 tablespoons of oats
- Flaxseed meal
- 3 tablespoons of water
- Salt and pepper

Addresses:
1. Preheat the fryer to 200°C.
2. Place the steamed cauliflower on a paper towel and a ring to remove excess water.
3. Transfer to a bowl and add the rest of the ingredients, except the breadcrumbs.
4. Mix until well combined and roll into balls with your hands.
5. Roll the tater tots in the breadcrumbs and place them in the fryer basket.
6. Cook for a few minutes. Once done, increase the cooking temperature to 200°C and cook for another 10 minutes.

880. Spinach and feta triangles

Servings: 4
Cooking time: 20 minutes
Ingredients:
- 1 cup steamed spinach
- 1 cup crumbled feta cheese
- ¼ teaspoon garlic powder
- 1 teaspoon oregano, chopped
- ¼ teaspoon salt

Addresses:
1. Preheat the fryer to 180°C.
2. Roll out the dough on a lightly floured flat surface.
3. Combine the feta, spinach, oregano, salt and garlic powder in a bowl. Cut the dough into 4 equal pieces.
4. Divide the spinach and cheese mixture between the pieces of dough. Fold the dough over and secure with a fork.
5. Place in a lined baking dish and then in the deep fryer. Cook for 1 minute, until lightly browned.

881. Crispy and tasty spring rolls

Servings: 4
Cooking time: 15 minutes
Ingredients:
- ½ teaspoon ginger, finely minced
- 1 stalk celery, chopped
- 1 cup shiitake mushrooms, thinly sliced
- 1 medium carrot, grated
- 1 tablespoon soy sauce
- 1 teaspoon coconut sugar
- 1 teaspoon corn starch
- 2 tablespoons of water
- 1 teaspoon nutritional yeast
- 8 spring roll wrappers

Addresses:
1. In a bowl, mix together the celery stalk, carrots, ginger, coconut sugar, soy sauce and nutritional yeast.
2. Take a spoonful of the vegetable mixture and place it in the centre of the spring roll wrappers.
3. Roll up and seal the edges of the wrapper with the cornflour mixture.
4. Cook in a preheated air fryer at 200°C until the spring roll wrapper is crispy.

882. Rice salad with cauli and tomatoes

Servings: 4
Cooking time: 25 minutes
Ingredients:
- 450 grams of cauliflower rice
- 2 cloves garlic, pressed
- 1/3 cup chopped cilantro
- 1 cup chopped shallots
- 115 grams of tomato, sliced
- 1 cup rocket lettuce, cut into pieces
- 2 tablespoons apple cider vinegar
- Sea salt and ground black pepper

Addresses:
1. Place the cauliflower rice in the basket of the Air Fryer.
2. Cook at 190°C. Shake the basket and continue cooking for a further 10 minutes.
3. Transfer the prepared couscous to a nice salad bowl.
4. Add the rest of the ingredients, stir to combine and enjoy!

883. Corn cakes

Servings: 8
Cooking time: 25 minutes
Ingredients:
- 2 eggs, lightly beaten
- 1/3 cup finely chopped green onions
- ¼ cup chopped parsley
- 1 cup flour
- ½ teaspoon baking powder

- Salt and black pepper

Addresses:
1. In a bowl, add the corn, eggs, parsley and green onions, season with salt and pepper and mix well to combine.
2. Sieve the flour and baking powder into the bowl and stir. Line the fryer basket with baking paper and place spoonfuls of batter in it, making sure they are at least one centimetre apart.
3. Cook for a few minutes at 200°C, turning once halfway through.
4. Serve with sour cream.

884. Paneer cutlet

Servings: 1
Cooking time: 15 minutes
Ingredients:
- 1 cup grated cheese
- ½ teaspoon chai masala
- 1 teaspoon butter
- ½ teaspoon garlic powder
- 1 small onion, finely chopped
- ½ teaspoon oregano
- ½ teaspoon salt

Addresses:
1. Preheat the air fryer to 180°C, and grease a baking dish.
2. Mix all ingredients in a bowl until well incorporated.
3. Make cutlets from the mixture and place them in the greased baking dish.
4. Transfer the baking dish to the fryer and cook the cutlets until crispy.

885. Famous buffalo cauliflower

Servings: 4
Cooking time: 30 minutes
Ingredients:
- 450 grams of cauliflower florets
- 1/2 cup all-purpose flour
- 1/2 cup rice flour
- Sea salt and ground black pepper
- 1/2 teaspoon cayenne pepper
- 1/2 teaspoon chilli powder
- 1/2 cup soy milk
- 2 tablespoons soy sauce
- 2 tablespoons tahini
- 1 teaspoon vegetable oil
- 2 cloves garlic, minced
- 6 scotch bonnet peppers, seeded and sliced
- 1 small onion, chopped
- 1/2 teaspoon salt
- 1 cup of water
- 2 tablespoons white vinegar
- 1 tablespoon granulated sugar

Addresses:
1. Rinse the cauliflower florets and pat dry.
2. Spray the Air Fryer basket with cooking spray.
3. In a bowl, mix the all-purpose flour and rice flour, add the salt, black pepper, cayenne pepper and chilli powder.
4. Add the soy milk, soy sauce and tahini. Stir until a thick batter forms. Dip the cauliflower florets into the batter.
5. Cook the cauliflower at 180°C for 16 minutes, turning halfway through cooking.
6. Meanwhile, heat the vegetable oil in a saucepan over medium-high heat, then sauté the garlic, peppers and onion for a minute or so or until fragrant.
7. Add the rest of the ingredients and bring the mixture to a rapid boil. Now reduce the heat to a simmer and continue cooking for a further 10 minutes or until the sauce has reduced by half.
8. Pour the sauce over the prepared cauliflower and serve - bon appetit!

886. Crispy green beans with Pecorino Romano

Servings: 3
Cooking time: 15 minutes
Ingredients:
- 2 tablespoons buttermilk
- 1 egg
- 4 tablespoons almond flour
- 4 tablespoons golden flaxseed meal
- 4 tablespoons Pecorino Romano cheese, finely grated
- Coarse salt and ground black pepper
- 1 teaspoon smoked paprika
- 170 grams of green beans, chopped

Addresses:
1. In a shallow bowl, whisk together the buttermilk and egg.
2. In a separate bowl, combine the almond flour, golden flaxseed meal, pecorino romano cheese, salt, black pepper and paprika.
3. Dip the green beans into the egg mixture and then into the cheese mixture. Place the green beans in the lightly greased baking basket.
4. Cook in the preheated Air Fryer at 200°C. Shake the basket halfway through cooking.
5. Taste, adjust seasoning and serve with dipping sauce if desired - bon appetit!

887. Spicy roasted cashew nuts

Servings: 4
Cooking time: 20 minutes
Ingredients:
- 1 cup whole cashew nuts
- 1 teaspoon olive oil
- Salt and ground black pepper
- 1/2 teaspoon smoked paprika
- 1/2 teaspoon ancho chili powder

Addresses:
1. Mix all the ingredients in the mixer bowl.

2. Line the basket of the Air Fryer with baking paper. Spread the spiced cashew nuts in a single layer in the basket.
3. Roast for 6 to 8 minutes, shaking the basket once or twice. Work in batches.

888. Quick Crunchy Cheese Larks

Servings: 4
Cooking time: 15 minutes
Ingredients:
- 1 cup all-purpose flour
- 1 tablespoon butter
- 1 tablespoon baking powder
- ¼ teaspoon chilli powder
- ¼ teaspoon salt
- 2 tablespoons of water

Addresses:
1. In a bowl, mix the flour and baking powder. Add the chili powder, salt, butter, cheese and 2 tablespoons of water.
2. Make a stiff dough. Knead the dough for a while and sprinkle with a spoonful of flour.
3. With a rolling pin, roll the dough to a thickness of 1.25 centimetres. Cut into shapes.
4. Cook for 6 minutes at 190°C.

889. Chives 'n Thyme Spiced Veggie Burger

Servings: 8
Cooking time: 15 minutes
Ingredients:
- ¼ cup desiccated coconut
- ½ cup of oatmeal
- ½ pound cauliflower, steamed and diced
- 1 cup breadcrumbs
- 1 flax egg
- 1 flaxseed egg
- 3 tablespoons of water
- 1 teaspoon mustard powder
- 2 teaspoons chives
- 2 teaspoons coconut oil, melted
- 2 teaspoons minced garlic
- 2 teaspoons parsley
- 2 teaspoons thyme
- 3 tablespoons plain flour
- Salt and pepper

Addresses:
1. Preheat the fryer to 200°C.
2. Place the cauliflower in a tea towel and ring out excess water. Place in a bowl and add all the ingredients except the breadcrumbs. Mix well until well combined.
3. Form the mixture into 8 patties using your hands.
4. Roll the patties in the breadcrumbs and place them in the fryer basket. Make sure they do not overlap.
5. Cook for 10 minutes or until the patties are crispy.

890. Celery croquettes with chive mayonnaise

Servings: 4
Cooking time: 15 minutes
Ingredients:
- 2 medium celery stalks, trimmed and grated
- 1/2 cup leek, finely chopped
- 1 tablespoon garlic paste
- 1/4 teaspoon freshly ground black pepper
- 1 teaspoon fine sea salt
- 1 tablespoon fresh dill, finely chopped
- 1 egg, lightly beaten
- 1/4 cup almond flour
- 1/2 cup freshly grated parmesan cheese
- 1/4 teaspoon baking powder
- 2 tablespoons fresh chives, chopped
- 4 tablespoons mayonnaise

Addresses:
1. Place the celery on a paper towel and squeeze to remove excess liquid.
2. Combine the vegetables with the other ingredients except the chives and mayonnaise. Form into balls using 1 tablespoon of the vegetable mixture.
3. Then gently flatten each ball with the palm of your hand or a wide spatula. Spray the croquettes with non-stick cooking oil.
4. Fry the vegetable croquettes in a single layer for 6 minutes at 180°C.
5. In the meantime, mix the fresh chives and mayonnaise. Serve the croquettes hot with the chive mayonnaise - bon appetit!

891. Bacon and Cheese Stuffed Mushrooms

Servings: 4
Cooking time: 20 minutes
Ingredients:
- 1 clove garlic, minced
- Salt and pepper
- 4 slices of chopped bacon
- ¼ cup shredded Cheddar cheese
- 1 tablespoon of olive oil
- 1 tablespoon chopped parsley

Addresses:
1. Preheat the fryer to 200°C.
2. In a bowl, add the oil, bacon, cheddar cheese, parsley, salt, pepper and garlic. Mix well with a spoon.
3. Cut the stems off the mushrooms and fill each cup with the bacon mixture.
4. Press the bacon mixture into the lids.
5. Place the stuffed mushrooms in the fryer basket and cook at 200°C for 8 minutes.
6. Once browned and crispy, plate and serve with a green salad.

892. Fried okra with chilli

Servings: 4
Cooking time: 15 minutes
Ingredients:
- 3 tablespoons sour cream

- 2 tablespoons flour
- 2 tablespoons semolina
- ½ teaspoon red chilli powder
- Salt and black pepper to taste

Addresses:
1. Preheat the air fryer to 200°C. Spray the air fryer basket with cooking spray.
2. In a bowl, pour the sour cream. In another bowl, mix the flour, semolina, chili powder, salt and pepper.
3. Dip the okra into the sour cream and then into the flour mixture.
4. Place in the basket of your air fryer and cook for 5 minutes.
5. Remove the basket and shake. Cook for a further 5 minutes. Allow to cool and serve.

893. Herb roasted potatoes and peppers

Servings: 4
Cooking time: 30 minutes
Ingredients:
- 450 grams of russet potatoes, cut into 2.5-centimetre chunks
- 2 bell peppers, seeded and cut into 2.5 centimetre pieces
- 2 tablespoons olive oil
- 1 teaspoon dried rosemary
- 1 teaspoon basil, dried
- 1 teaspoon dried oregano
- 1 teaspoon dried parsley flakes
- Sea salt and ground black pepper
- 1/2 teaspoon smoked paprika

Addresses:
1. Place all ingredients in the fryer basket.
2. Roast at 200°C for 15 minutes, stirring the basket occasionally. Work in batches.
3. Serve hot and enjoy.

894. Hasselback potatoes

Servings: 4
Cooking time: 30 minutes
Ingredients:
- 4 potatoes
- 2 tablespoons grated Parmesan cheese
- 1 tablespoon chopped fresh chives
- 2 tablespoons olive oil

Addresses:
1. Preheat the fryer to 180°C and grease the fryer basket.
2. Cut slits along the length of each potato about 6 millimetres apart with a sharp knife, ensuring that the slices remain connected at the bottom.
3. Brush the potatoes with olive oil and place them in the fryer basket.
4. Cook for about 30 minutes and serve on a platter.
5. Top with chives and Parmesan cheese to serve.

895. Rosemary roasted pumpkin

Servings: 2
Cooking time: 30 minutes
Ingredients:
- 1 tablespoon dried rosemary
- Cooking spray
- Salt for seasoning

Addresses:
1. Place the pumpkin on a cutting board and peel it, cut it in half and remove the seeds. Cut the flesh into wedges and season with salt.
2. Preheat the fryer to 180°C, spray the squash with cooking spray and sprinkle with rosemary.
3. Grease the fryer basket with cooking spray and place the wedges inside.
4. Insert the fryer basket and cook for a few minutes, turning them once halfway through.
5. Serve with maple syrup and goat's cheese.

896. Easy granola with sultanas and walnuts

Servings: 8
Cooking time: 40 minutes
Ingredients:
- 2 cups oat flakes
- ½ cup chopped walnuts
- ⅓ cup chopped almonds
- ¼ cup sultanas
- ¼ cup whole wheat pastry flour
- ½ teaspoon cinnamon
- ¼ teaspoon nutmeg, preferably freshly grated
- ½ teaspoon salt
- ⅓ cup melted coconut oil
- ⅓ cup agave nectar
- ½ teaspoon coconut extract
- ½ teaspoon vanilla extract

Addresses:
1. Combine all ingredients thoroughly. Then spread the mixture into the trays of the Air Fryer. Spray with cooking spray.
2. Bake at 180°C for 25 minutes, turn the trays and bake for a further 10 to 15 minutes.
3. This granola can be stored in an airtight container for up to 2 weeks - enjoy!

897. Corn on the Cob with Spicy Avocado Spread

Servings: 4
Cooking time: 15 minutes
Ingredients:
- 4 ears of corn
- 1 avocado, pitted, peeled and mashed
- 1 pressed garlic clove
- 1 tablespoon fresh lime juice
- 1 tablespoon soy sauce
- 4 teaspoons nutritional yeast
- 1/2 teaspoon cayenne pepper
- 1/2 teaspoon dried dill

- Sea salt and ground black pepper
- 1 teaspoon hot sauce
- 2 heaped tablespoons fresh coriander leaves, coarsely chopped

Addresses:
1. Spray the corn with cooking spray.
2. Cook at 200°C for 6 minutes, turning halfway through cooking.
3. Meanwhile, mix the avocado, lime juice, soy sauce, nutritional yeast, cayenne pepper, dill, salt, black pepper and hot sauce.
4. Spread the avocado mixture all over the corn on the cob. Garnish with fresh coriander leaves - bon appetit!

898. Cauliflower and ricotta fritters

Servings: 4
Cooking time: 30 minutes
Ingredients:
- 1 tablespoon of olive oil
- 1/2 lb cauliflower
- 1/2 cup ricotta cheese
- 1/4 cup ground flaxseed meal
- 1/4 cup almond flour
- 1/2 teaspoon baking powder
- 1/2 onion, chopped
- 1 clove garlic, minced
- Sea salt and ground black pepper
- 1 cup grated Parmesan cheese

Addresses:
1. Start by preheating your air fryer to 200°C.
2. Drizzle the olive oil all over the cauliflower. Place the cauliflower in the basket of the Air Fryer and cook for approximately 15 minutes, shaking the basket periodically.
3. Next, mash the cauliflower and combine it with the other ingredients. Form the mixture into patties.
4. Bake in the preheated air fryer at 190°C for 1 minute, turning them over halfway through cooking to ensure even cooking. Enjoy!

899. Mediterranean Falafel with Tzatziki

Servings: 4
Cooking time: 30 minutes
Ingredients:
For Falafel you need:
- 2 cups shredded cauliflower
- 1/4 teaspoon baking powder
- 1/3 cup hot water
- 1/2 teaspoon salt
- 1 tablespoon coriander leaves, finely chopped
- 2 tablespoons fresh lemon juice

For the vegan Tzatziki you will need:
- 1 cup plain Greek yoghurt
- 2 tablespoons freshly squeezed lime juice
- 1/4 teaspoon ground black pepper
- 1/3 teaspoon of flaked sea salt
- 2 tablespoons of extra virgin olive oil
- 2 tablespoons chopped fresh dill
- 1 pressed garlic clove
- 1/2 fresh cucumber, grated

Addresses:
1. In a bowl, thoroughly combine all the ingredients for the falafel. Let the mixture stand for a few minutes.
2. Now air fry them at 200°C for 15 minutes, making sure to turn them over halfway through the cooking time.
3. To make the Greek tzatziki, blend all the ingredients in your food processor.
4. Serve the falafel hot with cold tzatziki. Enjoy.

900. Wasabi Gourmet Popcorn

Servings: 2
Cooking time: 30 minutes
Ingredients:
- 1/2 teaspoon brown sugar
- 1 teaspoon salt
- 1/2 teaspoon wasabi powder, sieved
- 1 tablespoon avocado oil
- 3 tablespoons popcorn kernels

Addresses:
1. Add the dried corn kernels to the basket of the Air Fryer, mix with the rest of the ingredients.
2. Bake at 200°C for 15 minutes, shaking the basket every 5 minutes. Work in two batches.
3. Taste, adjust the seasoning and serve immediately - bon appetit!

901. Radish and mozzarella salad with balsamic vinaigrette

Servings: 4
Cooking time: 30 minutes
Ingredients:
- 680 grams of radishes, trimmed and cut in halves
- 225 grams of fresh mozzarella cheese, sliced
- Salt and freshly ground black pepper
- 3 tablespoons olive oil
- 1 teaspoon honey
- 1 tablespoon balsamic vinegar

Addresses:
1. Preheat the fryer to 180°C and grease the fryer basket.
2. Combine the radishes, salt, black pepper and tablespoons of olive oil in a bowl and toss to coat well.
3. Place the radishes in the fryer basket and cook for a few minutes, turning them twice.
4. Place in a bowl and add the rest of the ingredients to serve.

902. Mediterranean-style fries with vegetable sauce

Servings: 4
Cooking time: 1 hour
Ingredients:
- 1 large potato, cut into slices approximately 5 millimetres thick
- 1 tablespoon of olive oil
- Sea salt
- 1/2 teaspoon crushed red pepper flakes
- 1 teaspoon fresh rosemary
- 1/2 teaspoon fresh sage
- 1/2 teaspoon fresh basil

For the dipping sauce you need:
- 1/3 cup of raw cashew nuts
- 1 tablespoon tahini
- 1 ½ tablespoons olive oil
- 1/4 cup raw almonds
- 1/4 teaspoon prepared yellow mustard

Addresses:
1. Soak the potatoes in a large bowl of cold water for 20 to 30 minutes.
2. Drain the potatoes and dry them with a kitchen towel.
3. Mix with olive oil and seasoning.
4. Place in the lightly greased baking basket and bake at 180°C for 30 minutes. Work in batches.
5. Meanwhile, puree the sauce ingredients in your food processor until smooth.
6. Serve the chips with the Vegveeta dipping sauce and enjoy!

903. French fries with polenta

Servings: 4
Cooking time: 80 minutes
Ingredients:
- 2 cups of milk
- 1 cup instant polenta
- Salt and black pepper
- Cooking spray
- Fresh thyme, chopped

Addresses:
1. Line a tray with paper.
2. Pour the water and milk into a saucepan and bring to a simmer. Continue to whisk while pouring in the polenta and whisk a little more to get the polenta to thicken and bubble. Season to taste.
3. Add the polenta to the lined tray and spread it out. Refrigerate for 45 minutes.
4. Cut the cold and set polenta into sticks and drizzle with oil.
5. Place the polenta pieces in the basket of the air fryer and cook for 16 minutes at 190°C, turning once halfway through. Serve when the fries are golden brown and crispy.

904. Elegant Garlic Mushroom

Servings: 3
Cooking time: 20 minutes
Ingredients:
- 2 tablespoons vermouth
- ½ teaspoon garlic powder
- 1 tablespoon of olive oil
- 2 teaspoons herbs
- 1 tablespoon duck fat

Addresses:
1. Preheat your fryer to 180°C.
2. Add the duck fat, garlic powder and herbs in a blender, and process. Pour the mixture over the mushrooms and top with vermouth.
3. Place the mushrooms in the cooking basket and cook for minutes.
4. Cover with more vermouth and cook for a further 5 minutes.

905. Traditional Indian Bhaji

Servings: 4
Cooking time: 40 minutes
Ingredients:
- 2 beaten eggs
- 1/2 cup almond flour
- 1/2 cup coconut flour
- 1/2 teaspoon baking powder
- 1 teaspoon curry paste
- 1 teaspoon cumin seeds
- 1 teaspoon chopped fresh ginger root
- Salt and black pepper
- 2 red onions, chopped
- 1 Indian green chilli, mashed
- Non-stick cooking spray

Addresses:
1. Whisk the eggs, almond flour, coconut flour and baking powder in a bowl to make a thick batter, adding cold water if necessary.
2. Add the curry paste, cumin seeds, ginger root, salt and black pepper.
3. Now add the onion and chilli, mix until everything is well incorporated.
4. Shape into balls and press them lightly to make patties. Drizzle the patties with cooking oil on all sides.
5. Place a sheet of aluminium foil in the food basket of the Air Fryer. Place the fritters on the foil.
6. Then air fry them at 180°C for 15 minutes, turn them over, press the on button and cook them for another 20 minutes. Serve immediately.

906. Delicious mushrooms

Servings: 4
Cooking time: 22 minutes
Ingredients:
- 2 cups mushrooms, sliced
- 2 tablespoons grated cheddar cheese
- 1 tablespoon chopped fresh chives
- 2 tablespoons olive oil

Addresses:

1. Preheat the fryer to 180°C and grease the fryer basket.
2. Brush the mushrooms with olive oil and place them in the fryer basket.
3. Cook for about 20 minutes and serve on a platter.
4. Top with chives and cheddar cheese and cook for a further 2 minutes.
5. Serve hot.

907. Okra with green beans

Servings: 2
Cooking time: 20 minutes
Ingredients:
- ½ bag (280 grams) frozen sliced okra
- ½ bag (280 grams) frozen chopped green beans
- ¼ cup nutritional yeast
- 3 tablespoons balsamic vinegar
- Salt and black pepper

Addresses:
1. Preheat the fryer to 200°C and grease the fryer basket.
2. Place the okra, green beans, nutritional yeast, vinegar, salt and black pepper in a bowl and toss to coat well.
3. Place the okra mixture in the fryer basket and cook for about 20 minutes.
4. Transfer to a serving dish and serve hot.

908. Grilled drunken mushrooms

Servings: 4
Cooking time: 20 minutes
Ingredients:
- 2 cloves garlic, finely chopped
- 3 tablespoons chopped fresh thyme and/or rosemary leaves
- A large pinch of crushed red pepper flakes
- 1 teaspoon kosher salt,
- 6 spring onions, cut crosswise into about 5-centimetre pieces
- Cherry tomatoes
- 1 pint cremini, button or other small mushrooms
- 1/2 cup extra virgin olive oil
- 1/2 tsp freshly ground black pepper, more to taste
- 1/4 cup red wine vinegar or sherry vinegar

Addresses:
1. In a Ziploc bag, thoroughly mix together the black pepper, salt, red pepper flakes, thyme, vinegar, oil and garlic. Add the mushrooms, tomatoes and spring onions.
2. Mix well and leave to marinate for half an hour.
3. Skewer the mushrooms, tomatoes and spring onions. Reserve the sauce for basting. Place on the skewer rack of the air fryer. If necessary, cook in batches.
4. Cook at 200°C for 10 minutes. Halfway through the cooking time, turn the skewers over and baste them with the reserved sauce.
5. Serve and enjoy.

909. Vegetable sauce wraps

Servings: 4
Cooking time: 15 minutes
Ingredients:
- 1 cup sliced red onion
- 1 courgette, chopped
- 1 poblano chilli, deveined and finely chopped
- 1 head of lettuce
- 1/2 cup salsa (homemade or store-bought)
- 225 grams of mozzarella cheese

Addresses:
1. Start by preheating your air fryer to 200°C.
2. Cook the red onion, courgette and poblano peppers until tender and fragrant or about 7 minutes.
3. Divide the sautéed mixture between the lettuce leaves, top with the sauce. Finish with the mozzarella cheese.
4. Wrap the lettuce leaves around the filling. Enjoy.

910. Versatile stuffed tomato

Servings: 4
Cooking time: 22 minutes
Ingredients:
- 4 tomatoes, tops and seeds removed
- 1 carrot, peeled and chopped
- 1 onion, chopped
- 1 cup frozen peas, thawed
- 2 cups of cold cooked rice
- 1 teaspoon olive oil
- 1 clove garlic, minced
- 1 tablespoon soy sauce

Addresses:
1. Preheat the fryer to 180°C and grease the fryer basket.
2. Heat the olive oil in a frying pan over low heat and add the carrots, onions, peas and garlic.
3. Cook for about 2 minutes and add the soy sauce and rice.
4. Fill the tomatoes with the rice mixture and place them in the fryer basket.
5. Cook for about 20 minutes and serve hot.

Other recipes for the air fryer

911. Turkey cutlets in Dijon and Curry Sauce

Servings: 4
Cooking time: 30 minutes + marinating time
Ingredients:

- 1/2 tablespoon Dijon mustard
- 1/2 teaspoon curry powder
- Sea salt flakes and freshly ground black peppercorns
- 150 grams turkey cutlets
- 1/2 cup fresh lemon juice
- 1/2 tablespoon tamari sauce

Addresses:
1. Set the air fryer to cook at 190°C.
2. Place turkey cutlets in a mixing bowl. Add fresh lemon juice, tamari and mustard, marinate for at least 2 hours.
3. Coat each turkey cutlet with the curry powder, salt and freshly ground black peppercorns.
4. Roast in the air fryer, work in batches - bon appetit!

912. Egg Salad with Asparagus and Spinach

Servings: 4
Cooking time: 25 minutes + cooling time
Ingredients:
- 4 eggs
- 450 grams of asparagus, chopped
- 2 cups baby spinach
- 1/2 cup mayonnaise
- 1 teaspoon mustard
- 1 teaspoon fresh lemon juice
- Sea salt and ground black pepper

Addresses:
1. Place the rack in the basket of the Air Fryer, lower the eggs onto the rack.
2. Bake at 180°C for 15 minutes.
3. Place them in an ice water bath to stop the cooking process. Peel the eggs under cold running water, chop the hard-boiled eggs and set aside.
4. Increase the temperature to 200°C. Place the asparagus in the lightly greased basket of the air fryer.
5. Cook for a few minutes or until tender. Place in a nice salad bowl. Add the baby spinach.
6. In a mixing bowl, mix the rest of the ingredients well. Drizzle this dressing over the asparagus in the salad bowl and top with the chopped eggs - bon appetit!

913. Peppery egg salad

Servings: 3
Cooking time: 20 minutes + cooling time
Ingredients:
- 6 eggs
- 1 teaspoon mustard
- 1/2 cup mayonnaise
- 1 tablespoon white vinegar
- 1 habanero chilli, chopped
- 1 red pepper, seeded and sliced
- 1 green pepper, seeded and sliced
- 1 shallot, cut into slices
- Sea salt and ground black pepper

Addresses:
1. Place the rack in the basket of the Air Fryer, lower the eggs onto the rack.
2. Bake at 180°C for 15 minutes.
3. Transfer them to an ice water bath to stop the cooking process. Peel the eggs under cold running water, chop the hard-boiled eggs and set aside.
4. Mix with the rest of the ingredients and serve well chilled. Enjoy!

914. Famous Western Eggs

Servings: 6
Cooking time: 20 minutes
Ingredients:
- 6 eggs
- 3/4 cup milk
- 30 grams cream cheese, softened
- Sea salt
- 1/4 teaspoon ground black pepper
- 1/4 teaspoon paprika
- 170 grams of cooked ham, diced
- 1 onion, chopped
- 1/3 cup shredded cheddar cheese

Addresses:
1. Preheat your air fryer to 180°C.
2. Spray the sides and bottom of a baking sheet with cooking oil.
3. In a mixing bowl, beat the eggs, milk and cream cheese until pale.
4. Add the spices, ham and onion, stir until everything is well incorporated.
5. Pour the mixture into the baking dish, top with the cheddar cheese.
6. Bake in the preheated Air Fryer for 12 minutes. Serve hot and enjoy.

915. Potato and kale croquettes

Servings: 6
Cooking time: 9 minutes
Ingredients:
- 4 eggs, lightly beaten
- 1/3 cup flour
- 1/3 cup crumbled goat cheese
- 1 ½ teaspoons fine sea salt
- 4 cloves garlic, minced
- 1 cup steamed kale
- 1/3 cup breadcrumbs
- 1/3 teaspoon red pepper flakes
- 3 potatoes, peeled and cut into quarters
- 1/3 teaspoon of dried dill weed

Addresses:
1. First, boil the potatoes in salted water.
2. Once the potatoes are cooked, mash them, add the kale, goat's cheese, minced garlic, sea salt, red pepper flakes, dill and an egg, stir to combine well.
3. Now roll the mixture into small croquettes.
4. Take three shallow bowls. Put the flour in the first shallow bowl.

5. Beat the remaining 3 eggs in the second bowl. Then pour the breadcrumbs into the third shallow bowl.
6. Dredge each croquette in the flour, then dredge in the bowl of eggs, and finally dredge each croquette in the breadcrumbs.
7. Air fry at 170°C for 7 minutes or until golden brown. Then add seasoning and serve hot.

916. Fluffy omelette with beef leftovers

Servings: 4
Cooking time: 20 minutes
Ingredients:
- Non-stick cooking spray
- 225 grams of leftover beef, coarsely minced
- 2 cloves garlic, pressed
- 1 cup kale, chopped and wilted
- 1 pepper, chopped
- 6 beaten eggs
- 6 tablespoons sour cream
- 1/2 teaspoon turmeric powder
- 1 teaspoon red pepper flakes
- Salt and ground black pepper

Addresses:
1. Spray the inside of four ramekins with cooking spray.
2. Divide all the above ingredients between the prepared moulds. Stir until everything is well combined.
3. Air fry for 16 minutes, check with a wooden toothpick and return the eggs to the air fryer for a few more minutes if necessary. Serve immediately.

917. Fruit skewers with a Greek twist

Servings: 2
Cooking time: 10 minutes
Ingredients:
- 6 strawberries cut in half
- 1 banana, peeled and sliced
- 1/4 pineapple, peeled and diced
- 1 teaspoon fresh lemon juice
- 1/4 cup Greek yogurt
- 2 tablespoons honey
- 1 teaspoon vanilla

Addresses:
1. Mix the fruit with the lemon juice in a bowl. Thread the fruit pieces on skewers.
2. Bake at 170°C for 5 minutes.
3. Meanwhile, whisk the Greek yoghurt with the honey and vanilla. Serve the fruit skewers with the Greek sauce on the side - bon appetit!

918. Cajun Turkey Meatloaf

Servings: 6
Cooking time: 45 minutes
Ingredients:
- 600 grams of ground turkey breasts
- ½ cup vegetable stock
- 2 eggs, lightly beaten
- 1/2 sprig thyme, chopped
- 1/2 teaspoon Cajun seasoning
- 1/2 sprig chopped coriander
- ½ cup seasoned breadcrumbs
- 2 tablespoons butter at room temperature
- 1/2 cup chopped onions
- 1/3 teaspoon ground nutmeg
- 1/3 cup tomato ketchup
- 1/2 teaspoon table salt
- 2 teaspoons whole grain mustard
- 1/3 teaspoon mixed peppercorns, freshly ground

Addresses:
1. First, heat the butter in a medium saucepan over medium heat, sauté the spring onions together with the chopped thyme and coriander leaves until tender.
2. While the spring onions are sautéing, set your air fryer to cook at 185°C.
3. Combine all ingredients except the ketchup in a mixing bowl, add the sautéed mixture and mix again.
4. Form into a meatloaf and cover with the tomato sauce. Fry in the open air for at least 45 minutes - bon appetit!

919. Spring chocolate doughnuts

Servings: 6
Cooking time: 20 minutes
Ingredients:
- 1 tin of buttermilk biscuits

For the chocolate glaze you will need:
- 1 cup icing sugar
- 4 tablespoons unsweetened cocoa for baking
- 2 tablespoons melted butter
- 2 tablespoons milk

Addresses:
1. Bake your biscuits in the preheated air fryer at 180°C for 8 minutes, turning them over halfway through the baking time.
2. While the biscuits are baking, prepare the glaze.
3. Beat the ingredients with a stick blender until smooth, adding enough milk for the desired consistency, set aside.
4. Dip the doughnuts in the chocolate glaze and transfer them to a cooling rack to set. Bon appetit!

920. Double Cheese Balls with Mushrooms

Servings: 4
Cooking time: 30 minutes
Ingredients:
- 1 ½ tablespoons olive oil
- 115 grams of cauliflower florets
- 3 cloves garlic, peeled and minced
- 1/2 yellow onion, finely chopped
- 1 small red chilli, seeded and chopped

- 1/2 cup roasted vegetable stock
- 2 cups white mushrooms, finely chopped
- Sea salt and ground black pepper
- 1/2 cup grated Swiss cheese
- 1/4 cup pork rinds
- 1 beaten egg
- 1/4 cup shredded Romano cheese

Addresses:
1. Puree the cauliflower florets in your food processor until they are shredded, i.e. they look like grains of rice.
2. Heat a saucepan over moderate heat, now heat the oil and sweat the cauliflower, garlic, onion and chilli until tender.
3. Add the mushrooms and fry until fragrant and the liquid has almost evaporated.
4. Add the vegetable stock and boil for 18 minutes.
5. Now add the salt, black pepper, Swiss cheese pork rinds and beaten egg, mix to combine.
6. Allow the mixture to cool completely. Form the mixture into balls.
7. Roll the balls in the grated romano cheese and put them in the air fryer to cook at 200°C for 7 minutes. Bon appetit!

921. Crispy Wontons with Asian Sauce

Servings: 4
Cooking time: 20 minutes
Ingredients:
- 1 teaspoon sesame oil
- 350 grams of minced meat
- Sea salt
- 1/4 teaspoon Sichuan pepper
- 20 wonton wrappers

For the dipping sauce you need:
- 2 tablespoons low sodium soy sauce
- 1 tablespoon of honey
- 1 teaspoon Gochujang
- 1 teaspoon rice wine vinegar
- 1/2 teaspoon sesame oil

Addresses:
1. Heat a teaspoon of sesame oil in a wok over medium-high heat. Cook the minced beef until no longer pink. Season with salt and Sichuan pepper.
2. Place a piece of the wonton wrapper in the palm of your hand, add the meat mixture to the centre of the wrapper. Then fold it over to form a triangle, pinch the edges to seal it well.
3. Place the wontons in the lightly greased fryer basket. Cook for 10 minutes in the Air Fryer preheated to 180°C. Work in batches.
4. Meanwhile, mix all the ingredients for the sauce. Serve hot.

922. Bagel 'n' Egg Melts

Servings: 3
Cooking time: 25 minutes
Ingredients:
- 3 eggs
- 3 slices of chopped smoked ham
- 1 teaspoon Dijon mustard
- 1/4 cup mayonnaise
- Salt and white pepper
- 3 buns
- 85 grams Colby cheese, grated

Addresses:
1. Place the rack in the basket of the Air Fryer, lower the eggs onto the rack.
2. Bake at 180°C for 15 minutes.
3. Place them in an ice water bath to stop the cooking process. Peel the eggs under cold running water, chop coarsely and set aside.
4. Combine the chopped eggs, ham, mustard, mayonnaise, salt and pepper in a bowl.
5. Cut the rolls in half. Spread the egg mixture on top and sprinkle with the grated cheese.
6. Grill for 7 minutes in the Air Fryer preheated to 190°C or until the cheese is melted, enjoy!

923. Homemade pork scratchings

Portions: 10
Cooking time: 50 minutes
Ingredients:
- 450 grams of raw pork rind, butcher's marked
- 1 tablespoon sea salt
- 2 tablespoons of smoked paprika

Addresses:
1. Sprinkle and rub salt on the skin side of the pork rind. Leave to stand for 30 minutes.
2. Roast them at 190°C for 8 minutes, turn them over and cook them for another 8 minutes or until they open.
3. Sprinkle the smoked paprika on top of the cracklings and serve, enjoy!

924. Breakfast eggs with chard and ham

Servings: 2
Cooking time: 20 minutes
Ingredients:
- 2 eggs
- 1/4 teaspoon dried or fresh marjoram
- 2 teaspoons chilli powder
- 1/3 teaspoon kosher salt
- 1/2 cup steamed chard
- 1/4 teaspoon dried or fresh rosemary
- 4 slices of pork ham
- 1/3 teaspoon ground black pepper

Addresses:
1. Divide the chard and ham into 2 moulds and place an egg in each. Sprinkle with the seasoning.

2. Cook for 15 minutes at 170°C or until the eggs reach the desired texture.
3. Serve hot with spicy tomato ketchup and pickles, enjoy!

925. Filipino minced meat omelette (tortang Giniling)

Servings: 3
Cooking time: 20 minutes
Ingredients:
- 1 teaspoon lard
- 300 grams of minced meat
- 1/4 teaspoon chilli powder
- 1/2 teaspoon ground bay leaf
- 1/2 teaspoon ground pepper
- Sea salt
- 1 green pepper, seeded and chopped
- 1 red pepper, seeded and minced
- 6 eggs
- 1/3 cup double cream
- 1/2 cup Colby cheese, grated
- 1 tomato, sliced

Addresses:
1. Melt the butter in a cast iron skillet over medium-high heat.
2. Add the minced meat and cook for 4 minutes until it is no longer pink, breaking it up with a spatula.
3. Add the minced meat mixture together with the spices to the baking tray. Now add the peppers.
4. In a bowl, beat the eggs with the cream. Pour the mixture over the meat and peppers in the pan.
5. Cook for 10 minutes in the preheated air fryer at 180°C.
6. Top with the cheese and tomato slices. Continue cooking for a few more minutes or until the eggs are golden brown and the cheese has melted.

926. Baked Denver omelette with sausages

Portions: 5
Cooking time: 14 minutes
Ingredients:
- 3 minced pork sausages
- 8 eggs, well beaten
- 1 ½ peppers, seeded and chopped
- 1 teaspoon smoked cayenne pepper
- 2 tablespoons Fontina cheese
- 1/2 teaspoon tarragon
- 1/2 teaspoon ground black pepper
- 1 teaspoon salt

Addresses:
1. In a cast-iron frying pan, sweat the peppers together with the chopped pork sausages until the peppers are fragrant and the sausage begins to release liquid.
2. Lightly grease the inside of a baking dish with cooking spray.
3. Pour all of the above ingredients into the prepared baking dish, including the sautéed mixture, stir to combine.
4. Bake for approximately 9 minutes at 190°C. Serve immediately with the salad of your choice.

927. Cauliflower and Manchego Croquettes

Servings: 4
Cooking time: 15 minutes
Ingredients:
- 1 cup grated manchego cheese
- 1 teaspoon paprika
- 1 teaspoon freshly ground black pepper
- 1/2 tablespoon fine sea salt
- 1/2 cup spring onions, finely chopped
- 450 grams of cauliflower florets
- 2 tablespoons canola oil
- 2 teaspoons basil, dried

Addresses:
1. Grind the cauliflower florets in a food processor until finely chopped.
2. Next, combine the broccoli with the rest of the above ingredients.
3. Form the balls with your hands. Now flatten the balls to make patties.
4. Then cook your burgers for about 10 minutes, enjoy!

928. Keto Rolls with Halibut and Eggs

Servings: 4
Cooking time: 25 minutes
Ingredients:
- 4 keto rolls
- 450 grams of smoked halibut, minced
- 4 eggs
- 1 teaspoon dried thyme
- 1 teaspoon basil, dried
- Salt and black pepper

Addresses:
1. Cut off the top of each keto roll, then remove the inside to make the shells.
2. Place the prepared keto roll shells in the lightly greased cooking basket.
3. Drizzle with cooking oil, add the halibut. Crack an egg into each keto roll shell, sprinkle with thyme, basil, salt and black pepper.
4. Bake in the preheated Air Fryer at 160°C for 20 minutes, enjoy!

929. Apple crisps country style

Servings: 4
Cooking time: 20 minutes
Ingredients:
- 1/2 cup milk
- 1 egg
- 1/2 all-purpose flour
- 1 teaspoon baking powder
- 4 tablespoons brown sugar
- 1 teaspoon vanilla extract

- 1/2 teaspoon ground cloves
- A pinch of kosher salt
- A pinch of grated nutmeg
- 1 tbsp melted coconut oil
- 2 Pink Lady apples, cored, peeled, cut into chunks (conforms to and the size of crisps)
- 1/3 cup granulated sugar
- 1 teaspoon ground cinnamon

Addresses:
1. In a bowl, whisk together the milk and eggs, gradually add the flour, add the baking powder, brown sugar, vanilla, cloves, salt, nutmeg and melted coconut oil. Mix to combine well.
2. Dip each apple slice into the batter, covering all sides. Spray the bottom of the cooking basket with cooking oil.
3. Cook the apple crisps in the preheated Air Fryer at 190°C for approximately 8 minutes, turning them over halfway through cooking.
4. Cook in small batches to ensure even cooking.
5. Meanwhile, mix the granulated sugar with the ground cinnamon, sprinkle the cinnamon sugar over the fried apples. Serve hot.

930. Creamy Italian Frittata with Kale

Servings: 3
Cooking time: 20 minutes
Ingredients:
- 1 yellow onion, finely chopped
- 170 grams of wild mushrooms, cut into slices
- 6 eggs
- 1/4 cup double cream
- 1/2 teaspoon cayenne pepper
- Sea salt and ground black pepper
- 1 tablespoon melted butter
- 2 tbsp. chopped fresh Italian parsley
- 2 cups chopped kale
- 1/2 cup shredded mozzarella cheese

Addresses:
1. Start by preheating the fryer to 180°C.
2. Spray the sides and bottom of a baking sheet with cooking oil.
3. Add the onions and wild mushrooms, and cook in the preheated air fryer at 180°C for 4 to 5 minutes.
4. In a mixing bowl, beat the eggs and double cream until pale. Add the spices, butter, parsley and kale, stir until well incorporated.
5. Pour the mixture into the mould with the mushrooms.
6. Top with the cheese. Cook in the preheated Air Fryer for 10 minutes. Serve immediately and enjoy.

931. Mini sweet monkey rolls

Servings: 6
Cooking time: 25 minutes
Ingredients:
- 3/4 cup brown sugar
- 1 stick of melted butter
- 1/4 cup granulated sugar
- 1 teaspoon ground cinnamon
- 1/4 teaspoon ground cardamom
- 1 can (450 grams) refrigerated buttermilk biscuit dough

Addresses:
1. Spray 6 standard-size muffin tins with non-stick spray.
2. Mix the brown sugar and butter together, spread the mixture into the muffin tins.
3. Combine the granulated sugar with the cinnamon and cardamom.
4. Separate the dough into 16 biscuits, cut each into 6 pieces.
5. Dredge the pieces in the cinnamon-sugar mixture to coat them. Divide between the muffin tins.
6. Bake at 180°C for about 20 minutes or until golden brown.

932. Chicken avocado sliders dinner

Servings: 4
Cooking time: 10 minutes
Ingredients:
- 225 grams of ground chicken meat
- 4 hamburger buns
- ½ cup romaine lettuce, loosely packed
- ½ teaspoon dried parsley flakes
- ⅓ teaspoon of mustard seeds
- 1 teaspoon onion powder
- 1 fresh ripe avocado, smashed
- 1 teaspoon garlic powder
- 1 ½ tablespoons extra virgin olive oil
- 1 clove garlic, minced
- Non-stick cooking spray
- Salt and black peppercorns

Addresses:
1. First, spray the air fryer basket with non-stick cooking spray.
2. Mix the ground chicken meat, mustard seeds, garlic powder, onion powder, parsley, salt and black pepper until well combined. Be sure not to overwork the meat to avoid tough chicken patties.
3. Form patties from the meat mixture and dredge in breadcrumbs, place patties in the prepared cooking basket. Coat patties with cooking spray.
4. Air fry at 180°C for 9 minutes, working in batches. Cut the hamburger buns into halves.
5. Meanwhile, combine the olive oil with the mashed avocado and pressed garlic.
6. To finish, place the romaine lettuce and avocado spread on the bun bottoms, now

add the burgers and bun tops - bon appetit!

933. Easy broccoli with cheese

Servings: 4
Cooking time: 25 minutes
Ingredients:
- 1/3 cup yellow cheese, grated
- 1 large head of broccoli, stalk removed, cut into small florets
- 2 ½ tablespoons canola oil
- 2 teaspoons dried rosemary
- 2 teaspoons basil, dried
- Salt and ground black pepper

Addresses:
1. Bring a medium saucepan of lightly salted water to the boil. Then boil the broccoli florets for about 3 minutes.
2. Drain the broccoli florets well, mix with the canola oil, rosemary, basil, salt and black pepper.
3. Set your air fryer to 180°C, place the seasoned broccoli in the cooking basket, set the timer for 17 minutes. Stir the broccoli halfway through the cooking process.
4. Serve hot with grated cheese and enjoy.

934. Famous Bacon Cheese Rolls

Servings: 6
Cooking time: 10 minutes
Ingredients:
- 1/3 cup grated Swiss cheese
- 10 slices of bacon
- 280 grams of canned crescent rolls
- 2 tablespoons yellow mustard 6

Addresses:
1. Preheat your air fryer to 160°C.
2. Then form the crescent rolls into "leaves". Spread the sheets with mustard. Place the chopped Swiss cheese and bacon in the centre of each sheet of dough.
3. Create the rolls and bake them for about 9 minutes.
4. Then set the machine to 195°C, bake for a few more minutes in the preheated air fryer. Eat hot with a little extra yellow mustard.

935. Celery and bacon cakes

Servings: 4
Cooking time: 25 minutes
Ingredients:
- 2 eggs, lightly beaten
- 1/3 teaspoon freshly ground black pepper
- 1 cup grated Colby cheese
- 1/2 tbsp. fresh dill, finely chopped
- 1/2 tablespoon garlic paste
- 1/3 cup finely chopped onion
- 1/3 cup chopped bacon
- 2 teaspoons fine sea salt
- 2 medium celery stalks, chopped and grated
- 1/3 teaspoon baking powder

Addresses:
1. Place the celery on a paper towel and squeeze to remove excess liquid.
2. Combine the vegetables with the other ingredients in the order given. Form into balls using 1 tablespoon of the vegetable mixture.
3. Then gently flatten each ball with the palm of your hand or a wide spatula. Spray the croquettes with non-stick cooking oil.
4. Bake the vegetable cakes in a single layer for 17 minutes at 160°C. Serve hot with sour cream.

936. The best sweet potato crisps

Servings: 4
Cooking time: 20 minutes
Ingredients:
- 1 ½ tablespoons olive oil
- ½ teaspoon smoked cayenne pepper
- 3 sweet potatoes, peeled and cut into slices approximately 6 millimetres in length
- ½ teaspoon shallot powder
- ⅓ teaspoon of freshly ground black pepper
- ¾ teaspoon garlic salt

Addresses:
1. First of all, preheat your air fryer to 180°C.
2. The sweet potatoes are then added to a mixing bowl and mixed with the other ingredients.
3. Cook the sweet potatoes for approximately 14 minutes. Serve with a dipping sauce of your choice.

937. Stuffed Chicken with Double Cheese

Servings: 6
Cooking time: 30 minutes
Ingredients:
- 2 eggs, well beaten
- 1 cup grated Parmesan cheese
- 1 ½ tablespoons of extra virgin olive oil
- 1 ½ tablespoons fresh chives, chopped
- 3 chicken breasts, cut in half, lengthwise
- 1 ½ cup mozzarella cheese
- 2 teaspoons sweet paprika
- 1/2 teaspoon whole grain mustard
- 1/2 teaspoon cumin powder
- 1/3 teaspoon fine sea salt
- 1/3 cup chopped fresh cilantro
- 1/3 teaspoon freshly ground black pepper, or more to taste

Addresses:
1. Flatten each piece of chicken breast with a rolling pin. Then find three mixing bowls.
2. On the first plate, combine the mozzarella cheese with the coriander, fresh chives, cumin and mustard.

3. In the second, beat the eggs with the sweet paprika. In the third dish, combine the salt, black pepper and Parmesan cheese.
4. Spread the cheese mixture over each piece of chicken. Repeat with the remaining chicken breast pieces, now roll them up.
5. Coat each chicken roll with the beaten egg, dip each chicken roll in the Parmesan mixture.
6. Lower the rolls into the cooking basket of the Air Fryer. Drizzle the rolls with extra virgin olive oil.
7. Fry in the open air at 175°C for 28 minutes, working in batches. Serve hot, garnished with sour cream if desired.

938. Chicken with super-easy tomato sauce

Servings: 4
Cooking time: 20 minutes + marinating time
Ingredients:
- 1 tablespoon balsamic vinegar
- ½ teaspoon crushed red pepper flakes
- 1 fresh garlic, coarsely chopped
- 2 ½ large sized chicken breasts, cut into halves
- 1/3 handful of fresh coriander, coarsely chopped
- 2 tablespoons olive oil
- 4 roma tomatoes, diced
- 1 ½ tablespoons butter
- 1/3 handful fresh basil, loosely packed, chopped
- 1 teaspoon kosher salt
- 2 cloves garlic, minced
- Bucatini, cooked, to serve

Addresses:
1. Place the first seven ingredients in a medium bowl, marinate for a couple of hours.
2. Preheat the air fryer to 180°C.
3. Air fry the chicken for 32 minutes and serve hot.
4. Meanwhile, prepare the tomato sauce by preheating a deep saucepan. Simmer the tomatoes until the mixture is chunky. Add the garlic, basil and butter, stir well.
5. Serve the cooked chicken breasts with the tomato sauce and the cooked bucatini, enjoy!

939. Quinoa with baked eggs and bacon

Servings: 4
Cooking time: 40 minutes
Ingredients:
- 1/2 cup quinoa
- 1/2 lb. potatoes, diced
- 1 onion, diced
- 6 slices of pre-cooked bacon
- 1 tablespoon melted butter
- Sea salt and ground black pepper
- 6 eggs

Addresses:
1. Rinse the quinoa under cold running water. Place the rinsed quinoa in a saucepan and add one cup of water.
2. Bring to the boil. Lower the heat and simmer for 13-15 minutes or until tender, set aside.
3. Dice the potatoes and onion in a lightly greased casserole dish. Add the bacon and the reserved quinoa. Drizzle the melted butter over the quinoa and sprinkle with salt and pepper.
4. Bake in the preheated Air Fryer at 200°C for 10 minutes.
5. Lower the temperature to 180°C.
6. Make six holes for the eggs, put one egg in each hole. Bake for 12 minutes, turning the pan once or twice to ensure even baking, bon appetit!

940. Salted pretzel croissants

Servings: 4
Cooking time: 20 minutes
Ingredients:
- 1 can crescent rolls
- 10 cups of water
- 1/2 cup bicarbonate of soda
- 1 egg beaten with 1 tablespoon of water
- 1 tablespoon poppy seeds
- 2 tablespoons sesame seeds
- 1 teaspoon coarse sea salt

Addresses:
1. Roll out the dough on the work surface and separate into 8 triangles.
2. In a large saucepan, bring the water and baking soda to a boil over high heat.
3. Cook each roll for a few seconds. Remove from the water with a skimmer, place on a kitchen towel to drain.
4. Repeat with the rest of the rolls. Now brush the top with the egg wash, sprinkle each roll with the poppy seeds, sesame seeds and coarse sea salt. Cover and leave to rest for 10 minutes.
5. Place the pretzels in the lightly greased fryer basket.
6. Bake in the Air Fryer preheated to 170°C. Bake for 7 minutes or until golden brown - bon appetit!

941. Toast with blueberries and honey

Servings: 6
Cooking time: 20 minutes
Ingredients:
- 1/4 cup milk
- 2 eggs
- 2 tablespoons melted butter
- 1/2 teaspoon ground cinnamon
- 1/4 teaspoon ground cloves
- 1 teaspoon vanilla extract
- 6 slices of day-old French baguette

- 2 tablespoons honey
- 1/2 cup blueberries

Addresses:
1. In a bowl, beat eggs with milk, butter, cinnamon, cloves and vanilla extract.
2. Dip each piece of baguette into the egg mixture and place in the parchment-lined air fryer basket.
3. Cook in the preheated air fryer at 200°C for 6 to 7 minutes, turning them halfway through the cooking time to ensure even cooking.
4. Serve garnished with honey and cranberries - enjoy!

942. Winter Baked Eggs with Italian Sausage

Servings: 4
Cooking time: 30 minutes
Ingredients:
- 450 grams of Italian sausage
- 2 sprigs of rosemary
- 1 celery, sliced
- 225 grams broccoli, cut into small florets
- 2 sprigs of thyme
- 1 pepper, trimmed and cut into small sticks
- 2 cloves garlic, crushed
- 2 tablespoons of extra virgin olive oil
- 1 leek, cut in halves lengthways
- A pinch of grated nutmeg
- Salt and black pepper
- 4 whole eggs

Addresses:
1. Place the vegetables on the bottom of the Air Fryer baking tray.
2. Sprinkle with seasoning and top with sausage.
3. Roast approximately 20 minutes at 180°C, stirring occasionally. Cover with the eggs and reduce the temperature to 165°C.
4. Bake for 5 to 6 minutes more, bon appetit!

943. Spicy Cheese Risotto Balls

Servings: 4
Cooking time: 26 minutes
Ingredients:
- 85 grams of cooked rice
- 1/2 cup roasted vegetable broth
- 1 beaten egg
- 1 cup white mushrooms, finely chopped
- 1/2 cup seasoned breadcrumbs
- 3 cloves garlic, peeled and minced
- 1/2 yellow onion, finely chopped
- 1/3 teaspoon ground black pepper, or more to taste
- 1 ½ chopped seeded peppers
- 1/2 chipotle chilli, seeded and chopped
- 1/2 tbsp grated Colby cheese
- 1 ½ tablespoons canola oil
- Sea salt, to taste

Addresses:
1. Heat a saucepan over medium heat, now heat the oil and sweat the garlic, onion, pepper and chipotle chilli until tender.
2. Stir in the mushrooms and fry until fragrant and the liquid has almost evaporated.
3. Add the cooked rice and stock, boil for 18 minutes. Now add the cheese and spices, stir to combine.
4. Allow the mixture to cool completely. Form the risotto mixture into balls. Roll the risotto balls in the beaten egg, then roll them in the breadcrumbs.
5. Fry the risotto balls for 6 minutes at 200°C. Serve with marinara sauce and enjoy!

944. Za'atar Eggs with Chicken and Provolone Cheese

Servings: 2
Cooking time: 20 minutes
Ingredients:
- ⅓ cup of milk
- 1 ½ chopped roma tomatoes
- ⅓ cup grated Provolone cheese
- 1 teaspoon freshly ground pink peppercorns
- 3 eggs
- 1 teaspoon Za'atar
- ½ cooked chicken breast
- 1 teaspoon fine sea salt
- 1 teaspoon freshly ground pink peppercorns

Addresses:
1. Preheat your deep fryer to 185°C. In a medium bowl, whisk the eggs together with the milk, Za'atar, sea salt and pink peppercorns.
2. Spray the ramekins with cooking oil, spread the prepared egg mixture between the greased ramekins.
3. Shred the chicken with two forks or a blender. Add the shredded chicken to the ramekins, followed by the tomato and cheese.
4. To finish, air fry for 18 minutes or until done - bon appetit!

945. Cajun creamed chicken

Servings: 6
Cooking time: 10 minutes
Ingredients:
- 3 green onions, thinly sliced
- ½ tablespoon Cajun seasoning
- 1 ½ cup buttermilk
- 2 large sized chicken breasts, cut into strips
- 1/2 teaspoon garlic powder
- 1 teaspoon salt
- 1 cup corn flour mix
- 1 teaspoon shallot powder

- 1 ½ cup flour
- 1 teaspoon ground black pepper, or to taste

Addresses:
1. Prepare three mixing bowls. In one bowl, combine 2 cups of the plain flour along with the cornmeal and Cajun seasoning. In another bowl, place the buttermilk. Finally, pour the remaining 1 cup of flour into the third bowl.
2. Sprinkle the chicken strips with all the seasonings. Next, dip each chicken strip in the 1 cup flour, then in the buttermilk, then dredge in the cornmeal mixture.
3. Cook the chicken strips in the frying pan of the air fryer for 16 minutes at 185°C.
4. Serve garnished with green onions - bon appetit!

946. Scrambled Eggs with Sausage

Servings: 6
Cooking time: 25 minutes
Ingredients:
- 1 teaspoon lard
- 225 grams of turkey sausage
- 6 eggs
- 1 chopped spring onion
- 1 clove garlic, minced
- 1 sweet pepper, seeded and minced
- 1 chilli, seeded and chopped
- Sea salt and ground black pepper, to taste
- 1/2 cup grated Swiss cheese

Addresses:
1. Start by preheating your Air Fryer to 165°C.
2. Spray 6 silicone moulds with cooking spray.
3. Melt the lard in a saucepan over medium-high heat. Now cook the sausage for 5 minutes or until no longer pink.
4. Chop the sausage, add the eggs, spring onions, garlic, peppers, salt and black pepper. Divide the egg mixture between the silicone moulds. Top with the grated cheese.
5. Bake in the preheated air fryer at 180°C for 15 minutes, checking halfway through the cooking time to ensure even cooking. Enjoy.

947. Pea fritters with yoghurt and parsley sauce

Servings: 4
Cooking time: 20 minutes
Ingredients:
For the pea fritters you will need:
- 1 ½ cups frozen green peas
- 1 tablespoon sesame oil
- 1/2 cup chopped onions
- 2 cloves garlic, minced
- 1 cup chickpea flour
- 1 teaspoon baking powder
- 1/2 teaspoon sea salt
- 1/2 teaspoon ground black pepper
- 1/4 teaspoon of dried dill
- 1/2 teaspoon dried basil

For the yoghurt dip with parsley you will need:
- 1/2 cup Greek yoghurt
- 2 tablespoons mayonnaise
- 2 tablespoons fresh parsley, chopped
- 1 tablespoon fresh lemon juice
- 1/2 teaspoon crushed garlic

Addresses:
1. Place thawed green peas in a mixing bowl, pour in hot water. Drain and rinse well.
2. Mash the green peas, add the rest of the ingredients for the pea fritters and mix well.
3. Form the mixture into patties and transfer to the lightly greased cooking basket.
4. Bake at 180°C for 14 minutes or until heated through.
5. Meanwhile, prepare the dipping sauce by whisking together the rest of the ingredients. Place in your refrigerator until ready to serve.
6. Serve the pea fritters with the cold sauce on the side. Enjoy.

948. Spicy paprika chicken

Servings: 4
Cooking time: 30 minutes
Ingredients:
- 1 ½ tablespoons freshly squeezed lemon juice
- 2 small boneless chicken breasts, boneless
- 1/2 teaspoon ground cumin
- 1 teaspoon mustard powder
- 1 teaspoon paprika
- 2 teaspoons cup pear cider vinegar
- 1 tablespoon of olive oil
- 2 cloves garlic, minced
- Kosher salt and freshly ground peppercorns

Addresses:
1. Heat the olive oil in a non-stick frying pan over moderate heat. Sauté the garlic for a few minutes.
2. Remove the pan from the heat, add the cider vinegar, lemon juice, paprika, cumin, mustard powder, kosher salt and black pepper. Pour the paprika sauce into a baking dish.
3. Pat the chicken breasts dry and transfer them to the prepared sauce. Bake in the preheated air fryer for about 28 minutes at 180°C, check for doneness with a thermometer or fork.
4. Let stand for 8 to 9 minutes before slicing and serving. Serve with dressing.

949. Sweetcorn and grain fritters

Servings: 4

Cooking time: 20 minutes
Ingredients:
- 1 medium carrot, grated
- 1 yellow onion, finely chopped
- 115 grams canned sweetcorn kernels, drained
- 1 teaspoon flaked sea salt
- 1 heaped tablespoon of chopped fresh coriander
- 1 medium egg, beaten
- 2 tablespoons of regular milk
- 1 cup grated parmesan cheese
- 1/4 cup self-raising flour
- 1/3 teaspoon baking powder
- 1/3 teaspoon brown sugar

Addresses:
1. Press the grated carrot in the colander to remove excess liquid. Then spread the grated carrot between several sheets of kitchen paper and pat dry.
2. Then mix the carrots with the rest of the ingredients in the order given.
3. Roll a tablespoon of the mixture into a ball and gently flatten it with the back of a spoon or your hand. Now repeat with the rest of the ingredients.
4. Spray the balls with non-stick cooking oil.
5. Bake in a single layer at 180°C for 8 to 11 minutes or until firm to the touch in the centre. Serve hot and enjoy.

950. Spicy Eggs with Sausage and Swiss Cheese

Servings: 6
Cooking time: 25 minutes
Ingredients:
- 1 teaspoon lard
- 225 grams of turkey sausage
- 6 eggs
- 1 chopped spring onion
- 1 clove garlic, minced
- 1 pepper, seeded and chopped
- 1 chilli, seeded and chopped
- Sea salt and ground black pepper
- 1/2 cup grated Swiss cheese

Addresses:
1. Start by preheating your Air Fryer to 165°C. Now, spray 4 silicone moulds with cooking spray.
2. Melt the lard in a saucepan over medium-high heat. Now cook the sausage for 5 minutes or until no longer pink.
3. Chop the sausage, add the eggs, spring onions, garlic, peppers, salt and black pepper. Divide the egg mixture between the silicone moulds. Top with the grated cheese.
4. Bake in the preheated air fryer for 15 minutes, checking halfway through the cooking time to ensure even cooking. Enjoy.

951. Decadent Frittata with roasted garlic and sausage

Servings: 6
Cooking time: 20 minutes
Ingredients:
- 6 large eggs
- 2 tablespoons melted butter
- 3 tablespoons cream
- 1 cup chopped chicken sausage
- 2 tablespoons roasted, pressed garlic
- 1/3 cup goat cheese, such as Caprino, shredded
- 1 teaspoon smoked cayenne pepper
- 1 teaspoon freshly ground black pepper
- 1/2 red onion, peeled and chopped
- 1 teaspoon fine sea salt

Addresses:
1. First, grease six baking tins with melted butter. Next, divide the roasted garlic and red onion among the ramekins. Add the chicken sausage and stir to combine.
2. Beat the eggs with the cream until well combined and pale, sprinkle with cayenne pepper, salt and black pepper, beat again.
3. Spoon the mixture into the moulds and fry for 1 minute at 180°C.
4. Top with shredded cheese and serve immediately.

952. Deviled eggs for farmer's breakfast

Servings: 3
Cooking time: 25 minutes
Ingredients:
- 6 eggs
- 6 slices of bacon
- 2 tablespoons mayonnaise
- 1 teaspoon hot sauce
- 1/2 teaspoon Worcestershire sauce
- 2 tablespoons chopped green onions
- 1 tablespoon pickle relish
- Salt and ground black pepper
- 1 teaspoon smoked paprika

Addresses:
1. Place the rack in the basket of the Air Fryer, lower the eggs onto the rack.
2. Cook at 190°C for 15 minutes.
3. When ready, transfer the eggs to a bowl of ice water to stop the cooking process. Then peel the eggs under cold running water and cut them into halves.
4. Cook the bacon at 200°C for 3 minutes, turn the bacon over and cook for another 3 minutes, chop the bacon and set aside.
5. Mash the egg yolks with the mayonnaise, hot sauce, Worcestershire sauce, green onions, pickle relish, salt and black pepper, add the reserved bacon and spoon the egg yolk mixture into the egg whites.
6. Garnish with smoked paprika and enjoy!

953. Vegetable casserole with ham and baked eggs

Servings: 4
Cooking time: 30 minutes
Ingredients:
- 2 tablespoons melted butter
- 1 courgette, diced
- 1 pepper, seeded and cut into slices
- 1 red chilli, seeded and minced
- 1 medium-sized leek, cut into slices
- 350 grams of cooked and diced ham
- 5 eggs
- 1 teaspoon cayenne pepper
- Sea salt
- 1/2 teaspoon ground black pepper
- 1 tablespoon chopped fresh coriander

Addresses:
1. Start by preheating the fryer to 190°C.
2. Grease the sides and bottom of a baking dish with the melted butter.
3. Place the courgette, peppers, leeks and ham on the baking tray. Bake in the preheated Air Fryer for 6 minutes.
4. Crack the eggs over the ham and vegetables, season with the cayenne pepper, salt and black pepper. Bake for a further 20 minutes or until the egg whites are completely set.
5. Garnish with fresh coriander and serve - bon appetit!

954. Baked eggs with cheese and cowrie rice

Servings: 4
Cooking time: 30 minutes
Ingredients:
- 450 grams of cauliflower rice
- 1 onion, diced
- 6 slices of pre-cooked bacon
- 1 tablespoon melted butter
- Sea salt and ground black pepper
- 6 eggs
- 1 cup shredded cheddar cheese

Addresses:
1. Place the cauliflower rice and onion in a lightly greased casserole dish. Add the bacon and the reserved quinoa.
2. Drizzle the melted butter over the cauliflower rice and sprinkle with salt and pepper.
3. Bake in the preheated Air Fryer at 200°C for 10 minutes.
4. Lower the temperature to 180°C.
5. Make six holes for the eggs, putting one egg in each hole. Bake for 10 minutes, turning the pan once or twice to ensure even cooking.
6. Cover with cheese and bake for another few minutes. Enjoy.

955. Baked Eggs Florentine style

Servings: 2
Cooking time: 20 minutes
Ingredients:
- 1 tablespoon melted ghee
- 2 cups baby spinach, chopped into small pieces
- 2 tablespoons chopped shallots
- 1/4 teaspoon red pepper flakes
- Salt
- 1 tablespoon fresh thyme leaves, coarsely chopped
- 4 eggs

Addresses:
1. Start by preheating your fryer to 180°C.
2. Brush the sides and bottom of a gratin dish with the melted ghee.
3. Place the spinach and shallots in the bottom of the gratin dish. Season with red pepper, salt and fresh thyme.
4. Make four holes for the eggs, place one egg in each hole. Bake for 12 minutes, turning the pan once or twice to ensure even cooking. Enjoy.

956. Baked Eggs with Linguica Sausage

Servings: 2
Cooking time: 18 minutes
Ingredients:
- 1/2 cup shredded Cheddar cheese
- 4 eggs
- 55 grams of Linguica (Portuguese pork sausage), minced
- 1/2 onion, peeled and chopped
- 2 tablespoons olive oil
- 1/2 teaspoon chopped rosemary
- ½ teaspoon marjoram
- 1/4 cup sour cream
- Sea salt and freshly ground black pepper
- ½ teaspoon chopped fresh sage

Addresses:
1. Lightly grease 2 baking tins with olive oil. Now, divide the sausage and onions between these ramekins.
2. Place one egg in each casserole dish and add the rest of the elements, except the cheese.
3. Air fry at 180°C for approximately 13 minutes.
4. Top immediately with Cheddar cheese, serve and enjoy.

957. Masala Baked Eggs

Servings: 6
Cooking time: 25 minutes
Ingredients:
- 6 medium eggs, beaten
- 1 teaspoon garam masala
- 1 cup spring onions, finely chopped
- 3 cloves garlic, finely chopped
- 2 cups of shredded chicken scraps
- 2 tablespoons sesame oil
- Hot sauce (for drizzling)
- 1 teaspoon turmeric

- 1 teaspoon of mixed peppercorns, freshly ground
- 1 teaspoon kosher salt
- 1/3 teaspoon smoked paprika

Addresses:
1. Heat the sesame oil in a frying pan over medium heat, then sauté the spring onions and garlic until fragrant, about 5 minutes.
2. Now pour in the leftover chicken and stir until heated through.
3. In a medium bowl or measuring cup, thoroughly combine the eggs with all the seasonings.
4. Next, coat the inside of six ovenproof baking pans with non-stick cooking spray. Spread the chicken and egg mixture into the ramekins.
5. Fry in the open air for approximately 18 minutes at 180°C. Drizzle with hot sauce and eat hot.

958. Country style pork pie

Servings: 4
Cooking time: 25 minutes
Ingredients:
- 225 grams of lean pork, minced
- 1/3 cup breadcrumbs
- 1/2 tablespoon chopped green garlic
- 1½ tablespoons fresh coriander, chopped
- 1/2 tablespoon fish sauce
- 1/3 teaspoon dried basil
- 2 leeks, chopped
- 2 tablespoons tomato puree
- 1/2 teaspoon dried thyme
- Salt and ground black pepper

Addresses:
1. Add all the ingredients, except the breadcrumbs, to a large bowl and mix everything together with your hands.
2. Finally, add the breadcrumbs to form a meatloaf.
3. Bake in the air fryer at 185°C. Then let the meatloaf rest for 10 minutes before slicing and serving - bon appetit!

959. Jamaican Cornmeal Pudding

Servings: 6
Cooking time: 1 hour + cooling time
Ingredients:
- 3 cups coconut milk
- 55 grams butter, softened
- 1 teaspoon cinnamon
- 1/2 teaspoon of grated nutmeg
- 1 cup sugar
- 1/2 teaspoon fine sea salt
- 1 ½ cups yellow maize flour
- 1/4 cup plain flour
- 1/2 cup water
- 1/2 cup sultanas
- 1 teaspoon rum extract
- 1 teaspoon vanilla extract

For the custard you need:
- 1/2 cup whole coconut milk
- 30 grams of butter
- 1/4 cup honey
- 1 dash vanilla

Addresses:
1. Place the coconut milk, butter, cinnamon, nutmeg, sugar and salt in a large saucepan, bring to a rapid boil and turn off the heat.
2. In a bowl, combine the cornflour, flour and water, stir to combine well.
3. Add the milk/butter mixture to the cornflour mixture, stir to combine. Bring the cornflour mixture to the boil, then reduce the heat and simmer for approximately 7 minutes, whisking continuously.
4. Remove from the heat. Now add the sultanas, rum extract and vanilla.
5. Place the mixture in a lightly greased baking tin and bake at 160°C for 12 minutes.
6. In a saucepan, whisk together the coconut milk, butter, honey and vanilla, simmer for 2 to 3 minutes. Now prick your pudding with a fork and cover with the prepared custard.
7. Return to your Air Fryer and bake for a further 35 minutes or until a toothpick inserted comes out dry and clean. Place in your refrigerator until ready to serve - bon appetit!

960. Egg muffins for breakfast

Servings: 4
Cooking time: 20 minutes
Ingredients:
- 1/2 cup almond flour
- 1 teaspoon baking powder
- 1 tablespoon granulated sweetener of your choice
- 4 eggs
- 1 teaspoon cinnamon powder
- 1 teaspoon vanilla paste
- 1/4 cup coconut oil
- 4 tablespoons peanut butter

Addresses:
1. Start by preheating your fryer to 165°C.
2. Now, spray the silicone muffin tins with cooking spray.
3. Combine all ingredients well in a mixing bowl. Fill muffin tins with batter.
4. Bake in the preheated Air Fryer for approximately 1 minute. Check with a toothpick, when the toothpick comes out clean, your muffins are done.
5. Place them on a wire rack to cool slightly before removing them from the muffin tins - enjoy!

961. Grilled lemon grilled pork chops

Portions: 5
Cooking time: 34 minutes
Ingredients:
- 5 pork chops
- 1/3 cup vermouth
- 1/2 teaspoon paprika
- 2 sprigs thyme, crushed leaves only
- 1/2 teaspoon dried oregano
- Fresh parsley, to serve
- 1 teaspoon garlic salt
- ½ lemon, cut into wedges
- 1 teaspoon freshly ground black pepper
- 3 tablespoons lemon juice
- 3 cloves garlic, minced
- 2 tablespoons canola oil

Addresses:
1. First, heat the canola oil in a frying pan over moderate heat. Then sauté the garlic until fragrant.
2. Remove the pan from the heat and pour in the lemon juice and vermouth. Now pour in the seasoning. Pour the sauce into a baking dish, along with the pork chops.
3. Place the lemon wedges between the pork chops and fry for 27 minutes at 180°C. Enjoy!

962. Cheese and garlic stuffed chicken breasts

Servings: 2
Cooking time: 20 minutes
Ingredients:
- 1/2 cup cottage cheese
- 2 beaten eggs
- 2 medium chicken breasts, cut in halves
- 2 tablespoons chopped fresh coriander
- 1 teaspoon fine sea salt
- Seasoned breadcrumbs
- 1/3 teaspoon freshly ground black pepper, to taste
- 3 cloves garlic, finely chopped

Addresses:
1. First, flatten the chicken breast with a meat tenderiser.
2. In a medium bowl, mix the cottage cheese with the garlic, coriander, salt and black pepper.
3. Spread some of the mixture over the first chicken breast. Repeat with the rest of the ingredients. Roll the chicken around the filling, making sure to secure with toothpicks.
4. Now, beat the egg in a shallow bowl. In another shallow bowl, combine the salt, ground black pepper and seasoned breadcrumbs.
5. Dredge the chicken breasts in the beaten egg, then coat them in the breadcrumbs.
6. Cook in the cooking basket of the air fryer at 180°C for 22 minutes. Serve immediately.

963. Chive, feta cheese and chicken frittata

Servings: 4
Cooking time: 10 minutes
Ingredients:
- 1/3 cup crumbled feta cheese
- 1 teaspoon dried rosemary
- ½ teaspoon brown sugar
- 2 tablespoons fish sauce
- 1 ½ cups cooked, boneless, shredded chicken breasts
- 1/2 teaspoon coriander sprig, finely chopped
- 3 medium eggs, beaten
- 1/3 teaspoon ground white pepper
- 1 cup chopped fresh chives
- 1/2 teaspoon garlic paste
- Fine sea salt
- Non-stick cooking spray

Addresses:
1. Find a baking sheet that will fit in your air fryer.
2. Lightly coat the inside of the baking dish with a non-stick spray of your choice.
3. Stir in all ingredients except Feta cheese. Stir to combine well.
4. Cook in the air fryer for 180°C for 8 minutes, check regularly for doneness.
5. Sprinkle the crumbled Feta cheese on top and eat immediately.

964. Rum roasted cherries

Servings: 3
Cooking time: 40 minutes
Ingredients:
- 255 grams of dark sweet cherries
- 2 tablespoons brown sugar
- 1 tablespoon of honey
- 3 tablespoons rum
- A pinch of grated nutmeg
- 1/4 teaspoon ground cloves
- 1/4 teaspoon ground cardamom
- 1 teaspoon vanilla

Addresses:
1. Place the cherries in a lightly greased baking dish.
2. Whisk together the remaining ingredients until well combined, add this mixture to the baking dish and stir gently to combine.
3. Bake in the preheated Air Fryer at 190°C for 35 minutes. Serve at room temperature - enjoy!

965. Omelette with smoked tofu and vegetables

Servings: 2
Cooking time: 20 minutes
Ingredients:
- 2 beaten eggs
- 1/3 cup chopped cherry tomatoes
- 1 pepper, seeded and chopped
- 1/3 teaspoon freshly ground black pepper
- 1/2 red onion, peeled and cut into slices

- 1 teaspoon smoked cayenne pepper
- 5 medium eggs, well beaten
- 1/3 cup smoked tofu, crumbled
- 1 teaspoon seasoned salt
- 1 ½ tablespoons fresh chives, chopped

Addresses:
1. Coat a baking dish with a layer of cooking spray.
2. Put all the ingredients, except the fresh chives, into the baking dish, stir well.
3. Cook for about 15 minutes at 190°C. When serving, garnish with freshly chopped chives and enjoy!

966. Eggs Florentine style with spinach

Servings: 2
Cooking time: 20 minutes
Ingredients:
- 2 tablespoons melted ghee
- 2 cups baby spinach, chopped into small pieces
- 2 tablespoons chopped shallots
- 1/4 teaspoon red pepper flakes
- Salt
- 1 tablespoon fresh thyme leaves, coarsely chopped
- 4 eggs

Addresses:
1. Start by preheating your Air Fryer to 180°C.
2. Brush the sides and bottom of a gratin dish with the melted ghee.
3. Place the spinach and shallots in the bottom of the gratin dish. Season with red pepper, salt and fresh thyme.
4. Make four holes for the eggs, crack an egg into each hole. Bake for 12 minutes, turning the pan once or twice to ensure even cooking. Bon appetit!

967. Award-winning breaded chicken

Servings: 4
Cooking time: 10 minutes + marinating time
Ingredients:
For the marinade you need:
- 1 ½ teaspoons olive oil
- 1 teaspoon crushed red pepper flakes
- 1/3 teaspoon of chicken bouillon granules
- 1/3 teaspoon shallot powder
- 1 ½ tablespoons tamari soy sauce
- 1/3 teaspoon cumin powder
- 1 ½ tablespoons mayonnaise
- 1 teaspoon kosher salt

For the chicken you need:
- 2 beaten eggs
- Breadcrumbs
- 1 ½ chicken breasts, boneless and skinless
- 1 ½ tablespoons plain flour

Addresses:
1. Butterfly the chicken breasts, then marinate for at least 55 minutes.
2. Dredge the chicken in flour, then in the beaten eggs and finally in the breadcrumbs.
3. Lightly grease the cooking basket. Fry the breaded chicken at 190°C for 12 minutes, turning them halfway through.

968. Sausage, Pepper and Fontina Frittata

Portions: 5
Cooking time: 14 minutes
Ingredients:
- 3 minced pork sausages
- 5 eggs, well beaten
- 1 ½ peppers, seeded and chopped
- 1 teaspoon smoked cayenne pepper
- 2 tablespoons Fontina cheese
- 1/2 teaspoon tarragon
- 1/2 teaspoon ground black pepper
- 1 teaspoon salt

Addresses:
1. In a cast-iron frying pan, sweat the peppers together with the chopped pork sausages until the peppers are fragrant and the sausage begins to release liquid.
2. Lightly grease the inside of a baking dish with cooking spray.
3. Pour all of the above ingredients into the prepared baking dish, including the sautéed mixture, stir to combine.
4. Bake at 190°C for approximately 9 minutes. Serve immediately with the salad of your choice.

969. Nachos with mozzarella sticks

Servings: 4
Cooking time: 40 minutes
Ingredients:
- 1 packet (450 grams) mozzarella cheese sticks
- 2 eggs
- 1/2 cup flour
- 1/2 (7 x 340 gram bags of multigrain tortilla chips, crushed
- 1 teaspoon garlic powder
- 1 teaspoon dried oregano
- 1/2 cup salsa, preferably homemade
-

Addresses:
1. Prepare your breading station. Put the flour in a shallow bowl, whisk the eggs in another shallow bowl, in a third bowl, mix the crushed tortilla chips, garlic powder and oregano.
2. Dredge the mozzarella sticks in flour, then in the egg and finally in the tortilla mixture. Place in your freezer for 30 minutes.
3. Place the breaded cheese sticks in the lightly greased basket of the Air Fryer. Cook at 180 °C for 6 minutes.
4. Serve with sauce on the side and enjoy.

970. Broccoli bites with spicy sauce

Servings: 6
Cooking time: 20 minutes
Ingredients:
For the broccoli bites you will need:
- 1 medium sized head of broccoli, cut into florets
- 1/2 teaspoon freshly grated lemon zest
- 1/3 teaspoon fine sea salt
- 1/2 teaspoon hot paprika
- 1 teaspoon shallot powder
- 1 teaspoon boletus powder
- 1/2 teaspoon granulated garlic
- 1/3 teaspoon celery seeds
- 1 ½ tablespoons olive oil

For the hot sauce you need:
- 1/2 cup tomato sauce
- 3 tablespoons brown sugar
- 1 tablespoon balsamic vinegar
- 1/2 teaspoon ground allspice

Addresses:
1. Mix all the ingredients for the broccoli bites in a bowl, coating the broccoli florets on all sides.
2. Cook them in the preheated Air Fryer at 180°C for 13 to 15 minutes. Meanwhile, mix all the ingredients for the hot sauce.
3. Pause your Air Fryer, mix the broccoli with the prepared sauce and cook for a few more minutes, enjoy!

971. Cheese Sticks with Ketchup

Servings: 4
Cooking time: 15 minutes
Ingredients:
- 1/4 cup coconut flour
- 1/4 cup almond flour
- 2 eggs
- 1/2 cup grated Parmesan cheese
- 1 tablespoon Cajun seasoning
- 8 cheese sticks
- 1/4 cup ketchup, low-carb

Addresses:
1. To begin, prepare your breading station. Place the flour in a shallow dish. In another plate, beat the eggs.
2. Finally, mix the Parmesan cheese and Cajun seasoning in a third dish.
3. Start by dredging the cheese sticks in the flour and then dip them in the egg. Press the cheese sticks into the parmesan mixture, coating them evenly.
4. Place the breaded cheese sticks in the lightly greased basket of the Air Fryer.
5. Cook at 190°C for 6 minutes.
6. Serve with ketchup and enjoy.

972. Salted Italian Crespelle

Servings: 3
Cooking time: 35 minutes
Ingredients:
- 3/4 cup plain flour
- 2 beaten eggs
- 1/4 teaspoon allspice
- 1/2 teaspoon salt
- 3/4 cup milk
- 1 cup ricotta cheese
- 1/2 cup Parmigiano-Reggiano cheese, preferably freshly grated
- 1 cup marinara sauce

Addresses:
1. Mix the flour, eggs, allspice and salt in a large bowl. Gradually add the milk, whisking continuously, until well combined.
2. Let it stand for a few minutes.
3. Spray the mould of the Air Fryer with cooking spray. Pour the batter into the prepared pan.
4. Cook at 110°C for 3 minutes. Turn and cook until golden brown in spots, 2 to 3 minutes more.
5. Repeat with the rest of the dough. Serve with cheese and marinara sauce and enjoy!

973. Onion rings with mayonnaise sauce

Servings: 3
Cooking time: 25 minutes
Ingredients:
- 1 large onion
- 1/2 cup almond flour
- 1 teaspoon salt
- 1/2 teaspoon ground black pepper
- 1 teaspoon cayenne pepper
- 1/2 teaspoon dried thyme
- 1/2 teaspoon dried oregano
- 1/2 teaspoon ground cumin
- 2 eggs
- 4 tablespoons milk

Pata mayo dip is needed:
- 3 tablespoons mayonnaise
- 3 tablespoons sour cream
- 1 tablespoon drained horseradish
- Kosher salt and freshly ground black pepper

Addresses:
1. Cut off the top 5 cm of the Vidalia onion, peel the onion and place it cut side down.
2. Starting 1 cm from the root, cut the onion in half. Make a second cut dividing each half in two. You will have 4 quarters joined at the root.
3. Repeat these cuts, dividing the 4 quarters into eighths, then divide again until you have 16 evenly spaced cuts. Turn the onion over and gently separate the outer pieces with your fingers.
4. In a bowl, mix well the almond flour and spices. In another bowl, whisk together the eggs and milk. Dip the onion into the egg mixture, followed by the almond flour mixture.

5. Spray the onion with cooking spray and transfer to the lightly greased cooking basket.
6. Cook at 185°C for 12 to 15 minutes.
7. Meanwhile, make the mayonnaise sauce by whisking together the rest of the ingredients. Serve and enjoy.

974. Two cheese and shrimp dip

Servings: 8
Cooking time: 25 minutes
Ingredients:
- 2 teaspoons melted butter
- 225 grams shrimps, peeled and deveined
- 2 cloves garlic, minced
- 1/4 cup chicken broth
- 2 tablespoons fresh lemon juice
- Salt and ground black pepper
- 1/2 teaspoon red pepper flakes
- 115 grams of cream cheese, at room temperature
- 1/2 cup sour cream
- 4 tablespoons mayonnaise
- 1/4 cup shredded mozzarella cheese

Addresses:
1. Preheat your air fryer to 200°C.
2. Grease the sides and bottom of a baking sheet with the melted butter.
3. Place the prawns, garlic, chicken stock, lemon juice, salt, black pepper and red pepper flakes in the baking dish.
4. Transfer the baking dish to the baking basket and bake for 10 minutes. Add the mixture to your food processor, pulse until coarsely chopped.
5. Stir in the cream cheese, sour cream and mayonnaise. Top with the mozzarella cheese and bake in the preheated Air Fryer at 180°C for 6 to 7 minutes or until the cheese is bubbly.
6. Serve immediately with breadsticks if desired - bon appetit!

975. Philadelphia mushroom omelette

Servings: 2
Cooking time: 20 minutes
Ingredients:
- 1 tablespoon of olive oil
- 1/2 cup chopped onions
- 1 pepper, seeded and thinly sliced
- 170 grams of mushrooms, thinly sliced
- 4 eggs
- 2 tablespoons milk
- Sea salt and freshly ground black pepper
- 1 tbsp fresh chives (to serve)

Addresses:
1. Heat the olive oil in a frying pan over medium-high heat. Now, sauté the spring onions and peppers until aromatic.
2. Add the mushrooms and continue cooking for a further 3 minutes or until tender. Set aside.
3. Generously grease a baking dish with non-stick cooking spray.
4. Next, whisk together the eggs, milk, salt and black pepper. Pour the mixture into the prepared mould.
5. Cook in the preheated Air Fryer at 180°C for 4 minutes. Turn over and cook for another 3 minutes.
6. Place the reserved mushroom filling on one side of the tortilla. Fold the omelette in half and slide onto a serving plate. Serve immediately garnished with fresh chives - bon appetit!

976. Delicious hot fruit tart

Servings: 4
Cooking time: 40 minutes
Ingredients:
- 2 cups blueberries
- 2 cups of raspberries
- 1 tablespoon corn starch
- 3 tablespoons maple syrup
- 2 tbsp. melted coconut oil
- A pinch of freshly grated nutmeg
- A pinch of salt
- 1 cinnamon stick
- 1 vanilla pod

Addresses:
1. Place the berries in a lightly greased baking dish. Sprinkle the cornflour over the fruit.
2. Whisk together the maple syrup, coconut oil, nutmeg and salt in a bowl, add this mixture to the berries and stir gently to combine.
3. Add the cinnamon and vanilla. Bake in the preheated Air Fryer at 180°C for 35 minutes. Serve warm at room temperature. Enjoy.

977. Omelette with mushrooms and peppers

Servings: 2
Cooking time: 20 minutes
Ingredients:
- 1 tablespoon of olive oil
- 1/2 cup chopped onions
- 1 pepper, seeded and thinly sliced
- 170 grams of mushrooms, thinly sliced
- 4 eggs
- 2 tablespoons milk
- Sea salt and freshly ground black pepper
- 1 tbsp fresh chives (to serve)

Addresses:
1. Heat the olive oil in a frying pan over medium-high heat. Now, sauté the spring onions and peppers until aromatic.

2. Add the mushrooms and continue cooking for a further 3 minutes or until tender. Set aside.
3. Generously grease a baking dish with non-stick cooking spray.
4. Next, whisk together the eggs, milk, salt and black pepper. Pour the mixture into the prepared mould.
5. Cook in the preheated Air Fryer at 180°C for 4 minutes. Turn over and cook for another 3 minutes.
6. Place the reserved mushroom filling on one side of the tortilla. Fold the omelette in half and slide onto a serving plate. Serve immediately garnished with fresh chives - bon appetit!

978. Broccoli Parmesan Fritters

Servings: 6
Cooking time: 30 minutes
Ingredients:
- 1 ½ cups Monterey Jack cheese
- 1 teaspoon of dried dill weed
- ⅓ teaspoon of ground black pepper
- 3 beaten eggs
- 1 teaspoon cayenne pepper
- ½ teaspoon kosher salt
- 2 ½ cups broccoli florets
- ½ cup Parmesan cheese

Addresses:
1. Shred the broccoli florets in a food processor until finely chopped. Then combine the broccoli with the rest of the above ingredients.
2. Form the mixture into balls, put the balls in the fridge for about half an hour.
3. Preheat your Air Fryer to 350°C and set the timer for 14 minutes, cook until the broccoli croquettes are golden brown and serve hot.

979. Cheese and chive stuffed chicken rolls

Servings: 6
Cooking time: 20 minutes
Ingredients:
- 2 eggs, well beaten
- Crushed tortilla chips
- 1 ½ tablespoons of extra virgin olive oil
- 1 ½ tablespoons fresh chives, chopped
- 3 chicken breasts, cut in half, lengthwise
- 1 ½ cup soft cheese
- 2 teaspoons sweet paprika
- ½ teaspoon whole grain mustard
- ½ teaspoon cumin powder
- ⅓ teaspoon fine sea salt
- ⅓ cup chopped fresh coriander
- ⅓ teaspoon freshly ground black pepper, or more to taste

Addresses:
1. Flatten each piece of chicken breast with a rolling pin. Then take three mixing plates.
2. In the first, combine the soft cheese with coriander, fresh chives, cumin and mustard.
3. In another bowl, beat the eggs with the paprika. In the third bowl, combine the salt, black pepper and crushed tortilla chips.
4. Spread the cheese mixture over each piece of chicken. Repeat with the remaining pieces of chicken breasts, now roll them up.
5. Coat each chicken roll with the beaten egg, dip each chicken roll in the tortilla chip mixture. Lower the rolls into the cooking basket of the air fryer. Drizzle the rolls with extra virgin olive oil.
6. Air fry at 170°C for 28 minutes, working in batches. Serve hot, garnished with sour cream if desired.

980. Asparagus and Creamed Egg Salad

Servings: 4
Cooking time: 25 minutes + cooling time
Ingredients:
- 2 eggs
- 450 grams of asparagus, chopped
- 2 cups baby spinach
- ½ cup mayonnaise
- 1 teaspoon mustard
- 1 teaspoon fresh lemon juice
- Sea salt and ground black pepper

Addresses:
1. Place the rack in the basket of the Air Fryer, lower the eggs onto the rack.
2. Cook for 15 minutes.
3. Transfer them to an ice water bath to stop the cooking process. Peel the eggs under cold running water, chop the hard-boiled eggs and set aside.
4. Increase the temperature to 180°C. Place the asparagus in the lightly greased fryer basket.
5. Cook for a few minutes or until tender. Place in a nice salad bowl. Add the baby spinach.
6. In a mixing bowl, mix the rest of the ingredients well. Drizzle this dressing over the asparagus in the salad bowl and top with the chopped eggs - bon appetit!

981. Easy Frittata with chicken sausage

Servings: 2
Cooking time: 15 minutes
Ingredients:
- 1 tablespoon of olive oil
- 2 chicken sausages, cut in slices
- 4 eggs
- 1 clove garlic, minced
- ½ yellow onion, chopped
- Sea salt and ground black pepper
- 4 tablespoons Monterey-Jack cheese

- 1 tbsp chopped fresh parsley leaves

Addresses:
1. Grease the sides and bottom of a baking dish with olive oil.
2. Add the sausages and cook in the preheated Air Fryer at 180°C for 4 to 5 minutes.
3. In a bowl, beat the eggs with the garlic and onion. Season with salt and black pepper.
4. Pour the mixture over the sausages. Top with cheese. Cook in the Air Fryer for a further 6 minutes.
5. Serve immediately with fresh parsley leaves and enjoy!

982. Carrot crisps with romano cheese

Servings: 3
Cooking time: 20 minutes
Ingredients:
- 3 carrots, cut into sticks
- 1 tablespoon coconut oil
- ⅓ cup Romano cheese, preferably freshly grated
- 2 teaspoons granulated garlic
- Sea salt and ground black pepper

Addresses:
1. Mix all the ingredients in a bowl until the carrots are coated on all sides.
2. Cook at 190°C for 15 minutes, shaking the basket halfway through cooking.
3. Serve with your favourite dipping sauce and enjoy!

983. Breakfast eggs and seafood casserole

Servings: 2
Cooking time: 30 minutes
Ingredients:
- 1 tablespoon of olive oil
- 2 cloves garlic, minced
- 1 small yellow onion, chopped
- 115 grams of tilapia pieces
- 115 grams of rockfish chunks
- ½ teaspoon dried basil
- Salt and white pepper
- 4 eggs, lightly beaten
- 1 tablespoon dry sherry
- 4 tablespoons grated cheese

Addresses:
1. Start by preheating your Air Fryer to 180°C, add the olive oil to a baking tray. Once hot, cook the garlic and onion for 2 minutes or until fragrant.
2. Add the fish, basil, salt and pepper. In a bowl, thoroughly mix the eggs with the sherry and cheese. Pour the mixture into the baking dish.
3. Cook for approximately 20 minutes - bon appetit!

984. Greek Revithokeftedes easy

Servings: 3
Cooking time: 30 minutes
Ingredients:
- 340 grams of canned chickpeas, drained
- 1 red onion, sliced
- 2 cloves garlic
- 1 chilli
- 1 tablespoon fresh coriander
- 2 tablespoons plain flour
- ½ teaspoon cayenne pepper
- Sea salt and freshly ground pepper
- 3 large pita bread loaves (approximately 16.5 centimetres)

Addresses:
1. Pulse the chickpeas, onion, garlic, chilli and coriander in your food processor until the chickpeas are ground.
2. Add all-purpose flour, cayenne pepper, salt and black pepper, stir to combine well.
3. Form the chickpea mixture into balls and place them in the lightly greased fryer basket.
4. Cook at 190°C for about 15 minutes, shaking the basket occasionally to ensure even cooking.
5. Then heat the pita bread in your Air Fryer at 200°C for about 6 minutes.
6. Serve the revithokeftedes in pita bread with tzatziki or your favourite Greek topping. Enjoy.

985. Spicy potato wedges

Servings: 4
Cooking time: 23 minutes
Ingredients:
- 1 ½ tablespoons melted butter
- 1 teaspoon dried parsley flakes
- 1 teaspoon ground coriander
- 1 teaspoon seasoned salt
- 3 large red potatoes, cut into pieces
- ½ teaspoon chilli powder
- ⅓ teaspoon garlic pepper

Addresses:
1. Place the potato pieces in the cooking basket of the air fryer.
2. Drizzle with melted butter and bake for 20 minutes at 190°C. Be sure to stir a couple of times during the cooking process.
3. Add the rest of the ingredients and mix to coat the potato pieces on all sides. Enjoy!

986. Keto Brioche with Caciocavallo

Servings: 6
Cooking time: 15 minutes
Ingredients:
- 1/2 cup shredded ricotta cheese
- 1 cup part-skim mozzarella cheese, grated
- 1 egg
- 1/2 cup coconut flour
- 1/2 cup almond flour
- 1 teaspoon bicarbonate of soda
- 2 tablespoons natural whey protein isolate

- 3 tablespoons sesame oil
- 2 teaspoons dried thyme
- 1 ½ cups of grated Caciocavallo
- 1 cup shredded chicken leftovers
- 3 eggs
- 1 teaspoon kosher salt
- 1 tsp freshly ground black pepper
- 1/3 teaspoon gremolata

Addresses:
1. To make the keto brioche, heat the cheese in the microwave for 30 seconds, stirring twice.
2. Add the cheese to the bowl of a food processor and blend well. Add the egg and blend again.
3. Add the flour, baking soda and whey protein isolate, beat again. Scrape the dough into the centre of a lightly greased cling film.
4. Form the dough into a disc and place in the freezer to chill, cut into 6 pieces and transfer to a parchment-lined baking dish (be sure to grease your hands).
5. First cut off the top of each brioche, then scoop out the inside.
6. Spread each brioche with sesame oil. Add the remaining ingredients in the order given.
7. Place the prepared brioche in the bottom of the baking basket. Bake for 7 minutes at 170°C. Enjoy!

987. Baked eggs with meat and tomatoes

Servings: 4
Cooking time: 20 minutes
Ingredients:
- Non-stick cooking spray
- 1/2 lb of leftover beef, coarsely chopped
- 2 cloves garlic, pressed
- 1 cup of kale, chopped and wilted
- 1 chopped tomato
- 4 beaten eggs
- 4 tablespoons of cream
- 1/2 teaspoon turmeric powder
- Salt and ground black pepper
- 1/8 teaspoon ground allspice

Addresses:
1. Spray the inside of four ramekins with cooking spray.
2. Divide all the above ingredients between the prepared moulds. Stir until everything is well combined.
3. Air fry at 160 °C for 16 minutes, check with a wooden toothpick and return the eggs to the air fryer for a few more minutes if necessary. Serve immediately.

988. Veal and Kale Omelette

Servings: 4
Cooking time: 20 minutes
Ingredients:
- Non-stick cooking spray
- 225 grams of leftover beef, coarsely minced
- 2 cloves garlic, pressed
- 1 cup kale, chopped and wilted
- 1 chopped tomato
- 1/4 teaspoon brown sugar
- 4 beaten eggs
- 4 tablespoons of cream
- 1/2 teaspoon turmeric powder
- Salt and ground black pepper
- 1/8 teaspoon ground allspice

Addresses:
1. Spray the inside of four ramekins with cooking spray.
2. Divide all the above ingredients between the prepared moulds. Stir until everything is well combined.
3. Air fry at 180°C for 16 minutes, check with a wooden toothpick and return the eggs to the air fryer for a few more minutes if necessary. Serve immediately.

989. Cauliflower balls with cheese

Servings: 4
Cooking time: 26 minutes
Ingredients:
- 115 grams of cauliflower florets
- 1/2 cup roasted vegetable stock
- 1 beaten egg
- 1 cup white mushrooms, finely chopped
- 1/2 cup grated Parmesan cheese
- 3 cloves garlic, peeled and minced
- 1/2 yellow onion, finely chopped
- 1/3 teaspoon ground black pepper, or more to taste
- 1 ½ chopped seeded peppers
- 1/2 chipotle chilli, seeded and chopped
- 1/2 cup grated Colby cheese
- 1 ½ tablespoons canola oil
- Sea salt

Addresses:
1. Shred the cauliflower florets in your food processor until they are shredded (about the size of rice).
2. Heat a saucepan over medium heat, now heat the oil and sweat the garlic, onions, pepper, cauli rice and chipotle chilli until tender.
3. Add the mushrooms and fry until fragrant and the liquid has almost evaporated.
4. Add the stock and boil for 18 minutes. Now add the cheese and spices, stir to combine.
5. Allow the mixture to cool completely. Form the mixture into balls. Roll the balls in the beaten egg, then roll them in the grated Parmesan.
6. Fry these balls for a few minutes at 200°C. Serve with marinara sauce and enjoy!

990. Super easy sage and lime wings

Servings: 4
Cooking time: 30 minutes + marinating time
Ingredients:
- 1 teaspoon onion powder
- 1/3 cup fresh lime juice
- 1/2 tablespoon maize flour
- 1/2 heaped tablespoon of chopped fresh parsley
- 1/3 teaspoon mustard powder
- 225 grams of turkey wings, cut into small pieces
- 2 heaped tablespoons of chopped fresh sage
- 1/2 teaspoon garlic powder
- 1/2 teaspoon seasoned salt
- 1 teaspoon freshly ground black or white peppercorns

Addresses:
1. Simply pour all the above ingredients into a bowl.
2. Cover and marinate for a few hours in the refrigerator.
3. Fry the turkey wings for a few minutes at 180°C. Enjoy!

991. Spring Frittata with Chicken and Goat Cheese

Servings: 4
Cooking time: 10 minutes
Ingredients:
- 1 cup crumbled goat's cheese
- 1 teaspoon dried rosemary
- 2 cups cooked, boned and shredded chicken breasts
- 1/4 teaspoon mustard seeds
- 1 teaspoon red pepper flakes, crushed
- 5 medium eggs, beaten
- 1/3 teaspoon ground white pepper
- 1/2 cup chopped green onions
- 1 stalk of green garlic, chopped
- Fine sea salt
- Non-stick cooking spray

Addresses:
1. Take a baking tray that fits in your Air Fryer.
2. Lightly coat the inside of the baking sheet with a non-stick spray of your choice.
3. Stir in all ingredients except cheese. Stir to combine well.
4. Transfer to the air fryer to cook at 180°C for 8 minutes. Before removing, check for doneness.
5. Sprinkle the crumbled goat's cheese on top and eat immediately.

992. Potatoes with cashew sauce

Servings: 4
Cooking time: 20 minutes
Ingredients:
- 450 grams of fingerling potatoes
- 1 tablespoon melted butter
- Sea salt and ground black pepper
- 1 teaspoon shallot powder
- 1 teaspoon garlic powder

For the cashew nut sauce you need:
- 1/2 cup raw cashew nuts
- 1 teaspoon cayenne pepper
- 3 tablespoons nutritional yeast
- 2 teaspoons white vinegar
- 4 tablespoons of water
- 1/4 teaspoon dried rosemary
- 1/4 teaspoon of dried dill

Addresses:
1. Mix the potatoes with the butter, salt, black pepper, shallot powder and garlic powder.
2. Place the potatoes in the lightly greased fryer basket and cook at 200°C for 6 minutes, shake the basket and cook for another 6 minutes.
3. Meanwhile, prepare the sauce by blending all the ingredients in your food processor or high-speed blender.
4. Drizzle the cashew sauce over the potato pieces. Cook for a further 2 minutes or until heated through. Enjoy.

993. Potato appetizer with garlic and mayonnaise sauce

Servings: 4
Cooking time: 19 minutes
Ingredients:
- 2 tablespoons vegetable oil of choice
- Kosher salt and freshly ground black pepper
- 3 Russet potatoes, cut into chunks

For the dipping sauce you need:
- 2 teaspoons crushed dried rosemary
- 3 cloves garlic, minced
- ⅓ teaspoon dried marjoram, crushed
- ¼ cup sour cream
- ⅓ cup mayonnaise

Addresses:
1. Lightly grease the potatoes with a thin layer of vegetable oil. Season with salt and ground black pepper.
2. Place the seasoned potato wedges in a cooking basket of the air fryer. Bake at 200°C for 15 minutes, stirring once or twice.
3. Meanwhile, prepare the dipping sauce by mixing all the dipping sauce ingredients together. Serve the potatoes with the dipping sauce and enjoy.

994. The easiest vegan burrito ever

Servings: 6
Cooking time: 35 minutes
Ingredients:
- 2 tablespoons olive oil
- 1 small onion, chopped
- 2 sweet peppers, seeded and chopped

- 1 chilli, seeded and chopped
- Sea salt and ground black pepper
- 1 teaspoon crushed red pepper flakes
- 1 teaspoon dried parsley flakes
- 280 grams of cooked pinto beans
- 340 grams of canned sweet corn, drained
- 6 large corn tortillas
- ½ cup vegan sour cream

Addresses:
1. Start by preheating your Air Frye to 200°C.
2. Heat the olive oil in a frying pan. Once hot, cook the onion and peppers until tender and fragrant, about 15 minutes.
3. Stir in the salt, black pepper, red pepper, parsley, beans and sweetcorn to combine well.
4. Divide the bean mixture among the corn tortillas. Roll the tortillas and place them in the parchment-lined basket of the Air Fryer.
5. Bake in the preheated Air Fryer for 15 minutes. Serve garnished with sour cream - bon appetit!

995. Eggs with turkey bacon and green onions

Servings: 4
Cooking time: 25 minutes
Ingredients:
- 225 grams of turkey bacon
- 4 eggs
- 1/3 cup milk
- 2 tablespoons yoghurt
- 1/2 teaspoon sea salt
- 1 pepper, finely chopped
- 2 green onions, finely chopped
- 1/2 cup Colby cheese, grated

Addresses:
1. Place the turkey bacon in the cooking basket.
2. Bake at 180°C for 9 to 11 minutes. Work in batches. Reserve the fried bacon.
3. In a bowl, beat the eggs well with the milk and yoghurt. Add the salt, pepper and green onions.
4. Spread the sides and bottom of the pan with the reserved teaspoon of bacon fat.
5. Pour the egg mixture into the baking dish. Cook for about 5 minutes. Top with grated Colby cheese and cook for 5 to 6 minutes more.
6. Serve the scrambled eggs with the reserved bacon and enjoy.

996. The easiest pork chops to make

Servings: 6
Cooking time: 22 minutes
Ingredients:
- ⅓ cup Italian breadcrumbs
- Chopped fresh coriander
- 2 teaspoons Cajun seasoning
- Non-stick cooking spray
- 2 beaten eggs
- 3 tablespoons white flour
- 1 teaspoon seasoned salt
- Garlic and onion spice mixture
- 6 pork chops
- ⅓ teaspoon of freshly ground black pepper

Addresses:
1. Coat the pork chops with the Cajun seasoning, salt, pepper and spice mixture on all sides.
2. Then add the flour to a plate. In a shallow dish, beat the egg until pale and smooth. Place the Italian breadcrumbs in the third dish.
3. Dredge each piece of pork in the flour, then dredge in the egg, and finally dredge in the breadcrumbs. Spray them with cooking spray on both sides.
4. Now air fry the pork chops for about 18 minutes at 190°C, test for doneness after the first 12 minutes of cooking.
5. Finally, garnish with fresh coriander - bon appetit!

997. English muffins with a twist

Servings: 4
Cooking time: 15 minutes
Ingredients:
- 4 English muffins, halved
- 2 eggs
- 1/3 cup milk
- 1/4 cup heavy cream
- 2 tablespoons honey
- 1 teaspoon pure vanilla extract
- 1/4 cup confectioner's sugar

Addresses:
1. Cut the rolls crosswise into strips.
2. In a bowl, whisk together the eggs, milk, cream, honey and vanilla extract.
3. Dip each muffin piece into the egg mixture and place in the parchment-lined Air Fryer basket.
4. Cook in the preheated air fryer at 180°C for 6 to 7 minutes, turning them halfway through the cooking time to ensure even cooking.
5. Sprinkle with icing sugar and serve hot.

998. Easy fried mushrooms

Servings: 4
Cooking time: 15 minutes
Ingredients:
- 450 grams of mushrooms
- 1 cup corn starch
- 1 cup all-purpose flour
- ½ teaspoon baking powder
- 2 beaten eggs
- 2 cups of seasoned breadcrumbs
- 1/2 teaspoon salt

- 2 tbsp fresh parsley leaves, coarsely chopped

Addresses:
1. Dry the mushrooms with a paper towel.
2. To begin, prepare your breading station. Mix the cornflour, flour and baking powder in a shallow dish. In another plate, beat the eggs.
3. Finally, place the breadcrumbs and salt in a third dish.
4. Start by dredging the mushrooms in the flour mixture, then dip them in the eggs. Press the mushrooms into the breadcrumbs, coating them evenly.
5. Spray the Air Fryer basket with cooking oil.
6. Add the mushrooms and cook at 200°C for 6 minutes, turning halfway through cooking.
7. Serve garnished with fresh parsley leaves and enjoy!

999. Onion rings wrapped in bacon

Servings: 4
Cooking time: 25 minutes
Ingredients:
- 12 bacon torreznos
- ½ teaspoon ground black pepper
- Fresh chopped parsley
- ½ teaspoon paprika
- ½ teaspoon chilli powder
- ½ tablespoon soy sauce
- ½ teaspoon salt

Addresses:
1. Start by preheating your air fryer to 180°C.
2. Season the onion rings with paprika, salt, black pepper and chilli powder. Wrap the onion rings with the bacon and sprinkle with soy sauce.
3. Bake for 17 minutes, garnish with fresh parsley and serve - bon appetit!

1000. Roasted green bean salad with goat's cheese

Servings: 4
Cooking time: 10 minutes + cooling time
Ingredients:
- 450 grams of trimmed green beans, cut into bite-size pieces
- Salt and freshly ground mixed pepper
- 1 shallot, thinly sliced
- 1 tablespoon lime juice
- 1 tablespoon of cava vinegar
- ¼ cup extra virgin olive oil
- ½ teaspoon of mustard seeds
- ½ teaspoon celery seeds
- 1 tbsp. chopped fresh basil leaves
- 1 tbsp fresh parsley leaves
- 1 cup crumbled goat's cheese

Addresses:
1. Toss the green beans with salt and pepper in a lightly greased Air Fryer basket.
2. Cook in the preheated Air Fryer at 200°C for 5 minutes or until tender.
3. Add the shallots and stir gently to combine.
4. In a bowl, whisk together the lime juice, vinegar, olive oil and spices. Dress the salad and top with the goat cheese. Serve at room temperature or chilled. Enjoy.

1001. Japanese fried rice with eggs

Servings: 2
Cooking time: 30 minutes
Ingredients:
- 2 cups cauliflower rice
- 2 teaspoons sesame oil
- Sea salt and freshly ground black pepper
- 2 beaten eggs
- 2 spring onions, white and green parts separated, chopped
- 1 tablespoon Shoyu sauce
- 1 tablespoon of sake
- 2 tablespoons Kewpie Japanese mayonnaise

Addresses:
1. Combine the cauliflower rice, sesame oil, salt and pepper in a baking dish.
2. Cook at 170°C for about 13 minutes, stirring halfway through cooking.
3. Pour the eggs over the cauliflower rice and continue cooking for about 5 minutes.
4. Then add the spring onions and stir to combine. Continue cooking for 2 to 3 minutes more or until heated through.
5. Meanwhile, prepare the sauce by whisking the Shoyu sauce, sake and Japanese mayonnaise in a bowl.
6. Divide the fried cauliflower rice into individual bowls and serve with the prepared sauce. Enjoy.

21-DAY MEAL PLAN

Eating does not involve much, but it is pertinent that we have a planned meal to help maintain a healthy body. Among a plethora of meal plans, 21 Days gained popularity due to its ability to promote weight loss, giving man a healthy body. Some studies have shown that eliminating added sugars and processed foods are effective ways to lose body fat. Why other studies provided us with an obvious fact that people who consume added sugar and sugar-sweetened beverages are more likely to be obese or gain more fat compared to those with low sugar intake or those with regulated sugar intake? A 21-day meal plan may be just what you need to keep your body in shape. You may have heard a lot of people say the well-known quote, "abs start from the kitchen" from that statement, you can easily deduce that everything we consume as humans is having a long way to go in our body, physically or internally, Guide your food.

It is important that I provide my reader with information obtained from previous studies that say that those who consume fast food are more likely or have the propensity to become obese than those who did not, the conclusion of all this information is to create an indulgence in your mind that unguided eating could or will eventually lead to unwanted or unplanned repercussions. During the 21-day meal plan, cover a high-protein, high-fibre diet and drink plenty of water, methods that have also been shown to be particularly powerful in promoting weight loss, the foods in this meal plan are well guided with nutrient-rich healthy foods that cut across vegetables, complex carbohydrates and lean proteins. This 21-day meal plan has provided the participant the fact that preparing their food at home will be preferable to seeking comfort in fast food or unhealthy junk meals. We must proceed to the full explanation of the 21-day meal plan.

WEEK 1

Day	Breakfast	Sandwich	Lunch	Sandwich	Dinner	Beverages
Monday	KETO BLUEBERRY CAKE	Olive oil Roasted sugar Peas	Tomato and rocket salad with avocado	Vegan Pumpkin Parmesan Chips	Spicy Red Curry Roasted Cauliflower Soup	Baked Courgette Tomato Pesto
Tuesday	KETO BROWNIE MUFFINS	Keto Low Carb Crackers (Almond Flour, Paleo)	Fresh pepper Basil pizza	COCONUT COCONUT	Courgette and avocado walnut pesto ribbons	Oven-roasted asparagus with lemon and garlic
Wednesday	MUSHROOM RISOTTO WITH CAULIFLOWER RICE	Vegan Pumpkin Parmesan Chips	TRIPLE PALEO GREEN KALE TRIPLE PALEO SALAD	HAY BITES	Roasted cauliflower tofu vegan tacos	Roasted radishes with garlic recipe
Thursday	GRILLED AUBERGINE CAPRESE ROLLS	Low carb fried Mac and vegan cheese	Crispy Tofu and Bok Choy Salad	Pizza Dip Bread	Zoodle Sesame Almond Bowl	Keto Margarita
Friday	PEANUT BUTTER CHIA PUDDING	HAY BITES	Spaghetti Squash with Tomato and Mushroom {Whole30 Recipe}	Low-carb biscuits	Ginger Cauliflower Fried Rice	Guilt-free Chai Tea Smoothie
Saturday	SPINACH AND COURGETTE LASAGNE	COCONUT COCONUT	Asian ginger salad	Bread pizza Dip	Vegan recipe for courgette noodles with pesto	Tropical Keto Shake
Sunday	CURRIED TOFU SCRAMBLE	Keto Fat Bombs Cheesecake	Vegan sesame tofu and aubergine	Vegan Pumpkin Parmesan Chips	CAULIFLOWER PUREE WITH GARLIC AND HERBS	These indentations

WEEK 2

Day	Breakfast	Sandwich	Lunch	Sandwich	Dinner	Beverages
Monday	VEGETARIAN SPAGHETTI SQUASH LASAGNE WITH CHEESE	LOW-CARB ROASTED CABBAGE WITH LEMON	Low-carb Margherita pizza with Portobello mushroom crust	Vanilla Keto Overnight Oatmeal	INSTANT POT WHOLE ROASTED CAULIFLOWER IN INDIAN MASAA	Ketoproof coffee
Tuesday	VEGAN KETO PORRIDGE	KETO CHOCOLATE CHIP BISCUITS	Guacamole Mason Jar Salad	Low-carb biscuits	vegan thai soup	Pure MCT oil Keto Coffee
Wednesday	SMOOTHIE BOWL WITH CAULIFLOWER AND VEGETABLES	PEANUT BUTTER FAT BOMBS	Thyme waffles with cheese	Sun-Dried Tomato Pesto Cup Cake	Vegan Seitan Negimaki	Instant Creamy Coffee MCT Oil
Thursday	QUICK SPIRAL COURGETTE AND GRAPE TOMATOES	Sun-Dried Tomato Pesto Cup Cake	Vegetarian Greek Kale Wraps	KETO CHOCOLATE CHIP BISCUITS	ROASTED GARLIC AND RED PEPPER NOODLES	Keto coffee with cocoa flavour
Friday	LEMON RASPBERRY SWEET ROLLS	Cucumber sting	Keto Vegan Grilled Cheese Sandwich	Low carb fried Mac & Cheese	VEGAN KETO HICKORY CHILI	Simple Blueberry Shae
Saturday	VEGAN LOW-CARB CHILI RELLENOS BAKED IN THE OVEN	Olive oil Roasted sugar Peas	Tomato and Basil and Mozzarella Vegan Galette	Vegan Parmesan Pumpkin Chips	Courgette noodles with avocado sauce	Word Keto
Sunday	LOW CARB MAPLE OATS	Slow Cooker Balsamic glazed mushrooms	Keto Club Vegetarian Salad	Baked courgette chips recipe	Zoodle Sesame Almond Bowl	Keto Margarita

WEEK 3

Day	Breakfast	Sandwich	Lunch	Sandwich	Dinner	Beverages
Monday	MEDITERRANEAN PASTA	Baked courgette chips recipe	Vegetarian red coconut curry	Olive oil Roasted sugar Peas	VEGAN KETO HICKORY CHILI	Keto Bloody Mary cocktail

Tuesday	CRISPY PEANUT TOFU AND CAULIFLOWER RICE STIR-FRY	Low-carb biscuits	Fresh pepper Basil pizza	Vegan Parmesan Pumpkin Chips	Egg roll in a bowl	Strawberry daisies
Wednesday	KETO FALAFEL WITH TAHINI SAUCE	Keto Fat Bombs Cheesecake	Fettuccine Crepe with tomatoes, fresh vegan mozzarella and pesto	Low carb fried Mac and vegan cheese	Keto Creamy Avocado Paste with Shirataki	Low-carb vodka drink
Thursday	GUACAMOLE	Ketogenic fat bombs with cocoa and cashew nuts	Low-carb Margherita pizza with Portobello mushroom crust	Baked courgette chips recipe	Veggie Noodle Pad Thai	Low Carb Vodka Mojito recipe
Friday	KETO CANNOLI STUFFED PANCAKES	Cheesy Hearts of Palm Dip	Crispy Tofu and Bok Choy Salad	Vanilla Keto Overnight Oatmeal	CAULIFLOWER PARMESAN STEAK	Low-carb Moscow Mule (sugar-free)
Saturday	GREEN CURRY KALE WITH CRISPY COCONUT TEMPEH	Pizza Dip Bread	Vegan sesame tofu and aubergine	PEANUT BUTTER FAT BOMBS	Keto Tabbouleh	Sex on the beach
Sunday	ASPARAGUS AND TOMATO FRITTATA WITH HAVARTI AND DILL	Pizza Dip Bread	Keto Club Vegetarian Salad	Low-carb biscuits	HEALTHY VEGAN QUICHE	Green juice

Thank you!

Printed in Great Britain
by Amazon